SWORD COAST ADVENTURER'S GUIDE

GREEN RONIN
PUBLISHING

CREDITS

This book was a collaboration between Wizards of the Coast and Green Ronin Publishing. Members of the Green Ronin creative team are marked with an asterisk below.

Lead Designer: Steve Kenson*
Designers: Joseph Carriker,* Brian Cortijo,* Jeremy Crawford, Peter Lee, Jon Leitheusser,* Mike Mearls, Jack Norris,* Sean K Reynolds, Matt Sernett, Rodney Thompson
Managing Editor: Jeremy Crawford
Editor: Kim Mohan*
Editorial Assistance: Chris Sims, Matt Sernett, Dan Helmick
Producer: Greg Bilsland
D&D Lead Designers: Mike Mearls, Jeremy Crawford

Art Directors: Kate Irwin, Hal Mangold,* Shauna Narciso
Graphic Designer: Emi Tanji
Cover Illustrator: Tyler Jacobson
Interior Illustrators: Conceptopolis, Olga Drebas, Jason A. Engle, Randy Gallegos, Ilich Henriquez, David Heuso, Tyler Jacobson, McLean Kendree, Howard Lyon, William O'Connor, Claudio Pozas, Bryan Syme, Eva Widermann
Cartographers: Jared Blando, Mike Schley
Font Designer: Daniel Reeve

Project Management: Neil Shinkle, John Hay
Production Services: Cynda Callaway, Jefferson Dunlap, David Gershman
Brand and Marketing: Nathan Stewart, Liz Schuh, Chris Lindsay, Shelly Mazzanoble, Hilary Ross, John Feil, Greg Tito, Kim Lundstrom, Trevor Kidd

Playtesters: Adam Hennebeck, Anthony Caroselli, Arthur Wright, Bill Benham, Bryce Haley, Christopher Hackler, Claudio Pozas, Daniel Oquendo, David "Oak" Stark, Gregory L. Harris, Jason Baxter, Jason Fuller, Jay Anderson, Jeff Greiner, Jonathan Longstaff, Jonathan Urman, Josh Dillard, Karl Resch, Ken J Breese, Keoki Young, Kevin Neff, Krupal Desai, Kyle Turner, Liam Gulliver, Logan Neufeld, Lou Michelli, Matt Maranda, Mik Calow, Mike Mihalas, Naomi Kellerman-Bernard, Paul Hughes, Paul Melamed, Richard Green, Robert Alaniz, Rory Madden, Shane Leahy, Shawn Merwin, Stacy Bermes, Teos Abadia, Tom Lommel, Travis Brock, Yan Lacharité

BIBLIOGRAPHY

Here are the Forgotten Realms works that most influenced this book.

Athans, Philip. *A Reader's Guide to R.A. Salvatore's Legend of Drizzt.* 2008.
Baker, Richard, Ed Bonny, and Travis Stout. *Lost Empires of Faerûn.* 2005.
Boyd, Eric L. *City of Splendors: Waterdeep.* 2005.
———. *Drizzt do'Urden's Guide to the Underdark.* 1999.
Connors, William W. *Hordes of Dragonspear.* 1992.
Cordell, Bruce R., Ed Greenwood, and Chris Sims. *Forgotten Realms Campaign Guide.* 2008.
Crawford, Jeremy, and Christopher Perkins. *Ghosts of Dragonspear Castle.* 2013.
Cunningham, Elaine. *Thornhold.* 2001.
Greenwood, Ed. *Dwarves Deep.* 1990.
———. *Volo's Guide to Baldur's Gate II.* 2000.
———. *Volo's Guide to the North.* 1993.
———. *Volo's Guide to the Sword Coast.* 1994.
———. *Volo's Guide to Waterdeep.* 1992.
———. *Waterdeep and the North.* 1987.
———. *Waterdeep.* 1989.
———. *City of Splendors.* 1994.
Greenwood, Ed, and Jason Carl. *Silver Marches.* 2002.
Greenwood, Ed, Matt Sernett, and others. *Murder in Baldur's Gate.* 2013.
Greenwood, Ed, Sean K Reynolds, Skip Williams, and Rob Heinsoo. *Forgotten Realms Campaign Setting.* 2001.
Grubb, Jeff, Kate Novak, and others. *Hall of Heroes.* 1989.
Jaquays, Paul. *The Savage Frontier.* 1988.
Leati, Tito, Matt Sernett, and Chris Sims. *Scourge of the Sword Coast.* 2014.
Perrin, Steve. *Under Illefarn.* 1987.
Salvatore, R.A. *The Crystal Shard.* 1988.
———. *Rise of the King.* 2015.
Salvatore, R.A., James Wyatt, and Jeffrey Ludwig. *Legacy of the Crystal Shard.* 2013.
Sernett, Matt, Erik Scott de Bie, and Ari Marmell. *Neverwinter Campaign Setting.* 2011.
slade, Ed Greenwood, Jeff Grubb, and others. *The North: Guide to the Savage Frontier.* 1996.

Disclaimer: Wizards of the Coast cannot be held responsible for any actions undertaken by entities native to or currently inhabiting the Forgotten Realms, including necromancer lords of distant magocracies, resident mages of any or all Dales but especially Shadowdale, drow rangers wielding one or more scimitars and accompanied by one or more panthers, mad wizards inhabiting sprawling dungeons accessible via a well in the middle of a tavern, beholders who head up criminal cartels, and anyone with the word Many-Arrows in their name. In the event of a catastrophic encounter with any or all such entities, blame your Dungeon Master. If that doesn't work, blame Ed Greenwood, but don't tell him we told you that. He knows more archmages than we do.

ON THE COVER

Tyler Jacobson illustrates this band of adventurers as they engage in aggressive negotiations with a fierce delegation of orcs. Featured (left to right): Skip Brickard, a halfling fighter with an orc-sized chip on his shoulder; Illydia Maethellyn, an aged moon elf cleric of Sehanine Moonbow; Hitch, a brash rogue whose shady past ties him to the Zhentarim; Makos, a tiefling warlock hell-bent on revenge against his infernal father; and Nayeli Goldflower, a powerful human paladin driven by an oath of vengeance.

620B2438000001 EN
ISBN: 978-0-7869-6580-9
First Printing: November 2015

9 8 7 6 5 4 (includes corrections)

$C\epsilon$

Contents

PREFACE

AIL AND WELL MET, TRAVELER! WELCOME to a world of magic and adventure. Originally created by Ed Greenwood, the Forgotten Realms setting has been home to DUNGEONS & DRAGONS stories and games for decades. Built for tales of swords and sorcery, the Realms initially grew and flourished in Ed's D&D campaign, which featured heroes like the Knights of Myth Drannor in the Dalelands. Ed also shared glimpses of the Realms in the pages of *Dragon* magazine, giving D&D players their first tales from the wizard Elminster, the old sage of Shadowdale, who occasionally found his way through a portal between Faerûn and our world and into Ed's living room.

When TSR, the company that owned D&D at the time, sought a new world to expand the D&D multiverse, they chose the Forgotten Realms, and in 1987, the gates were flung wide for players and Dungeon Masters all over the world to come to Faerûn and create their own heroic tales. A year later, author R.A. Salvatore introduced readers to the adventures of the drow outcast Drizzt Do'Urden in his first novel, *The Crystal Shard*, establishing the Underdark as an essential part of the Realms.

In the years since, the Forgotten Realms have played host to a vast number of game products, novels, video games, and more, making it one of the most widely visited fantasy settings ever created. The lost portals to the Realms have returned and remained open in the depths of our imaginations and do so to this day, as more and more visitors find their way there.

It is no surprise, then, that the Forgotten Realms became the setting for the first adventures for fifth edition DUNGEONS & DRAGONS. Already, new heroes have saved Faerûn from terrible evil and will continue to do so, as long as the flame of imagination draws them there.

In these pages, you'll learn about the history, lands, and peoples of Faerûn, of the great city-states of the Sword Coast and the North, of the world's gods, and of the factions and forces that support and threaten civilization. Chapter 1 gives an overview of the Sword Coast and nearby lands, its history, the role of magic, and its religions. Chapter 2 goes into detail about the cities and other locations of the Sword Coast. Chapter 3 gives history and some game material for various races, both common and uncommon, that can be met on the Sword Coast and in the North. Chapter 4 shows how the character options in the *Player's Handbook* fit into this region and presents new character class options. Chapter 5 gives backgrounds designed to link your characters to the great places, people, and events of Faerûn.

While this book is only an introduction to the vastness of the Realms, the setting—like D&D itself—is yours, and has been ever since Ed opened that first portal and invited us to visit. The Realms are a place to tell your stories, about your adventurers and their deeds. The lands and peoples of Faerûn welcome you, traveler, for it is a place of peril sorely in need of the heroes you will bring forth. Go now, through the portal of imagination and into vast and wonderful realms awaiting beyond.

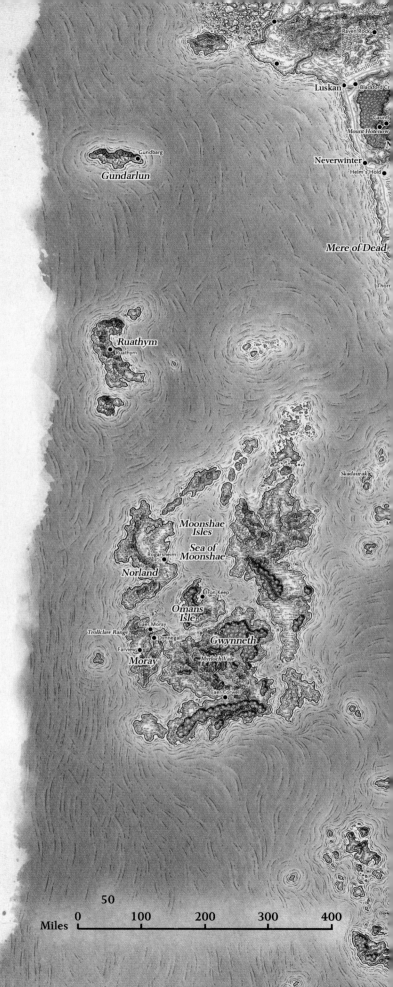

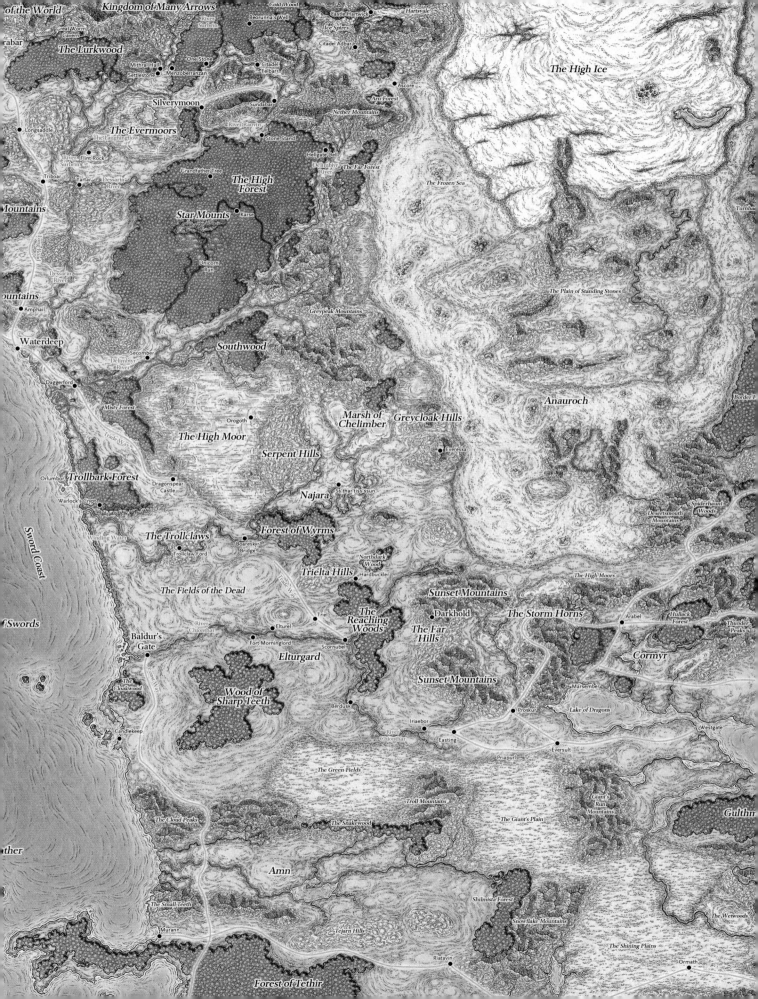

Chapter 1: Welcome to the Realms

O N THE WORLD OF TORIL, BETWEEN THE windswept Sea of Swords to the west and the mysterious lands of Kara-Tur to the east, lies the continent of Faerûn. A place of varied cultures and races, Faerûn is dominated by human lands, be they kingdoms, city-states, or carefully maintained alliances of rural communities. Interspersed among the lands of humans are old dwarven kingdoms and hidden elven enclaves, assimilated populations of gnomes and halflings, and more exotic folk.

A great deal of adventure is to be had in the Realms, for those willing to seek it out. The routes between cities and nations often cross into the territory of brigands or marauding humanoids. Every forest, swamp, and mountain range has its own perils, whether lurking bandits, savage orcs and goblinoids, or mighty creatures such as giants and dragons. Ruins dot the landscape and the caverns that wind beneath the surface. In these places, treasures of every living race—and a number of dead ones—wait for adventurers intrepid enough to come and claim them.

Faerûn is filled with rich history and wondrous tales of adventure and magic, but the lifeblood of its common people is agriculture and trade. Most rural folk depend on farming to eat, and Faerûnians who live in cities ply skilled trades or use brawn to earn their keep, so they can purchase the goods and food provided by others. News and gossip are carried between population centers by caravans and ships that bring in supplies for trade and by traveling bards and minstrels who recount (or invent) stories to inform and entertain people in taverns, inns, and castles. Adventurers also spread news— while also creating it!

The common folk of Faerûn look on adventurers with a mixture of admiration, envy, and mistrust. Folk believe that any stalwarts willing to risk their lives on behalf of complete strangers should be lauded and rewarded. But such adventurers, if they become successful, amass wealth and personal status at a rate that some people find alarming. Even people who admire these adventurers for their energy and their acts of valor might have misgivings: what horrors will be unleashed if adventurers, heedless or unknowing of the danger, unlock a ruin or a tomb and release an ancient evil into the world?

Most of the people who populate the continent have little or no knowledge of lands outside Faerûn. The most educated among the populace agree that Faerûn is but one continent and that Toril is the whole of the world, but for the majority of people, who don't experience intercontinental travel or extraplanar exploration, "Faerûn" is more than large enough of a concept for them to comprehend.

Except in the most remote or insular places, Faerûnians are accustomed to seeing people of different cultures, ethnicities, and races. Only in the most cosmopolitan areas does such casual acceptance extend to evil humanoid races—such as goblinoids, orcs, and drow—to say nothing of even more dangerous creatures. Adventurers tend to be more tolerant, accepting exiles, misfits, and redeemed folk from strange lands and with unusual shapes.

The Sword Coast and the North

Running along the Sea of Swords from north of Amn to the Sea of Moving Ice, the Sword Coast is a narrow band of territory dominated by the city-states of the area that use the sea for trade. For most who care about such things, the area is delimited by Neverwinter in the north and Baldur's Gate in the south, but territory farther to the north and south that isn't under the sway of a more influential power is usually also included in maps of the Sword Coast.

More broadly, the North refers to all the territory north of Amn, split into two general regions: the Western Heartlands and the Savage Frontier. The Western Heartlands encompasses a narrow strip of civilization running from the Sunset Mountains to the Sea of Swords, and northward from the band of territory marked by the Cloud Peaks and the Troll Mountains to the Trade Way. The Savage Frontier is the name given to the rest of the unsettled or sparsely settled territory in the North, not including the major cities and towns and any settlements in their immediate spheres of influence.

Most of the communities, nations, and governments of the North can be grouped into five categories: the cities and towns that are members of the Lords' Alliance, the dwarfholds that have been built throughout the area, the island kingdoms off the coast, the independent realms scattered up and down the coast, and the subterranean environs of the Underdark. Each category is discussed briefly here; more details can be found in chapter 2.

The Lords' Alliance

The Lords' Alliance is a confederation among the rulers of various northern settlements. The number of members on the Council of Lords, the group's governing body, shifts depending on the changing status of member cities and political tensions in the region. Currently, the Lords' Alliance counts these individuals as council members:

- Laeral Silverhand, the Open Lord of Waterdeep
- Dagult Neverember, Lord Protector of Neverwinter
- Taern Hornblade, High Mage of Silverymoon
- Ulder Ravengard, Grand Duke of Baldur's Gate and Marshal of the Flaming Fist
- Morwen Daggerford, Duchess of Daggerford
- Selin Ramur, Marchion of Mirabar
- Dowell Harpell of Longsaddle
- Dagnabbet Waybeard, Queen of Mithral Hall
- Lord Dauner Ilzimmer of Amphail
- Nestra Ruthiol, Waterbaron of Yartar

The Lords' Alliance includes the strongest mercantile powers of the North. In addition to providing military support and a forum for the peaceful airing of differences, the Alliance has always acted under the principle that communities with common cause that engage in trade are less likely to go to war with one another. By maintaining strong trade ties within the alliance as well as outside it, the Lords' Alliance helps to keep the peace.

Dwarfholds of the North

The various dwarven communities of the North are the heirs and survivors of Delzoun, the great Northkingdom of long ago. Despite continually warring over the centuries with the orcs and goblinoids of the region, and having to fight off assaults from below by duergar and drow, the shield dwarves have stood fast, determined to hold their halls against all threats—and, when necessary, reclaim them.

Holds that survive from the days of Delzoun include Mithral Hall, Citadel Adbar, and Citadel Felbarr. The fabled city of Gauntlgrym, built by the Delzoun dwarves and recently taken back from the drow, stands as a beacon of resurgent dwarven strength in the North. Stoneshaft Hold and Ironmaster are lonely settlements continually girding themselves for threats real and imagined. Sundabar and Mirabar are also generally considered dwarfholds, despite their substantial human populations.

Until recently, many of the dwarfholds were members of the Silver Marches (also known as Luruar), an alliance of cities that provided mutual protection across the North. Disagreements and failed obligations during a war with the orc kingdom of Many-Arrows destroyed the remaining trust between members of the Marches, and that pact is no more. The dwarfholds still ally with one another, and individually with nearby human realms, but no longer pledge to stand unified with all their neighbors.

Island Kingdoms

Off the western coast of Faerûn are a number of island realms of varying size. The most distant, and yet perhaps the most symbolically important to the mainland, is Evermeet, the island paradise of the elves, reputed to be a part of the divine realm of Arvandor. Much closer to Faerûn are the Whalebones and Ruathym, ancient homes of the ancestors of the Illuskan people, and the Moonshaes, where many of those same people now share the islands with the Ffolk and an elf offshoot known as the Llewyr. The free port of Mintarn lies nearby, a neutral site for meetings between enemies and a recruitment spot that offers abundant jobs for sailors. Despite its size, the tiny island of Orlumbor, with its treacherous harbor and its skilled, in-demand shipwrights, is an independent and influential nation unto itself.

In the seas to the south, pirates of many races and predilections sail from the Nelanther Isles, preying on trade running north and south along the coasts. Since the beginning of the Sundering, fabled Lantan and Nimbral have returned. Both the center of invention and the isle of Leira-worshiping illusionists are even more secretive and less welcoming of strangers than before their disappearance.

Independent Realms

Interspersed among the fortresses of the dwarves and the settlements protected by the Lord's Alliance are significant sites that have no collective character, except that they exist largely outside the protection or purview of the great powers of the region. Even the civilized locales among these places, such as Elturgard, exist, at best, in an uneasy tension with the denizens of the wilder lands within and just outside their borders, and survive only through constant vigilance and the steady recruitment of new defenders.

A great variety of independent nations and notable locations is encompassed within the wild lands of the North. Among them are the great library of Candlekeep, home of the greatest collection of written lore in Faerûn; the imposing, giant-scale castle of Darkhold; the fortified abbey of Helm's Hold; sites of great battles such as Boareskyr Bridge and the Fields of the Dead; realms of some security, such as Elturgard and Hartsvale; and the yuan-ti realm of Najara. The lands of the Uthgardt, the towns of frigid Icewind Dale, the quiet Trielta Hills, the cutthroat city of Luskan, and the legendary Warlock's Crypt, dominion of the great lich Larloch, are all independent realms, as are the High Moor, the Trollclaws, and the High Forest.

There is much danger and adventure to be had in the free places of the North, and a great deal of wealth and treasure as well. The ruins of ancient kingdoms and countless smaller settlements litter the countryside, waiting for the right explorers to happen upon them.

THE UNDERDARK

Extending miles downward and outward beneath the surface of Faerûn, and reaching to other continents as well, the great network of subterranean caverns known as the Underdark is home to all manner of strange and deadly creatures. Duergar and drow—dark reflections of dwarves and elves—live in these sunless lands, as do the svirfneblin, or deep gnomes. Most surface-dwelling folk aren't threatened or even disturbed by denizens of the deep places, but the creatures occasionally emerge to raid or to seek some kind of goal in the surface world.

Among the lands of the Underdark beneath the North are the svirfneblin city of Blingdenstone, the duergar city of Gracklstugh, and the infamous drow city of Menzoberranzan. Also prominent is Mantol-Derith, a trading post for Underdark merchants.

TORIL AND ITS LANDS

Toril is a vast and wondrous world, filled with an immense diversity of peoples and a rich, full history. For most folk of the Sword Coast, however, knowledge doesn't extend much beyond the confines of the North, and anything "known" outside of Faerûn proper is based more in rumor than in fact.

FAERÛN

The vast central continent of Toril, Faerûn is a land mass divided by a great sea known as the Inner Sea, or the Sea of Fallen Stars. The lands beyond the North can be roughly divided into those to the south and those to the east, becoming more foreign to the folk of the Sword Coast and the North the farther away they are.

LANDS TO THE SOUTH

To the south of the Sword Coast lie ancient nations, a tremendous, forbidding jungle, and all manner of lands destroyed or transformed by magical cataclysms and upheavals. Amid the ruin and the distress in these realms are signs of renewal and hope, as tenacious civilizations and peoples rebuild, reclaim, and create anew.

Amn. A nation led by the representatives of five noble families, Amn is a place where the wealthy rule, openly and without pretense. Shrewd traders and ruthless in business, Amnians believe that the end of a successful transaction is justified by any means, ethical or otherwise. Although the nation is richer by far than even the northern metropolises of Baldur's Gate and Waterdeep, its influence is curtailed by the unwillingness of its rulers to work together in the nation's best interest. The members of the Council of Five are fairly unified and tight-fisted in their control of Amn, but their ability to affect events outside their own borders is limited because they can't agree enough on major matters of foreign policy. The oligarchs utterly control their nation,

but beyond the areas that each rules, their families and businesses compete with one another and with the locals of far-flung places.

The use of arcane magic is illegal in Amn, meaning that the only authorized spellcasters in the nation are wielders of divine magic who enjoy the support and patronage of a temple, and users of arcane magic who have been given special dispensation by one of the oligarchs. So pervasive is the sway of Amn's oligarchy that few crimes merit physical punishment but those that involve the use of arcane magic or an offense against one of the council's merchant houses. Other infractions are forgiven after the miscreant makes payment of an appropriate fine.

Calimshan. This southern land has long been the battleground for warring genies. After years of struggling beneath their genasi masters, human slaves arose to follow a Chosen of Ilmater, at first using nonviolent resistance, and then erupting in full rebellion following his disappearance. They overthrew the genie lords of Calimport and Memnon, casting the remaining genies out of the cities and back to their elemental homes or into the depths of the deserts.

Much of Calimshan is a chaotic place dominated by wealth, political influence, and personal power. Many pray for the return of the Chosen and the completion of his work. Others are learning to live together without genie masters, and to grudgingly accept the remaining genasi among them.

Chult. The vast, choking jungles of Chult hide what many believe to be great mineral wealth, including large gemstones and veins of ore. Poisonous flora and fauna riddle the jungles, but some still brave the dangers to

seek their fortunes. Some of the exotic plants that grow only in Chult fetch high prices in mainland markets. Ruined Mezro stands across the sea from Calimshan, waiting for explorers and its displaced people to cleanse the city of its undead inhabitants and uncover the treasures that lie hidden there.

Eastward along the Chultan peninsula lie the remains of Thindol and Samarach. Despite the apparent fall of both civilizations, Thindol remains infested with yuan-ti, while the illusions cloaking Samarach's mountain passes conceal the activities in that nation.

Dambrath. Situated on a warm plain on the shore of the Great Sea, Dambrath is ruled by nomadic clans of human horse riders who revere Silvanus, Malar, and occasionally Selûne. Given the Dambrathans' history of domination by the Crinti, a ruling caste of half-drow, it is no surprise that they reserve their greatest hatred for the drow.

The clans meet twice a year at a sacred site known as the Hills of the Kings, where dozens of totem sculptures are preserved. At these gatherings, each clan updates its totem with an account of its exploits over the previous seasons. Many Dambrathans seek out lycanthropy as a means of showing reverence for their favored deity and honoring their heritage.

Elfharrow. A blasted near-desert north and east of the North Wall mountains bordering Halruaa, Elfharrow isn't a name bestowed by its residents, but rather the sobriquet that travelers use for this violent region. The tribes of xenophobic elves that claim this area don't hesitate to discourage uninvited guests by any means necessary. A simple group of pilgrims might be scared off with some arrows, while a band of hunters or explorers is likely to be killed outright.

Food is sparse in this region, with the forests long since vanished, and as a result the elves of Elfharrow fiercely protect the herds of animals they have cultivated. The elves have no interest in looting the cities of fallen Lapaliiya, but neither are they willing to allow "adventurers" free access to those lands through their territory.

Halruaa. Once believed destroyed in the conflagration of the Spellplague, Halruaa has largely been restored to the insular, magic-mighty nation it once was. Because of the foresight of their divinations, Halruaan wizards were able to use the raging blue fire that followed Mystra's death to propel their nation safely into the realm of Toril's twin, Abeir (displacing part of that world into the Plane of Shadow).

Now that the events of those times have mostly been undone, the famed Halruaan skyships and waterborne vessels have spread out from their home once again, seeking to establish trading routes and political connections, as well as to learn what has changed of the world in their century of absence.

The Lake of Steam. Far to the south and east of the Sword Coast, the Lake of Steam is more accurately an inland sea, its waters tainted by volcanism and undrinkable. Around its perimeter is a conglomeration of city-states and minor baronies typified by the shifting domains known as the Border Kingdoms. Here, along the southern shore of the lake, explorers and fortune seekers squander their amassed wealth building castles, founding communities, and drawing loyal vassals to them—only to have all those good works disappear within a generation or two. In some cases, one of these realms is fortunate to be saved from its inevitable decline by another group of successful adventurers, who inject enough wealth and wisdom to keep the enterprise going a few more decades.

Luiren. Long the homeland of halflings and thought to be the place where their race had its genesis, Luiren was lost during the Spellplague to a great inundation of the sea. In the century since that great disaster, the waters receded, and now stories told by travelers from the south tell of halfling communities that survived as island redoubts.

Tethyr. Tethyr is a feudal realm ruled by Queen Anais from its capital of Darromar. The queen commands her dukes, who in turn receive homage from the counts and countesses of the realm, appoint sheriffs over their counties, and generally maintain order. The farmlands of Tethyr are abundant, and its markets flow freely with trade from the Western Heartlands.

Tethyr has seen more than its share of noble intrigue and royal murder, and adventurers who are native to Tethyr or merely passing through that land are often drawn into such plots, either as unwitting accomplices or as easy scapegoats.

LANDS TO THE EAST

To the east lie many of the older nations of the Realms, including the Western Heartlands of Faerûn—those civilizations centrally located on the continent, and thereby best able to take advantage of trade routes and access to the Sea of Fallen Stars. As in the North, there are cold lands to the east, as well as more temperate regions. As one travels farther from the Sword Coast, one moves from lands not so different from one's own to places so foreign they might as well exist on other continents or worlds—which a few of them actually have done.

Aglarond. The great peninsula of Aglarond juts out into the Inner Sea, and that body of water and the forests of the Yuirwood define much of the nation's character. A realm of humans living in harmony with their elf and half-elf neighbors, Aglarond has been a foe of Thay for centuries, in part due to the temperament of its former ruler, the Simbul. The nation is now ruled by a Simbarch Council, which has backed away from open hostilities with Thay. With the restoration of the Weave, the ongoing changes to the political landscape, and calls for elven independence within the nation, it is unclear what

REGIONS OF THE REALMS

Just as "the North" describes an area that includes a number of nations and governments, a number of collective terms exist for other regions across Faerûn. Not all such names are used universally, and opinions vary as to which lands qualify in which groups. Here are some currently recognized regional groupings:

The Cold Lands: Damara, Narfell, Sossal, and Vaasa
The Heartlands: Cormyr, the Dalelands, the Moonsea, and Sembia
The Lands of Intrigue: Amn, Calimshan, and Tethyr, also known as the Empires of the Sands
The Old Empires: Chessenta, Mulhorand, and Unther

sort of place Aglarond will be in a generation's time, except that its potential for great change will be realized.

Chessenta. A collection of city-states bound by common culture and mutual defense, Chessenta isn't truly a nation. Each city boasts its own heroes, worships its own gladiatorial champions, and spends as much time insulting and competing with the other cities as it does on any other activity. The city of Luthcheq is dominated by worship of the bizarre deity known as Entropy, while Erebos is ruled by the latest incarnation of the red dragon known as Tchazzar the Undying. Heptios contains the largest library in Chessenta, a center of learning where all nobles aspire to send their children for tutoring. That city is looked on with disdain by the people of Akanax, whose militant contempt for the "fat philosophers" of Heptios is widely known. Toreus welcomes all visitors, even those from lands that are despised or mistrusted, and foreign coin can buy nearly anything there. The floating city of Airspur still flies somehow, its earthmotes unaffected by the fall of its fellows when the Sundering came to a close.

Cormyr. For most folk in central Faerûn, the notion of a human kingdom is inextricably linked to Cormyr. A strong realm bolstered by its loyal army (the Purple Dragons), a cadre of magical defenders and investigators (the War Wizards), and numerous wealthy and influential nobles, Cormyr is recovering from its war with Sembia and Netheril—a conflict that cost the nation much, but left the kingdom standing, and which, in the end, Netheril didn't survive. The pride of that victory remains strong in Cormyr's collective consciousness, even as Queen Raedra draws back from plans to permanently welcome into the realm towns that lie beyond Cormyr's traditional borders.

Cormyreans are justly proud of their homeland, and go to great lengths to guard it and its honor. Still, there is no shortage of danger in the Forest Kingdom, whether from scheming, treacherous nobles, monsters out of the Hullack Forest or the Stonelands, or some ancient, hidden magic. Cormyr is many things, but dull isn't one of them.

The Cold Lands. The nations of Damara, Narfell, Sossal, and Vaasa, known collectively to most Faerûnians as the Cold Lands, rest near the Great Glacier in the cold, dry environs of the northeast. Few outside the region have much interest in what goes on here, except for those in the immediately surrounding lands, who fear a resurgence of the ancient evils of the region—though they aren't fearful enough to do more than send an adventuring party or two into the area to investigate.

In Damara, the usurper King Yarin Frostmantle sits on the throne of the Dragonbane dynasty, while his people complain about his tyranny and the growing threat from demons across the country. In Narfell, skilled riders and archers hunt, raid, and are gradually reclaiming their heritage as a great nation of mages who treated with devils. The Warlock Knights of Vaasa threaten to break the bounds of their nation and invade Damara, the Moonsea, or both, while some of its members suspiciously eye the ominously silent Castle Perilous, perhaps planning another excursion to the place. The tiny nation of Sossal trades with its neighbors, but shares little of itself with the wider world.

The Dalelands. The humans who call the Dalelands home want nothing more than lives untroubled by the concerns of larger nations. They take great pride in their peaceful coexistence with the elves of Cormanthor, and in their ability to remain largely self-sufficient and autonomous even when their homeland was used as a battlefield by Cormyr, Netheril, Sembia, and Myth Drannor in the recent conflicts. Featherdale and Tasseldale have reasserted their independence since the end of the war, and rejoined Archendale, Battledale, Daggerdale, Deepingdale, Harrowdale, Mistledale, Scardale, and Shadowdale on the Dales Council. The High Dale did the same shortly afterward.

Dalesfolk are mistrustful of anyone unwilling to sacrifice for the common good, but those who put in good work—whether in defense or labor—are accepted as equals, entitled to share in the rewards from their toil.

The Hordelands. Formerly known as the Endless Wastes, this land has gained a new name among Faerûnians, styled after the vast Tuigan horde that roared out of the east and rode against Faerûn more than a century ago. After these tribesfolk were defeated, some of the fierce, mounted warriors who survived the conflict gathered to form the small nation of Yaïmunnahar. Some others cling to the old ways, mastering the sword and the bow and riding across the steppes on their short-legged horses. Brave merchants still traverse the Golden Way to and from Kara-Tur, but those who return from such a voyage are fewer than they once were.

Impiltur. With the rising of the waters of the Sea of Fallen Stars, some of Impiltur's wealth and influence is returning, leading to whispers among the populace that a lost king of the line of old will rise up to lift Impiltur out of its woes and back to the great nation it once was.

Impiltur is a nation of humans with pockets of dwarves and halflings among its populace. Where once a long royal line sat its throne and ruled over a unified kingdom, now a Grand Council sits around a table and struggles to combat the presence of demons, and demon worship, within the nation's borders.

The Moonsea. The shores of the Moonsea have long been home to cities that rise swiftly, relying on vigorous trade and gathering powerful mercenaries to their banners, only to overextend themselves and fall—sometimes crumbling over time, and sometimes dropping like stones from the sky.

Now that Netheril and Myth Drannor have fallen, those two great powers can no longer exert their influence over the Moonsea, allowing the city of Hillsfar to spread its wings and eye southward expansion, and Mulmaster to once again further the worship of Bane. Phlan, Teshwave, Thentia, and Voonlar—all Moonsea cities where greater powers jockeyed for influence—now work to find their own identities before an unchecked or malevolent realm swallows them, one by one.

This region is also home to the ruins of the Citadel of the Raven and Zhentil Keep, former strongholds of the Zhentarim, which the Black Network shows occasional interest in restoring.

Mulhorand. Since the Chosen of the gods began to appear in the last few years, Mulhorand has become a land transformed. Its deities manifested fully in the forms of some of their descendants, and swiftly rallied the Mulan to overthrow the Imaskari. Aided by the mighty wizard Nezram, known as the World-Walker, the Mulhorandi overthrew the rulers of High Imaskar, who fled into the Plains of Purple Dust or to extraplanar safeholds.

When the upheaval ended and the Chosen began to disappear, the gods of Mulhorand remained to rule their people, focusing their attention on defending their restored homeland to keep the war in Unther and Tymanther from spilling over its borders. For the first time in centuries, the people in Mulhorand are free, with the gods declaring that slavery shall no longer be practiced among the Mulan since their return.

Rashemen. A harsh, cold land filled with hardy folk, Rashemen is a fiercely traditional nation. It is ruled by its Iron Lord, Mangan Uruk, who speaks for the power behind the throne: the Wychlaran, the society of masked witches that determine Rashemen's course. These witches wield great powers tied to the land and its magic and guard against evil fey and vengeful spirits. A small number of male spellcasters, known as the Old Ones, create magic items and weave arcane rituals for the witches. Rashemi witches revere the Three, a triumvirate of goddesses they call Bhalla (the Den Mother), Khelliara (the Forest Maiden), and the Hidden One. Over the centuries, scholars in other lands have speculated that these deities might be faces of Chauntea, Mielikki, and Mystra, respectively.

The nation's warriors are a fierce, stoic lot, famed for their strength, endurance, and stubbornness in battle. Rashemen is a long-standing enemy of Thay, and has often thwarted that nation's ambitions to rule Faerûn. Little pleases a Rashemi warrior more than the chance to strike down a Red Wizard in battle.

Sembia. Following a period of subjugation at the hands of Netheril, Sembia is already on its way to becoming the economic power it was in prior years. Although relations are cool with the Dales and Cormyr following the most recent war, Sembian merchants are quick to dismiss previous conflicts as the work of the Netherese, and remind their former trading partners of the long and mutually profitable relationships they previously enjoyed. To prove its good intentions, Sembia has "allowed" Featherdale and Tasseldale to regain their independence, even though Sembian investors had owned much of Featherdale for nearly seventy years when the war came to an end.

Before Netheril claimed Sembia as a vassal state, mercenary work and adventuring were popular livelihoods among Sembians who didn't have local families to feed. Those endeavors are even more popular now among veterans of the war, who are better trained than their predecessors were. A few of Sembia's less scrupulous former soldiers have taken to banditry, which offers other Sembians more opportunities for guard work.

Thay. For centuries one of the greatest concentrations of magical might in Faerûn, Thay is ruled by the ancient lich, Szass Tam, and the nation's Council of Zulkirs in a ruthless magocracy. The council's will is enacted by regional tharchions and bureaucrats, leaving the ruling Red Wizards to focus on magical study and more important arcane matters.

For a time, living mages couldn't hope to advance to prominence in Thay: Szass Tam promoted undeath as a means of existence with boundless possibilities, and held back those who didn't agree with this philosophy. The recent battles with the demon Eltab, however, have prompted Szass Tam to loosen this stricture—the living now have hope of ascending within the Red Wizards, even if that hope is merely to advance to a high station within the cadre of Tam's servants.

Thesk. Reminders of the century-old war with the Tuigan horde remain throughout Thesk, in the many and varied features of its present-day inhabitants, particularly the half-orc descendants of the mercenaries who fought in that great conflict.

Thesk is known to many as the Gateway to the East because it is the western terminus of the Golden Way, which runs through the Hordelands and into Kara-Tur. Because their city is a crossroads of sorts between Faerûn and the east, it should come as no surprise that Theskians don't judge outsiders quickly, and don't bristle at visitors who demonstrate strange quirks in speech or behavior. The people of Thesk trade readily with any folk, even nearby orcs and goblins that are willing to treat with them peacefully. They aren't fools, however, and have no patience for violent or raiding humanoids of all sorts.

Turmish. On the southern shore of the Sea of Fallen Stars, Turmish is a nation of mercantile cities ruled by its Assembly of Stars, representatives of each of its cities in a parliamentary democracy. After being much diminished by the devastation wrought in this area a century ago, Turmish is currently enjoying a revival of its fortunes, as the rising of the waters of the Inner Sea has returned some of the trade that was lost in the cataclysm. Turmish is the birthplace of the Emerald Enclave, which has proudly taken credit for the rebirth of Turmishan agriculture, the cessation of the great rains that plagued the region a few years ago, and the restoration of the god Lathander.

Tymanther. In decades past, the land of the dragonborn claimed as its territory part of what had been the vanished nation of Unther. Then Unther suddenly returned to Faerûn a few years ago and promptly went to war against Tymanther. The realm has since been reduced to small tracts mainly along the coast of the

COIN OF THE REALMS

Nearly every major power of Faerûn has its own currency: coins minted within its borders that represent both its influence and material wealth. Most coins of pure composition and standard weight are accepted at face value across the continent, though not every city-state or nation bothers to mint every sort of coin.

Some of the most commonly found, and widely accepted, currency in the Realms is summarized below. Each grouping is arranged in order of value: copper, silver, electrum, gold, and (when present) platinum. Most people across Faerûn refer to coins by whatever name the issuing government uses, regardless of origin, except for Zhentil Keep—for some reason, all Zhent coins have unflattering epithets associated with them.

Amn: fander, taran, centaur, danter, roldon
Cormyr: thumb, falcon, blue eye, golden lion, tricrown
Sembia: steelpence (an iron coin), hawk, blue eye, noble
Silverymoon: glint, shield, sword, dragon, unicorn
Waterdeep: nib, shard, sambar, dragon, sun
Zhentil Keep: fang ("dung-piece"), talon/naal ("flea-bit"), tarenth ("hardhammer"), glory ("weeping wolf"), platinum glory ("flat metal gem")

Silverymoon also mints two special coins: the moon and the eclipsed moon. The moon is a crescent-shaped, shining blue coin of electrum, valued at 2 unicorns in Silverymoon and nearby settlements, and 1 unicorn everywhere else. The eclipsed moon stamps an electrum moon with a darker silver wedge to complete a round coin. It is worth 5 unicorns within the city, but only 2 unicorns elsewhere.

Waterdeep has its own coins. The taol is a square piece of brass, worth 2 dragons in the city—and virtually worthless to anyone not trading with Waterdeep. Most traders exchange their taols for standard coins before traveling. The "harbor moon" is a palm-sized crescent of platinum inset with electrum, and is worth 50 dragons in the city, 30 dragons elsewhere. Its name comes from its common use in buying large amounts of cargo. Both taols and harbor moons are pierced to enable the bearer to string multiple coins together.

Baldur's Gate sets the standard for minting trade bars—ingots of metal (usually silver) of an accepted size and weight used in lieu of great piles of coins or gems for larger transactions. The most common such trade bar is a 5-pound bar 6 inches long, 2 inches wide, and 1 inch thick, valued at 25 gp.

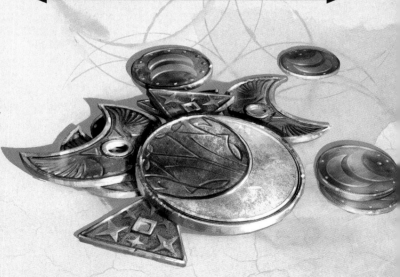

Alamber Sea and Ash Lake. The dragonborn that have withdrawn to those areas have lost none of their military tradition, and their ability to hold this smaller amount of territory makes it unlikely that Unther will push farther any time soon—particularly since the Untherite navy has been unable to overcome the great beast that guards the harbor of Djerad Kethendi and the nearby waters of the Alamber.

Some of Tymanther's dragonborn have spread across Faerûn and gained reputations as competent, highly sought-after mercenaries.

Unther. Trapped in another world, the people of Unther had succumbed to domination by others. Then among them arose one who called himself Gilgeam, and he reminded them of their former greatness. Under the leadership of this reincarnated god, the people of Unther rose up as an army to face their masters. On the eve of a great battle, the people of Unther were miraculously returned to their home, and Gilgeam wasted no time in leading them against the dragonborn occupying their ancestral lands. The Untherites have retaken much of the land they formerly held, while seeking to wipe out the "godless lizards" they blame for their time of oppression in Abeir.

Gilgeam wants nothing short of a complete return to Unther's former glory. This achievement will require utterly destroying Tymanther, of course, and eventual war with Mulhorand to reclaim lands lost centuries ago, but as every Untherite knows, the great God-King is patient, for he is eternal.

Westgate. The dismal city of Westgate isn't a romantic place, but someone seeking employment for shady work, or looking to hire someone for the same, will find few places better suited in all of Faerûn.

Westgate is considered by some Faerûnians as a harbinger of the eventual fate of places like Amn and Sembia, where coin rules over all other considerations. As in many such places, one's moral outlook is less important in Westgate than one's attitude toward bribery. The city's proximity to Cormyr makes it a breeding ground for that nation's enemies, including the Fire Knives, a guild of thieves and assassins that the naive pretend doesn't exist.

Kara-Tur

Far to the east, past the wastes of the Hordelands, lie the empires of Shou Lung, Kozakura, Wa, and the other lands of the vast continent of Kara-Tur. To most people of Faerûn, Kara-Tur is like another world, and the tales told by travelers from its nations seem to confirm it. The gods that humans worship in Faerûn are unknown there, as are common peoples such as gnomes and orcs. Other dragons, neither chromatic nor metallic, dwell in its lands and fly its skies. And its mages practice forms of magic mysterious even to archwizards of Faerûn.

Stories of Kara-Tur tell of gold and jade in great abundance, rich spices, silks, and other goods rare or unknown in western lands—alongside tales of shapechanging spirit-people, horned giants, and nightmare monsters absent in Faerûn.

Zakhara

Far to the south of Faerûn, beyond Calimshan and even the jungles of Chult, are the Lands of Fate. Surrounded by waters thick with pirates and corsairs, Zakhara is a place less hospitable than most, but still braved by travelers who hope to profit from its exotic goods and strange magics. Like Kara-Tur, Zakhara seems a world away to Faerûnians. It is thought of as a vast desert, sprinkled with glittering cities like scattered gems. Romantic tales abound of scimitar-wielding rogues riding flying carpets and of genies bound in service to humans. Their mages, called sha'ir, practice their magic with the aid of genies and, it is said, might carry the lineage of these elemental beings in their blood.

Beyond the Trackless Sea

Farther to the west, past even Evermeet, are untold, unknown lands beyond the Trackless Sea. Many explorers have visited such lands, and some have even returned, bearing tales that change from generation to generation about exotic locales, from island chains that are the sites of countless shipwrecks, to fearsome feather-clad warriors, and vast continents that suddenly appeared where nothing—or something very much different—had rested only seasons prior.

Time in the Realms

Although a number of means exist for marking the days and the passage of time during a year, nearly all folk in Faerûn have adopted the Calendar of Harptos. Even the cultures and races that don't favor this method of marking time are aware of it, with the result that it is recognized across nearly all races, languages, and cultures.

A year on Toril consists of 365 days. In the Calendar of Harptos, the year is divided into twelve months of thirty days, loosely following the synodic cycle of Selûne, the moon. A month is made up of three tendays, also known as rides. Five annual holidays, falling between the months, complete the 365-day calendar. Once every four years, the Calendar of Harptos includes Shieldmeet as a "leap day" following Midsummer.

Individual days of a tenday have no special names. Instead, they are denoted by counting from the beginning of the period ("first day," "second day," and so on). Days of the month are designated by a number and the month name. For example, sages would record an event as occurring on "1 Mirtul" or "27 Uktar." People might also refer to a given day by its relationship to the current date ("two tendays from today") or the nearest holiday ("three days past Greengrass").

Special Calendar Days

Every nation, faith, and culture across Faerûn has its own special festivals and holidays, the observances of which are governed by the cycles of the sun, the moon, the stars, or some other event. In addition, the Calendar of Harptos specifies five annual festivals keyed to the changing of the seasons and one quadrennial festival that are observed in almost every land, with particular celebrations varying based on local traditions and popular faiths.

Midwinter. The first festival day of the year is known generally as Midwinter, though some people name it differently. Nobles and monarchs of the Heartlands look to the High Festival of Winter as a day to commemorate or renew alliances. Commoners in the North, the Moonsea, and other, colder climes celebrate Deadwinter Day as a marking of the midpoint of the cold season, with hard times still ahead, but some of the worst days now past.

Greengrass. The traditional beginning of spring, Greengrass is celebrated by the display of freshly cut flowers (grown in special hothouses wherever the climate doesn't permit flowers so early) that are given as gifts to the gods or spread among the fields in hopes of a bountiful and speedy growing season.

Midsummer. The midpoint of summer is a day of feasting, carousing, betrothals, and basking in the pleasant weather. Storms on Midsummer night are seen as bad omens and signs of ill fortune, and sometimes interpreted as divine disapproval of the romances or marriages sparked by the day's events.

Shieldmeet. The great holiday of the Calendar of Harptos, Shieldmeet occurs once every four years immediately after Midsummer. It is a day for plain speaking and open council between rulers and their subjects, for the renewal of pacts and contracts, and for treaty making between peoples. Many tournaments and contests of skill are held on Shieldmeet, and most faiths mark the holiday by emphasizing one of their key tenets.

The next Shieldmeet will be observed in 1492 DR.

Highharvestide. A day of feasting and thanks, Highharvestide marks the fall harvest. Most humans give thanks to Chauntea on this day for a plentiful bounty before winter approaches. Many who make their living by traveling road or sea set out immediately following the holiday, before winter comes on in full force and blocks mountain passes and harbors.

The Feast of the Moon. As nights lengthen and winter winds begin to approach, the Feast of the Moon is the time when people celebrate their ancestors and their honored dead. During festivals on this day, people gather to share stories and legends, offer prayers for the fallen, and prepare for the coming cold.

KEEPING TIME FROM DAY TO DAY

Most people don't keep track of the time of day beyond notions such as "mid-morning" or "nigh sunset." If people plan to meet at a particular time, they tend to base their arrangements around such expressions.

The concept of hours and minutes exists mainly where wealthy people use clocks, but mechanical clocks are often unreliable, and rarely are two set to the same time. If a local temple or civic structure has a clock that tolls out the passing of the hours, people refer to hours as "bells," as in "I'll meet you at seven bells."

THE SHIFTING OF THE SEASONS

The worlds of Abeir and Toril drifted apart in 1487 and 1488 DR. In some places this change was accompanied

THE CALENDAR OF HARPTOS

Month	Name	Common Name
1	Hammer	Deepwinter
	Annual Holiday: Midwinter	
2	Alturiak	The Claw of Winter
3	Ches	The Claw of Sunsets
4	Tarsahk	The Claw of Storms
	Annual Holiday: Greengrass	
5	Mirtul	The Melting
6	Kythorn	The Time of Flowers
7	Flamerule	Summertide
	Annual Holiday: Midsummer	
	Quadrennial Holiday: Shieldmeet	
8	Eleasis	Highsun
9	Elient	The Fading
	Annual Holiday: Highharvestide	
10	Marpenoth	Leaffall
11	Uktar	The Rotting
	Annual Holiday: The Feast of the Moon	
12	Nightal	The Drawing Down

by cataclysm, while in others the shift went without notice. Astronomers and navigators who closely watched the stars couldn't fail to see that there were nights when they seemed to hang in the sky. The winter of 1487–1488 lasted longer than normal. It was then noted that the solstices and equinoxes had somehow shifted, beginning with the spring equinox falling on Greengrass of 1488 DR. The seasons followed suit, with each starting later and ending later.

This shift in seasons has caused some sages, and the priests of Chauntea, to consider changing the marking of some of the annual feast days, but most folk counsel patience, believing that the seasons will fall back to their previous cycle over the coming years.

A BRIEF HISTORY

The known history of the Sword Coast region spans thousands of years, extending back into the misty epochs of the creator races and the ages of the first nations of the elves and dwarves. Comparatively recent history is the story of the rise and deeds of humans and other younger races.

Much of what follows in this section is known mainly by sages, some of whom have been alive for the last few centuries of Faerûn's history. The common folk across the continent have little knowledge of, and little use for, events that have transpired far away in time and space. News does travel, of course, so even people who live in a village along the Sword Coast might get wind of happenings in distant lands.

THE DAYS OF THUNDER

Tens of thousands of years ago, empires of reptilian, amphibian, and avian peoples—known in Elvish as *Iqua'Tel'Quessir*, the creator races—dominated the world. They built great cities of stone and glass, carved paths through the wilderness, tamed the great lizards, worked mighty magics, shaped the world around them, and warred upon each other. Those were the Days of Thunder.

The age of the creator races came to a sudden end some thirty thousand years ago. Perhaps their wars reached a terrible and inevitable crescendo, or they tampered with forbidden forces. For whatever reason, the world changed, and their vast empires vanished. All that remains of them are ruins and the scattered lizardfolk, bullywug, and aarakocra tribes, barbaric descendants of those who once ruled the world.

THE FIRST FLOWERING

From the ruins of the Days of Thunder arose the first nations of the Proud People—the elves and dwarves—in the region.

The elves raised up the nations of Aryvandaar, Ardeep, and Ilythiir. They settled Illefarn along the Sword Coast, from the Spine of the World to the River Delimbiyr—its capitol Aelinthaldaar in the shadow of what is now Mount Waterdeep. Wood elves and moon elves founded the kingdom of Eaerlann in the Delimbiyr Valley and the High Forest, and separatists from Aryvandaar settled Miyeritar in the lands of the present-day High Moor and Misty Forest.

The dwarf clans united as the nation of Delzoun, named for its forge-founder, with dwarfholds built on sites ranging from the Ice Mountains to the Nether Mountains and the Narrow Sea, and settlements and halls westward to the Crags and the Sword Mountains.

The Proud People regularly defended their homelands against orc hordes that arose from the mountains of the Spine of the World and surged southward to attack and pillage.

THE FIRST SUNDERING

Thousands of years after the rise of the great elven nations, hundreds of elf high mages united to cast a spell intended to create a glorious homeland for their race. The spell succeeded, but it rippled backward and forward in time, and the land was sundered, changing the face of the world. The largest continent of this new world is now called Faerûn. Far from its western shores rose the isle of Evermeet, considered a part of Arvandor, the home of the elven gods on the plane of Arborea, and a bridge between worlds.

THE CROWN WARS

Some thirteen thousand years ago, war broke out between the elven nations of Aryvandaar and Miyeritar, beginning a series of conflicts known as the Crown Wars. Lasting some three thousand years, these conflicts culminated in the Dark Disaster, in which terrible storms engulfed Miyeritar, turning it into a wasteland within a single season, leaving behind the area now known as the High Moor. The high mages of Aryvandaar are blamed for the destruction, although no proof was ever produced.

The vengeful dark elves of Ilythiir turned to corrupt and demonic powers, unleashing them against Aryvandaar. In the centuries of destruction that followed, elf priests and high mages fervently prayed to Corellon Larethian and the gods of the elven pantheon for salvation.

THE DESCENT OF THE DROW

Corellon interceded in the Crown Wars and cursed the dark elves so that they might never dwell comfortably under the sun. Now finding themselves pained by exposure to daylight, the drow—in a mere two months' time—retreated from the sunlit lands of the World Above into the Underdark. They abandoned all loyalty to the elven gods who betrayed and banished them, turning instead to Lolth, the Demon Queen of Spiders, as their patron. Wars soon began between the drow and the underground cities of the dwarves.

THE AGE OF HUMANITY

For millennia following the end of the Crown Wars, humans spread and settled throughout Faerûn as the elven and dwarven nations stagnated and then began a long, slow decline. Deep in the Underdark, the drow fought wars of survival and conquest in their new domain.

THE RISE AND FALL OF NETHERIL

More than five thousand years ago, a group of human fishing villages on the shores of the Narrow Sea joined under the rule of the shaman-king Nether, becoming known as the empire of Netheril. The Netherese learned the use of magic from the Eaerlanni elves and became renowned wizards. Centuries later, they discovered the arcane texts known as the *Nether Scrolls* in the ruins of Aryvandaar and subsequently abandoned the practices of the Eaerlanni in order to procure even greater magical power.

Netheril grew to become an invincible nation of magic and wonders, dominating much of the North for three thousand years. Then the power-mad Netherese arcanist Karsus attempted to usurp the role of the goddess of magic. The resulting disruption in the fabric of magic sent Netheril's floating cities crashing to the ground, destroyed a host of other wards and enchantments, and brought about the end of the great empire.

THE GREAT CITIES

In the decades and centuries following the collapse of Netheril, many cities of the Sword Coast and the North, such as Illusk and Citadel Sundbarr, took in refugees from the fallen empire, and new settlements made up entirely or primarily of human survivors from Netheril and their descendants were established throughout the North and in the Western Heartlands.

Nearly fifteen hundred years ago, the human settlers of the Dalelands and the elves of Cormanthor pledged their alliance in an agreement known as the Dales Compact. A monument called the Standing Stone was erected to mark the occasion, and the advent of Dalereckoning was decreed, beginning with the year 1 DR. This method of numbering the years in Toril's history has spread across Faerûn and is commonly understood (if not universally accepted).

The city of Neverwinter—called Eigersstor when it was a mere settlement—was founded in 87 DR. On the banks of the River Raurin, the humble community of Silverymoon Ford came into being in 384 DR, and less than two centuries later it had grown to become the city of Silverymoon.

In 882 DR, a village and trading post on the shore of a deep bay in the shadow of a great mountain was named Nimoar's Hold, after the Uthgardt chieftain who claimed the area and fortified it. The place became known to sea captains as "Waterdeep," a name that displaced the original within a few generations. In 1032 DR, Ahghairon, heir to the arts of Netheril, saved the city from itself by unseating Waterdeep's warlord and would-be emperor, Raurlor. Ahghairon declared that wisdom, not strength of arms, would rule in the city from now on, and created the Lords of Waterdeep.

These and other nations and great city-states rose to prominence along the Sword Coast, forming a chain along the Trade Way from Illusk in the far north to Baldur's Gate in the south, near the borders of Amn. Like their elven and dwarven predecessors, they fought off attacks by savage humanoids, including orc hordes from the Spine of the World. Waterdeep, guided by its mysterious Lords, became a rising power, while old Illusk fell to the orcs for decades, until it was eventually reclaimed and the city of Luskan built upon its ruins.

The Present Age

The four and a half centuries since the establishment of the Lords of Waterdeep have been tumultuous times for the Sword Coast and the world. Throughout this period, civilization struggles against the savage forces of chaos, and life attempts to persevere against the agents of death and strife, sometimes in places where even the gods themselves have not been exempt from destruction.

The last one hundred fifty years have comprised one of the most cataclysmic periods in Faerûn's history. On no fewer than three occasions, Toril has been shaken to its core by forces that have repeatedly rewritten the laws of reality.

The Time of Troubles

In 1358 DR, the gods were cast out of their otherworldly domain and made to wander the land incarnated as mortals. In seeking to recover their divinity, they warred among themselves. Magic became unpredictable, and the prayers of the faithful went unanswered. Some of the gods-turned-mortal were slain, while a handful of mortals ascended to godhood, assuming the responsibilities of the dead deities.

The Return of Netheril

In 1374 DR, the Empire of Netheril rose again when the floating city of Thultanthar, commonly known as Shade, returned from a nearly two-thousand-year-long excursion in the Shadowfell, to hover above the Anauroch desert. The shadow-touched nobles of the city almost immediately began hunting for ancient Netherese ruins and artifacts and preparing for a restoration of their once-great empire.

The Spellplague

In 1385 DR, the ascended deity Cyric, aided by Shar, murdered Mystra, the goddess of magic, in her domain of Dweomerheart. This act ripped asunder the fabric of magic in the world, unleashing its raw power in a catastrophe called the Spellplague. Thousands of practitioners of the Art were driven mad or killed, while the face of Faerûn was reshaped by waves and veils of mystic blue fire. Entire nations were displaced or exchanged with realms from other worlds, and parts of the earth were torn free to float in the air.

The Second Sundering

A century after the Spellplague, the lands and peoples of Faerûn had become accustomed to the state of things—just in time for everything to change again.

The first indication of new turmoil came in 1482 DR, when Bhaal, the long-dead god of murder, was reborn in Baldur's Gate amid chaos and bloodshed, leaving two of the city's dukes and many of its citizens dead. The return of Bhaal and his apparent reclamation of the domain of murder from Cyric led some scholars and sages to believe that the rules by which all deities must abide were in flux.

In 1484, strange calamities began to occur throughout Faerûn. An earthquake struck Iriaebor. A plague of locusts afflicted Amn. Droughts gripped the southern lands as the sea steadily receded in places. Amid this tumult, conflict broke out in many regions of the continent. The orcs of Many-Arrows warred against the dwarfholds of the North and their allies. Sembia invaded the Dalelands, and Cormyr raised an army to come to the aid of the Dalesfolk. Netheril brought forces to Cormyr's border, and Cormyr was drawn into a war on both fronts.

Throughout this period, tales began to spread of individuals who had been touched by the gods and granted strange powers. Some of these so-called Chosen were at the root of the conflicts that grip the land. Some seemed driven by divine purpose, while others claimed to be mystified as to why they would be singled out.

In 1485, in Icewind Dale, the Chosen of Auril foments war with Ten-Towns and is defeated. In Anauroch, seeing that Netherese forces were spread thin, the long-subjugated Bedine people rebelled. Having defeated or besieged the dwarfholds of the North, orcs march on Silverymoon. In Cormyr and Sembia, the Netherese and the Cormyreans traded ground, while the Dalelands became a war zone. As if to offset the drought in the south, in the autumn of 1485 the Great Rain began to fall around the Sea of Fallen Stars and continued unceasingly.

While the waters rose to the east in early 1486, the tide turned against the orcs in the North, and by the end of the year their armies were broken and scattered. Also during that year, the elves of Myth Drannor came to the aid of the Dalelands and helped push back Sembian forces. On the Sword Coast, the Hosttower of the Arcane rose again in Luskan, along with the Arcane Brotherhood. In Waterdeep and Neverwinter, efforts were made to clear those cities of century-old rubble and neglect. Cormyr repulsed the last of the Sembian and Netherese forces from the nation, reclaiming its territory, and recalled its forces, turning inward to address issues of rebuilding.

Late in 1486, the Great Rain finally abated, but this event didn't signify an end to the chaos. The Sea of

Fallen Stars had grown, submerging great swaths of land beneath its waves.

Early in 1487, earthquakes and volcanic eruptions abounded for months, as if the whole world was convulsing. Rumors spread of chasms caused by the Spellplague suddenly vanishing, and stories circulated of known destinations being farther away from one another, as if the world had quietly added miles of wilderness to the distance between them. Word began to spread of places and peoples not heard from since the Spellplague. It became apparent that some of the effects of that terrible time had been reversed. During the year, ships claiming to be from Evermeet, Lantan, and Nimbral—nations thought vanished or destroyed—sailed into ports on the Sword Coast and in the Shining South. Tales spread of the legendary skyships of Halruaa being spotted in southern skies. No longer engaged in Cormyr, Netheril attacked Myth Drannor by floating the City of Shade over it. In a struggle for control of Myth Drannor's *mythal* and the Weave itself, the flying capital of Netheril was brought crashing down on Myth Drannor, resulting in the cataclysmic destruction of both.

As the year drew to a close, there were nights when the heavens seemed to hang motionless. Throughout much of Faerûn, the winter of 1487 and 1488 lasted longer than any on record. The solstices and equinoxes had somehow drifted. Later seasons followed suit, with each starting and ending later than expected. Prayers to the gods for knowledge and mercy seemed to go unacknowledged, apart from the presence of their Chosen.

Although the orcs were defeated in the North, the League of Silver Marches was disbanded in 1488, as former allies blamed one another for failures in the war. Sembia divided into separate city-states only nominally allied with one another. While a handful of settlements survived, the Netherese Empire was no more. The remainder of the Netherese forces battle with the Bedine over control of the Memory Spire, thought to be a tomb of the phaerimm, Netheril's ancient enemies. The battle awakens what turns out to be a hive of the creatures, and they use the life and magic-draining power of the spire against the lands below.

By 1489, many of the wars that began during the Sundering had ground to a close. Other conflicts arose, and mighty threats still imperiled the world, but the deities ceased interfering with the world through their Chosen. The gods were no longer silent but quiet, and in many places new priesthoods arose to interpret the gods' now subtle signs.

The world today seems a place filled with new lands and opportunities, where those who dare can leave their mark. Students of history and those elves and dwarves who recall the past that short-lived humans see as distant perceive a world much like it was over a century ago. For most folk, wild tales of people empowered by the gods, and of far-off lands returned to the world, are the subjects of fireside chatter. Daily concerns and the dangers and opportunities just beyond their doors take precedence, and plenty of both remain on the Sword Coast and in the North.

Magic in the Realms

From the simplest cantrip to the mightiest workings of High Magic, from the blessings of healing mercy to the raising of mighty heroes from the dead, magic permeates the Realms. Any understanding of magic begins, and ends, with an understanding of the Weave.

The Weave

The Weave is an essential element of the universe, running through everything in unseen threads. Some creatures, objects, and locations have deep, intrinsic ties to the Weave and can perform extraordinary feats that come naturally to them (a beholder's flight, a vampire's charming gaze, a dragon's breath weapon, and so forth). Creatures with the necessary talent and skill can also manipulate the Weave to perform magic by casting spells.

The Weave isn't normally visible or detectable, even through the use of spells. *Detect magic* doesn't let you perceive the Weave, for instance. The Weave isn't magic, precisely, any more than a collection of threads is a garment; it's the raw material from which the tapestry of magic is woven.

In two senses, both the metaphorical and the real, the goddess Mystra is the Weave. She is its keeper and tender, but all three times the goddess of magic has died or been separated from her divinity (twice as Mystra, and once as her predecessor, Mystryl), magic has been twisted or has failed entirely. With Mystra's last death and the coming of the Spellplague, the Weave was thought destroyed, and the term lost its significance. Since the end of the most recent Sundering, both Mystra and the Weave have returned to their roles of centuries past, and spells and magic items are more reliable than they had been while the Spellplague raged.

Supernatural Powers and Psionics

The inborn magical abilities of certain creatures, the acquired supernatural powers of people such as monks, and psionic abilities are similar in that their users don't manipulate the Weave in the customary way that spellcasters do. The mental state of the user is vitally important: monks and some psionics-users train long and hard to attain the right frame of mind, while creatures with supernatural powers have that mind-set in their nature. How these abilities are related to the Weave remains a matter of debate; many students of the arcane believe that the use of the so-called Unseen Art is an aspect of magical talent that can't be directly studied or taught.

Magic Items

Where a spell effect is brought to life by manipulating the threads of the Weave, the creation of a magic item ties some of those threads together in a specific way, to produce the desired effect for as long as the item lasts. The Weave provides immediately available energy for spells and also enables those who know the craft to harness that energy inside an object until it is called forth by its user (who, of course, need not be a spellcaster).

In some cases, the magic of an item must be tied to its wielder, representing an entwining of the threads of the Weave between wielder and object known as attunement. As with all matters related to magic, the number of items to which a single being can be attuned is limited, but the benefits of such a relationship can be considerable.

MYTHALS

Mythals are some of the most powerful magic in the world of Toril, constructs that bind and shape the Weave in a particular location, sometimes so powerfully that the rules of magic or even reality can be bent or rewritten.

A *mythal* is a permanent field of overlapping magical wards and effects tied to a specific location. In its original usage, this term applied to the works of High Magic that protected ancient elven cities. It has since been expanded to cover all manner of similar protections, from the immense floating cities of fallen Netheril to the wards of Silverymoon to the smaller—but no less effective—workings of magic that keep safe important locations like Candlekeep. Even the many-layered wards and effects of Undermountain, beneath Waterdeep, are considered a *mythal* by some.

Most *mythals* are defensive in nature, designed to restrict the kinds of magic that can be employed in the area they govern, and the most common restrictions are concerned with teleportation and conjuration magic. Evereska's *mythal* influences the weather of the area and wards its inhabitants against disease, while the *mythal* of undersea Myth Nantar makes its waters breathable and more comfortable for creatures not suited to underwater life.

In many ways, a *mythal* is less like a spell or a magic item than a living creation of magic, capable of growing stronger or weaker, absorbing damage, or dying. *Mythals* can also sometimes heal themselves, as did the *mythal* of Silverymoon, blossoming out of the Moonbridge following Mystra's most recent return. Each active *mythal* has one or more beings attuned to its effects, who can ignore any restrictions on spellcasting, can direct targetable effects of the *mythal*, and can teach others of appropriate skill how to access its secrets.

Except in cities such as Silverymoon and Evereska, adventurers are most likely to encounter damaged or failing *mythals* in ruined locations where magic once had great influence. Although an *identify* spell might reveal some of the simplest effects of a *mythal*, active restrictions on spellcasting can be discovered only by trying (and failing) to cast a prohibited spell. A powerful spellcaster might learn how to access or repair a *mythal* without assistance, but such feats are legendary, and rarely attempted by even the most renowned of mages. Any elven city with Myth in its title (Myth Drannor, Myth Glaurach, Myth Nantar, and others) has, or had, a *mythal* protecting it. The ruins of such places are certain to have unpredictable effects related to their damaged or destroyed *mythals*.

WEAVE-AFFECTING MAGIC

Certain spells allow casters to perceive or manipulate the effects of the Weave in particular ways. The Weave itself also has irregularities that affect spells.

Detect Magic. Detect magic reveals threads of the Weave woven together through spellcasting, or the "knots" of the Weave in a magic item. A magic item appears enmeshed in the silvery-blue threads of the Weave, and the way the threads are arranged reveals what type of magic is used (necromancy, abjuration, and so on). Similarly, active spells and areas imbued with magic are limned in a silvery network of threads, which might twist and reknit themselves depending on the magic involved.

Dispel Magic. Dispel magic unwinds and prematurely ends magic, unraveling whatever construct of the Weave was put in place.

Antimagic. Antimagic effects can dispel existing spells and unravel any magic woven from the Weave. Permanent effects, such as those from magic items, are usually suppressed by antimagic: while the effect is within an area of antimagic, the construct of the Weave unravels, but the threads snap back into place once the magic is outside the area.

Dead Magic. In rare areas of dead magic, the Weave is absent. Not only do spells and magic items cease to function, but even the supernatural abilities of creatures that are innately tied to the Weave might fail as the knot of the Weave they carry with them unravels.

Wild Magic. In an area of wild magic, the Weave becomes "tangled," spontaneously forming its own constructs and resulting magic. It also tends to twist the constructs of the Weave created by spellcasting, causing unexpected results.

RELIGION IN THE REALMS

Though wizards work wonders with their Art, and adventurers take their fates into their own hands, it is on the gods that most folk in the Forgotten Realms depend when they have need. The gods play a role in the lives of nearly everyone, from the mightiest lord to the meanest urchin.

The various races of Toril worship their pantheons, which remain largely the same from region to region, with different cultures and societies emphasizing some deities over others. Although exceptions exist—the gods of Mulhorand, for example—all the gods are revered across all of Faerûn.

FORMS OF WORSHIP

The average person worships different gods in different contexts. Most vocations have a patron deity: farmers make offerings to Chauntea for the prosperity of their crops, clerks sharpen their quills with a prayer to Deneir, while pious merchants remember to set coins aside for Waukeen at the end of the day. Most people worship a deity associated with their livelihood, family, or home, while others feel called to a particular god for a variety of reasons. Individuals often carry or wear a small token of their favored deity: a pendant or a pin in the image of the god's holy symbol, or some other personal keepsake.

In addition, people regularly venerate gods based on their needs and circumstances: a farmer whose favored deity is Chauntea would pray to Amaunator for a few clear, sunny days, and a Waterdhavian noble who habitually worships Denier would give thanks to Sune after a successful coming-out party for her son. Even priests of particular gods acknowledge the roles that other deities play in the world and in their lives.

In general, worshipers view their relationships with the gods as practical and reciprocal: they pray and make offerings because that is how one invites the blessings of the gods and turns away their wrath. These prayers and other acts of devotion are generally performed quietly at the shrine in one's household or community, or occasionally in a temple dedicated to one's deity, when a worshiper feels the need to "come knocking upon a god's door" to ask for attention.

Forms of worship are often acts of veneration: giving thanks for favor shown, making requests for future blessings, and offering praise for the deity's intercessions, large and small. Because most folk in Faerûn don't want to attract the ire of the cruel or savage gods, beseeching them to keep the peace is also an act of worship. A hunter or a farmer might make offerings to Malar in hopes of keeping predators at bay, and a sailor might pray to Umberlee that she withhold her wrath for the duration of a voyage.

NEW AND FOREIGN GODS

The Faerûnian pantheon isn't the only one known on Toril. Nonhuman races honor their own gods, for example, and people in faraway lands are known to worship altogether different gods. Occasionally, foreigners bring the worship of these gods to Faerûn. In addition, on rare occasions a new god comes into being, perhaps a mortal elevated to godhood or a deity whose arrival was foretold by prophets and leaders of new religions. In cosmopolitan places such as Waterdeep and Calimshan, small shrines and temples to strange gods spring up from time to time.

The burgeoning worship of a new deity is rarely a concern to the other gods of the Faerûnian pantheon, and the people who revere those deities, except when the newcomer's area of concern directly competes with that of an established deity. The methods of resolving such conflicts range from friendly dueling festivals or rites meant to emphasize the glory of one god over another, to campaigns of outright religious bloodshed.

Over generations, a new god might become a settled-in member of the pantheon. Indeed, some scholars posit that Faerûn has many "immigrant" gods, who joined the pantheon's ranks so long ago that their foreign origins are lost in antiquity.

DEAD AND RESURRECTED GODS

Over and over, mourning bells have tolled for some of the deities of the Realms. Gods were struck down during the Time of Troubles, when the Spellplague wrought its destruction, and most recently when Netheril fell. Some deities have even been slain by mortals wielding impossibly powerful magic.

When a god withdraws from a pantheon, divine magic stops flowing to the faithful, and miracles and omens associated with that god cease, that deity's priesthood loses faith, and holy sites are abandoned or taken over by other faiths. To the deity's worshipers in the world,

it is immaterial whether the god is truly dead or merely dormant—the consequences for them are the same either way. Yet, as recent events have borne out, a god who is gone might not remain absent forever. More than a few supposedly dead gods have returned and amassed a new body of worshipers. Indeed, the legends of some gods speak of a cycle of death and resurrection.

As the Sage of Shadowdale once noted, "If the gods can grant the power to raise mortals from death, why do ye assume they should be laid low by it forever?"

THE AFTERLIFE

Most humans believe the souls of the recently deceased are spirited away to the Fugue Plane, where they wander the great City of Judgment, often unaware they are dead. The servants of the gods come to collect such souls and, if they are worthy, they are taken to their awaited afterlife in the deity's domain. Occasionally, the faithful are sent back to be reborn into the world to finish work that was left undone.

Souls that are unclaimed by the servants of the gods are judged by Kelemvor, who decides the fate of each one. Some are charged with serving as guides for other lost souls, while others are transformed into squirming larvae and cast into the dust. The truly false and faithless are mortared into the Wall of the Faithless, the great barrier that bounds the City of the Dead, where their souls slowly dissolve and begin to become part of the stuff of the Wall itself.

RELIGIOUS INSTITUTIONS

Those who serve as priests of a god aren't necessarily clerics. Indeed, the power invested in clerics and other divine spellcasters by the gods is given out only rarely (see "Divine Magic" below). The work of a priest is to serve one's deity and that deity's faithful, a task that doesn't necessarily require the use of magic.

The kind of person attracted to a deity's priesthood depends on the tenets of that god: the cunning rogues who venerate Mask have little in common with the upright law-keepers of Tyr, and the delightful revelers who revere Lliira are different from both.

TEMPLES AND SHRINES

The core religious institutions of Faerûn are temples and shrines. Whether a small, out-of-the-way building, or a complex made up of multiple structures and tracts of land, each temple operates according to the traditions of its faith, although powerful or charismatic figures who rise to prominence within the temple hierarchy might motivate or inspire changes to those traditions.

Temples in Faerûn don't have regular services as such. Group observances in a temple occur only at specific festival times, and priests also go out into the community to perform rites such as marriages and funerals. Temples are places where worshipers go either to spend personal or family time in a space consecrated to a deity or to seek the aid of the priests for some reason.

Small shrines and private chapels, as distinct from full-fledged temples, are common throughout Faerûn, particularly in areas where a temple doesn't exist.

The Faerûnian Pantheon

Deity	Alignment	Domains	Symbol
Akadi, goddess of air	N	Tempest	Cloud
Amaunator, god of the sun	LN	Life, Light	Golden sun
Asmodeus, god of indulgence	LE	Knowledge, Trickery	Three inverted triangles arranged in a long triangle
Auril, goddess of winter	NE	Nature, Tempest	Six-pointed snowflake
Azuth, god of wizardry	LN	Arcana, Knowledge	Left hand pointing upward, outlined in fire
Bane, god of tyranny	LE	War	Upright black hand, thumb and fingers together
Beshaba, goddess of misfortune	CE	Trickery	Black antlers
Bhaal, god of murder	NE	Death	Skull surrounded by ring of bloody droplets
Chauntea, goddess of agriculture	NG	Life	Sheaf of grain or a blooming rose over grain
Cyric, god of lies	CE	Trickery	White jawless skull on black or purple sunburst
Deneir, god of writing	NG	Arcana, Knowledge	Lit candle above an open eye
Eldath, goddess of peace	NG	Life, Nature	Waterfall plunging into a still pool
Gond, god of craft	N	Knowledge	Toothed cog with four spokes
Grumbar, god of earth	N	Knowledge	Mountain
Gwaeron Windstrom, god of tracking	NG	Knowledge, Nature	Paw print with a five-pointed star in its center
Helm, god of watchfulness	LN	Life, Light	Staring eye on upright left gauntlet
Hoar, god of revenge and retribution	LN	War	A coin with a two-faced head
Ilmater, god of endurance	LG	Life	Hands bound at the wrist with red cord
Istishia, god of water	N	Tempest	Wave
Jergal, scribe of the dead	LN	Knowledge, Death	A skull biting a scroll
Kelemvor, god of the dead	LN	Death	Upright skeletal arm holding balanced scales
Kossuth, god of fire	N	Light	Flame
Lathander, god of dawn and renewal	NG	Life, Light	Road traveling into a sunrise
Leira, goddess of illusion	CN	Trickery	Point-down triangle containing a swirl of mist
Lliira, goddess of joy	CG	Life	Triangle of three six-pointed stars
Loviatar, goddess of pain	LE	Death	Nine-tailed barbed scourge
Malar, god of the hunt	CE	Nature	Clawed paw
Mask, god of thieves	CN	Trickery	Black mask
Mielikki, goddess of forests	NG	Nature	Unicorn's head
Milil, god of poetry and song	NG	Light	Five-stringed harp made of leaves
Myrkul, god of death	NE	Death	White human skull
Mystra, goddess of magic	NG	Arcana, Knowledge	Circle of seven stars, nine stars encircling a flowing red mist, or a single star
Oghma, god of knowledge	N	Knowledge	Blank scroll
The Red Knight, goddess of strategy	LN	War	Red knight lanceboard piece with stars for eyes
Savras, god of divination and fate	LN	Arcana, Knowledge	Crystal ball containing many kinds of eyes
Selûne, goddess of the moon	CG	Knowledge, Life	Pair of eyes surrounded by seven stars
Shar, goddess of darkness and loss	NE	Death, Trickery	Black disk encircled with a purple border
Silvanus, god of wild nature	N	Nature	Oak leaf
Sune, goddess of love and beauty	CG	Life, Light	Face of a beautiful red-haired woman
Talona, goddess of poison and disease	CE	Death	Three teardrops in a triangle
Talos, god of storms	CE	Tempest	Three lightning bolts radiating from a point
Tempus, god of war	N	War	Upright flaming sword
Torm, god of courage and self-sacrifice	LG	War	White right gauntlet
Tymora, goddess of good fortune	CG	Trickery	Face-up coin
Tyr, god of justice	LG	War	Balanced scales resting on a warhammer
Umberlee, goddess of the sea	CE	Tempest	Wave curling left and right
Valkur, Northlander god of sailors	CG	Tempest, War	A cloud and three lightning bolts
Waukeen, goddess of trade	N	Knowledge, Trickery	Upright coin with Waukeen's profile facing left

THE DWARVEN PANTHEON

Deity	Alignment	Domains	Symbol
Abbathor, god of greed	NE	Trickery	Jeweled dagger, point-down
Berronar Truesilver, goddess of hearth and home	LG	Life, Light	Intertwined silver rings
Clangeddin Silverbeard, god of war	LG	War	Crossed silver battleaxes
Deep Duerra, duergar goddess of conquest and psionics	LE	Arcana, War	Mind flayer skull
Dugmaren Brightmantle, god of discovery	CG	Knowledge	Open book
Dumathoin, god of buried secrets	N	Death, Knowledge	Mountain silhouette with a central gemstone
Gorm Gulthyn, god of vigilance	LG	War	Bronze half-mask
Haela Brightaxe, goddess of war-luck	CG	War	Upright sword whose blade is spiraled in flame
Laduguer, duergar god of magic and slavery	LE	Arcana, Death	Broken arrow
Marthammor Duin, god of wanderers	NG	Nature, Trickery	Upright mace in front of a tall boot
Moradin, god of creation	LG	Knowledge	Hammer and anvil
Sharindlar, goddess of healing	CG	Life	Burning needle
Vergadain, god of luck and wealth	N	Trickery	Gold coin with the face of a dwarf

Shrines tend to be unstaffed, kept up by the locals and visitors who use the place for prayer. A shrine might be as modest as a roadside well, where traveling merchants can drop a coin to request good fortune from Waukeen, or as grand as a statue of Amaunator surrounded by braziers in a pavilion in the middle of a village.

Traveling priests often seek out and visit these sites, and they act as meeting places for the faithful. When word gets around that a traveling priest of Eldath has come into town, the faithful seek her out at the holy spring dedicated to the goddess at the edge of town.

A family or business might maintain a shrine or a chapel to its favored deity, perhaps a set of wind chimes consecrated to Akadi hung from the high branches of a tree in the garden, or a wooden symbol shaped like the hand of Azuth in miniature displayed on a prominent wall with a space nearby to burn a candle or some incense.

COMMUNING WITH THE GODS

Though many tales are told of times past when the gods appeared in physical form and walked the land, occasions of that sort are few and far between. For the most part, the gods communicate with their faithful through signs and omens, appreciated by those able to interpret them. Of course, some signs are more subtle—and thus more open to interpretation—than others.

The most common kind of communion that worshipers and priests find with their deities is in prayer, song, or meditation. Such experiences are intensely personal, and it is common wisdom to keep them that way. After all, "advice" from one's god that appears during morning prayer and gives one a good turn to the day is worthwhile only for oneself. Let each worshiper commune in their own way, as the saying goes.

Divine magic also provides a means of communing with the gods and can be used to call upon their guidance. Divine pronouncements of this sort are often personal in scope and brief, and those edicts that concern broader matters tend to be open to interpretation or debate.

PRIESTHOOD

Priesthood is a vocation like any other, with those who undertake it often honing their abilities through a system of apprenticeship. At a small temple, a novice or an acolyte might study under the only priest available. Larger temples can accommodate groups of acolytes, each learning under the direction of one or more mentors responsible for training them in the duties and skills of the priesthood.

Once acolytes complete their education, they are often ordained in a ritual in which a successful candidate is invested with the responsibilities of the priesthood.

CONFLICTS AND PERSECUTION

The moral and ethical values of the deities in Faerûn run the gamut, representing all the outlooks that their mortal followers demonstrate, from the principled agents of good to the vicious proponents of evil. Most cultures and societies aren't nearly as cosmopolitan as the population of Faerûn taken as a whole; as a result, religious persecution (from the viewpoint of those who garner the attention) is practiced in places where worship of certain deities is frowned on.

Most governments that engage in persecution limit such restrictions to the establishment of formal temples, priesthoods, and organized festivals. (On a practical level, it's impossible to prevent individuals from innocuously or secretly worshiping whichever deities they choose.) For instance, although worship of Talona—like that of many evil gods—is forbidden in Waterdeep, this prohibition extends only to the creation of a temple and the presence of her priesthood within the city. Individual citizens or families who revere Talona might be viewed as misguided, but they aren't taken into custody or punished as long as they obey the laws of the city.

Some places take this form of persecution a step further, for a variety of reasons. A tyrant might outlaw worship of Torm, lest it inspire rebellion, and an otherwise fair-minded mayor of a river-mill community might demand that worshipers of Silvanus find elsewhere to

THE ELVEN PANTHEON

Deity	Alignment	Domains	Symbol
Aerdrie Faenya, goddess of the sky	CG	Tempest, Trickery	Bird silhouetted against a cloud
Angharradh, triple goddess of wisdom and protection	CG	Knowledge, Life	Triangle with three interlocking circles within
Corellon Larethian, god of art and magic	CG	Arcana, Light	Crescent moon
Deep Sashelas, god of the sea	CG	Nature, Tempest	Dolphin
Erevan Ilesere, god of mischief	CN	Trickery	Asymmetrical eight-armed star
Fenmarel Mestarine, god of outcasts	CN	Trickery	Two peering elven eyes
Hanali Celanil, goddess of love and beauty	CG	Life	Golden heart
Labelas Enoreth, god of time, history, and philosophy	CG	Arcana, Knowledge	Setting sun
Rillifane Rallathil, god of nature	CG	Nature	Oak
Sehanine Moonbow, goddess of divination, dreams, travel, and death	CG	Knowledge	Full moon under a moonbow
Shevarash, god of vengeance	CN	War	Broken arrow over a tear
Solonor Thelandira, god of archery	CG	War	Silver arrow with green fletching

THE DROW PANTHEON

Deity	Alignment	Domains	Symbol
Eilistraee, goddess of song and moonlight	CG	Light, Nature	Sword-wielding dancing drow female silhouetted against the full moon
Kiaransalee, goddess of necromancy	CE	Arcana	Female drow hand wearing many silver rings
Lolth, goddess of spiders	CE	Trickery	Spider
Selvetarm, god of warriors	CE	War	Spider over crossed sword-and-mace
Vhaeraun, god of thieves	CE	Trickery	Black mask with blue glass lenses inset over eyes

THE HALFLING PANTHEON

Deity	Alignment	Domains	Symbol
Arvoreen, god of vigilance and war	LG	War	Crossed short swords
Brandobaris, god of thievery and adventure	N	Trickery	Halfling footprint
Cyrrollalee, goddess of hearth and home	LG	Life	An open door
Sheela Peryroyl, goddess of agriculture and weather	N	Nature, Tempest	Flower
Urogalan, god of earth and death	LN	Death, Knowledge	Silhouette of a dog's head
Yondalla, goddess of fertility and protection	LG	Life	Cornucopia on a shield

live because of recent problems the timber-cutters have had with local druids.

DIVINE MAGIC

The gods show their favor toward mortals in myriad ways. A chosen few have their minds and souls opened to the power of magic. There is no formula for who does and doesn't receive this divine insight, as the gods keep their own counsel concerning their selections. Some who are favored seek to ignore or deny their gift, while others embrace it wholeheartedly.

Some who display the potential for divine magic develop and practice their abilities in a temple, a sacred grove, or some other spiritual place, perhaps in the company of other students. Other practitioners of divine magic discover and nurture their gods-given power entirely on their own.

THE GODS OF FAERÛN

The gods that make up the pantheon of Faerûn are much like the population of some of the Realms' greatest cities: an eclectic blend of individuals from a variety of sources. The makeup of the pantheon has shifted over the ages, as a result of changes in the Realms and its people (or vice versa, depending on which scholars you believe). The following pages describe the most prominent members of the pantheon.

The deities of the Faerûnian pantheon are by no means the only powers worshiped in the Realms. The nonhuman races have pantheons of their own (described in chapter 3), and scattered other cults and local divinities can be found across Faerûn.

THE GNOMISH PANTHEON

Deity	Alignment	Domains	Symbol
Baervan Wildwanderer, god of woodlands	NG	Nature	Face of a raccoon
Baravar Cloakshadow, god of illusion and deception	NG	Arcana, Trickery	Dagger against a hooded cloak
Callarduran Smoothhands, god of mining and carving stone	N	Knowledge, Nature	Golden signet ring with six-pointed star
Flandal Steelskin, god of metalwork	NG	Knowledge	Flaming hammer
Gaerdal Ironhand, god of protection	LG	War	Iron band
Garl Glittergold, god of trickery and gems	LG	Trickery	Gold nugget
Nebelun, god of invention and luck	CG	Knowledge, Trickery	Bellows and a lizard tail
Segojan Earthcaller, god of earth and the dead	NG	Light	Glowing gemstone
Urdlen, god of greed and murder	CE	Death, War	White clawed mole emerging from ground

THE ORC PANTHEON

Deity	Alignment	Domains	Symbol
Bahgtru, god of strength	LE	War	Broken thigh bone
Gruumsh, god of storms and war	CE	Tempest, War	Unblinking eye
Ilneval, god of strategy and hordes	LE	War	Upright blood-spattered sword
Luthic, mother-goddess of fertility and healing	LE	Life, Nature	Orcish rune meaning "cave entrance"
Shargaas, god of stealth and darkness	NE	Trickery	Red crescent moon with a skull between the moon's horns
Yurtrus, god of death and disease	NE	Death	White hand, palm outward

AMAUNATOR

The Keeper of the Eternal Sun, the Light of Law, the Yellow God

The rule of law and the glory of the sun are both in Amaunator's dominion. His priests help establish bureaucracies and lawful order in communities. They often witness contracts and signed agreements, stamping such documents with the sun-symbol of Amaunator to signify their validity.

His priests teach that Amaunator has died and been reborn time and again. Like the sun, he might pass into the realm of darkness, but inevitably his bright gaze will fall on the world once again. Amaunator is seen as a stern and unforgiving deity, not unlike Silvanus in comportment, but his concern isn't for the balance of life—he cares that things proceed according to the celestial order, that promises are kept, and that the rule of law persists.

Farmers and travelers beseech him when they pray for rain or sun, as do any others looking for a favorable change in the weather. But the most common form of propitiation to Amaunator is the practice of swearing oaths, signing contracts, and declaring laws under the light of the sun. So ingrained in the common perception is the connection between a solemn oath and the sun that those engaged in closing deals or issuing edicts often pause and wait for a passing cloud to clear the sun before completing the transaction or pronouncement.

ASMODEUS

The Lord of the Ninth, The Cloven, Old Hoof and Horn

Open worship of Asmodeus began roughly a century ago when small cults with charismatic leaders sprang up in the aftermath of the Spellplague. That catastrophe left many asking why the gods were angry or had abandoned them. To those questioners, the faithful of Asmodeus provided answers and a god who would forgive all

SYMBOL OF AMAUNATOR

SYMBOL OF ASMODEUS

their faults. Still, for the next few decades, the cult of Asmodeus struggled for acceptance.

In the beliefs of the people of the North—which coincide with many tales told by dwarves, elves, and others—Asmodeus is Lord of the Ninth, the leader of all devils of the Nine Hells. People know devils to be iron-minded and silver-tongued purveyors of temptation, whose price for their boons can be as dear as one's soul. It's said that when a soul waits on the Fugue Plane for a deity to take it to its appropriate afterlife, devils approach the soul and offer it a chance at power and immortal pleasures. All a soul needs to do is take one step out of the dust and the milling crowd and put a foot on the first rung of the infernal ladder that represents the hierarchy of the Nine Hells.

The faithful of Asmodeus acknowledge that devils offer their worshipers a path that's not for everyone—just as eternally basking in the light of Lathander or endlessly swinging a hammer in the mines of Moradin might not be for everyone. Those who serve Asmodeus in life hope to be summoned out of the moaning masses of the Fugue Plane after death. They yearn for the chance to master their own fates, with all of eternity to achieve their goals.

To those not so dedicated, priests of Asmodeus offer the prospect of a reprieve in the afterlife. All souls wait on the Fugue Plane for a deity's pleasure, which determines where a soul will spend the rest of eternity. Those who lived their lives most in keeping with a deity's outlook are taken first. Others, who have transgressed in the eyes of their favored god or have not followed any particular ethos, might wait centuries before Kelemvor judges where they go. People who fear such a fate can pray to Asmodeus, his priests say, and in return a devil will grant a waiting soul some comfort.

Today, shrines to Asmodeus are still rare and temples are almost unheard of, but many folk have adopted the habit of asking Asmodeus for reprieve from their sins. After transgressing against a god in some way, a person prays to Asmodeus for something to provide respite during the long wait. Asmodeus is known to grant people what they wish, and thus people pray for all the delights and distractions they desire most from life. Those who transgress in great ways often ask Asmodeus to hide their sins from the gods, and priests say that he will do so, but with a price after death.

AURIL

The Frostmaiden, Lady Frostkiss, Icedawn

Auril, the merciless goddess of cold and winter, is worshiped mostly in regions that are affected by deep winters. Folk propitiate Auril with offerings and prayers for mercy. Her priests warn others to prepare for winter, and to stock extra provisions in order to have some to spare as offerings to the goddess.

Few favor Auril except for those who make their livelihood from winter or those who truly love the season. Her rare priests tend to be folk who would, but for their status, likely be outcasts from their communities. They practice celibacy and remain aloof from others when not serving in their official capacity.

Luskan has a temple dedicated to Auril, the white-spired Winter Palace. The structure is a roofless array of pillars and arches carved of white stone. The rituals of Auril's worship often seem cruel to outsiders. In Luskan, visitors gather at the temple to watch the frequent "wet parades," a ritual in which supplicants don garments packed with ice. They then journey between six white pillars known as the Kisses of Auril, which are dispersed throughout the city. The worshipers move from pillar to pillar, chanting prayers to the goddess. Upon reaching a pillar, a supplicant must climb it and then "kiss the lady," touching lips to a rusty iron plate at the top. In winter, these events resemble frantic footraces, with the added risk of frostbite and injuries caused by falling from the slippery pillars. The parade runners are cheered on by patrons who come out of nearby taverns to place bets on the stamina of the participants. Those who finish the race are thought to have helped make the winter easier, and they rarely have to pay for food or ale all winter long.

AZUTH

The High One, the Lord of Spellcraft, the First Magister

Few pay homage to Azuth aside from wizards. For them, the High One is the ultimate embodiment of all that they hold dear.

Mystra serves as goddess of magic; Oghma is god of knowledge; and Deneir is god of writing and language. Azuth takes aspects of these general fields and applies them to the specific practices of wizards. For instance, while Mystra is the deity who represents the soul, art, and wonder of magic, Azuth is god of a wizard's long hours of study, exacting standards of movement and

SYMBOL OF AURIL

SYMBOL OF AZUTH

speech, and cramped, ink-stained fingers. Wizards invoke Azuth when they scribe scrolls, inscribe magic circles, attempt to memorize spells, and even when they cast spells. Often this acknowledgment comes in the form of silently forming Azuth's holy symbol, pointing the index finger of the left hand to the sky. For many wizards, the gesture is so commonplace in their lives that it becomes an unconscious habit.

Temples dedicated to Azuth are scarce, and clerics of the deity are extremely rare. Even in magic-saturated Halruaa, only a handful of holy places are dedicated to Azuth. Sometimes a statue or a shrine dedicated to him stands in a corner of a temple to Mystra or another deity. More often, a wizard has a personal shrine at home. Azuth is represented at such sites as a hooded and bearded figure with left hand held high, finger pointed up. Sometimes he is represented by merely the hand. In either case, the finger often serves as a candleholder or as the point of origin for a *light* spell.

BANE

The Black Hand, the Lord of Darkness

Bane has a simple ethos: the strong have not just the right but the duty to rule over the weak. A tyrant who is able to seize power must do so, for not only does the tyrant benefit, but so do those under the tyrant's rule. When a ruler succumbs to decadence, corruption, or decrepitude, a stronger and more suitable ruler will rise.

Bane is vilified in many legends. Throughout history, those who favor him have committed dark deeds in his name, but most people don't worship Bane out of malice. Bane represents ambition and control, and those who have the former but lack the latter pray to him to give them strength. It is said that Bane favors those who exhibit drive and courage, and that he aids those who seek to become conquerors, carving kingdoms from the wilderness, and bringing order to the lawless.

At many times and in many places in Faerûn, the faithful of Bane have been seen as saviors for their efforts in slaughtering raiders, throwing down corrupt rulers, or saving armies on the brink of defeat. But in just as many other places, the worship of Bane has created or supported cruel dictatorships, aided mercantile monopolies, or brought about the practice of slavery where before it didn't exist.

SYMBOL OF BANE

BESHABA

The Maid of Misfortune, Lady Doom, Black Bess

Beshaba is the counterpoint to Tymora and is just as frequently acknowledged in daily life as is her more benevolent "sister." She is seen as a cruel and capricious goddess who must be propitiated to avoid attracting her attention and interest in a negative way.

Beshaba's name is invoked when someone is beset by bad luck—which could be as minor as stubbing a toe or breaking a wagon wheel, or as catastrophic as slipping and accidentally falling off a cliff. It is also invoked to ward off her attentions when someone is doing something in which good luck wouldn't play a part but bad luck might. For example, someone rolling dice would invoke Tymora because they want random chance to fall in their favor, but someone about to cross a rickety bridge would ask Beshaba to keep the bridge intact.

Folk make the symbol of Beshaba by folding in their thumbs and extending their fingers on one or both hands (mimicking the horns of her holy symbol) to ward off misfortune. The same gesture raised to the head signifies a salute; when pointed at someone, the "horns" indicate ill favor directed toward that individual.

Many druids worship Beshaba as one of the First Circle. They propitiate her with dances while wearing fire-blackened antlers dipped in blood. According to these druids, her holy symbol is the horns of a stag because when Beshaba was first worshiped, humans were simple hunter-gatherers and she was believed to bring misfortune to hunters, such as being gored by a stag.

Although most people tremble in fear at the prospect of Beshaba's attendance at any event (even in spirit), Beshaba is almost always invoked and welcomed formally in the opening speeches or ceremonies of formal functions such as marriages and coronations, contests of sport or martial prowess, and at the naming ceremonies of children. If she isn't invited to such an event, she might take offense and wreak misfortune on those involved.

Temples to Beshaba are virtually unknown. It's common, however, for rural folk to erect a post and mount antlers on it at the site of some roadside accident or murder. In cities, where antlers are hard to come by and murders and accidents more prevalent, the fashion is to draw the black antlers of Beshaba with charcoal on a nearby wall, leaving the symbol on display until weather scours it away. These "shrines," in either form, serve as warnings to others about places of ill fortune.

SYMBOL OF BESHABA

More formal shrines to Beshaba exist in places where folk frequently hope to ward off misfortune. These sites tend to be posts or stones painted red with blackened antlers attached to them, or a red, triangular wall-mounted plaque with attached antlers. Both types have a stone or bronze bowl where coins can be tossed or burnt offerings made. The Red Wizards of Thay commonly erect such shrines outside their ritual chambers to guard against unfortunate mistakes.

Few dare to take Beshaba as a patron. The rare clerics of the Maid of Misfortune are those who have been deeply affected by great misfortunes and who seek to warn others of the essential unfairness of life—or to inflict that unfairness upon them.

BHAAL

The Lord of Murder

The folk of Faerûn don't normally pray to or acknowledge Bhaal. He is seen as a deeply evil and destructive deity who hungers for death—meaning the death of any sentient beings through unlawful means.

Some people pray to Bhaal when they want to commit murder. A person might have good reason to resort to murder, such as when one is unable to redress some injustice through lawful means. But it's far more common for prayers to Bhaal to be uttered by those who seek to kill someone out of jealousy, greed, or wrath. It's rare for anyone but assassins or compulsive killers to take Bhaal as a patron, and clerics who revere Bhaal often qualify on both counts.

Murder cults of Bhaal have arisen in the past, each led by a charismatic, self-styled priest of Bhaal, but organized worship of the Lord of Murder is extremely uncommon. Temples and shrines are similarly rare. Those who erect a shrine to Bhaal usually do so to thank him for a successful murder. Such shrines typically feature a skull or a severed head surrounded by drops of blood (often both from the murdered victim).

CHAUNTEA

The Great Mother, the Grain Goddess

Chauntea is goddess of agriculture: sowing and reaping, seeding and harvest, breeding and butchery, shearing and weaving. In this aspect she is a rural deity rarely prayed to behind the walls of a city except by kitchen gardeners. But Chauntea is also the Great Mother, a goddess of crib, hearth, and home. And as such she is

THE EARTHMOTHER

The druids of the Moonshae Isles worship the Earthmother, she who is the generative power of the land itself. To some mainlanders, the Earthmother is an aspect or manifestation of Chauntea, but to the Ffolk, she is simply the Earthmother, and always will be. The moonwells of the isles are her sacred sites and her windows onto the world. See "Druids" in chapter 4 for more information.

welcomed into all homes at mealtimes and at the birth of children, and folk give her thanks whenever they experience the pleasure of settling by a fire and feeling safe and loved.

Chauntea's faith is one of nurturing and growth. Agricultural aphorisms and farming parables dot her teachings. Growing and reaping, the eternal cycle, is a common theme in the faith. Destruction for its own sake, or leveling without rebuilding, is anathema to her.

Temples of Chauntea maintain a great body of lore about farming and cultivation. Her priests work closely with communities in rural areas, and they are willing to roll up their sleeves and dig their hands into the dirt.

CYRIC

The Prince of Lies, the Dark Sun

The worship of Cyric derives directly from the story of his ascension to godhood. Cyric was a mortal during the Time of Troubles and the key to how that chaotic period resolved, but he was also a selfish traitor and a murderer. When he became a god, Cyric continued to work various plots of deceit and murder—the most famous of which is that, according to legend, Cyric murdered Mystra and thus caused the Spellplague over a century ago.

Those who don't worship Cyric see him as a god of madness, strife, and deceit, although his priests consider such claims to be heresy. Their Prince of Lies isn't a twisted madman, but a god of dark majesty who proves that, ultimately, all bonds between folk corrupt and wither away.

Cyric's church works openly in Amn, where the citizens espouse the principles of ambition, self-reliance, and "buyer beware." Those who take Cyric as their patron tend to be sadists, con artists, power-mad connivers, and worse. Other folk pray to Cyric when they want to do wrong but don't want others to find out about it.

"The Dark Sun," originally one of Cyric's epithets, has become a metaphor for strife in the Realms. "A Dark Sun has risen o'er this court" might be spoken as a

SYMBOL OF BHAAL

SYMBOL OF CHAUNTEA

SYMBOL OF CYRIC

warning that intrigues and infighting have gotten out of hand in a noble household; and married couples know to seek advice from others if "a Dark Sun shines through the window" in their relationship.

DENEIR

The Lord of All Glyphs and Images, the First Scribe, the Scribe of Oghma

Deneir is the god of literature and literacy, the patron of the artist and the scribe. His is the power to accurately render and describe, to write and to read, and to pass on information. In legend, Deneir is often portrayed as being a scribe in service to Oghma, and he is sometimes thought of as Oghma's right hand.

It's common practice for someone who writes a letter or records information to say a prayer to Deneir to avoid mistakes. Similarly, artists acknowledge Deneir before beginning and upon completing paintings, particularly illuminations on manuscripts, tapestries that relate stories, and any such attempt to use art to capture the truth.

Followers of Deneir believe that information not recorded and saved for later use is information lost. They consider literacy an important gift of the gods, one that should be spread and taught. His followers are scribes and scholars devoted, like their patron, to preserving written works, and also to experiencing them, for they say that Deneir himself is hidden within the lines, shapes, and passages of all written works. Priests of Deneir take an oath of charity as well, compelling them to accept the requests of others to write letters and transcribe information.

The god's followers tend to be individualists, united by their shared faith but not overly concerned with religious hierarchy and protocol. This behavior is supported by the fact that Deneir's blessings of divine magic are more often bestowed on those who lose themselves in written works than on those who fancy themselves part of any temple or religious order. Contemplation of the faith's most holy book, the *Tome of Universal Harmony*, is the most effective way to become deserving of Deneir's blessings.

SYMBOL OF DENEIR

ELDATH

The Quiet One, the Guardian of Groves, the Mother of the Waters

Eldath is the goddess of waterfalls, springs, pools, stillness, peace, and quiet glades. She is thought to be present at many such places, particularly those that serve as druid groves. Eldath is a goddess of comfort, healing, and calm. Her blessed waters heal the sick, cure madness, and comfort the dying.

Most rural places have a pond or a glade that locals ascribe to Eldath. Tradition dictates that it be a place of quiet reflection where others are left to their thoughts. A body of water such as a pond or a spring typically serves as a repository of offerings. If the holy site is a glade, a stream one crosses along the way might serve as the repository, or a prominent bush or tree in the glade might be the place where people tie offerings. Typical offerings are broken weapons or items that are remembrances of arguments, which the faithful discard while making a wish for peace in the future. Many of those who favor Eldath are pacifists or people who are troubled by violence they have witnessed or experienced.

Eldath's priests don't organize into large sects. Indeed, many are itinerant, wandering between various holy sites and shrines, seeing that the locations are cared for and that they remain places of sweet serenity. The faithful of Eldath are usually close to nature, and allied to druids, who count Eldath among the First Circle. It is taboo to strike a priest of Eldath, and killing one is said to bring great misfortune. Despite the measure of protection that this belief affords them, most priests of Eldath avoid conflicts rather than attempting to quell them. Those who serve Eldath are happy to preside over peaceful negotiations and to certify treaties, but they can't force others to engage in harmony.

GOND

The Wonderbringer, the Inspiration Divine, the Holy Maker of All Things

Gond is the god of artifice, craft, and construction. He is revered by blacksmiths, woodworkers, engineers, and inventors. Anyone who is crafting something might say a prayer to Gond to guide the work, but folk know that Gond smiles most brightly upon new inventions that others find useful.

Priests of Gond wander the North dressed in saffron vestments, adorned with sashes that contain within

SYMBOL OF ELDATH

their folds gears, locks, hooks, and bits of steel, tin, and wood that might prove useful in a pinch. They also wear belts of large, linked metal medallions and enormous sun hats. A traveling priest of Gond offers services to distant villages as a tinker, a carpenter, and a civil engineer rolled into one, ready to help build a better paddock gate, dig a new well, or mend pots or furniture that might otherwise go to waste. All priests of Gond keep journals in which they record ideas, inventions, and innovations discovered in their travels, and take great delight in meeting fellow priests and sharing their finds. In large cities, the Gondar construct temples that serve as great workshops and inventors' labs. Wandering priests turn their journals over to the resident scribes at such temples, who then record the priests' observations for posterity and the benefit of all.

Most who favor Gond practice time-honored crafting professions: they are smiths and engineers, architects and weavers, leatherworkers and jewelers. Even so, this faith has a well-earned reputation as a haven for crackpot inventors and visionaries.

The center of Gond's worship on the Sword Coast lies in Baldur's Gate, where the faithful have erected two huge structures in honor of the Wonderbringer: a temple called the High House of Wonders and a museum of craft and design called the Hall of Wonders. Lantan had been the preeminent place of Gond's worship in the world until a century ago, when the island nation disappeared, and since its return the few Lantanese merchants seen in Sword Coast ports have said little about the present state of their homeland.

GWAERON WINDSTROM

The Mouth of Mielikki, the Master Tracker, the Tracker Never Led Astray

Few aside from rangers of the North pray to Gwaeron Windstrom. Said to have been a mortal man elevated to godhood by Mielikki, Gwaeron serves rangers as their intercessor with Mielikki. He is seen as a master ranger, the perfect tracker, a peerless animal handler, and a dedicated foe of rapacious creatures such as trolls and orcs. He is said to look like an old man with a long white beard who is still hale and mighty, and he is believed to take rest and sleep in a stand of trees near Triboar.

Rangers pray to Gwaeron because he represents much of the work they do, and because he can speak to Mielikki on their behalf. In the North, most rangers view Mielikki as too mysterious, holy, and wild to be addressed directly with their requests, but they consider Gwaeron Windstrom to be one of them and thus understanding of their needs.

Gwaeron has no temples, but shrines dedicated to him can be found in many places that serve wilderness wanderers as trail markers. Each one is denoted by a carving of Gwaeron's symbol, a paw print with a star on the palm, on a prominent tree or stone.

HELM

The Watcher, He of the Unsleeping Eyes, the Vigilant One

The god of vigilance and protection, Helm is seen as the epitome of the guardian, the watcher, and the guard. He is venerated by those who need to remain watchful for enemies or danger. Helm is a favorite deity of people who make a living by protecting someone or something, such as bodyguards, members of the city watch, and the guards of a treasury vault.

Helm embodies the spirit of watchfulness without regard to good or evil. In legends, he is honorable and keeps his word to a fault, such as when he guarded the celestial stairways during the Time of Troubles, preventing the gods from ascending them and continuing the chaos of that period, until the Tablets of Fate were found.

Although his faith has known dark days, worship of Helm never truly faded away. Most of his followers believe that the Watcher can never be vanquished utterly, and recent events have borne out that assertion.

Helm's priests teach that one must be ever vigilant, ever aware, ever prepared for one's enemies. Patience, clear thought, and careful planning will always defeat rushed actions in the end. Those who favor Helm strive to be alert, clear-headed, and true to their word. These traits don't necessarily make them nice people, however, and as such many consider the faithful of Helm to be inflexible and merciless.

HOAR

The Doombringer, Poet of Justice

Hoar, known in the lands along the Inner Sea as Assuran, is a god of revenge and retribution. He isn't typically worshiped habitually, but his name is invoked by those who seek vengeance. When a guilty party falls prey to fate—such as when a murderer escapes prosecution, but is then accidentally slain himself—the hand of Hoar

SYMBOL OF GOND

SYMBOL OF HELM

SYMBOL OF HOAR

is given credit. When one hears three rolls of thunder in succession, it is thought to be a sign from Hoar that some act of vengeance has been performed. Many human societies have the custom of ringing a bell or a gong three times when judgment of a crime is rendered or an execution takes place.

Folk speak Hoar's name when they want revenge, particularly when they are incapable of avenging themselves. This invocation might be in response to a petty slight or a true injustice, and the acknowledgment of Hoar might be a short prayer said aloud or might be written down somewhere. It's generally believed that the more permanent the form of the prayer, the more likely it is to be fulfilled. For this reason, some etch their prayers in lead and bury it or hide their prayers inside diaries. Aside from bounty hunters and those on crusades of vengeance, few truly revere Hoar, and he is served by fewer still who would call themselves priests. Temples or shrines of Hoar are almost nonexistent except for ancient sites in Chessenta and Unther.

Hoar became a member of the Faerûnian pantheon when his worship extended beyond the lands that originally revered him. Most consider Tyr to be the arbiter of laws, and Hoar to be the god who metes out punishment that comes as a result of breaking those codes. A judge might favor the worship of Tyr, while a jailor or a headsman is more likely to pray to Hoar.

ILMATER

The Crying God, the Rack-Broken Lord, He Who Endures

Ilmater is the god of suffering, martyrdom, and perseverance, renowned for his compassion and endurance. It is he who offers succor and calming words to those who are in pain, victimized, or in great need. He is the willing sufferer, the one who takes the place of another to heft the other's burden, to take the other's pain. He is the god of the oppressed and the unjustly treated.

It is said that if he had his way, the Crying God would take all the suffering in the world onto himself, so as to spare others. Since he can't, he blesses those who endure on others' behalf, and he alleviates suffering when he can. Martyrs who die that others may live are always blessed by Ilmater with a final rest and reward in the god's afterlife, should they so choose.

Ilmater's priests take in the ill, the starving, and the injured, and his temples give most of what they receive to help offset the suffering of the world. His followers provide succor when they can, but also use force to put an end to torture and suffering inflicted on others. Ilmater's priests travel to places where the worst possible conditions exist, ministering to the needs of the oppressed, the deceased, and the poor. They put others ahead of themselves, are sharing of all they have, and emphasize the spiritual nature of life over the welfare of the material body.

Priests of Ilmater who are on a quest to aid others can be recognized by their hair shirts, vests of coarse fur worn against the bare skin. It is taboo to harm such priests as they go about their duties, such as when they administer to the wounded on a battlefield. The taboo is so strongly felt among humans that other races respect the custom. Even orcs and goblinoids will avoid directly attacking a peaceful priest of Ilmater, as long as the priest administers to their fallen warriors as well.

Most folk deeply respect the work and the sacrifice of Ilmater's faith, and lend aid to such endeavors where they can. When a temple of Ilmater sends its faithful to help refugees of war or victims of plague, their willingness to sacrifice their own well-being always prompts ordinary people to support them, whether they are inspired or shamed into action.

JERGAL

The Final Scribe, the Pitiless One, the Bleak Seneschal

Legend has it that Jergal is an ancient deity. The story goes that in the time of Netheril he was worshiped as the god of death, murder, and strife. Yet with the passing of time, he became bored with his position. Then one day three mortals, each a powerful adventurer, met Jergal in the lands of the dead, determined to destroy him and take his power. Instead, Jergal calmly abdicated his throne of bones and allowed each of the three mortals to take part of his divinity. Thus it was that Bane assumed the portfolio of strife, Myrkul the rulership of the dead, and Bhaal the portfolio of murder. Jergal lost his former stature and became a scribe of the dead.

Jergal is now seen as an uncaring custodian of the dead. He is thought to record the passing of the living and to aid Kelemvor in seeing that souls are properly bound to their appropriate afterlife. He is rarely acknowledged directly, except for being mentioned at funerals and among those who practice the custom of writing the name of the deceased on a sheet of parchment and placing it in the corpse's mouth. This rite is

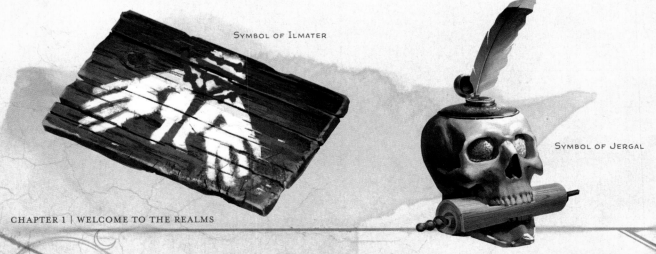

SYMBOL OF ILMATER

SYMBOL OF JERGAL

THE LEGEND OF KNUCKLEBONES, SKULL BOWLING, AND THE EMPTY THRONE

Long ago there was but one god of strife, death, and the dead, and he was known as Jergal, Lord of the End of Everything. Jergal fomented and fed on the discord among mortals and deific entities alike. When beings slew each other in their quest for power or in their hatred, he welcomed them into his shadowy kingdom of eternal gloom. As all things died, everything came to him eventually, and over time he built a kingdom unchallenged by any other god. But he grew tired of his duties, for he knew them too well, and without challenge there is nothing—and in nothingness there is only gloom. In such a state, the difference between absolute power and absolute powerlessness is undetectable.

During this dark era arose three powerful mortals—Bane, Bhaal, and Myrkul—who lusted after the power Jergal possessed. The trio forged an unholy pact that they would gain such ultimate power or die in the attempt. Over the length and breadth of the world they strode, seeking powerful magic and spells and defying death at every turn. No matter what monster they confronted or what spells they braved, the three mortals emerged unscathed at every turn. Eventually, the trio journeyed into the Gray Waste and sought out the Castle of Bone. Through armies of skeletons, legions of zombies, hordes of wraiths, and a gauntlet of liches they battled. Eventually they reached the object of their lifelong quest—the Bone Throne.

"I claim this throne of evil," Bane the tyrant shouted to Jergal.

"I'll destroy you before you can raise a finger," threatened Bhaal the assassin.

"And I shall imprison your essence for eternity," promised Myrkul the necromancer.

Jergal arose from his throne with a weary expression and said, "The throne is yours. I have grown weary of this empty power. Take it if you wish—I promise to serve and guide you as your seneschal until you grow comfortable with the position." Then, before the stunned trio could react, the Lord of the Dead asked, "Who among you shall rule?"

The trio immediately fell to fighting among themselves while Jergal looked on with indifference. When eventually it appeared that either they would all die of exhaustion or battle on for an eternity, the Lord of the End of Everything intervened.

"After all you have sacrificed, would you come away with nothing? Why don't you divide the portfolios of the office by engaging in a game of skill for them?" asked Jergal.

Bane, Bhaal, and Myrkul considered the god's offer and agreed to it. So Jergal took the skulls of his three most powerful liches and gave them to the trio so they could compete in skull bowling. Each mortal rolled a skull across the Gray Waste, having agreed that the winner would be he who bowled the farthest.

Malar the Beastlord arrived to visit Jergal at this moment. After quickly ascertaining that the winner of the contest would receive all of Jergal's power, he chased off after the three skulls to make sure that the contest would be halted until he had a chance to participate for part of the prize. Bane, Bhaal, and Myrkul again fell to fighting, as it was obvious their sport had been ruined, but again Jergal intervened. "Why don't you allow Lady Luck to decide, so you don't have to share with the Beast?"

The trio agreed to this alternative, and Jergal broke off his skeletal finger bones and gave them to the contestants. When Malar returned from chasing the skulls, he found that the trio had just finished a game of knucklebones.

Bane cried out triumphantly, "As winner, I choose to rule for all eternity as the ultimate tyrant. I can induce hatred and strife at my whim, and all will bow down before me while in my kingdom."

Myrkul, who had won second place, declared, "But I choose the dead, and by doing so I truly win, because all that you are lord over, Bane, will eventually be mine. All things must die—even gods."

Bhaal, who finished third, proclaimed, "I choose death, and it is by my hand that all that you rule, Lord Bane, will eventually pass to Lord Myrkul. Both of you must pay honor to me and obey my wishes, since I can destroy your kingdom, Bane, by murdering your subjects, and I can starve your kingdom, Myrkul, by staying my hand."

Malar growled in frustration, but could do nothing, and so yet again only the beasts were left for him.

And Jergal merely smiled, for he had been delivered.

---

common in places where an individual's grave or tomb isn't marked with the person's name.

Few people favor Jergal as a deity, and most who do are concerned with the dispensation of the dead in some way. Priests of Jergal serve communities as undertakers and caretakers of gravesites. Jergal has no temples dedicated to him aside from abandoned places devoted to his old, darker incarnation, but his priests are welcome in the temples of Kelemvor, Deneir, and Myrkul. His faithful send their annual recordings of mortality to holy sites where records of that sort are kept.

KELEMVOR

The Lord of the Dead, the Judge of the Damned

Kelemvor is seen as a just, fair, and comforting god of death. Death comes to all, and when it occurs Kelemvor is there to take each soul by the hand and lead it to the

SYMBOL OF KELEMVOR

proper afterlife. Kelemvor's priests teach that those who revere the gods according to the rites of their religion have done their proper service and will be offered the afterlife they seek.

The faithful of Kelemvor provide people with peaceful transitions into the care of the Lord of the Dead. They help the dying put their affairs in order, and they officiate at funeral rites for those who can't afford the lavish ceremonies of their faith. The tenets of Kelemvor's faithful compel them to forestall or prevent untimely deaths whenever possible. Different sects and worshipers define "untimely" in different ways. One group might concentrate on stopping the spread of disease, another on the prevention of murder, and yet another on eliminating the scourge of the undead. In fact, all the faithful of Kelemvor despise the undead and work to some degree to eliminate them, for undead of any sort are seen as an abomination of the natural order. This belief obviously puts Kelemvor's faithful at odds with necromancers, priests of Myrkul, and others who promote the creation of the undead, and it also causes conflict from unexpected sources. For instance, priests of Kelemvor routinely destroy any writings about the creation of the undead that they find—an act that offends those who value knowledge for its own sake, such as the faithful of Oghma and Deneir. And there also exist undead that aren't evil, such as the baelnorn, which the elves consider holy. Kelemvor's devotees seek the end of such beings regardless of that fact.

LATHANDER

The Morninglord, Inspiration's Dawn, the Rose-and-Gold God

Lathander is the god of the spring, birth, and renewal, a deity of conception, vitality, youth, renewal, and self-perfection. He is god not of the sun but of the dawn, which represents the start of a new day filled with potential.

Lathander is a god of beginnings. People commonly offer a prayer to him before undertaking any journey or endeavor. Lathander's name is invoked to seal alliances and christen new ventures or companies. As a result, the god is very popular among the merchant classes, and the church has benefited accordingly.

The rising sun is his symbol, and his colors are the rose, gold, and violet of the dawn. Lathander's temples and shrines host a wide range of functions both municipal and personal. At such places folk get married in dawn ceremonies, announce the start of civic projects,

and even give birth when possible, to provide the baby good fortune.

The faithful of Lathander embrace the founding of new communities and the growth of civilization, as long as that civilization gives everyone the potential to succeed. They despise the undead, seeing them as both a corruption of the natural order and a disavowal of new beginnings, because undead cling to their old existence rather than moving on.

LEIRA

The Lady of the Mists, Mistshadow, the Lady of Deception

Leira has worn many masks, and more than once has been thought to be dead or to be another deity altogether. Perhaps such a reputation is only natural for the goddess of illusion and deception. Her faithful agree that whatever the "truth" might be, their Lady takes great delight in the confusion sown by her various incarnations. Even the faithful of Cyric once taught that their god killed Leira, but now they espouse the strange idea that somehow she is his daughter.

Leira isn't viewed as malicious or as a trickster but is seen as enigmatic, quiet, and retiring. She is credited with inventing Ruathlek, the language of illusionists and the spoken tongue of Nimbral.

The faithful of Leira seem to be scarce, although it is difficult to know this for certain, because those who favor her rarely make their inclinations known. Leira is the patron of illusionists and liars. She receives little regular worship except from illusionists, who pray to the Mistshadow for potency in their magic, and con artists, for whom she is a kind of champion. Most people pray to her when they hope to keep something secret, or placate her with a prayer before making an important decision when they fear being deceived. Some folk perform a swirling motion with a finger behind their backs when telling a lie as a way of beseeching her for aid.

Her priests wear vestments of white and mist-gray, and their faces are covered by smooth, featureless masks. Only in Nimbral do temples to Leira exist, and shrines dedicated to her found across the continent are usually disguised as other kinds of sites, marked with signs that only the faithful would recognize.

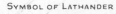
SYMBOL OF LATHANDER

SYMBOL OF LEIRA

LLIIRA

Our Lady of Joy, Joybringer, the Mistress of Revels

Lliira is a beloved goddess, a deity of contentment, release, joy, happiness, dance, and freedom. As the patron of festivals, she is honored at any celebration, and dance is the primary way to worship her. The Mistress of Revels is said to abhor violence, and any fighting or drawing of weapons (except in ceremony) at a celebration will cause her to withhold her favor. Her priests and priestesses, known as joybringers, take it as their mission to make other people happy, even if just for a moment.

Her faithful always wear at least one clothing item of a bright, cheerful color, and her priests' vestments have more in common with festival attire than with somber ecclesial garments. Rubies and sapphires are sacred to Our Lady of Joy, and her priests bless anyone they see wearing such adornments.

Lliira's followers aren't frivolous, however. To them, divine joy is a very real gift to the world of mortals, and one much needed. To that end, they fight those who would bring misery to others. They are fierce against their foes, and joyous revelers when their work is done.

LOVIATAR

The Maiden of Pain, the Scourge Mistress, the Willing Whip

Pain isn't a means to an end for Loviatar's faithful, but an end unto itself. To them, nothing is as transcendent as suffering, and all pain is holy, from the crudest barbarism, to the most sublime torture, to the emotional suffering of the heartbroken or the betrayed.

The pain that one feels is proof of the Lady's attention, and so her faithful are notorious self-flagellants. Pain is also a path to power, in terms of both one's ability to inflict it and one's ability to endure it. A cold, cruel demeanor is considered ideal because it best emulates the Scourge Mistress, and for the same reason her faithful appreciate beauty, cultural refinement, and a certain adeptness at manipulation.

Though temples to Loviatar are rare, her faithful are more numerous than might be expected. Loviatar is the chosen deity of those who inflict pain as a matter of course, including torturers and others who need to break the will of their victims. She is favored by sadists and masochists, and some of her followers form cultish cells of secret adherents. Each of these groups is led by someone who takes pleasure in administering pain and dominating others, supported and backed up by a number of submissive sycophants.

Worshipers of Loviatar rarely gather in numbers except in the more populous cities. When small cadres of faithful operate quietly in such places, few citizens take notice or raise a fuss if they do witness cult activity. The sufferers who endure the lash, however, aren't always willing participants, and Lovatar's cults sometimes operate secret slavery rings, which can draw the attention of the authorities. The open worship of Loviatar and temples clearly dedicated to her are rarely seen except in lands where slavery is an accepted practice.

MALAR

The Beastlord, the Black-Blooded One

Malar epitomizes the dark side of nature, the world that is red in tooth and claw. His faithful believe the hunt is the center point between life and death—the facing off of hunter and prey, forcing the issue of who lives and who dies. People believe that Malar can't be propitiated and knows no mercy, so he receives prayers only from those engaging in a hunt. Such supplicants pray to Malar for two reasons: to beg the aid of his peerless skill as a hunter, or to adopt his fearsome mantle and thus ward off other predators. Malar is the god of those who delight in the hunt, don't shy from bloodshed, and savor the fear of their prey.

Many lycanthropes consider Malar to be their divine father, as do some other intelligent predators. He has many devotees who are druids and rangers of particularly savage inclination, and many barbarians take Malar as a patron for his ferocity and cruelty. His priests use claw bracers, impressive gauntlets bedecked with stylized claws that jut out from the ends of the fists, as ceremonial weapons.

MASK

The Lord of Shadows, the Master of All Thieves

Mask is a trickster god, the patron of ne'er-do-wells, spies, and thieves. All that occurs within shadow is in the purview of Mask. People whisper a prayer to Mask whenever stealth is required or intrigue is afoot. Courtiers and diplomats invoke the god's name in hopes of a smooth negotiation.

Those who favor Mask usually pursue thievery and other forms of acquisition of what belongs to others, such as pickpocketing, burglary, mugging, and con

SYMBOL OF LLIIRA

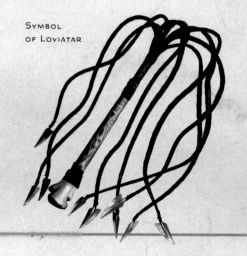

SYMBOL OF LOVIATAR

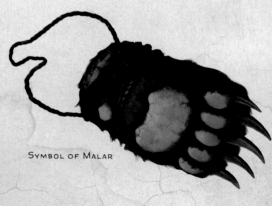

SYMBOL OF MALAR

games. Ordinary folk pray to him to avert his eyes from their valuables, but the cautious sometimes employ "Mask's purse," a small, cheap cloth pouch worn in plain sight (thus easily cut or lifted) containing a small offering of coin. By convention, a pickpocket pilfers Mask's purse when encountering another person wearing one, and considers the gain a gift from the god, while the one who lost the purse is grateful to the Lord of Shadows for accepting a respectful sacrifice of a small portion of his goods. Of course, nothing prevents another pickpocket from targeting someone who has lost Mask's purse, but anyone with the ill luck to attract multiple pickpockets in a single outing has probably earned Mask's ire anyway.

Priests of Mask are usually thieves by profession, and often serve as higher-ups in the local underworld or criminal syndicate. They go by the title of demarche or demarchess, and wear veil-masks when acting in their priestly capacity.

MIELIKKI

Our Lady of the Forest, the Forest Queen

People rarely speak of Mielikki except in quiet forest spaces. Woodlands that evoke wonder are where she reigns supreme, but she is said to keep watch over good folk in any forest, not matter how dark or cruel. When children are lost in the woods, people beseech Mielikki to protect them until they are found.

Mielikki is the goddess of the forest and the creatures that live within it. She is seen as a remote and spiritual deity—less human-like than many other gods. She's not unmindful of people, but her attention and favor are difficult to attract. She is the patron of rangers in the same way that Milil is the patron of bards, but even rangers rarely pray to her directly. They instead pray to Gwaeron Windstrom, who they believe will carry their words to the goddess by tracking her to whichever forest she hides in.

Mielikki's symbol is a unicorn, which prompts some to think of her as such and conflate her with Lurue, Queen of the Unicorns and the actual goddess of their kind. But most tales depict Mielikki as a beautiful woman whom Lurue allows upon her back as a rider, and the two are thought to be boon companions. Mielikki's relationships with other deities of the natural world are more complex. Silvanus is sometimes thought of as her father and Eldath is considered her sister, but Mielikki walks her own path through the wilds.

She has many shrines, particularly in the Savage Frontier. Most consist of a dead tree trunk into which has been carved a likeness of her holy symbol, a unicorn's head. Alternatively, the likeness might be carved on a separate piece of wood and tacked to a living tree. These shrines typically mark the point in a forest beyond which locals know not to cut timber or hunt. Often these tributes are created by loggers at the end of a logging excursion as a mark of thanks to the goddess for providing the wood and for keeping the timber cutters safe during the work.

MILIL

The Lord of Song, the One True Hand of All-Wise Oghma

Milil is the god of poetry, eloquence, and song. He is a god of creativity and inspiration, of the entire song more than just the lyrics or the music. He represents the finished thought, the result of the process that takes an idea from conception to realization. Milil is most venerated by bards, troubadours, and other entertainers, but anyone preparing to entertain or speak before a crowd might offer Milil a brief prayer for a successful performance. Those who seek inspiration in a creative endeavor also pray to Milil.

His icons depict him as a handsome male, sometimes a human, sometimes an elf, and even a half-elf in places (such as Aglarond) that have a large half-elf population. He is variously depicted as young or old, but his identity is always apparent because of his five-stringed harp made of silvery leaves, which he carries constantly. He is the ideal to which all performers aspire: poised and confident, winningly charismatic, and a source of inspiration for those who listen to him. He is said to have total recall of anything he hears or that is spoken while music plays, as well as utmost skill at improvisation.

Holy sites dedicated to Milil are often found in performance venues and schools of music. Whether the site is a vast concert hall or a small choral chamber, it must have excellent acoustic qualities. Milil's priests are patrons of the arts in addition to being performers themselves, and they frequently act as tutors in the arts of performance at his shrines and temples.

Like Deneir, Milil is sometimes thought of as being in service to Oghma. In these portrayals of the deity, Milil is the god's left hand, also referred to as the One True Hand. This expression isn't meant to denigrate the right hand (Deneir); rather, it stems from the fact

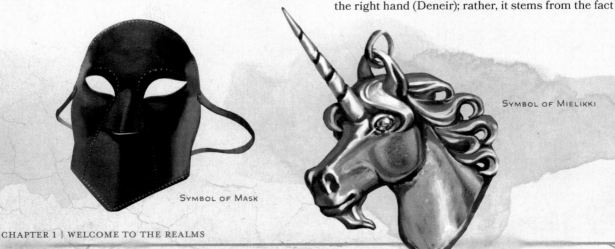

SYMBOL OF MASK

SYMBOL OF MIELIKKI

that left-handedness is more often associated with great artistic ability and the belief that the greatest art comes from the acceptance of truth.

MYRKUL

The Lord of Bones, Old Lord Skull, the Reaper

Myrkul is an ancient god, one of three former mortals who were raised to deityhood when Jergal grew weary of his divine duties and distributed his influence between them. Myrkul became the god of death and the dead, and ruled over the City of the Dead for centuries until he, in turn, was slain. In time Myrkul returned, for can death itself truly ever die? Myrkul's faithful see him as the Reaper, who lays claim to souls and brings them to Kelemvor to be judged.

Myrkul is a deity of death, decay, old age, exhaustion, dusk, and autumn. He's the god of the ending of things and hopelessness, as much as Lathander is the god of beginnings and hope. Folk don't pray to Myrkul so much as dread him and blame him for aching bones and fading vision. Myrkul is thought to be passionless and uncaring even of his most devout worshipers. Those who take Myrkul as a patron tend to be morose, taciturn, and obsessed with the dead and the undead. Like many followers of Kelemvor and Jergal, priests of Myrkul serve as undertakers and typically keep their patron's identity secret.

Shrines to Myrkul or engravings of his holy symbol appear in many places where humans bury their dead, but full-fledged temples are rare. The few that exist are hallowed places where the dead from hundreds of miles around are brought for internment, even if they were not of Myrkul's faith. There is little space set aside for the living in such a location, usually a single modest shrine, but its catacombs and ossuaries are vast. In the deepest chamber of each temple rests a throne, and upon that throne sits the doomwarden—the preserved corpse of the most revered saint in the history of the temple (often its founder). Initiates to the faith are brought to kneel before a temple's doomwarden, where they must spend a night and a day fasting and meditating in complete darkness.

MYSTRA

The Lady of Mysteries, Our Lady of Spells, the Mother of All Magic

Mystra is the goddess of magic, and with that the goddess of possibilities. She is venerated by mages and by those who use magic or magical objects in their daily lives. She also receives the prayers of those who find magic wondrous or encounter magic they fear. Mystra is the goddess of the essential force that makes all spellcasting possible. She provides and tends the Weave, the conduit through which mortal spellcasters and magical crafters can safely access the raw force of magic.

The faith of Mystra is pervasive in Faerûn, which is to be expected for a land as touched by magic as it is. Her worshipers include those who use magic or work closely with it, such as alchemists and sages. The blue-clad priests of Mystran temples count wizards and sorcerers among their numbers, as well as the occasional bard. The goal of Mystra's faithful is simple: that magic be preserved and promulgated throughout the Realms. It isn't unusual for her followers to keep an eye out for those who demonstrate high potential for using magic and help arrange for such persons to find tutelage with a suitable mentor.

OGHMA

The Binder, the Lord of Knowledge

Oghma is the god of inspiration, invention, and knowledge. Above all else, Oghma represents knowledge in its most supreme, raw form—the idea. An aphorism cited by his faithful about this concept serves them as a prayer when it is repeated aloud: "An idea has no heft but it can move mountains. An idea has no authority but it can dominate people. An idea has no strength but it can push aside empires. Knowledge is the greatest tool of the mortal mind, outweighing anything made by mortal hands. Before anything else can exist, the idea must exist."

Oghma's faithful spread knowledge and literacy as widely as possible, believing that minds ought never to be shackled by ignorance and thus not be able to bequeath the benefit they might otherwise provide their fellows. Not surprisingly, those who follow Oghma oppose those who foster deceit, trickery, and ignorance.

Folk of many professions favor the Binder: wizards, cartographers, artists, bards, clerks, inventors, sages, scribes, and all manner of others who uncover, preserve, and create knowledge and learning. The worship of Oghma was, at one point, one of the few organized faiths in Faerûn that had an established orthodoxy and a complete network of temples that adhered to that orthodoxy. Schisms during the Time of Troubles shattered that network, and now the structures that house the

SYMBOL OF MYRKUL

SYMBOL OF MYSTRA

SYMBOL OF OGHMA

faith are individual temples or small networks of allied temples, much in the manner of other faiths.

THE RED KNIGHT

The Lady of Strategy, the Crimson General, the Grandmaster of the Lanceboard

The Red Knight is the goddess of planning and strategy. Those who favor her call themselves the Red Fellowship. They believe wars are won by the best planning, strategy, and tactics. The worship of the Red Knight is filled with doctrine about strategy, such as: "Every war is a series of battles. Losing one doesn't mean losing the war." "In war, plan for peace. In peace, plan for war." "Seek allies among your enemy's enemies."

Worship of the Red Knight arose among a hero-venerating monastic order of Tempus in Tethyr shortly after the Time of Troubles. The Red Knight has since grown in popularity because of what her followers call the Great Stratagem: for decades, her priests have been traveling to places of warfare to educate generals and kings in the arts of strategy and battlefield tactics. Many of the leaders they approached turned them away at first, but it soon became apparent that those who accepted the counsel of the Crimson General's followers gained a distinct benefit. Grateful victors built temples to the Lady of Strategy, and gradually her faith spread.

Today, followers of the Red Knight can be found in nearly any land that has seen warfare in the past century. Worshipers of the Red Knight are rare in the general population, but those who revere her can frequently be found among high-ranking commanders of armies, instructors in colleges of war, quartermasters, and the authors of tomes of strategy. Each temple to the Red Knight includes an altar dedicated to Tempus, and so such a place is likely to be frequented by mercenaries and soldiers. A temple is surrounded by a vast pavilion and courtyard, which can be rented by companies of soldiers and mercenaries for practice and training. Her priests believe that drilling one's troops in a temple courtyard is a form of propitiation that the Red Knight looks upon with special favor.

SAVRAS

The All-Seeing, the Third Eye, Divination's Lord

Savras is a god of divination and fortunetelling. Few people worship him, but many pray to him when performing small rituals of foresight. For example, young

men and women sometimes attempt to divine the names of their future spouses by saying a rhyming chant that calls upon Savras while gazing in a mirror.

Savras has no currently active temples in Faerûn, and his shrines are few and far between, tucked away in the corners of libraries and scriptoria. Despite this lack of prominence, certain folk pay regular homage to Savras, including investigators, diviners, judges, and others who have a need to uncover the truth. Such individuals can sometimes be identified by the elaborate staffs they carry in homage to Savras. According to legend, Savras was trapped in Azuth's staff for ages. Azuth eventually freed Savras so long as Savras swore fealty, and today the staff is a potent symbol for those who revere Savras. Devout worshipers take great pains to decorate and embellish their staffs, each hoping that Savras might find it a welcoming place to stop for a time.

SELÛNE

Our Lady of Silver, the Moonmaiden, the Night White Lady

Selûne is thought to be among the most ancient of Faerûn's deities. Most humans in Faerûn consider the moon in the sky to literally be the goddess gazing down on the world, and the trailing motes of light behind it her tears. She is also a goddess of stars and navigation as well as motherhood and reproductive cycles. She is seen as a calm power, frequently venerated by female humans as well as by a mix of other folk: navigators and sailors, those who work honestly at night, those seeking protection in the dark, the lost, and the questing.

There are many legends about Selûne, chief among them being the tale of the battle at the beginning of time between Selûne and her sister, Shar. The Tears of Selûne, the cluster of starry lights that follow the moon around the sky, are thought to be brought about by the goddess's joy, sorrow, or both.

Milk, a symbol of motherhood, is used in many rites performed by the worshipers of Selûne, as are trances and meditation. Those who favor her typically set a bowl of milk outside on each night of the full moon.

SHAR

The Mistress of the Night, the Dark Lady, Our Lady of Loss

The dark twin of Selûne, Shar is the goddess of darkness, both in its physical form and as it exists in the minds and souls of mortals. People worship Shar as

SYMBOL OF THE
RED KNIGHT

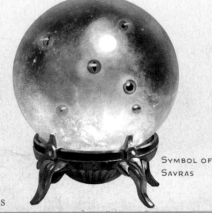

SYMBOL OF
SAVRAS

SYMBOL
OF SELÛNE

the goddess of night, secrets, loss, and forgetfulness. She represents pains hidden but not forgotten, and vengeances carefully nurtured away from the light. She is said to have the power to make folk forget their pain or become inured to a loss, and many people in distress pray to Shar for such a blessing.

Shar is revered by those who must venture into dark places and so pray to her for protection, such as miners, as well as by those who have fallen into melancholy and despair, who wish to forget something, or who have lost something and wish to recover it. Priests drawn to serve Shar often nurture their own deep wounds or dark secrets, which in their minds makes them best suited to console those who suffer from a similar ill. Throughout the world's history, many followers of Shar have done dark deeds in her name—most notably the shadovar of Netheril, an entire society dedicated to Shar. The tragedies and losses brought about by the fanaticism of her followers have caused many places to outlaw her worship and thus driven most of her priests into secrecy, but such prohibitions only heighten the priests' umbrage at authorities and make the faithful a focal point for rebellion and revenge against whoever rules.

SILVANUS

Oak Father, the Old Oak, Old Father Tree

Silvanus represents the entirety of nature, deserts as well as forests, sharks as much as deer. But folk in the North, who contend with the dangers of forests, mountains, and plains, see Silvanus more as a god of those places. Silvanus is thought of as a grim and severe father figure who metes out flood and drought, fire and ice, and life and death in the wilderness. In legends he often commands other nature deities, dealing out rewards and punishments to them as is fitting.

Nature and its impartial fairness is central to the dogma of Silvanus's faith. His priests seek to know the total situation, to view the macrocosm; their viewpoint isn't confined to one person's or one nation's idea of what is best. The loss of a farming community to goblin raids is a tragedy for some, but the event provides an opportunity for the wilderness to grow up and make the land fertile again, which in turn provides new challenges for those who would return to tame it.

The creed of Silvanus dictates that nature's glory must be preserved not merely because nature is beautiful, but because wild nature is the true state of the world. Its expanses refresh and revitalize the mortal soul, and give breath to all the world. Many of his faithful oppose the expansion of settlements into wild places, and consider excessive consumption of natural resources to be not only wasteful but blasphemous.

Silvanus often receives veneration from travelers in wild lands, explorers, and residents of rural communities far from the protection of a local lord or a great city. The oak leaf is Silvanus's symbol, and a grove of oak trees within a village or on its outskirts is often dedicated as a shrine to him. In rural places where oak trees don't grow, an oak leaf etched into the bark of another kind of tree signifies a sacred site.

SUNE

Lady Firehair, the Lady of Love, the Princess of Passion

Sune Firehair is a deity of passion and the delights of the senses. She is the goddess of beauty in all its forms—not just pleasing sights, but also enchanting sounds, luxurious tastes and scents, and the exquisite pleasures of the flesh, from a lover's caress to the brush of silk on the skin. Her worshipers seek out these pleasures in life, not out of mere decadence, but because the experience of pleasure is the touch of Sune herself.

The followers of Sune have a reputation as hedonists, and so they are, to a degree. More than that, her priests foster beauty in the world. They do so by creating art, by acting as patrons for promising talents, and by investing in merchants who bring luxuries to far-off places that have never seen satin or tasted a luscious wine.

Her priests consider loveliness to be one of their greatest callings, and all are trained in comportment, fashion, and cosmetics. Indeed, so talented are Sune's priests in the creation of beautiful appearances that many take pride in their ability to present themselves as stunningly attractive examples of either gender.

But beauty is more than skin deep, say the Sunites; it issues from the core of one's being and shows one's true face to the world, whether fair or foul. The followers of Sune are believers in romance, true love winning over all, and following one's heart to one's true destination. Fated matches, impossible loves, and ugly ducklings becoming swans are all in the purview of Sune.

Temples dedicated to Sune are common in human lands, and they frequently serve as public baths and places of relaxation. A temple usually features a mirrored and well-lit salon where folks can primp, as well as see others and be seen. Where a temple doesn't exist, or in a large city where the nearest temple might be too

SYMBOL OF SILVANUS

SYMBOL OF SUNE

far to walk to, a small shrine to Sune often stands near a street corner. These sites consist of a mirror hung beneath a small roof where one can say a prayer while checking one's appearance. The spot might feature a shelf or a cupboard holding various perfumes and cosmetics so that those without the funds to purchase such items can still make themselves feel beautiful.

TALONA

Lady of Poison, Mistress of Disease, the Plague-crone

One of the most often beseeched of Faerûn's deities, Talona is the goddess of disease and poison, blamed for everything from common illnesses to crop failure to brackish wells to plague. Depicted in temple iconography as a withered crone with a cup or a vase that holds all the varieties of disease and poison, Talona is a fearsome goddess, and many are the prayers that beg her for protection from illness and poison. Various rituals to placate her involve the use of three drops of blood or three tears—to be dropped into a well that has gone bad, dripped into the handkerchief of someone beset by coughing, dropped into a fire made by burning a withered crop, dripped into the mouth of a plague sufferer, and so on. It's common practice to mark a container of poison with her holy symbol, three droplets in a triangle, and during epidemics folk paint the same image on the homes of the infected.

Though she is often the recipient of prayers, Talona has almost no temples and few cults dedicated to her. A cult or a shrine to her might arise in an area after it suffers from pestilence, when some of those who survived decide to revere her or even become priests.

TALOS

Stormlord, the Destroyer

Talos is the dark side of nature, the uncaring and destructive force that might strike at any time. He is the god of storms, forest fires, earthquakes, tornadoes, and general destruction. He counts the ravager, the raider, the looter, and the brigand among his followers. Those who favor him see life as a succession of random effects in a sea of chaos, so the devout should grab what they can, when they can—for who can say when Talos will strike and send them into the afterlife?

Talos is portrayed as a broad-shouldered, bearded young man with a single good eye, the other covered by a dark patch. He is said to carry a collection of three staffs, made from the first tree cut down in the world, the first silver smelted, and the first iron forged. He uses these staffs to raise destructive winds, cause terrible storms, and split the land in acts of rage. The three lightning bolts of his holy symbol represent these staffs, and when he vents his wrath on the world, he is thought to hurl them down from the sky as lightning strikes.

Although Talos is a popular deity, his name is invoked more often out of fear than out of reverence. He does have priests, mostly traveling doomsayers, who warn of disasters to come and accept charity in exchange for blessings of protection. Many of his faithful wear a black eyepatch, even if both eyes are intact.

TEMPUS

The Foehammer, the Lord of Battles

Tempus is a war god concerned with brave conduct during war, using force of arms over talk for settling disputes, and encouraging bloodshed. The god of war is random in his favors, meaning that his chaotic nature favors all sides equally. Lord Tempus might be an army's ally one day, and its enemy the next. He might seem to manifest before a battle, appearing to one side or the other. If he is seen riding a white mare (Veiros), then the army will succeed. If he rides a black stallion (Deiros), then defeat is certain. Most often he appears to be riding with one foot in each mount's stirrup, signifying the unpredictable nature of battle. In such visions, Tempus is always a powerfully built warrior dressed for battle in the style of those who envision him.

Tempus's favor might be randomly distributed, but over the centuries his priests have made an effort to spread and enforce a common code of warfare—to make war a thing of rules, respect for reputations, and professional behavior. This code, called Tempus's Honor, has the purpose of making conflicts brief, decisive, and as safe as possible for those not directly involved. The rules in the code include the following: arm anyone who has need of a weapon; disparage no foe; acquit oneself with bravery; train all for battle; and don't engage in feuds. Those who poison wells, taint fields, kill noncombatants, or engage in torture in the name of war are all considered sinners.

Worshipers of Tempus are legion, and his name is often on the lips of soldiers. His priests are tacticians, often skilled in the art of war. Many of his ordained don't serve in temples, but as battlefield chaplains with armies and mercenary companies, encouraging their fellow soldiers with both word and blade. Priests of

SYMBOL OF TALONA

SYMBOL OF TALOS

Tempus teach that war conducted properly is fair in that it oppresses all sides equally, and that in any given battle, a mortal might be slain or might become a great leader among his or her companions. Mortals shouldn't fear war but should see it as a natural force, the storm that civilization brings about by its very existence.

TORM

The Loyal Fury, the True, the Hand of Righteousness

Torm is the god of duty and loyalty, revered by those who face danger to bring about a greater good. Those who favor Torm believe that one's salvation can be found through service, that every failure to perform one's duty diminishes Torm, and that every success adds to his luster. Those who take Torm to heart must strive to fulfill his commandment to go out into the world and be an active force for good, to right wrongs, and to help the hopeless. They must strive to maintain peace and order while opposing unjust laws. Followers of Torm stand ever alert against corruption and are expected to strike quickly and hard against any evidence of rot in the hearts of mortals. As the sword arm of justice, Torm's faithful are expected to bring quick deaths to betrayers. Considering these tenets, it should be no surprise that most human paladins have Torm as their patron.

Most temples dedicated to Torm are fortresses built on heights. These structures offer austere quarters for residents and visiting knights, drilling grounds, and stables. White granite, lion statues, and armored figures predominate in the architecture, with the coats of arms of fallen heroes decorating the walls of the great halls.

Torm is seen as the good right hand of Tyr, and a such his symbol is a white gauntlet made for the right hand. It represents Tyr's sword hand, but it is also a symbol of forbearance. Torm is frequently depicted with his right gauntlet extended palm forward, which worshipers call the Hand Resolute. It signifies the principle that the just and true must pause before acting to judge whether their intentions uphold Torm's ideals. Temples, civic structures, and the homes of the faithful are often decorated with images of the Hand Resolute as a constant reminder of this principle.

Worshipers of Torm come from most walks of life, for he welcomes any who seek the best in themselves and others, who uphold his tenets of loyalty, responsibility, duty, and kindness, or who are willing to sacrifice to keep evil from gaining ascendancy in the world. The faithful know that all of them will stumble from time to time while following in Torm's footsteps, but Torm's priests teach that the shame of a minor fall from grace is far less severe than declining to rise oneself up to Torm's standards.

TYMORA

Lady Luck, Our Smiling Lady

Tymora is the bright-faced goddess of fortune, the one to whom gamblers and game-players pray in Faerûn. Our Smiling Lady is said to love none so much as those who gamble with the utmost skill and daring. Yet she is thought to watch over all who take risks to better their fortunes.

The battle cry of the followers of Tymora is "Fortune favors the bold." Someone might say words to Tymora before any endeavor in which a little good luck would help, but not when an incidence of bad luck might occur. (On such occasions folk pray to Beshaba to spare them from bad luck; praying to both is thought to anger both goddesses.) One common method of divining the future is to toss a coin to a stranger (typically a beggar) and ask if it's heads. If it is, the coin is left with the stranger as payment for Tymora's favor. If it's not, the stranger can choose to keep it (and the bad luck) or return it.

Those who favor Tymora—as distinct from folk who invoke her name by mumbling over the dice—tend to be daring sorts. Adventurers and gamblers make up much of their ranks. They all have the belief that what is good about their lives is the result of having both good luck and the bravery to seek it out. Tymora has worshipers among all sorts of folk: the dashing young noble, the risk-taking merchant, the daydreaming field hand, and the scheming ne'er-do-well.

Priests of Tymora and temples devoted to Lady Luck are scarce, since her faith tends not to stress a need for intermediaries: "Let the lucky man and the Smiling Lady suss it out," as the old saying goes. Shrines to Tymora at gambling parlors aren't unusual, however, and sometimes such establishments attract a priest and effectively become temples.

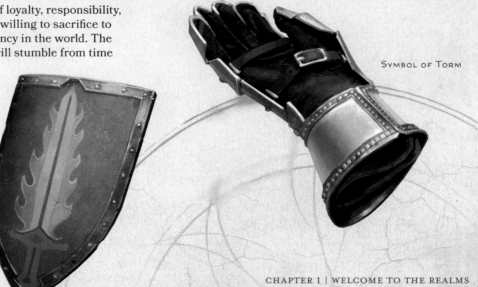

SYMBOL OF TORM

SYMBOL OF TEMPUS

The Legend of Tyche and Her Twin Daughters

Before the Dawn Cataclysm, there was but one goddess of luck, Tyche. Ever flirting with fortune and disaster, Lady Luck bestowed and withdrew her favor at a whim. When her current paramour, Lathander, started a fight among the gods, Tyche kissed the Morninglord with misfortune and wandered off to explore the world.

During her travels, Lady Luck discovered a budding rose of unequaled beauty. Delighted with this fortuitous happenstance, Tyche reached to pluck this delightful token, which she assumed was a peace overture from Lathander, who sought to regain her good graces. Much to her amazement, Lady Luck couldn't pluck the rose from its bush no matter how hard she tried. Frustrated, she cursed the rose with bad luck, and the flower's stem broke in her hands. Tyche put the plucked rose behind her ear and continued on her way. Unknown to Tyche, the rose was a manifestation of Moander, god of corruption and decay. The severed rose stem crept into Tyche's ear and subtly began to rot her from the inside out.

When Tyche returned home, she came across her dear friend, the goddess Selûne, waiting to speak with her. Also waiting for her were Lathander, who wished to regain her affections, and Azuth, who had come to mediate the dispute between the two. Selûne wept great tears as she saw the corruption destroying her friend from within, and before Tyche could discern her intent, Selûne lashed out with a bolt of purifying light. Tyche's rotted core split down the middle and a smaller, brighter version of the goddess of luck stepped out, allowing the goddess of the moon to save that which was good and pure in her friend. However, following this first figure out of the rotten shell was another form stunning to behold, but full of dark malice and capricious ill will. As the two forms emerged, they immediately fell upon each other in hate, struggling madly, and were separated only by the combined efforts of all three visitors.

It is said that Tymora, Tyche's Fair-Haired Daughter, embodies all the grace and kindness of her mother, while Beshaba, Tyche's Unpleasant Daughter, got only her looks. Since their birth, the twin aspects of Tyche—Tymora, Lady Luck, and Beshaba, Maid of Misfortune—have battled each other, contesting matters as great as the fate of nations and as small as the flip of a coin.

Tyr

Grimjaws, the Maimed God, the Evenhanded

Tyr Grimjaws, Tyr the Evenhanded, Wounded Tyr, the Maimed God, the Blind, Blind Tyr, the Lord of Justice—all of these names speak to the nature of the Faerûnian god of justice. Tyr appears as a noble warrior missing his right hand, which he lost to Kezef the Chaos Hound in an act of bravery and sacrifice, and with his eyes wrapped in cloth to signify his blindness, caused by a wound dealt to him by Ao when he questioned the justice of the Overgod's actions.

Tyr's followers devote themselves to the cause of justice, to the righting of wrongs and the deliverance of vengeance. This devotion isn't necessarily concerned with equality or fairness, but rather the discovery of truth and the punishment of the guilty. Those who favor Tyr tend to be stiff-necked about matters of theology and laws, seeing things in terms of black and white. Tyr's credo of lawfulness and honesty is a demanding one, and his priests remind the faithful not to hold in contempt others who can't live by it—it wouldn't be an honorable calling if everyone could muster the strength of will to follow it.

Many orders of knighthood are devoted to Tyr, including the Knights of Holy Judgment and the Knights of the Merciful Sword. Such knights—as well as judges and priests, clerics, and paladins who worship Tyr—sometimes wear thin strips of diaphanous cloth over their eyes to remind others of the blindness of justice.

Umberlee

The Bitch Queen, the Queen of the Depths, the Wavemother

No community that lives by the sea can ignore the influence of Umberlee, the furious goddess whose tempestuous nature reflects and is reflected by the waters of the deep. Any such community makes sure to host festivals to propitiate the Wavemother and seek her favor. Although mercurial in temperament, she can be generous to those who do her honor, as is any great queen.

The Bitch Queen is worshiped out of fear instead of adoration, and ship crews offer her gems, tossed over the side, to calm storm-tossed waters. As her most common moniker suggests, she is viewed as capricious and cruel with no firm ethical outlook; the sea is a savage place, and those who travel it had best be willing to pay the price of challenging her domain.

There is little in the way of an organized clergy of Umberlee. Her priests roam coastal cities, warning of doom and demanding free passage on ships in return for ensuring the goddess's pleasure. Often they wear the colors of waves and storms, and they decorate themselves

Symbol of Tyr

with items that remind others of the sea's dangerous nature—a necklace of shark teeth, seaweed wrapped about a human bone, and so on. The preserved hand of a drowned person is thought to be a particularly holy object, and some of her few clerics use such severed hands as holy symbols. Umberlee does have a large number of shrines in the coastal cities, and sailors often leave flowers or small candies at them in hopes that she will spare them on their next voyage. Both Waterdeep and Baldur's Gate have true temples dedicated to Umberlee, staffed largely by the widows of sailors lost at sea.

WAUKEEN

Our Lady of Gold, the Coinmaiden, the Merchant's Friend

Waukeen is the goddess of wealth and trade, on both sides of the law. Her most ardent worshipers include shopkeepers, members of trading costers, wealthy merchants, caravan guides, itinerant peddlers, moneychangers, and smugglers. She is interested in anything that increases trade and the flow of money, whether new trade routes, new inventions, or the whim of changing fashion. Those who take Waukeen as a patron can be reliably thought of as greedy, but the Coinmaiden is said to frown upon misers and smile upon the industrious and the profligate, and thus priests who bear her holy symbol find themselves welcome in many towns and cities.

Temples of Waukeen resemble guildhalls and often serve as meeting places for trade consortiums. Those who follow Waukeen's ethos seek to create more opportunity for all and see competition for wealth as one of society's main means of progress. Thus, the faithful of Our Lady of Gold often find themselves at odds with trade guilds and others who would form monopolies. It's common practice among those who seek Waukeen's favor to set aside a tithe of ten percent of their profits, but rather than being given to a temple, the money is meant to be spent to help a struggling business, to finance a new endeavor, or, if all else fails, on frivolous fun.

THE GODS OF MULHORAND

People of Faerûn refer to Mulhorand as one of the Old Empires, but most don't know that Mulhorand is in fact the oldest human empire still in existence on the continent. Mulhorand's pantheon of deities, sometimes called god-kings or pharaohs, can trace their lineage even farther back.

According to the demigods enthroned in Mulhorand, the ancestors of the Mulhorandi people were brought from another world and enslaved by the Imaskari in an ancient empire deep in what is now Raurin, the Dust Desert. When the gods of those ancestors heard the pleas of their distant faithful, they set out in a great celestial ark guided by the entity known as Ptah. Upon arriving in the world, two of the deities, Re and Enlil, set about empowering the slaves and fomenting rebellion.

The revolt succeeded, but Re and Enlil couldn't keep peace with one another. Each then founded a separate dynasty of divine mortals, Re in Mulhorand, and Enlil (father of Gilgeam) in Unther. Re and his related deities ruled Mulhorand through mortal incarnations for thousands of years.

Time took its toll, and the attention the deities of Mulhorand paid to their followers wavered and diminished. Each new incarnation of Isis, Osiris, and Thoth was a little more human and a little less divine. When the magically powerful Imaskari returned with a vengeance a little over a century ago, they stole the scepter of rulership from a grasp so weak it barely had any strength left.

Although Mulhorand's conquerors outlawed slavery in the area they now called High Imaskar, the Mulhorandi people recognized the yoke they now bore. The Imaskari were the new coming of the slavemasters of old, as depicted in the carvings in the pharaohs' tombs. Many prayed that the vanished gods would return and once again free them from Imaskari rule, and during the Sundering, that is what happened. What were referred to as Chosen in other lands were recognized in Mulhorand as living gods, come to lead the Mulhorandi in an uprising.

Today Mulhorand is ruled by demigods that call themselves by such names as Re, Anhur, Horus, Isis, Nephthys, Set, and Thoth. They take different forms, some human and others tieflings or aasimar, but all speak and act like the gods of legend come to life, which they must be. This family of deities bears the scars of all the past loves, rivalries, and wars between them, but for now they have set their differences aside for the betterment of Mulhorand and its people, and the people of Mulhorand love them for it.

SYMBOL OF UMBERLEE

SYMBOL OF WAUKEEN

CHAPTER 2: THE SWORD COAST AND THE NORTH

HIS CHAPTER DETAILS MANY OF THE locales of the Sword Coast and the North, as seen through the eyes and recollections of a person living in Faerûn. Rather than being exhaustive descriptions, what follows are snippets of information drawn from the experience of five individuals who have traversed, lived in, and explored these areas. Like any other narrators, they have opinions and biases, and may be drawing conclusions from incomplete information. No one in the Realms knows everything about any subject, even its oldest and most learned sages, and the views formed from such incomplete information can often suggest an inaccurate conclusion. This is not to say that any of the information the narrators provide is false, only that they may not be entirely knowledgeable in their declarations.

The details given here only begin to scratch the surface of the adventuring possibilities in the North. Although some of these locales are virtually unknown to outsiders, entire books longer than this one could be (and have been) written about others. If the descriptions leave you wanting to know more, consider them an inducement for you and your companions to visit these places and experience them firsthand.

Be aware, also, that there is a great deal more to the North than what is presented here. There are ruins without names, and settlements so small as to not even warrant mention in this tome. What lurks in the uncharted areas, waiting to tantalize or perhaps terrorize, is all the more formidable because it can't be anticipated.

THE LORDS' ALLIANCE

FOR A CENTURY AND A HALF, AND MORE, THE LORDS' Alliance has stood as the most important and influential group in the North. Its power has kept towns safe from the predations of larger powers, has kept the ambitions of Luskan in check, and has taught the rulers of many cities that it is better to cooperate, even for a time, then to merely shut one's doors and allow the storms to rage outside. It was this philosophy that led to the founding of Luruar, and when the lesson was lost, so too were the Silver Marches. But it serves no purpose to dwell on the folly of the past. Better instead to look to the future, repair the walls, and wait for word from the watching sentries.

—Andwe Cururen, agent of the Lords' Alliance

The Lords' Alliance isn't a nation unto itself, but a partnership of the rulers of towns and cities across the North, who have pledged peace with one another and promised to share information and effort against common threats such as orc hordes and Northlander pirates. It is a loose confederation of those settlements and their agents, all of whom owe allegiance first to their homelands, and second to the Lords' Alliance.

In the harsh lands of the North, where winters are cold and monsters and human barbarians regularly stream out of the mountains to pillage outlying settlements, large nations are rare indeed, particularly in the current state of the world. Instead, great city-states have emerged, enriched by trade and protected by stout walls and loyal defenders. Such cities—including Baldur's Gate, Mirabar, Neverwinter, Silverymoon, and Waterdeep—extend their influence into nearby regions, often creating or accepting vassal settlements, but in the end, these realms are cities, driven to consider their own protection and future before other concerns.

In the years soon after its founding more than one hundred fifty years ago, there was more interest in membership, and the Alliance accepted some members from farther south. Since then, events such as the growth of Elturgard into a power in its own right, and the recent fall of the Silver Marches, have caused the group to draw in on itself, restricting its membership to powers in the North. The current members of the Alliance are Amphail, Baldur's Gate, Daggerford, Longsaddle, Mirabar, Mithral Hall, Neverwinter, Silverymoon, Waterdeep, and Yartar. There is some doubt that Mithral Hall will be part of the alliance for much longer, but until rulership of the dwarven city is more firmly established, it remains a member.

It is impossible to ascribe an overall character to the individual members of the alliance. As a group, the agents of the members are interested in the preservation of civilization in the North, and they share what information they can—and oppose what threats they must—to further that goal. In the end, though, a merchant of Waterdeep and one of Baldur's Gate are concerned mainly for their own purses and the welfare of their home cities, and are unlikely to care what happens to the other, except inasmuch as it affects trade.

The advice and insights in this section come from Andwe Cururen, a half-elf native of Silverymoon who was once a Knight in Silver (a member of the city's army), and now serves as an emissary and, when necessary, an active agent for the Lords' Alliance. She travels the North on behalf of the Alliance, representing its interests and gathering and updating information on its settlements for her superiors, fellow agents, and potential recruits, including adventurers who might serve the Alliance or one of its members.

AMPHAIL

Named for its founder, a former warlord of Waterdeep, the small town of Amphail is home to just over seven hundred souls, yet it sought and received membership in the Lords' Alliance just under a century ago, thanks to the maneuverings of the noble families that control its lands. Where once it was simply an example of the extent of Waterdeep's reach, Amphail became the playground of that city's noble families, a place where they can scheme against their rivals and send their more rambunctious offspring to unleash some of their destructive tendencies without harming the family's reputation in proper society. As a result of being a member of the Lords' Alliance, Amphail is the equal of such great cities as Neverwinter and Baldur's Gate in matters that concern the other powers of the region, despite its clear inferiority in size and strength.

Amphail's sovereignty means that, although patrols from the Waterdeep City Guard sometimes ride north to check on matters in Amphail, the only true authority in the town is the will of the noble families that control it. The primary business of Amphail is horse ranching, and the town is a fine place to find replacement mounts, and all manner of tack, bridle, feed, and other goods necessary to keep up one's horse. Most farms have farriers, or at least hands that can swiftly shoe a horse, and spare shoes all but litter the town.

Visitors to Amphail often get a polite admonishment to "mind the high born" or "ware silver saddles" from the locals, but those who ignore such warnings should expect no help if they get into trouble with the nobility. Amphailans are by their nature suspicious of and quiet around folk who openly display wealth or status, having learned early in their lives that nobles are folk who like to throw their weight around, to the detriment of anyone nearby without enough coin or a grand enough title to stand up to them. I find that these common folk are ideal sources of information about the very people they distrust.

For their part, the young nobles that litter the town seem to make mischief mainly because they can. The feuds and rivalries that would generate only carefully worded insults in the city can escalate into brawls when these miscreants are far from the watchful eyes of their parents. Duels have long been prohibited by mutual agreement, due to the blood feuds they provoked in the past, but hands often drift to sword hilts when heated words are exchanged. Nearly every other sort of noble indiscretion is foisted on the residents of Amphail. Those who suffer property damage or worse at the nobles' hands are forced to forgive the offense in exchange for the application of coin or a promise made in the transgressor's name (suggesting that the youngster's relatives will handle any obligations). Some businesses survive entirely by bringing the comforts of Waterdeep to Amphail, creating gathering places where young nobles can feel at home.

The three greatest families with significant interests in Amphail are Houses Amcathra, Ilzimmer, and Roaringhorn; and most coin and business eventually passes through the hands one of those houses or its intermediaries. When Amphail joined the Lords' Alliance, these three houses were the loudest and most influential voices, and now control the rulership of the town, with the controlling family changing each Shieldmeet. The current Lord Warder is Dauner Ilzimmer, who speaks for the town to the Lords' Alliance. House Amcathra has yet to choose its successor for next Shieldmeet. Houses Jhansczil and Tarm have smaller breeding concerns in the area, and House Eagleshields has holdings near Amphail that it uses to continue its long tradition of caring for unhealthy animals from nearby farms, and offers fine tack and other gear for sale.

Among the common folk, the Oglyntyr family has the largest and oldest cattle and horse farm in Amphail, and supplies some of the finest Amphail grays (loyal, intelligent steeds favored as personal mounts) to nobles and travelers in the region. A new family, not noble but possessing much wealth, has purchased the old Baldasker ranch. We suspect that the Hemzar family, who were unknown in either Amphail or Waterdeep before the purchase, like most of the mysterious matters in Amphail, may have the secret backing of one noble house or another.

My contacts say the Oglyntyrs have petitioned the Ilzimmers to help crush this upstart business, a move that they are considering. I visited the Hemzar ranch, and I'd consider such a move inadvisable. A large family of Tashlutar descent, they seemed capable and confident of their position, despite my warning. I wasn't allowed the opportunity to explore the property fully, but I did note signs that the Hemzars are prepared to rear and train far more dangerous beasts than horses and cattle. I was then tempted to warn the Oglyntyrs, but that family can be as odious as the worst nobles. These things tend to sort themselves out.

The noble families of Waterdeep who send their children to Amphail, or allow them to go there, hope that their sons and daughters will learn some lessons about life while away from Waterdeep. If they are going to cause damage or hurt feelings in the process, at least they will do so far away from the watchful eyes of the other nobility of the city. To the young nobles, there is no one in Amphail of any real consequence who might be permanently harmed by any improprieties. They also believe there is no one of note nearby to hear these hot-headed youngsters issue their boasts and proclaim their schemes—I have more than once learned of a threat simply by listening to children of different houses brag to one another about matters that were meant only for the family.

Aside from the excesses of its nobles, Amphail is a peaceful town, with the threat of full-scale retaliation from both Waterdeep and the Lords' Alliance casting a long, dark shadow over any plans to disturb matters there. The nobles of Waterdeep have heavy purses, and are willing to spend as much coin as necessary to protect their favored playground—and to punish anyone that might disrupt their control over it. The only thing the nobles don't seem to be able to spend away is the smell of manure, which in the summer months hangs thick over the town. It is that manure that helps to feed the true business of Amphail: feeding Waterdeep with the produce from the many farms that surround the town.

Because so many of Amphail's farms are owned by House Ammakyl, members of that noble family are by far the most enriched by the commerce there. They consider themselves good landlords to the folk that farm their lands, and are sure to bring any threats to honest, hard-working commoners to the attention of both the Lord Warder and the Lords of Waterdeep. Anything that threatens farming in Amphail threatens the City of Splendors directly, and such situations are dealt with swiftly and surely by the city's Guard. As a result, even the most rebellious nobles are careful not to tread too heavily on Ammakyl turf in Amphail, as a house that does so might swiftly find its favorite foods suddenly difficult to procure for a revel or some other event where the family's status is at risk.

BALDUR'S GATE

On the Coast Way, some forty miles upstream along the River Chionthar from the Sword Coast, lies the bustling city of Baldur's Gate. Home to tens of thousands, the harbor city has poor soil, but its sheltered bay, well away from the tides that batter the coast, make it an ideal location for trading goods from locations to the west in the Sea of Swords, inland along the river, and up and down the coast. Baldur's Gate is a place of commerce, and the city enjoys great success handling the coins of other powers and making them its own.

Sadly, Baldur's Gate has a storied connection with the dark god, Bhaal. Just a few years ago, the city saw the terrifying return of the Lord of Murder. Following a number of deaths, one of the city's dukes, Torlin Silvershield, was revealed as the Chosen of Bhaal, and underwent a monstrous transformation, turning many citizens into bloodthirsty killers and inspiring a riot and much death before finally being put down by brave adventurers. Even now, murderous echoes ripple through the city and beyond, and reports of unexplainable, gruesome killings flow out of Baldur's Gate.

Baldur's Gate is ruled by the Council of Four, dukes who vote among themselves on matters of law and policy for the city. A single grand duke is chosen from among the four, and is empowered to break ties when the council is deadlocked. The current Grand Duke is Ulder Ravengard, who is joined by Dukes Thalamra Vanthampur, Belynne Stelmane, and Dillard Portyr, the former grand duke, who ceded the post to Ravengard after the city's recent troubles. Below the council sits the Parliament of Peers, a group of about fifty Baldurians who meet daily (though almost never in full number) to discuss the future of the city and recommend actions for the dukes to take on all matters, great and small. At any given time, roughly one-quarter of the peers are powerful members of Lower City society, with the rest drawn from the Upper City's noble families, called patriars.

Defense of the Upper City is handled by the Watch, the official constabulary of the city's elite. Their duty is to defend the patriars and enforce their laws, and little

else. For the rest of Baldur's Gate, security is enforced and order maintained by the Flaming Fist mercenary company, a supposedly neutral force which is free to fight in external conflicts, so long as it doesn't side against Baldur's Gate. By tradition, the highest officer of the Flaming Fist is one of the city's dukes, and Grand Duke Ulder Ravengard fulfills that tradition proudly. Membership in the Flaming Fist is fairly easy to achieve, and adventurers with much experience swiftly advance in rank (and, consequently, political influence) once they become permanent members. Many ranking officers are former adventurers who have "retired" to military life.

In both the Upper and Lower Cities, the underworld is controlled by a shadowy group known merely as the Guild. The dukes don't acknowledge the power of this group in any meaningful way—at least not publicly—but try (at least nominally) to curb its influence where and how they can. I lost count of how many gangs claim territory in the Lower and Outer City, and all of them seem to owe allegiance to the Guild. Efforts to destroy the Guild have thus far failed, due in part to the inability of outsiders to identify a clear leader of the group, but in no small measure to the shameful lack of effort on the part of the rulers of the city to protect its people.

UPPER CITY

The Upper City of Baldur's Gate is the enclosed haven of the city's nobility—the patriars. Sitting atop their hill, the patriars look down on the rest of Baldur's Gate in every real sense, wielding their wealth and influence to push the Council of Four to protect their lifestyle. Though at one time a wealthy merchant or powerful adventurer might hope to advance to the ranks of the patriars, there is no longer room, physically or otherwise, for the class of the Upper City to grow. Now, only those born into the patriar families inhabit the manors of this oldest part of Baldur's Gate. The poorest among these go so far as to sell furnishings and decorations from inside their homes in order to keep up appearances with their fellow patriars.

Most would say that the lives of patriars are marked by luxury and decadence, and for a great many of them, this is likely true. However, some families do make an honest attempt at improving the city, and nearly every family has at least one member who engages in major

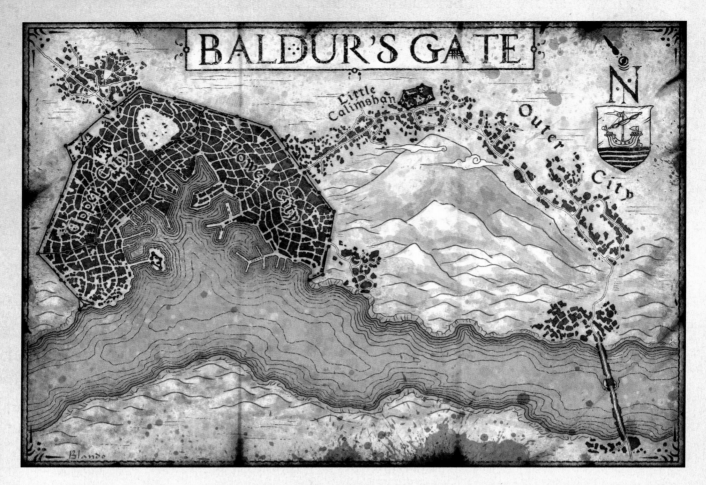

commerce—no matter one's heritage, everyone must have coin in order to eat. There is but one nonhuman family among the patriars, the dwarven Shattershields, who have been in Baldur's Gate for long enough that they are just as accomplished as their human peers at looking down on the rest of the citizenry.

A number of gates divide the Upper City from the Lower City, but the one to note is the famous Baldur's Gate, from which the city takes its name. Trade passes only through this gate, and is taxed by the city—despite the fact that it was just such taxes that led to the city's being overthrown by its first dukes and the Lower City enclosed by its ring wall. The other gates exist solely for the convenience of the patriars and their retinues. Any who aren't in the presence of a patriar, wearing a patriar's livery, or bearing a letter of proof of employment by a patriar must use Baldur's Gate to pass between the Upper and Lower Cities. Bear this in mind when trying to sneak from one part of the city to the next.

LOWER CITY

Hard against the harbor lies the Lower City, where stone, slate-roofed houses stand (sometimes unsteadily), and the folk who have long performed the real work of the city reside. Baldur's Gate depends on trade, and that trade flows in and out of the Gray Harbor. The hands that load and unload ships, that tally cargo and haul goods, that repair keels and mend sails, all live here. The damp clings heavily in this portion of the city— some say it's held in by the Old Wall—and lamps (lit and filled by citizens, not the city) pierce the fog. Most locals are wise enough to carry lanterns or lamps, and visitors that have not learned to do so can usually hire a young Baldurian to guide them through the streets.

The Lower City was long ago walled in to benefit from the protection of the city, but the divide between the two wards is as stark as it has ever been. The Flaming Fist is responsible for keeping order in the Lower City, and do so with brutal efficiency, deterring most from engaging in bold, public acts of theft, vandalism, or violence.

Where merchants in other cities might hope to one day join the nobility, in Baldur's Gate the best one can hope for is to become an absurdly wealthy and influential merchant. Becoming a patriar is out of the question. Still, the wealthiest Baldurians live as much like the patriars as they can, buying up adjacent properties in the hopes of demolishing them in order to build large homes to echo the manors of the Upper City. The Bloomridge district has a number of such homes, and some of the patriars grumble that these merchants are growing too comfortable with their new status.

OUTER CITY

Outside the walls, there are no laws barring construction or settlement, and so those who are too poor to reside within the city or to purchase property have slowly built up a third ward of the city, living in the shadow of its walls, paying its taxes, and covering both sides of the roads leading into Baldur's Gate. Here, the poorest of the poor live in the Outer City, but so too do those whose businesses are considered too troublesome, noisy, or foul-smelling to operate within the walls, so tanners, smiths, masons, dyers, and other tradesfolk abound. The city does woefully little to help the folk here, and charitable souls (myself included) sometimes start at one end of the road with a full purse, only to see it empty by the time they reach the other end.

The lack of laws in the Outer City has led to two strange phenomena, unrelated to one another. A walled Calishite district has grown up to the east of the city proper, known by Baldurians as Little Calimshan. Within the district, neighborhoods are divided by walls, but these walls have walkways atop them so that foot traffic can proceed unimpeded by the gates that slow carts and mounts. Here, refugees from Calimshan have found a home away from that southern nation, and largely depend on themselves for trade, culture, and defense.

Buildings have also been constructed along Wyrm's Crossing over the Chionthar. Shops, taverns, and tenements choke the bridge, hanging from both spans, and even in some cases built to hang from the supports that hold it up. Folk must pay a toll to cross on foot or by cart or wagon, but many swear they would pay yet more to be able to use the bridge without having to dodge the hawkers and urchins that infest the area.

DAGGERFORD

Built against the side of a low hill on the floodplains of the Delimbiyr, this small, walled town is dominated by the keep of the local duchess, Lady Morwen Daggerford. Counting the town itself and the nearby hamlets and farms that look to it for protection and guidance, some twelve hundred people call the area home. Lady Morwen is the sister of the previous duke, Maldwyn Daggerford, and she seems a capable and charismatic leader. The Daggerford family's authority over the area dates back to the ancient Kingdom of Man that succeeded Phalorm in the region. Though that realm has been dust for centuries, there are those that see Daggerford as the last bastion of a better time of peace, wealth, and influence—a time that, given the right leadership, has the smallest of chances of being restored.

Daggerford is a pastoral haven. Wide, sprawling hills nearby offer peaceful vistas, but are sometimes overrun by raiding orcs or goblins. The frequent caravans heading north to Waterdeep or south to Baldur's Gate need escort or guarding, and can offer news of both of those cities (and the settlements between them). Several inns stand ready to accept visitors, except in the busiest of trade or festival periods, when they fill swiftly, and many locals open up their homes to lodgers. Warriors in need of coin can help their purses by offering their services as trainers for the local militia, or accompanying the town guard on its patrols.

Daily rulership is in the hands of the Council of Guilds, composed of the heads of the town's informal trade groups. These guildmasters believe themselves more powerful and influential than they truly are, imitating the Lords of Waterdeep by going robed and masked to council meetings. This charade, in the eyes of most, borders on farce, as everyone in Daggerford knows precisely who the council members are, and no magic disguises the forms, voices, or mannerisms of the guild leaders, and a trained spy can learn which guildmaster is which after only an evening or two of proper observation.

The largest and oldest building in Daggerford is the ducal castle, a three-level keep enclosed by a two-story wall that contains its own smithy, a wide parade ground, and stabling for a large number of animals. The dukes of Daggerford have always kept a well-stocked larder, capable of feeding the castle's inhabitants and any citizens that might shelter inside during a siege.

Three gates lead into the town of Daggerford: River Gate, which provides access to the river, and through which shipping cargo is carted into the town proper; Caravan Gate, which handles most landgoing traffic, including land-based trade; and Farmers' Gate, which remains open at nearly all times, but is wide enough only to let one wagon or cart pass at a time.

A militia guards Daggerford. Militia service is mandatory for all able-bodied adults, and lasts for twenty years. All citizens living within the town receive instruction from the duchess's own soldiers in the use of spears and other weapons, and must spend at least one day a month in defense of the town, standing sentry on its walls or patrolling the nearby roads. Their training means that the common citizens of Daggerford aren't easily cowed by armed folk demanding goods, coin, or passage, and are slightly more likely to take up work as mercenaries, caravan guards, or adventurers.

Although she is less amiable than her brother was, Lady Morwen is acknowledged as more capable of ruling Daggerford than Duke Maldwyn had been. She is well liked by the people, who understand that she has an honorable heart, and wishes what is best for Daggerford. She regularly trains with the militia, and is seen in the town wearing armor just as often as she is adorned in the finery befitting her station. She often visits the local shrine to Tempus, which only enhances her reputation as a pious woman. Lady Morwen's features are only now starting to age, as though catching up with her white hair.

Most folk of Daggerford know one another, at least casually, by sight. Strangers are usually welcome, especially if they have coin to spend, unless such folk come armed and belligerent through the town. Guards stationed at each gate make note of new faces, but don't take action against those they don't recognize unless they are given reason to do so.

The largest of the town's inns, the River Shining Tavern, is the second biggest building in Daggerford, and the site of many local celebrations and gatherings. Here, the wealthy come to eat and relax. The inn is old—many locals claim it to be older even than the ducal castle—and to many, is the very soul of Daggerford. The Silver Flood Inn and Lizard's Gizzard also offer rooms, though the latter has no food to provide its guests, only beds.

One of Daggerford's most unusual businesses is the Sword Coast Traders' Bank, which accepts deposits from traveling merchants and enables them to receive these funds at a similar location in either Waterdeep

RUINED KINGDOMS OF THE NORTH

Many folk consider the start of civilization in the North to be marked by the founding of Waterdeep. More learned folk are aware of the deeper history of the region, and know of at least some of the kingdoms that have been built by the residents of the North down the centuries.

Ruins of these kingdoms are scattered throughout the North, and many present-day cities and towns are built atop their remains, sometimes with their residents ignorant of what lies just beneath their boots.

Eaerlann. The elven kingdom of Eaerlann, a survivor of the ancient Crown Wars, stretched from the High Forest to the Delimbiyr Vale. Weakened by the retreat of much of its populace to Evermeet and by orc attacks, Eaerlann finally fell six hundred years ago to the demons that burst forth from Ascalhorn (once known as Hellgate Keep and now as Hellgate Dell).

Illefarn. Ten thousand years ago, the capital city of Illefarn occupied the site where Waterdeep stands today. A kingdom of elves that accepted both humans and dwarves in its lands, Illefarn stood intact for seven millennia. It was eventually fragmented by increasing human settlement of the area, and repeated orc attacks spelled its doom.

Athalantar. The short-lived human kingdom of Athalantar lay south of the High Forest in territory claimed by its self-styled Stag King thirteen centuries ago. Its rulers were briefly supplanted by magelords, but then reclaimed the throne, only to be wiped out by orcs within a few generations.

Phalorm. Dwarf, elf, and human monarchs all shared the rule of Phalorm, also known as the Realm of Three Crowns, which was founded nearly a thousand years ago in the High Moor. Phalorm lasted barely a century before repeated orc and goblin attacks overcame it.

Kingdom of Man. When Phalorm fell, the surviving humans of the kingdom established the Kingdom of Man, formally known as Delimbiyran, which lasted only two generations. Its dissolution left behind a number of petty "kingdoms" that welcomed new human settlers in several locations, leading to the founding of new cities and towns on the Sword Coast and in its environs.

Netheril. For centuries, the legend of Netheril served as a lesson of human hubris and a lure for treasure hunters too prideful to learn from its story. Long before the Dales Compact and the advent of Dalereckoning, Netheril arose as a human empire founded on the might of magic learned from the golden Nether Scrolls, artifacts at least as old as the creator races. Flying Netherese cities drifted through the skies all over the North, but primarily they hung high over a verdant land that is now the desert of Anauroch.

Then Karsus, one of the mighty mages of Netheril, dared to believe that he could wrest control of the Weave and become a god himself. He almost succeeded, but in his failure Karsus killed the goddess of magic, shredded the Weave, and sent the floating enclaves that couldn't flee to other planes crashing to the ground. From the moments after the crash when the spilt blood was still fresh to the present day's moss-covered or dune-buried stones, the ruins of Netheril and its arcane secrets have drawn many to their doom.

or Baldur's Gate. Lady Belinda Anteos (of the Waterdeep noble house) promises that her business is secure and that the bank's magical means of communicating precise amounts of currency between cities can't be tampered with.

Members of local guilds that do business outside the town don't entirely trust the Traders' Bank, preferring instead to borrow coin from the Hardcheese family of halflings that run the Happy Cow tavern. The Alliance officially has no preference, but I find Lady Anteos trustworthy enough to be an alternative to carrying large sums on the road. It's easier to part with a small portion of one's purse than to lose everything to a band of brigands during a journey through the wilds.

Visitors to Daggerford are advised both to avoid the tannery to the west and to swiftly cross Tyndal's Bridge when approaching from the south. The tannery's location, up on the hill, does little to contain the stink of the process, and the Watermen's Guild dumps the city's waste over the side of the bridge. On hot days, the scents exuded from both sites can be overwhelming, which is why I have again asked the Alliance to assign a different agent to visit on next summer's rounds.

Tyndal's Bridge is a low stone structure over which travelers pass when approaching from the west, where a local boy named Tyndal held off a number of lizardfolk with only a dagger. He grew to manhood, married the local ruler's daughter, named himself duke, and built Daggerford atop the ruins of an older castle. This story, and most of the area's history, is happily related to any who ask by Sir Darfin Floshin, an elf older than Daggerford itself. He longs to see a rise in cooperation between humans, dwarves, and elves in the region, such as was once embodied in the realm of Phalorm. Darfin has been advisor to many dukes of Daggerford through the years. Though he was rebuffed by Duke Maldwyn during his reign, there are signs that Lady Morwen may be more receptive to the advice of a gold elf who has witnessed the fall of the human kingdom of Delimbiyran, the founding of Daggerford, and all the days since.

LONGSADDLE

The hamlet of Longsaddle is little more than a row of buildings on either side of the Long Road, halfway along the lengthy journey from Triboar to Mirabar. A path leaves the road here and winds to the Ivy Mansion, the great house of the wizards of the Harpell family. Since the Harpells founded the town more than four centuries ago, they have brooked little nonsense and less mayhem. Their own behavior sometimes borders on the bizarre and can be disturbing—they once turned two rival sects of Malarites into rabbits for disturbing Longsaddle with their squabbles, leaving them at the mercy of the predators they had honored—but they are one of the most potent gatherings of mages anywhere in the North.

The Harpells are a jovial, if insular, lot. All wizards, they tend to marry wizards as well, and the elder women of the family (by blood or marriage) set the course for the house and utterly rule matters within the Ivy Mansion. The family takes on a number of apprentice wizards, using them for menial tasks and for basic defense of Longsaddle. Some apprentices are often the inadvertent test subjects for an experimental spell, but such is the danger of apprenticing to the Harpells. It is likely this spirit of experimentation that caused the Harpells to found their town so far away from other settlements. Young wizards with oddly sized or shaped limbs, strange hair color, or shifting forms are fairly common sights in Longsaddle, not surprising to locals though they might give visitors pause.

Given the Harpells' reputation as powerful wizards, and the sheer number of them, there is no shortage of folk poking around Longsaddle and the nearby lands hoping to discover caches of magic, hidden like children's treasures. Of course, few, if any, such bundles exist, but the locals draw no shortage of entertainment from sending would-be thieves on grand chases for wands, rings, and other magic trinkets that any prudent person would realize simply don't exist. After all, if the average trader in Longsaddle knew where powerful magic was located, he would be more likely, down the years, to try to claim it.

The primary business of Longsaddle is ranching, and the lands surrounding the village are dominated by hundreds of ranches and farms of every sort and size, from tiny horse farms to great fields of cattle. During those days that livestock are brought in for trading, Longsaddle is a dusty, noise-filled place, with the sounds of the animals competing with the shouts of farmers hoping to sell their goods.

At all other times, it's a quiet, almost sleepy hamlet, except when the booming reverberation of a Harpell-crafted spell breaks the silence. The family is constantly researching magic both old and new, and twisting spells and rituals into interesting (to them) innovations. This proclivity has prompted them to surround Ivy Mansion with as many magical wards as the family can muster, in order to protect the populace from an errant explosion, terrifying illusion, or the odd, galloping horse of lightning speeding by.

Several businesses designed to attract travelers stand in Longsaddle, if for no other reason than travel along the well-named Long Road can be tiresome. The first is the Gilded Horseshoe, an old inn to the west of the road that serves fine food and drink, offers comfortable beds, and is close enough to the Ivy Mansion that no one would dare disturb it or its guests. The owners have access to some of the choicest cuts of meat in Longsaddle, and as a result, their roasts and stews are exquisite.

Across the road, the Ostever family serves as the local slaughterer and butcher for folk wishing to take meat, rather than live animals, away from Longsaddle. Rumor holds that the sausages have much improved down the years but buyers are advised to "mind the tusks" by locals, a reference to an old joke that none remember. Folk willing to wait can have the able hands of the Ostevers perform a slaughter, hanging, dressing, and packing for them, though this process is likely to take days longer than most travelers can spare.

There is entertainment to be had at the Gambling Golem, where cheaters in the card or dice games are tossed out into the street, and a local marbles game known as scattershields is popular. Dry goods, candles, lanterns, saddles, rope, and wagon wheels are available from a number of other shops.

It can't be stressed enough that while the Harpells have little interest in the daily running of Longsaddle, it is undeniably their town. They rarely suffer insults, and never tolerate violence against themselves, their family,

or the locals. A conflict involving the Harpells is likely to end swiftly and bloodily, and (unless the offender is convincingly apologetic, unconscious, dead, or forgiven of the wrongdoing) will often draw additional Harpells to support their kin. Harpell supports Harpell in all public matters, and no one bothers to record the numbers and names of those that forgot that fact.

Aside from the Harpells, the dominant families of Longsaddle are ranchers: the Cadrasz, Emmert, Kromlor, Mammlar, Sharnshield, Suldivver, and Zelorrgosz families have ranched in or near Longsaddle for generations, and influence most of the daily life there. They set the market days, help resolve disputes among families, and broker purchases when a farmer or businessperson dies without an heir. They settle smaller matters and keep the peace as best they can, knowing full well that if the Harpells need to get involved in a dispute, there is always the possibility of an offender's being blasted into nothingness.

These families are also the ones most likely to hire outsiders to deal with matters on the ranches, whether an orc raid or the appearance of lycanthropes in the area (though it's rumored that the latter creatures may be the descendants of one of the Harpells). The major ranching interests often hire adventurers not only to further their own aims or provide for defense, but to secretly hinder or harm one another and gain an advantage in their ongoing competition. Adventurers that go too far on such a mission can be explained away as foolish outlanders, and if they offend a Harpell and get blasted in the middle of the Low Road, there will be no one left to ask about the matter. My best advice is to be mindful of the scent of magic in the air and act accordingly.

The Spine of the World

Reghed Glacier

Raven Rock

Mirabar

River Mirar

Great Worm Cavern

The Lurkwood

Morgur's Mound

Gauntlgrym

MIRABAR

Mirabar is a human city that rests atop dwarven caverns. On the surface, humans dominate the population, with some dwarves mixed in, and a handful of gnomes and halflings. The uppermost level of the undercity is mostly dwarves, with some few humans. The mixing of races is due to convenience of trade, preference, or skill; just as some few humans like to mine, to imbibe strong dwarven drink, and to work underground, so do a minority of dwarves take to the open sky, doing dock work, or even manning and building ships. The lower levels beneath Mirabar are all dwarven, as even the most dwarf-like human can live so deep below ground for only so long. Almost all of its citizens, regardless of race, honor Moradin and the dwarven gods, making Mirabar a dwarven city in spirit and ethics, if not entirely by population, much in the way my own Silverymoon speaks to elven ideals of natural beauty.

Long ago, the great dwarven kingdom of Gharraghaur stood to the west of Delzoun, delving mines near the River Mirar and finding great, near-endless veins of gems. Like many of the dwarven realms, Gharraghaur fell to marauding orcs, which destroyed the kingdom and its capital city but couldn't take advantage of the wealth therein. For millennia the lower city lay empty, until some eight hundred years ago, when Prince Ereskas of Amn settled the same spot, creating the city of Mirabar (coincidentally echoing the dwarven "-bar" naming convention used for citadels throughout the North). It was only when dwarves returned to work the mines below that Mirabar began to see its fortunes increase.

Mirabar is ruled by its hereditary marchion, Selin Raurym, who issues edicts fed to him by the Council of Sparkling Stones. The council is a group of dwarves

EVERBRIGHT

The dwarves were the first to discover the secret of treating their metal with everbright. The technique has been imitated by other races, to varying degrees of success. Armor, weapons, and other metal objects to which everbright is applied maintain their luster without needing to be polished, and are resistant to natural (and, in some cases, magical) pitting, rusting, and tarnishing.

and some few humans elected to make policy for the city, who determine where the output of Mirabar's mines will be sold. Although the council has long kept Mirabar associated with the Lords' Alliance, it is the marchion who negotiates with his fellow lords. Thus far, Selin Raurym has proved far more capable than his predecessors at making beneficial decisions for the city, and the council has given him great leeway to speak for Mirabar outside the walls. His threat to pull out of the Alliance following its failure to aid the northern cities against the most recent orc hordes, though considered by some an empty gesture, has brought Mirabar more advantageous relationships with Waterdeep and Baldur's Gate, something which has not gone unappreciated by the council.

The city's guard, the Axe of Mirabar, exists primarily to deter and prevent sabotage of the mines, without which Mirabar would collapse. The guard also provides swift and capable defense and law enforcement within the city. The wealth of Mirabar is so great that it maintains docks, ships, and fortified harbors on many of the islands in the Sea of Swords, and as such the city is always seeking magical and military support for these defenses. Where other cities might use such vast mountains of coin as Mirabar possesses on shows of prosperity, Mirabarrens use it for more functional goals, making sure that the city's defenses are new, that its gates close securely when they are moved, that its buildings and walls are strong and secure. Given the recent destruction of Sundabar's surface city at the hand of orc armies, such expenditures are well justified, since no one in Mirabar wishes to see the surface city wiped out. It would simply be bad for business. Mirabar spares no expense in defending its wealth, and hires as many mages and adventurers as necessary to clear threats away from roads, investigate sabotage, and otherwise protect its vital trade.

With the rise of Mithral Hall in the last century, and now Gauntlgrym, Mirabar fears its place as the armory of the North is at risk. The miners, smelters, and smiths of Mirabar work ever harder to increase their output and improve their craft, while the jewelers and enamelers study ways to incorporate ancient techniques of melding dwarven, human, and elven designs together in their work, in the manner of old Phalorm.

Mirabarren (or to some, just Mierren) dwarves like to cultivate long, wide (as opposed to tapered or pointed) beards and tight braids of hair growing elsewhere than on the chin, a fashion copied by some local humans. They love polished, *everbright*-treated sheets of metal, particularly copper, used as doors or mirrorlike wall-panel inlays. They often set gems into the pommels and nonworking ends of tools and weapons. Mierren dwarves tend to be wealthy, to have personal collections of unusual and rare gems, to use seals made of gems carved into signet rings, and to be investors in ventures (rather than property) up and down the Sword Coast. They are sophisticated and worldly, and they decry the isolationist and xenophobic attitudes of some dwarves. Mierren dwarves demonstrate their own broader attitudes by being the diplomatic traders and power brokers in trademoots and agreements in Fireshear and Neverwinter and everywhere else they can worm their way into, among dwarves and between dwarves and non-dwarves.

To other dwarves, Mierren are translators and local guides and "the people who know the right people" in human-dominated cities everywhere along the Sword Coast and in much of the Heartlands. Most adult Mierren have dealings with a variety of human costers and merchants, taking care to avoid exclusivity or cultivate too narrow a range of business partners and contacts, so they control their own destinies and fortunes. They abhor the thought of humans having the slightest chance of dominating them.

The wealth that flows through Mirabar has not only extended the reach and worldly knowledge of all Mierren, it has enabled them to indulge all sorts of personal hobbies, such as art collections (statuettes and paintings in particular). The private living quarters of most Mierren feature comfortable furniture, painted artwork large and small, statuary, and hanging chimes—often metallic, but always soft and pleasant, never loud or strident. Gems are plentiful in Mierren families and are used as currency and in all manner of personal adornment, rather than being hidden away. Semiprecious stones line many of the streets in Mirabar, and gorgeous inlays mark important corners and intersections, some so new that one can still smell the jeweler's dust.

Still, despite the city's overall wealth, there are rich and (relatively) poor Mirabarrans. Not everyone shares in the coin the city's sales bring in, and wage workers whose income is determined by a day's labor or a month's output can't hope to expect that a well-worded contract by an employer will enrich them in the least. Wealthy merchants and business owners are careful not to show their success ostentatiously; their clothing might be of richer fabrics, but still in the same styles and colors as the garb of poorer folks. Waiting rooms and front halls in the fortified homes of the rich are just as sparsely furnished as those in poorer homes. Keeping up the appearance of relative equality in fortunes is vital, for if anyone in a position to commit a violent act—say, a weaponsmith with access to great stores of swords and axes—knew just how wealthy the wealthiest Mirabarrans were, there would very likely be bloodshed before the offended parties were satisfied.

Neverwinter

A short while ago, Neverwinter was beset by all manner of damage, danger, and gloom. Now, the orcs that once menaced the city have moved east to join their brethren in being crushed by the dwarves. The Chasm that rent the land has been sealed by powerful magic. The High Road has been cleared and rebuilt, and trade has resumed with Waterdeep and realms to the south. What was the blasted, wounded city of Neverwinter just a decade ago is now an exciting, humming place, where folk seem eager to throw off the hardships from which they have emerged and create a new, brighter future for their city.

Nearly half a century ago, Mount Hotenow (the nearby volcano that perpetually heats the river flowing through the city) violently erupted, destroying much of Neverwinter, killing thousands, and leaving in its wake a great,

gaping chasm that split the city. Neverwinter was in ruins, and external influences—from Netheril to Thay to Lord Dagult Neverember of Waterdeep to the agents of the Hells themselves—sought to exert control over the city. Many folk fought to stem all these dangers, and eventually, a measure of peace fell over Neverwinter.

Since Dagult Neverember was deposed as the Open Lord of Waterdeep, he has thrown his full attention and effort into the rebuilding of the city from which he claims descent. Whatever people's opinions are of his claim to Neverwinter's throne, he has proven a capable, inspiring leader over these last few years, and the population has embraced him as Lord Protector. He engineered the sealing of the Chasm and the restoration of the High Road, and is seeking other ways to repair and improve the city. Even if he can never prove his descent from Lord Nasher Alagondar, the people of Neverwinter have accepted his leadership. (My rumored personal dislike of Lord Neverember has nothing to do with my assessment of his leadership; I merely find him an intolerable flirt.)

Neverember's influence radiates outward from the Protector's Enclave, centered at the Hall of Justice. With Tyr restored to life and his worship returning to prominence, the Lord Protector has moved into a modest, private villa. This sacrifice—and the renewal of Tyr's faith in the previous center of his operations—is only further proof, to some, that Neverember deserves to rule Neverwinter. As yet, Castle Never remains a dangerous ruin, but Neverember has plans to reclaim and rebuild it as a symbol of the city's rejuvenation.

The faithful of Oghma have arrived in Neverwinter to restore the House of Knowledge to its former glory, but beyond that, shrines to all manner of gods have been cobbled together in every corner of the city.

As the city restores itself, there are likely to be requests for ennoblement and the privileges that provides, and certainly, trading interests will emerge. But Lord Protector Neverember is sure to point out that he is merely a protector, not a king, and so can't invest or recognize anyone. Guilds may form, but it is sure to be years, if not decades, before any prove strong enough to persevere over their rivals.

Increasingly, calls come from the citizenry for the enforcers out of Mintarn to be replaced by respectable, local guards who have a personal interest in the defense of Neverwinter. This public sentiment has led to some

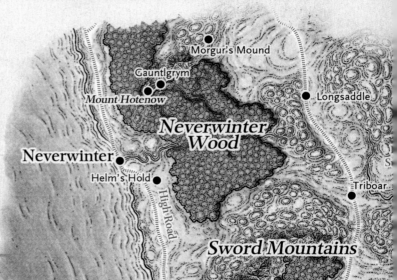

The city of: Neverwinter

Blando

neighborhoods organizing their own makeshift militias, and the Lord Protector wants to avoid conflict between them and the mercenaries he has hired. As a result, Neverember has slowly been drawing down the number of soldiers from Mintarn, as the citizens that grew up defending the makeshift Wall from threats out of the Chasm prove themselves capable of becoming a proper military force. Both Baldur's Gate and Waterdeep have offered to help train the new guards of Neverwinter, but Lord Neverember prefers the assistance of seasoned adventurers to the ignominy of seeking help from his former city.

With the restoration of nearby Gauntlgrym, Neverwinter hopes to have a close ally that can provide it with stout armor and strong weapons. Although the city presently has little to offer, trade activity is rapidly growing in Neverwinter, as word of its rebirth opens it up to shipping from the Sea of Swords, goods from the north, and coin from the south. Adventurers come to Neverwinter seeking work and following rumors of nearby treasures, and often find additional employment clearing out dangerous corners of the city and escorting the ever more numerous caravans up and down the High Road. It is the Lord Protector's hope that, with commerce and income both on the rise, and talented

craftfolk returning to ply their trades, that Neverwinter will someday again be worthy of its former epithet: the City of Skilled Hands.

Opposition to Neverember's authority still exists, but with no unified leadership and no other power in the city to which to appeal, the rebels are slowly turning away from their resistance and toward helping the city rebuild. Many of the Sons of Alagondar, a rebel group that initially opposed Lord Neverember, have begun to volunteer as replacements for the Mintarn mercenaries currently patrolling the city. If the Sons of Alagondar can be brought into line with his goals, Neverember hopes to use that achievement as a draw for wealthy Waterdhavian nobles—who have been reluctant to link their fortunes to a failed Open Lord who was effectively exiled from Waterdeep—to invest in the city and perhaps rebuild some of the noble villas in that district as places for them to stay when they do business.

With the Chasm closed, and the wall that separated the rest of the city from its horrors now torn down, a great swath of Neverwinter lies empty, with no inhabitants and plentiful chunks of stone plundered from ruins all across the city. Anyone who is willing to do so can come to this area, claim a portion of land, and build a structure in which to live or work. There aren't yet any guilds to restrict trade or construction, and no nobles to be petitioned or placated. Those seeking to create a home or start a business can simply do so, and even those without skills or money can use their hands and backs to provide until they can set up a place for themselves.

Along the river, many of the merchant villas are being claimed and restored by folk who have heard rumors of what Neverwinter once was, and might be again. Some have no skills to speak of, and many have no wealth, but all come with the desire to work and to enrich themselves in the process. New stores and workshops open by the tenday, and workers without training offer their services as laborers or apprentices; those that fail move on to other employment, taking advantage of the multitude of opportunities the city now offers. Those with no other options can get work dredging or mapping the city's sewers for the Lord Protector, a task made necessary by the cataclysm that created the Chasm.

Like any city, Neverwinter isn't without its drawbacks. Though most folk are willing to work, some steal as a means of making their living, and prey upon those who have little to be taken. Food is sometimes scarce, as inns and taverns underestimate the number of guests they will receive, or merchants simply run out of goods to sell. It's likely to be a few years before the city entirely shakes itself of these ills, but for some, the uncertainties of life in Neverwinter are what make the place exciting. For many traders, in particular those who produce or vend the grains and vegetables needed in the city, it is a vast opportunity to both aid a fledgling power and get quite rich in doing so.

SILVERYMOON

Long a powerful and influential member of the Lords' Alliance—and, for its entire existence, the Silver Marches of Luruar—Silverymoon is what many cities aspire to be: a quiet, peaceful realm, where many races live together for common knowledge, celebration, and defense. The city is peopled primarily by the "goodly" races (humans, dwarves, gnomes, elves, halflings, and half-elves), but no being is turned away from Silverymoon because of its race—though a drow or an orc proving true to one's blood is sure to be punished in full for transgressing against the peace of the city. I will make no secret of my love for my home in the following summary, but I will endeavor to be as evenhanded as I can in describing it.

The Gem of the North is a stunning place of sweeping curves, soaring towers, and structures built into the living trees. To many elves, the city is a reminder of the ancient elven cities of old; some call it the Myth Drannor of the North, even nowadays after the restoration and subsequent fall of that fabled city. Even where stone is employed in construction, ivy and other living plants grow through, over, or around most structural elements, giving most of the city a green cast.

Despite its arboreal architecture, Silverymoon is very much civilized, boasting schools of music and magic, a great library, bardic instruction, and temples or shrines to Mielikki, Oghma, Silvanus, Sune, Tymora, and Mystra. Knowledge, both the acquisition of it and the wisdom that comes from diligent study, is the real treasure of Silverymoon, as much as magic or wealth could ever be.

While it is easy and pleasing enough to get lost among the trees of the city, anyone who comes close enough to the River Raurin is awed by the vision of the Moonbridge: the great arch of silvery force that spans the water. Even for those native to the city, it is a powerful, moving sight, and some claim to see the goddess Lurue (for whom the city is named) dancing above the motes of the bridge when no one else is watching.

Given its beauty, a visit to Silverymoon is among the most memorable experiences most non-Silvaeren might have. Even among those that regularly fight monsters or handle magic, Silverymoon is a place of quiet, contemplative beauty, splendid opportunities for learning, and respite from the harsher realities of the North.

Folk seeking knowledge that has been lost or hidden often come to Silverymoon seeking a means to find it, whether by studying in the Vault of the Sages or perusing the Map House for the location of a lost city or grove. These are but two of the many buildings and houses of learning in the Conclave of Silverymoon, the great center of knowledge and wisdom that forms much of the city's southern part. If a map, a book, or a spell exists anywhere in Faerûn, knowledge of it likely exists here, even if only a mere mention in a tome or a recollection of one of the city's great sages. Candlekeep might be the greatest assembly of written knowledge anywhere in the world, but in the end, that place represents accumulation for its own sake. Silverymoon is where study and wisdom are honored. If your charge is to translate an ancient tome in a lost language, to learn the proper intonation of a complex song, or to better understand the cryptic writings of a long-dead sage, there is no better place to seek aid than Silverymoon.

It is an easy thing to come to Silverymoon seeking knowledge of one subject, and find oneself so enraptured by the study that it takes a lifetime to accomplish—or to realize that it was the study, rather than the sought-after fact, that one truly desired. Although tutors and sages in every field can be found In Silverymoon, rarely is interaction with one so simple as to ask a question and be provided an answer. Learning to cast a particular spell, to find an ancient ruin, or understand a specific secret might involve undergoing months of

instruction to prove to a teacher that the knowledge imparted is being entrusted to a deserving person.

In the east of the city is the High Palace, capital of the city and of the fallen state of Luruar. Lord Methrammar Aerasumé lives in this high, slender-spired structure. The merlons of its battlements are carved to resemble unicorn heads. The soldiers of the High Guard, clad in shining silver plate, protect the residence and seat of power, and keep those out that don't have business within.

Silverymoon has long been led by a high mage. One of the longest ruling, and certainly the most influential of these, Alustriel Silverhand, stepped down more than a hundred years ago to become the High Lady of Luruar, and was succeeded by Taern Hornblade. Though he ruled wisely over the last century, Taern recently relinquished the city's leadership to High Marshal Methrammar Aerasumé, Alustriel's half-elf son and the leader of Silverymoon's armed forces. Taern still speaks for the city on Methrammar's behalf at meetings of the Lords' Alliance, as the new ruler is far too blunt and impatient to suit the other lords of the compact.

Silverymoon is defended by several forces. First are the Knights in Silver, the shining-armored warriors that patrol the city and the nearby lands. Officers of the Knights are well trained in tactics and military history, and have high opinions of their own abilities and those of their comrades—opinions that are very often borne out. They are bolstered by the Spellguard, a cadre of powerful wizards and sorcerers that train in battle magic. Last is the city's own *mythal*, the great field of magical force that prevents the inhabitants of the city from engaging in all manner of spellcasting. In particular, spells that summon flame, conjure creatures, or permit teleportation fail when their target is within the bounds of the *mythal*. Should a foe try to traverse the Moonbridge, the span can be willed (by the city's rulers, and certain others specially attuned to the *mythal*) out of existence, dropping attackers into the river.

No city's prestige was harmed more than Silverymoon's by the recent war and the subsequent dismantling of the Silver Marches. Though they tried to bolster the nearby cities, the Silvaeren were accused of providing insufficient and incompetent support to Sundabar, the surface population of which was entirely wiped out. In the end, all of the dwarven states stepped away from Luruar, and without the support of those kingdoms or the leadership that Alustriel provided at its founding, the confederacy collapsed. Taern Hornblade isn't as powerful a voice in the Lords' Alliance as Alustriel was, either, in part because his affection and respect for the former High Lady has been extended, in large part, to her sister Laeral, now the Open Lord of Waterdeep.

Despite reports of her death decades ago, rumors have recently reached the city that High Lady Alustriel is in fact alive and active in southern lands. Seemingly, she has contacted neither her son nor her former comrade, Taern Hornblade—though given how widely known Taern's hopeless love for the High Lady was, and the long years he took to overcome his grief, it's not certain how he would react upon receiving proof of her survival.

Silverymoon has nonetheless long been known as a safe haven for Harpers in the North, because the city doesn't see the aims of the Alliance as conflicting with Those Who Harp. Where other cities' rulers might see the presence of the Harpers as a threat to their authority, Silverymoon desires an end to tyranny as fervently as the Harpers do, and thus the greater good is served. At the same time, some Silvaeren believe that the city's tolerance of certain other members of the Alliance (some mention Mirabar, others Baldur's Gate) is somewhat naive.

THE WARDS OF WATERDEEP

Waterdeep has long been divided into several large regions called wards. To locals these are essential to Waterdeep, but outsiders often lose track of which ward they're in or what a ward's name signifies. The names of the wards suggest the contents of the buildings and the character of the activity in each one, but no laws exist that restrict a given activity or class of people to any specific ward.

Castle Ward. As the name indicates, Castle Ward contains Castle Waterdeep, Piergeiron's Palace, and many other public buildings of the city. This ward is home to mainly the wealthy or influential who can't count themselves among the nobility. Other structures are taken up by educational or religious concerns that primarily serve the city at large, not the residents of the ward.

Dock Ward. Most of the city's harbor area is located in Dock Ward, as are the businesses and warehouses that depend on the city's newly restored harbor. It's a crowded neighborhood of many winding streets, where folk are comfortable making deals that might in other places provoke the displeasure of the law.

Field Ward. Of relatively recent vintage, the Field Ward stands between the inner and outer north walls of the city (an area formerly used as a caravan grounds). This ward grew up in a messy, unregulated fashion and is home to many of the poorest residents of the city.

North Ward. Home to many noble villas, townhouses, and a great many inns, North Ward is the neighborhood of the respectably wealthy.

Sea Ward. Those whose fortunes are on the rise build their homes in Sea Ward, and they join many long-established noble families in residence. This area in the northwest of the city is home to much of the city's wealth, the location of the grandest villas of the city's noble families (except for those in North Ward).

Southern Ward. Stables, warehouses, and shops related to overland trade dominate Southern Ward. Most residents are hardworking folk that load and unload caravan carts, and otherwise perform low-paying work.

Trades Ward. A narrow slice of land between the Castle Ward and the City of the Dead, Trades Ward is the center of commerce for the city, with most of the smaller transactions and respectable trade taking place here.

City of the Dead. The city's walled cemetery, the City of the Dead is the only place in Waterdeep where it is legal to bury the deceased. It is used by many citizens as a public park during the day, a lovely green space of pretty mausoleums and grand statues in which to escape the city's hustle and bustle.

Undercliff. While not considered by many to be a ward of the city, the little villages and many farms that sprawl across the land east of the city were lawfully incorporated into Waterdeep when it moved a barracks and training facility to the area.

WATERDEEP

Rising from the shores of its deep harbor to ring the great mountain standing tall out of the Sea of Swords is Waterdeep, the City of Splendors and the Crown of the North. To all of Faerûn, this great metropolis stands as the pinnacle of what a great city might be, in wealth, influence, and stability. Here, the citizens work, the nobles sneer, and the great masked lords plot and scheme, all while merchants dance between them to collect their coins and continue profiting as best they can. Waterdeep's shops and merchants offer goods of every sort from every corner of Toril, and even the rarest of items can be procured, given sufficient coin and patience. Adventurers lacking one or the other can very easily find all manner of employment, from simple escorting of caravans, to guarding nobility, to investigating a ruin or rumor of monsters anywhere in the North.

Though it has stood for hundreds of years, Waterdeep is only now returning to its status of a century and a half ago. The recent disruptions began when the gods walked the Realms and slew each other before the eyes of mortals, until they walked back to their divine domains through the very streets of Waterdeep itself. Decades later, more deities began dying off, magic failed, and all manner of catastrophes started altering the very nature of the city. Lord Neverember wasted the city's navy and then, instead of rebuilding it, hired sailors out of Mintarn (and profited from the endeavor).

Now, the City of Splendors is on the mend. The harbor has been cleared of the broken ships that made up the former district of Mistshore, and Waterdeep again has its own navy. The city's Guard (its army), Watch (police force), Navy, and it famous Griffon Cavalry are all being reformed, but all of that might be a matter of years in the settling. A plague chased most residents out of the Warrens and Downshadow, and living or digging below the city's surface has been deemed illegal except by those authorized by the lords to do so. Somehow, even the air seems fresher. In the words of one wise moon elf matron (whose status as my aunt has positively no bearing on her wisdom), "Waterdeep is back to where it was when I was a lass."

Perhaps most surprising of the newest developments is the return of Laeral Silverhand to Waterdeep. Long thought dead, she reemerged only recently, and swiftly rallied the masked lords to support her supplanting of Dagult Neverember as Open Lord of Waterdeep. Very few remember Lady Laeral from her previous time in the city, but those elves who have been living in there for the last century claim she is more reserved than she once was. The new Open Lord doesn't speak of her family—any mention of her children, her late husband (the fabled Blackstaff, Khelben Arunsun), or any of her famed sisters is cause for her to cut short whatever conversation may be in progress at the time. Her relationship with the current Blackstaff, Vajra Safahr, is cordial, but the two are seldom seen in one-on-one conversation, and most think that Lady Laeral has little to learn from a mage who isn't nearly her equal.

As always, the Open Lord is selected and supported by several masked lords, who bear masks, robes, and amulets to disguise themselves when publicly sitting in judgment or council, and who make policies for Waterdeep. Every Waterdhavian has suspicions as to whether this or that influential citizen is or isn't a lord of the city, and some are willing to make their beliefs public, but few who are confronted in such a way have ever claimed to be a lord, and none of those have also produced proof of that assertion.

Not hidden at all are the other lords of the city—the nobles of Waterdeep, whose high-nosed behavior and heavy-handed spending establish fashion in the city, which in turn creates trends all across the North for clothing, weaponry, favored trinkets, music, and any other preference that can be changed at a whim by those with enough coin to afford the expense. More than seventy-five noble families call Waterdeep home, representing between them all manner of business interests, rivalries, and internal strife.

Being a noble carries with it a great deal of advantage. Operating from one's place at the head of the economic and social hierarchy, a noble can easily lift a mediocre craftsperson out of obscurity, dash the hopes of a wealthy merchant of ever securing another contract within the city, or provide the backing an ambitious adventuring band needs to find fame and great wealth. The only true competition nobles face is from one another. Such rivalries are the source of much gossip and intrigue as

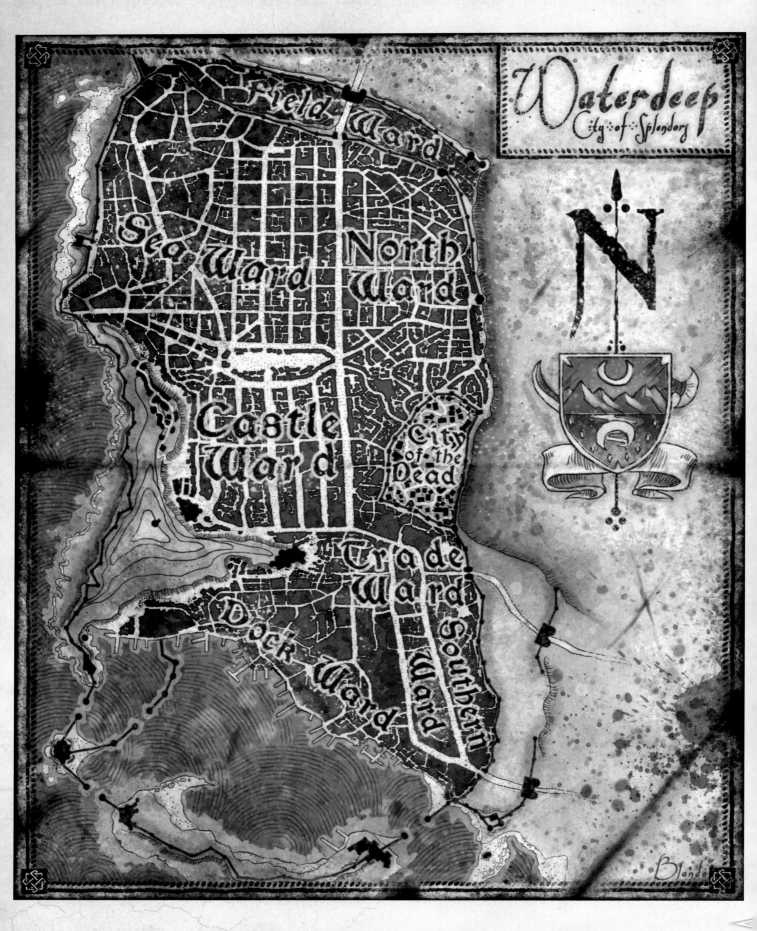

the nobles of Waterdeep always try to maintain at least a veneer of civility in their squabbles.

Although they seldom agree on much, one matter that all the noble houses see the same way is that their status should not be tainted by newcomers, and certainly not by anyone so brightcoin as to purchase one's way to a noble title. When during Lord Neverember's tenure it became legal for impoverished houses to sell their titles, and thus allow others to become noble, many leaders of the old-blood houses were apoplectic, particularly after some purchasers lost all their coin and sold their titles again within a season or two. Open Lord Laeral Silverhand has, to the relief of those leaders, seen the folly of this decision, and gathered enough support among the Lords of Waterdeep to not only reverse it, but to restore titles and lands to noble families who lost them through folly. The change has won her much support among the nobles. Now Zhents and Thayans and Baldurian merchants have coin enough to buy property within the city, if they choose, but that is no reason to award them noble titles and legal rights, instead of merely a mansion, for doing so.

YARTAR

Situated in the fork where the Rivers Surbrin and Dessarin join near the Evermoor Way, Yartar is a fortified town that, were it not for its own petty, internal squabbles, might wield more influence among its fellows in the North. Currently, it is most remarkable for its barge-building operation (and that industry's importance to the commerce of other settlements) and its annual fairs.

Each summer, except in years when Shieldmeet occurs, a vast Hiring Fair is held in Yartar, during which all sorts of undesirable folk gather north of the town looking for work as guards, miners, farmhands, guides, or other unskilled laborers. For the most part, those who attend this fair are brutes, bandits, freeholders whose lands can no longer sustain them, or Uthgardt who wish to be among "civilized" folk for a short time—but occasionally, a strong hand or a skilled warrior can be culled from the bunch. While this event is going on, Yartar is overrun with visitors it would rather not welcome, who steal goods, sell wares in the street (sometimes those they have just stolen), meet unscrupulous contacts to hand off coin, information, or purloined items, and engage in the occasional spell duel. It's quite common for a new adventuring company to come into being at one of these fairs, when those who stand out from the crowd because they have legitimate skills to sell gravitate toward one another and decide to form a group.

In those years when Shieldmeet falls, the town is instead treated to a great festival on that day, sponsored mainly by the local temple to Tymora, the Happy Hall of Fortuitous Happenstance. The Shieldmeet festival features a number of games of chance, skill, and bravery, from dice and darts, to drunken running, to wrestling and other physical contests. Occasionally, the Tymoran priests use this festival to identify adventurers whom the goddess has called to a particular task, selected for a blessing, or otherwise marked for some undetermined destiny.

Whether during the Hiring Fair or the Shieldmeet festival, each summer at least one adventuring band seems to get its start in Yartar. Most fall into obscurity, but the Smiling Company—the still-active portion of a larger band of warriors who gathered in Yartar nearly a decade ago—still enjoys moderate success, and makes annual contributions to the Happy Hall.

Yartar is ruled by a Waterbaron who is elected for life. The current Waterbaron is Nestra Ruthiol, a hot-tempered woman who is wickedly calculating; though she is free with her words and her insults, she seldom takes action against rivals unless she is sure such can be done to the most efficiently painful effect. During my last visit to Yartar, accusations arose against the Waterbaron that she had murdered a man, Kaidrod Palyr, who was later revealed to have been her lover. His body was found in the river, with the soaked remnant of what appeared to be Nestra Ruthiol's favorite cloak. That she loudly and publicly argued with Palyr's wife, Tiarshe, shortly before the accusations came to light did little to help her reputation, or the impression of her innocence. When she was finally cleared of the charges, Waterbaron Ruthiol made it clear that she didn't wish to speak of the matter again, and she would ensure that anyone who brought it up in official dealings would be quite unhappy with the results. Though there are whispers, it has not been mentioned in her presence since. Some blame the murder on the Hand of Yartar, the local thieves' guild, but I believe that Kaidrod was killed, and the Waterbaron was implicated, in order to free up the post for one of her rivals within the city.

It is conflicts and schemes such as this that keep Yartar from gaining prominence in the North. If the town can overcome its internal problems, take advantage of what its fellows in the Lords' Alliance can offer, and find a way to reap greater profit from its position along major trade routes—where it stands as the gateway to all the settlements of the northeast—Yartar might soon grow in size, wealth, and influence. Physical growth would require clearing terrain for further settlement and building another encircling wall to protect settlers—and additional guards hired to protect those who do the work.

With its location near two great rivers and its proximity to a third (the Laughingflow, forming a trio the locals creatively call the Three Rivers), Yartar is a fishing town, and its tables have fish as fare at every meal. Fresh crabs, eels, and other river life are available both to eat and to purchase, and serve as a primary means of income for the fisherfolk of the town.

The other major industry of Yartar is barge building. Most of the region's river barges are built, or at least begin their service, in Yartar, and the works of the town's bargewrights are famous all up and down the Dessarin and its tributaries. It is the importance of Yartar's barges to the commerce of the North that earned the town a place in the Lords' Alliance, to ensure that Yartar doesn't fall to enemies and cause upheaval in the trade network along the rivers.

What can't be transported to or from Yartar by barge comes and goes by caravan instead, and the town's location makes it a key stop for most caravans passing between Waterdeep and Silverymoon. In Yartar, a caravan can arrange for swift repairs, replacements of wagon wheels, carts, or full wagons, or the replenishment of tack and other accessories.

Because Yartar has so few industries, and fewer close neighbors, its merchants are often in direct competition with one another, and have neither the resources to seek new customers, nor the space or funds to explore new trades. As a result, a good deal of the gossip, thievery, and assault in Yartar has at its roots one merchant trying to get the upper hand on a rival, either through damage of goods, intimidation of workers, or theft of patrons and customers.

To curb and control rowdiness, the Waterbaron employs the Shields of Yartar, a mounted force of guards who police the town, keep order, and chase off the Uthgardt raids that occasionally menace the lands nearby. The Shields are housed in the Shield Tower, a fortified structure on the west bank of the Surbrin (the town sits primarily on the east), whose outer wall has frequently been torn down and rebuilt. It's rumored that guardian skeletons rise when unauthorized folk tread the ground between the walls, but no one has tested the area to see if its magic still functions; even if it doesn't, more than a hundred angry warriors charging out of the tower at trespassers is enough danger to scare people out of pursuing the idea. A fortified bridge connects the banks between the tower and the town proper.

More impressive than either the Shields or the Shield Tower is the Waterbaron's Barge. This massive vessel can carry two hundred soldiers or seventy-five Shields of Yartar with their horses. Its sides above the waterline are armored with iron. Behind its walls stand multiple crossbow contraptions, each able to fire a dozen bolts at once. When brought to bear against a force on the riverbank, the Shields loose two volleys against their enemies, then bring the Barge ashore and charge. No raiders have stood firm against such an assault.

In the center of town is the Waterbaron' Hall, a grand structure that is both the ruler's home and the location where she hears audiences. Feasts are often held here, though more often, the hall sees activity in its side rooms, where merchants dealing in large quantities of goods, or making deals and proposals that affect the entire community, can meet in comfort.

FALLEN DWARVEN KINGDOMS AND THEIR MARKS

The North is littered with the remnants of many dwarven realms. Although much of the wealth at these sites has been plundered by monsters and adventurers over the centuries, evidence of the settlements and their borders remains graven on cavern walls, trail markings, and scattered coins. Some of these realms, and the marks that bear testimony to their presence, are detailed below.

Haunghdannar. The oldest evidence of dwarven settlement in the North comes from the former site of Haunghdannar. This small coastal realm arose nearly sixty-five centuries ago in the northern Sword Mountains and along the Sword Coast, then fell quickly and mysteriously some fifteen hundred years later. Some records suggest that many of the citizens, driven mad by the sea, sailed westward and never returned. **Mark**: A mountain, with a left-facing fish, surmounted by a seven-pointed star.

Gharraghaur. The dwarves of Gharraghaur were the original delvers beneath the earth at the site of present-day Mirabar. The kingdom was founded soon after Haunghdannar but didn't last as long; twelve hundred years later it succumbed to a horde of ravaging orcs. **Mark**: Four vertical, diamond-shaped gems, three set in a triangle, with the largest in the center.

Besilmer. Nearly six thousand years ago, shield dwarves established an aboveground realm in the Dessarin valley that they named Besilmer. They were the builders of two noted landmarks on the Sword Coast: the Stone Bridge and the Halls of the Hunting Axe. Less than three hundred years after it came into being, Besilmer was overrun and destroyed by a horde of humanoids and giants. **Mark**: a wheel over a plow.

Delzoun. The great Northkingdom of the dwarves, Delzoun was carved out of the rock beneath the area known until recently as the Silver Marches. Founded soon after the fall of Besilmer, Delzoun remained a great power for nearly four thousand years, until orc hordes and subterranean monsters did it in. Many of Delzoun's greatest works, citadels such as Sundbarr and Adbar, survive and thrive yet today. **Mark**: a horizontal, double-headed hammer in a triangle of three sparkling gems.

DWARFHOLDS OF THE NORTH

WHO AM I? SON, I'VE GOT HAIRS ON MY BACK LONGER *than that little beard o' yours. I fought with Emerus to retake Felbarr, and marched with every dwarf king of the North to win back Gauntlgrym. Lost half my foot to an orc's blade, and slew every damned one that got in my way marching home. If I want to sit and enjoy my old age now that we finally drove the orcs back, I'll do just that, and courtesy be damned. I've earned my rest. Your little lordling don't like it, let him come and tell me himself. I'm not getting up until I finish my ale.*

—Drorn Waranvil, to the envoy of the Marchion of Mirabar

The history of the dwarves in the North is a long and violent one, dating back more than six millennia. Before there was a Standing Stone in the Dalelands, or a Waterdeep, or a Myth Drannor, there was the brief (in dwarven terms) glory of Besilmer, and the realms of Haunghdannar and Gharraghaur. Ruins now, to be sure, but these kingdoms lasted longer than almost any living realm of humans, even if their works have been forgotten by humans and dwarves alike.

The greatest and most recent of these dwarven realms was Delzoun, also called the Northkingdom. It stretched from the western edge of what was then the Narrow Sea (later, the Great Desert of Anauroch) west almost to present-day Silverymoon, and from the Ice Mountains to the Nether Mountains. Citadels Adbar and Felbarr were fortresses of Delzoun, and Mirabar, Mithral Hall, and Sundabar all owe their existence to that ancient kingdom or its descendants. Fabled Gauntlgrym, said to be touched by the presence of Moradin himself, was built by Delzoun's dwarves—first as a mine, and then as a city. It was the dwarves of Delzoun who built Ironmaster, too, and all the great mines and renowned forges of the North reside in the halls of the dwarves.

Now, when shield dwarves invoke the name of Delzoun, they are calling upon the glory of all their past accomplishments: every feat of architectural mastery, every fine blade or crushing warhammer forged, every kingdom and battle—won or lost—in defense of their people and the folk around them. The name is as much a battle cry and a badge of honor as it is a call into history, for although every dwarven settlement now has its own masters, kings, and queens, they all respect the memory of the great hammer of Delzoun and the glorious kingdom it represented.

The details in this section are drawn from the extensive teachings of Drorn Waranvil, a longbeard (dwarf elder) who is a retired veteran of the Iron Guard of Citadel Adbar *and* the Citadel Guards of Felbarr. Drorn fought in the orc wars of both this and the last century, and helped free Citadel Felbarr (twice) and Gauntlgrym before he put down his warhammer a few years ago and began to chronicle his experiences for the benefit of younger dwarves seeking to know more about their heritage and about the world of today from the proper perspective.

CITADEL ADBAR

In the extreme north of Faerûn, near the Cold Wood, lie the Ice Mountains. There, in the bitter cold, stands the eternal fortress of Citadel Adbar, the last great remnant of the Northkingdom, and glory of fallen Delzoun. For nearly eighteen centuries, Adbar has stood strong against every threat from every foe, and stood fast, to the great pride of its residents and our people throughout the region.

From the surface, Citadel Adbar looks less like a castle or a human city than a mountain carved to suit the purposes of the dwarves who live there. The two great towers that stand uppermost are ringed with vicious dragonspikes to keep large creatures from landing to attack the structures directly. The great chimney of the city's central foundry stands between them, belching smoke like a volcano about to erupt. Ringing the citadel is a host of platforms, battlements, and arrow slits from where defenders can fire crossbows at anyone foolish enough to attack the city.

For centuries, Adbar has stood as the living monument of the Northkingdom. Already the main fortress of Delzoun when that empire fell, it only grew in importance to the dwarves of the region as other settlements were overrun by orcs, assailed by goblins, or simply disappeared. An orc horde hoping to take Citadel Adbar might rage against its walls, but to little effect, until the great, unyielding granite became the anvil against which they were smashed. The great drawbridge allowed none to pass except welcomed guests, and such guests were few indeed. Standing unconquered, it was the bastion of dwarven hope, glory, and trade.

But now, for the first time in memory, my fellow Adbarran seem truly frightened at the prospect of opening the citadel to any outsiders. Perhaps they are reacting to the recent losses of the war, or the lack of leadership shown by our new king, or mere war-weariness, but for whatever reason Adbar's gates are even harder to move with soft words than they have been in the past, and there are fewer traders coming out of the city nowadays.

The recent orc wars have cost the kingdom dearly, both in warriors and in leadership. In a short time, our long-ruling king, Harbromm, died. His unprepared twin sons shared the rule until the elder, Bromm, was himself killed by a dragon, leaving young King Harnoth with the rule of the ancient citadel.

What followed was a great bleeding of the realm. Much was required to break the North out of the great siege the Many-Arrows orcs held it under. There are also whispers that King Harnoth led his Knights of the Mithral Shield out into the field to vent his rage and grief on the orcs in ill-advised assaults, winnowing down the once great Knights to fewer than two dozen. The Iron Guard, Adbar's army, appears as strong as ever it did, but given the extent of the losses against the orcs, it would be little surprise if their newer recruits were more smiths than warriors, serving their realm out of a sense of duty rather than a desire for battle. I served in the Guard for a century, but I've yet to test the newcomers to see just what they're made of.

If you are fortunate enough to be granted entry to Adbar, be wary of walking around on your own. Within the citadel are traps, deadfalls, and other hazards in various places waiting for someone to approach a protected location incorrectly. A guide, if you can find one, is necessary for newcomers to get around safely.

Beneath the citadel proper, miles of dwarf-sized caverns form a confusing maze that frustrates most non-dwarf visitors. These tunnels are what remain of the early mining efforts inside the mountain. Below them lie the great ore mines of today, constantly being worked by crews of engineers and laborers.

By law, the mines are forbidden to visitors—even non-Adbarran dwarves—except in times of great emergency. So, given the impregnable nature of the fortress, no one not of Adbar has yet been privileged enough to witness what occurs down below. The citadel's Great Wheel, a most impressive sight even to a dwarf, is an ever-turning water wheel that provides power to keep

CITADEL FELBARR

Among the eldest and grandest of the Delzoun holds, Citadel Felbarr was built more than three thousand years ago—a span of time beyond the ability of younger races to comprehend. With great wealth, obtained through profitable trade with Netheril and some of the older human settlements of the North, the dwarves forged themselves a mighty fortress.

Like most dwarven settlements, Felbarr was built around mining. With the fall of Netheril, the reduction of trade along the Lowroad, and signs that the mines beneath the city were reaching the end of their usefulness, the Felbarran abandoned the citadel after nearly two millennia, whereupon a force out of Silverymoon occupied the fortress shortly thereafter. Within half a century, the orcs had come to realize the weakness of the much smaller garrison, and Felbarr was taken by the savages following a four-month siege. The orcs gave the place their tribal name, and the Citadel of Many Arrows stood as a fortress for orcs for more than three hundred years.

The recent story of Citadel Felbarr is the story of my fallen friend, King Emerus Warcrown. In 1367 DR, Emerus led a force of dwarves to seize on the advantage when, to our surprise and delight, another orc horde assaulted the orcs inside the Citadel of Many Arrows. Biding his time until the invaders broke down the gates, Emerus vanquished both tribes of orcs and reclaimed the citadel for the dwarves. After a first, brutal winter, Citadel Felbarr was restored: its forges were relit, and the sound of dwarven hammers began ringing through its halls once again. It was a proud time when we welcomed the following summer with Felbarr back in dwarf hands.

In the most recent war, the orcs again took Citadel Felbarr, but with the help of King Bruenor Battlehammer and an alliance of dwarves from across the North, King Emerus again retook Felbarr, slaying every orc that managed to enter the city and the tunnels below. The grateful king and his loyal warriors then agreed to accompany Bruenor to Gauntlgrym, and there aided him in reclaiming that ancient city as well, but Emerus was mortally wounded in the effort. Bruenor honored

Adbar's foundries, mines, and other operations working at all times. Near the wheel is the Hall of Moradin's Forge, a place of worship that reminds every dwarf of the Soul Forger's strength and enduring protection. One can't help but feel safe in its presence, and a true dwarf is home in the warmth of Moradin's shadow.

Given the current state of the surface lands around the citadel, it is no surprise that Adbarran are even more suspicious than usual of caravans and visitors that approach the city by means of an underground route. One such road arrives from the west, connecting Adbar to Mithral Hall and Mirabar through the ancient tunnels of Old Delzoun. Another tunnel leads south from Adbar to meet the Lowroad, which connects the ruins of Ascore in the east to Citadel Felbarr in the west.

No matter where they come from, all roads leading to Adbar converge so that all travelers must confront the great pair of iron doors known as the Caravan Door. Like the rest of Citadel Adbar, this gate has never been breached. Mention the idea of that happening to an Adbarran dwarf, if you're looking to get a laugh.

King Emerus by naming him the second king of restored Gauntlgrym (after King Connerad was granted the honor of first kingship posthumously), but for most Felbarran dwarves, this honor is an empty comfort, because their beloved hero-king has been taken from them.

Now ruling Citadel Felbarr are King Emerus's distant kin, King Morinn and Queen Tithmel, who were recently married in a union designed to join separate claims to the throne into one family. Tithmel's claim to the throne is the stronger by a small degree of kinship, but Morinn is a quieter, more thoughtful ruler. Queen Tithmel has ever been a warrior, and some Felbarran are afraid she may run headlong into the wrong battle before the couple can provide the realm with an heir, and so they hope that King Morinn's softer influence will help to temper her impetuous nature and keep the city strong through the trying times following the recent conflicts. Although the two monarchs share the rule of the city, and speak with absolute authority, their citizens are wise to listen to what both have to say before deciding how to act on royal edicts.

Most humans know Citadel Felbarr from a distance. They see only a great raised road winding through a vale of broken rock, brooded over by two barbicans known as the Hammer and the Anvil. Two other fortifications loom higher still over the road, embedded in the nearby cliffs and built atop them. These are the North Vigil and the South Vigil. Far beyond them, the massive Rune Gate stands at the end of the road to give entrance into Felbarr, but visitors rarely pass through it.

Like most dwarven cities, Felbarr exists almost entirely underground. However, since it has been invaded by orcs more than once, no accurate maps of the city's full interior are known to exist, preventing would-be attackers from gaining their information. Dwarves, even those visiting from other realms through the connections with the Lowroad, have little trouble finding their way around, but humans, especially those who can't read Dwarvish or the shorthand runes carved throughout the city, have a far more difficult time.

Following the war, most Felbarran applauded the dissolution of the Silver Marches. In its time of greatest need, no races other than dwarves moved even the slightest to aid Citadel Felbarr, when more assistance and better coordination might have prevented not only that citadel's fall, but Sundabar's as well. Felbarran merchants remain willing to trade with the cities of the North, and will aid the other dwarven kingdoms when necessary, but it is doubtful that Queen Tithmel will ever consider an alliance with humans like the one that created Luruar, even if King Morinn might.

GAUNTLGRYM

Gauntlgrym has a complex and contradictory history, the gist of it depending on who's doing the telling. Humans have one story, of what they know from recent years, but for us dwarves, Gauntlgrym is an ancient place, first delved as a mine in the earliest days of Old Delzoun. All sorts of myths persist about the great mithral doors of the city, but at its start, Gauntlgrym was simply a mine. When they delved too deeply, the

dwarves there discovered the presence of a great being of flame, sealed the mines, and left. Only later, when the humans begged the Delzoun dwarves to build one, was there ever a city in Gauntlgrym. It arose because, this time, the dwarves succeeded in harnessing the primal power of fire in the depths, thus creating the Great Forge that made the city possible. Or so the stories go.

Despite all the quests undertaken by adventurers down the centuries, none ever truly found the ancient city until the ghosts of Gauntlgrym's former denizens began calling to living dwarves to seek out the city. And some did—or tried to, anyway. Shortly thereafter, the orc wars began anew, and nearly every dwarf's attention turned back to the existing dwarfholds and the dangers those places now faced. Gradually, as the orcs were pushed back and the dwarven cities secured anew, those delvers began to recall their promises to their ancestors. Further, when the war ended, King Bruenor Battlehammer of Mithral Hall promised to lead the dwarves to Gauntlgrym and reclaim it for the dwarves of the North.

It took fierce fighting to drive out the creatures that had claimed the city from below, and no one is quite sure who or what—aside from the drow—had tried to occupy Gauntlgrym, but in the end, the dwarven armies prevailed, and Bruenor claimed the victory. King Emerus Warcrown of Citadel Felbarr was gravely wounded, and Bruenor proclaimed him the second king of Gauntlgrym before his death. When dear Emerus passed on, Bruenor assumed the rule of Gauntlgrym, once again abdicating the leadership in Mithral Hall.

There are some who think that King Bruenor has designs on a great, restored empire of Delzoun, with the dwarves of all the North—from Ironmaster to Adbar and Sundabar—swearing him fealty. Others fear that he will punish those settlements that didn't contribute warriors to the cause to retake Gauntlgrym, but those folk don't know the returned king very well. If he wants a reborn Delzoun, may Moradin and his children grant him the wisdom to do it right, and the fortitude to see it through. It's a throne I wouldn't wish on anyone.

THE CANTICLE OF GAUNTLGRYM

Passed down by dwarves throughout the North for centuries, the Canticle of Gauntlgrym is now something of an anthem for the reclaimed city. It is often sung on the road by dwarven travelers on their way to make a life in Bruenor's halls.

> Silver halls and mithral doors
> Stone walls to seal the cavern
> Grander sights than e'er before
> In smithy, mine, and tavern
> Toil hard in endless night
> In toast, oh, lift yer flagon!
> Ye'll need the drink to keep ye right
> At forge that bakes the dragon.
> Come Delzoun, come one and all!
> Rush to grab yer kin
> And tell 'em that their home awaits
> In grandest Gauntlgrym!

The rise of a dwarven city so close to the coastal powers of Neverwinter and Waterdeep brings about its own special opportunities and concerns. Surely, once they get their forges going properly, the dwarves will sell armor and weapons similar to the excellent pieces they forged in the eastern cities of Old Delzoun, and this merchandise may lessen the demand for goods from more distant dwarven settlements. In particular, Sundabar is worried that its weapons will no longer be sought after along the Sword Coast, and is looking southward for new markets in Elturgard and elsewhere.

Beyond the great mithral doors of the city lies the great Iron Tabernacle, the holy center of Gauntlgrym, which the priests of all the Morndinsamman are meticulously restoring to honor the gods. Every portion of the city has a road or passageway that eventually leads back to this site, a vast cavern of crisscrossing walkways and great stairs. In its lowest levels, the Tabernacle holds the resting places of countless of Gauntlgrym's dead. Scholars have set about cataloging the lineages recorded here, to give King Bruenor a more complete picture of the bloodlines of the city, and to determine whether any of the living clans have relations or honored dead among those interred.

Deeper still is the Great Forge of Gauntlgrym, where in times past hammers rang off adamantine anvils to forge wonders from every conceivable type of metal. Now the forge might be brought back to life again, and soon—the priests and spellcasters of the city are working on a means of containing the great heat emanating from the Fiery Pit where the being of pure flame is contained, to harness the unquenchable fire as the dwarves of old did.

IRONMASTER

I've never set foot in Ironmaster myself, but I fought beside Storn Skulldark, a young warrior-priest of Clangeddin who was taking a sort of "vacation" from it in order to help reclaim Gauntlgrym. His descriptions of life in Ironmaster confirm much of what I've heard of the place, and so what I relate to you now is truth as solid as Moradin's anvil.

The dwarves of Ironmaster don't want you there, and they want little from the wider world that their traders can't bring back for them. Approaches to the vale in which their city lies are clearly marked with the symbol of Ironmaster: an anvil on a diamond. Such a mark is your only warning, and those ignorant of its meaning court death at the hands of dwarf patrols that will attack any interlopers. Some innocents have been spared and turned back, but no one should rely on the mercy of a dwarf of Ironmaster.

If you were to pass beyond the borders and into Ironmaster itself, you would behold one of the wonders of the world. The great Shaengarne river rushes through a deep canyon of rock and ice in a series of cascades and waterfalls, throwing up freezing froth as it bashes against massive spires of rock that rise from the riverbed. Ironmaster is built in these spires and into the walls of the canyon, the tunnels and towers strung together by high bridges and cliff-side walkways. To hear Storn talk of the place, you would think that dwarves scrabbling about at such heights through the open air was as normal as badgers in a burrow, but I don't mind saying I set aside my ale after he spoke of it.

Ironmaster owes its existence to the restlessness of Ilgostrogue Sstar, who left Citadel Adbar long ago with nearly a quarter of the population of the Northkingdom, headed for what is now Mirabar. By all accounts he was mad, and hoped to extend a dwarven empire to the sea. Once there, and settled, he grew restless again, and headed farther west with his troop, finally settling his nerves in sight of the sea over the Shaengarne River. There the dwarf leader died, and his heir demanded that the folk that followed him build a settlement in tribute to Clanmaster Sstar's grand vision of a dwarven empire. The dwarves found extensive deposits of iron in the hills surrounding their valley, and so named their city Ironmaster.

Ironmaster proved true to its name, and the dwarves have been tunneling out under to tundra for centuries, following the veins of metal. This brought them into contact with duergar of the Deepkingdom a generation back, and Ironmaster has been at war with them ever since. Storn was himself a veteran of many battles for tunnel territory, and despite being so young that not a hair of his beard was white, his knowledge of tunnel-fighting tactics rivaled my own.

Their war with the duergar isn't Ironmaster's only secret, however. My friend Storn wielded two silvered axes, as befits any devote follower of Clangeddin Silverbeard, but when I returned to him an axe he had thrown in the heat of battle, I noted its remarkable weight, and Storn told me that the blade was not steel beneath, but adamantine. I questioned him more about this, and his readiness to tell me of its origin speaks to both the abundance of adamantine among the Ironmaster dwarves and of my friend's innocence about the wider world. Apparently, the dragon-worshiping humans of the distant island of Tuern have long given raw adamantite mined from their island to the smiths of Ironmaster, and they render finished works of adamantine back to the Northlanders in return. Of course, not all the adamantine makes it back to the Northlanders, but since the humans are ignorant of the means of forging adamantine, they are likely none the wiser. What a trove of arms and armor must lie hidden beyond Ironmaster's borders! Ah well, surely they put it to good use against the duergar.

I don't think Storn will mind my sharing his city's secrets. You can go and ask him if you like. He'll no doubt enjoy another little "vacation" from the war in the tunnels.

MITHRAL HALL

The ancestral home of Clan Battlehammer, Mithral Hall was a place of great potential wealth when it was founded in the days of Old Delzoun. Dwarves of Clan Battlehammer left Citadel Adbar, heading west in the hope of finding mithral deposits hidden in the southern spurs of the Spine of the World. These they found, and so began the delving of Mithral Hall, with Clan Ironshield founding Settlestone nearby as a means of buffering the market for the products of the hall's ore.

Mithral Hall enjoyed centuries of profit before its delving permitted the shadow dragon, Shimmergloom, to break through into the world. A settlement of thousands was reduced to fewer than three hundred—all of them too young, too old, too weak, or too ill to fight—who fled to Settlestone. There, they waited for months for word from King Garumn that their lands were again safe. When messengers to the city didn't return, it was clear that Mithral Hall had been lost, and its dwarves headed north, first to Ironmaster, where they were treated with such distrust that they couldn't remain, and then to Icewind Dale.

When Garumn's grandson, Bruenor, was old enough, and sure of his path, he gathered allies to retake his former homeland, and went on a great many adventures with the group later known as the Companions of the Hall. At the end, Bruenor slew the dragon Shimmergloom and reclaimed Mithral Hall for Clan Battlehammer after almost two centuries.

After Bruenor regained the throne, his personal friends attracted some powerful enemies to Mithral Hall, including the drow of Menzoberranzan. This is one reason, his supporters claim, that the king abdicated in favor of his ancestor Gandalug Battlehammer: to protect the people from his personal enemies. Some of Bruenor's detractors claim it was wanderlust that made him leave, but none will bother (or dare) to ask him. In any case, when Gandalug died, Bruenor did his duty and resumed the throne.

Before Bruenor died, he was instrumental in gaining dwarven support for the Treaty of Garumn's Gorge, which brought peace between the dwarves and the orc Kingdom of Many-Arrows. When the orcs, in time, broke their treaty and made war on the North, he returned from the dead almost as though he had been summoned to rally the dwarves to defend themselves and punish their enemies. Some say he delayed receiving the rewards of Moradin's own Dwarfhome to return and aid his fellows and kinsfolk. Such sacrifice, such loyalty, makes a dwarf king worthy of the crown.

Bruenor Battlehammer, the Eighth and Tenth and Thirteen King of Mithral Hall, no longer leads Mithral Hall or the Battlehammer dwarves that live there. Since his return to life, he has refocused his attention on Gauntlgrym, and doesn't claim the kingship of his former home. Instead, the crown has been offered to General Dagnabbet Waybeard, granddaughter of Bruenor's ally, the great general Dagna.

When last I visited Mithral Hall a few years ago, I passed through the rebuilt ruin of Settlestone, where a garrison of two hundred stands to protect the approach to the Mithral Hall. Once I reached the gates, the

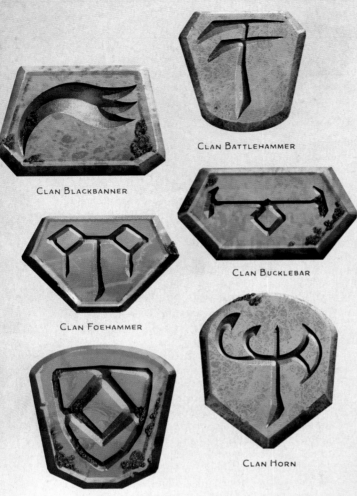

CLAN BLACKBANNER

CLAN BATTLEHAMMER

CLAN FOEHAMMER

CLAN BUCKLEBAR

CLAN STONESHIELD

CLAN HORN

massive granite doors proved to be heavily guarded, and nearly impossible to open from the outside. Mithral Hall's defenders call themselves the Host of the Hall, a disciplined, well-armored cohort that is willing to defend the city to the last dwarf. The famed Gutbuster Brigade is part of the Host, battleragers who strike fear into any enemy intelligent enough to realize whom it is they face.

Travelers allowed inside the city are housed in upper-level guest chambers just inside the labyrinth of caverns known as the Maze. From there, paths lead down into the middle levels of the city, past its various furnaces, and onward to either the lower levels and deeper mines (where guests aren't permitted) or the undercity (where non-dwarf visitors are prohibited).

Despite its recent reputation and the growing legend surrounding its most famous king, Mithral Hall is much more a mine than it is a city. Like most dwarven realms, it lost significant numbers to the orcs, and saw its population further depleted by Bruenor's quest for Gauntlgrym and the resulting permanent relocation of some of his people. As a result, Mithral Hall's numbers are sorely diminished at present, and it remains to be seen whether its fortunes will follow suit.

SUNDABAR

Like Mirabar, Sundabar was a dwarven settlement atop which a human city was built. Sundabar's recent fall should serve as an example to my fellow dwarves of what can happen when the balance of power shifts toward the surface and into human hands.

The city is descended from the citadel of Sundbarr, a stronghold of Delzoun constructed two thousand years ago around a strange volcanic rift that would come to be known as the Everfire—a mystical source of endless heat for the city's smithies and foundries that allowed Sundabar to produce works of great wonder. Sundbarr was led by a Forgemaster, the smith most skilled at working with the Everfire. When one Forgemeaster died or another surpassed his or her ability, leadership of Sundbarr changed hands.

So it was until the fleeing remnants of Ascalhorn were pursued to the citadel's doorstep some time later. Then the Forgemaster of Sundbarr aided the humans in fighting off the demons and other monsters that chased them. In recognition of a human saving his life during the fight, the Forgemaster permitted the refugees to settle on the surface, rather than forcing them to depart once the battle was done. The partnership that grew between dwarves and humans became renowned throughout the North, and the surface city of Sundabar was built up into a mighty fortress of commerce.

However, as the humans flourished above, the dwarf population dwindled, and eventually the Forgemaster was overtaken in prestige and influence by the Ruling Master of Sundabar, who came to speak for the human guilds and merchants of the surface city. One such ruling master, Helm Dwarf-Friend, was so beloved and respected that his descendants were able to crown themselves kings, something no dwarf before or since has dared to do in Sundabar.

King Firehelm, Helm's grandson, was the king in Sundabar when the city fell to the orc horde. He did not survive. Beyond that tragedy, the recent war did horrific damage to Sundabar and the humans on the surface. A dragon dropped great stones on many of the buildings above, and a good portion of the city's outer wall was destroyed. Most of Sundabar's military leadership was wiped out when the building they were meeting in was crushed. Despite the best efforts of Aleina Brightlance of Silverymoon's Knights in Silver to organize a defense, and the valiant efforts of the Sundabar garrison, orcs streamed into the city, slaughtering the human population on the surface and driving what few defenders remained into the caverns below, and from them many fled through the Underdark. The dwarves of the undercity barricaded themselves in the Everfire caverns, and waited. When the orc warlord Hartusk left only a token garrison behind in the city to slow pursuers, the dwarves emerged from below and set about slaughtering every orc and goblin in Sundabar.

Sundabar is now a dwarven city in its entirety; the human population is gone. Efforts to clear away rubble and debris from the attacks are slow, as most dwarves remain in the sheltered undercity, and those few who have duties on the surface have taken over the buildings with the least damage, scavenging stones from ruined structures to reinforce those that can be salvaged.

Before the war, Sundabar's surface streets were cobbled smooth, but many of those roads have been destroyed by falling stones, torn up for ammunition or to repair walls, or simply neglected. Now, the surface city is a hollowed-out ruin. Some believe that the city above will be allowed to wither into oblivion, with the exception of the sturdy double wall that surrounds it (and which the dwarves have already repaired). The temples of human deities stand abandoned. The walls are patrolled by a few sharp-eyed sentries, whose duty is to report what they see and to turn away unwanted visitors.

In the center of the upper city, the Circle still stands around the ruin of the Master's Hall, ready to receive visiting caravans, livestock, and merchants. However, few such visitors arrive, and fewer still are welcomed, as Sundabar prefers to engage in trade nowadays only with other dwarven cities through the Underdark. Were it within the Forgemaster's power, he would see to it that all commerce entering and leaving the city do so by means of underground traffic, so that most surface trade routes could be abandoned entirely.

Sundarren trust of outsiders is low, and their assessment of humans lower still. During the war, of all the human cities, only Silverymoon made any attempt to aid Sundabar, and that aid was (to dwarven minds) far too little and too late. As a result, with the Silver Marches dissolving, Sundabar wasted no time withdrawing from the Lords' Alliance as well, officially severing formal ties with the human realms of the North except for those necessary for trade. Given that such trade is now a rare occurrence, most of the human realms see Sundabar as jealously guarding its wealth and cravenly hiding beneath the surface, while the rest of the region does what it can to recover from the recent conflicts. Sundabar's losses in buildings and in population have done nothing to diminish the contents of its overflowing coffers, and despite its current state, the city remains one of the wealthiest in the North, though most of that coin rarely leaves the city now.

The notion of kingship has come up among the dwarves in the undercity, but the Forgemaster has rejected the idea. Let the dwarves tend to themselves, surely, but there should be no king in Sundabar. I don't know whether Flamestoker's reticence is false modesty or true wisdom, or if he is waiting for a warrior-king to claim Sundabar as part of a larger realm.

THORNHOLD

West of the High Road and hard to the coast near the Mere of Dead Men lies what humans refer to as Thornhold. Once the keep of a petty warlord of the Margaster family of Waterdeep, it was captured and claimed by a paladin as part of the Second Troll War. For many years the Knights of Samular, an order of Tyrran paladins founded by one Samular Caradoon, used Thornhold as its base, though the hold remained the personal property of the Margaster family.

For a brief time a little more than a century ago, Thornhold fell into Zhentarim hands. When the Zhentarim marched through the Underdark to claim

Thornhold, they passed through the caverns of Clan Stoneshaft, which had lived below since before the time the surface city was erected by humans. Though the Zhentarim killed or enslaved many of the dwarves there, they failed to destroy the clan. The survivors soon escaped, regrouped, and retook Thornhold by force under their leader, Ebenezer Stoneshaft, with the aid of Samular's descendant, the Harper Bronwyn Caradoon. After the fortress was reclaimed, in a gesture of respect and gratitude, Caradoon bequeathed its custody to Clan Stoneshaft.

The dwarves of Thornhold are all of the Stoneshaft clan, and because tunnels from their home connect to the castle, they refer to the place as Stoneshaft Hold; they use "Thornhold" only when a non-dwarf in a conversation is confused and an explanation must be made. By habit and nature, Stoneshaft dwarves are secretive (even for dwarves), but nonetheless always eager to hear what's afoot in Waterdeep, particularly any doings involving the Margaster family, whom they see as foes who will one day attack their home to regain it or destroy it if they can't take it back.

To most humans, Thornhold is merely the fortress above the surface, a castle of gray stone with a thick, curving wall and a two-towered central keep. They don't know of the caverns below that lead to the Stoneshaft clanhold. The cliff facing the sea is so sheer that no wall need be built to protect that side of the hill on which Thornhold sits. The castle is utterly without adornment or ornamentation, and only crenellations and arrow slits break the solid face of stone. Within the castle, surrounding the bailey, are small buildings of wood and plaster that hold animals and are used for smithwork, candlemaking, laundry, wood repairs (including wagons and the like), and brewing beer.

Long ago, Thornhold was a profitable stopover for caravanners, adventurers, and other travelers journeying north along the High Road past or through the Mere of Dead Men. For decades, the expansion of the Mere in the calamities of the Spellplague cut off most travel along the High Road. During that time, the Stoneshafts lived in relative isolation, stockpiling their ore, refined metal, and crafts. Stoneshafts are known for the fine metal- and gemwork they craft, considered by most to be works of art worn as personal adornment.

The Margasters of Waterdeep believe that they still have a right to Thornhold. The fortress sits on the reestablished High Road leading to Neverwinter, so it is no wonder that the nobles wish to profit from the fortress's location along that route. The Knights of Samular also show interest in restoring their outpost at Thornhold as a prelude to sorties into the Mere, and there is talk that these desires may lead to a curious alliance between the grasping human nobles and the high-minded paladins.

Stoneshafts fear the politics of powerful Waterdeep will lead to an assault on Thornhold. They have thus been preparing for siege by gathering supplies and reinforcing Thornhold's defenses.

Stoneshaft dwarves can taste the wealth, bustling energy, and constant excitement of nearby Waterdeep, and want to share in it. They don't want to be forced into isolationism, and kept away from Waterdhavian society and the riches of trade. The Stoneshafts aren't blind to House Margaster's ambitions, and they know that they must bring in profits if they hope to weather the challenges to their home. They're very careful to avoid being caught alone, fearing kidnap or torture at the hands of hired agents of the Margasters eager to learn the secrets of their defenses. For the same reason, only the Stoneshaft elders know and plan all the details of those defenses, so any single dwarf doesn't know everything and can't reveal it.

Stoneshafts like and are interested in the full variety of clothing and fashions, music, jokes and current news and rumors, and household goods and tools that Waterdeep offers. They tend to favor maces and morningstars and other bludgeoning weapons, plain armor with full-face helms that conceal a wearer's identity and that have plates to protect the vital areas of a knocked-down dwarf, and spicy foods.

Island Kingdoms

WHAT MAKES ME SUCH AN EXPERT ON SAILING OFF THE *Sword Coast? Well, experience, for one. Survival, for another. I've been doing this longer than most of my readers have been alive, and this is the third version of this book I'm offering. I write one of these only every half-century, and if you think the purchase price isn't worth the heaps of coin you'll make by selling my work to your customers, you're a fool. Don't want it? Don't buy it.*

– Gardorra Burr, to a Waterdhavian bookseller

West of the Sword Coast lies the Sea of Swords, and beyond that the Trackless Sea, a vast expanse separating Faerûn from whatever lies to the far west. Between the shore and the unknown are a number of islands, some large and others so small they lack names of their own. These island nations trade—and war—with Faerûn and one another, just like any mainland nation.

The information below is drawn from *Fifty Years at Sea, Volume the Third*, by Gardorra Burr, a gnome sailor who has spent most of her two hundred years traversing the Sea of Swords.

Mintarn

I don't know what the people of Mintarn did to attract Beshaba's ire, but they surely have her attention. For as long as I can remember, Mintarn has lived in the shadow of the dragon Hoondarrh—called the Red Rage of Mintarn since he dwells on an island close by—but for just as long, the people of Mintarn have been able to purchase the dragon's mercy. Now a series of events conspire to threaten their power to pay the dragon, as well as their other aspirations on the Sword Coast.

Mintarn has long been a neutral ground for various forces—a place aloof from the conflicts between the city-states of the coast and the rivalries of the Northlander isles. Any ship—be it pirate, privateer, or merchant vessel—could dock at Mintarn and find a warm welcome. Many treaties were struck on its shores, and when peace couldn't be achieved, soldiers and ships of Mintarn hired themselves out to various power groups, with no fear of retribution on Mintarn.

Not long ago, Mintarn was awash with coin. Dagult Neverember invested heavily in the island, creating a ship-building company, combat-training facilities, and even lending his coin to the yearly tribute to Hoondarrh when other means fell short. The White Sails company in which he invested grew to become Mintarn's preminent supplier of mercenary ships and soldiers.

Things only improved when Waterdeep wasted its navy chasing Northlander pirates. Then Neverember, acting as Open Lord of Waterdeep, relied on his connections to Mintarn to draft a new mercenary navy for the city. What's more, Neverember took it on himself to raise Neverwinter from the ashes, hiring more mercenaries of Mintarn to serve his needs as that city's Lord Protector.

With funds from two of the greatest cities of the Sword Coast filling its coffers, Mintarn knew a prosperity of which its people had never dreamed. It's true that the same tide that had coin flowing into Mintarn drew much of its young and vibrant people outward, but those they left behind were comforted by the knowledge that their family and friends didn't leave for war, but for much safer duties.

The trouble started, not surprisingly, with Hoondarrh. Though Mintarn made yearly tributes to the great wyrm and was always careful to neglect not a copper, old Hoondarrh was known to sleep for decades at a time, and the folk of Mintarn took their agreement with the dragon for granted. But something awoke him early a few years ago, and it was as if the red bastard could smell the gold coming into the island. Although Mintarn had made proper tribute, Hoondarrh landed atop Castle Mintarn, toppling two of its towers with his weight, and roared a demand for more treasure, right then, and in future tributes.

Of course, the folk of Mintarn scrambled to meet the impatient wyrm's demands. Even if they had all the soldiers shipped away to Neverwinter and Waterdeep, what could they hope to do to mighty Hoondarrh?

Things got worse recently when Neverember was deposed as Open Lord of Waterdeep. The Lords of Waterdeep have decided to reestablish their own navy, and they've told the soldiers of Mintarn to leave the city or take a commission among the navy or the city's other armed forces. Now in Neverwinter, Lord Neverember has decided to do away with a mercenary force as well. He says he wants to instill a sense of civic pride among the folk of Neverwitner, but many in Mintarn see it as a betrayal. Neverember is a cunning man. I think with Hoondarrh active, the Lord Protector is simply cutting his losses. He didn't get the nickname Dagger just because his first name is Dagult.

Mintarn had been playing the game well, but now it finds itself backed into a corner with few moves left to make. The coin is no longer flowing into its harbors, and many of its best and brightest have decided not to return. There's talk of hiring adventurers to slay Hoondarrh, but Hoondarrh's hoard must be massive. If that's not enough of a draw to dragon slayers, then there's

no amount of money Mintarn could offer that would sweeten the deal.

I like Mintarn. It has cozy inns, and they make a brilliant green wine unique to their island. But, there are safer harbors during the current storm. Maybe in another decade or two I'll try Mintarn again.

In the case that you visit, here are a few other things you should know of Mintarn.

Every five or six years, a new tyrant—yes, that's what they call themselves—emerges on Mintarn, ruling the island kingdom in the name of preserving its status as a neutral ground and a free port. A few years ago, Her Tyrancy was Bloeth Embuirhan, the supposed great-granddaughter of a tyrant from a century ago. She ruled the island through its most prosperous days, but odds are that the folk of Mintarn (and maybe herself as well, if she has her wits bout her) wants someone else on the throne now.

Despite its open harbors and many fine establishments, Mintarn remains a loosely settled island. There are farms and homesteads, to be sure, but also wide, open spaces between them, and enough land that anyone could make a small living if so inclined.

SKADAURAK

The Red Rage of Mintarn dwells in this mountain that rises from the sea north of Mintarn. I've never heard of any treasure hunters making it out alive, but those who give tribute to Hoondarrh say they sail into a sea cave and leave it on a sandy beach within. More caves are said to lead out from that bay, one even going straight up into the ceiling. Sometimes the tribute carriers can hear Hoondarrh's breathing from one of the caves: great inhalations, exhalations, and deep rumbles of slumber. When they can't hear such noises, you might think folk of Mintarn would be inclined to explore Skadaurak, but as it was explained to me, the lack of the dragon snoring might mean he is away hunting somewhere, but it could just as easily mean he is present, watching, and holding his breath.

THE MOONSHAES

Cloaked in mists, the rocky cliffs of the Moonshae Isles rise high above the surf of the Sea of Swords, their tops clothed in ancient forests. The Moonshaes lie due west from Mintarn—and Baldur's Gate, and Candlekeep, and even Amn, for that matter: this great stretch of islands is nearly half as long as the Sword Coast, enclosing the Sea of Moonshae.

On the southern isles live the Ffolk, humans ruled by their High King, Derid Kendrick, from the fortress of Caer Callidyr on Alaron. The Ffolk worship a goddess they call the Earthmother; her druids gather in sacred groves on the islands. Some of these groves hold moonwells, magical pools that the druids say the goddess uses as her windows onto the world.

The northern isles are the territory of the Northlanders, who spread south from Ruathym to settle here,

Northlander Isles

Korinn
Archipelago

Moonshae
Isles

Sea of
Moonshae

Rogarsheim

Fairheight Range

Norland

Dernal
Forest

Iron Keep

Omans
Isle

Alaron

Caer Moray

Trollclaw Range

Dynnegall

Gwynneth

Farview

Myrloch Vale

Moray

Caer Corwell

Snowdown

Caer Westphal

GWYNNETH

Over my lifetime, the isle of Gwynneth has become ever more fey and mysterious, home to the elven realm of Sarifal, under the rule of High Lady Ordalf.

Sarifal shares the island with the reclusive mountain kingdom of Synnoria, the home of the Llewyr elves, plus a few small shield dwarf settlements, and the ruins of Caer Corwell, the former Ffolk settlement on Gwynneth. High King Derid wants to reclaim the old citadel and rebuild it as an embassy, but has yet to secure Lady Ordalf's consent to do so.

Gwynneth is also home to Myrloch Vale, a lush valley nestled in the mountains with the shimmering waters of the Myrloch to the south. Druid circles are active in the Vale, allied with the elves and the fey creatures of this area.

In the north of the island, High Lady Ordalf's son, Prince Araithe, leads the struggle against the darker fey of the forest of Winterglen. The prince is a pragmatist willing to accept aid in fending off his people's foes, and so has been known to allow adventuring companies to cross the Strait of Alaron and land on Gwynneth, if they pledge to aid the cause.

KORINN ARCHIPELAGO

The Korinn Archipelago is dozens of rocky, rainy, and windswept islands populated mostly by Northlanders, who herd sheep, fish the nearby waters, and occasionally go raiding or pirating. Dozens of separate settlements are their own mini-kingdoms with little that unifies them besides a shared Northlander culture.

There's no safe harbor for outsiders; you just have no idea what you are dealing with. For other Northlanders, the settlement of Westhaven on Pandira serves as a neutral ground where Northlanders of all stripes who ply the waters of the Sea of Swords might come to port and wait out a storm or resupply.

MORAY

To the west of Gwynneth, Moray is a land at war with itself. The embattled Ffolk of Caer Moray struggle to keep the port town open so that Dynnegall, farther inland, can receive vital goods and supplies.

These supplies sometimes include reinforcements to deal with the threats of the island, which are many and varied: the Black Blood tribe of Malar-worshiping werefolk, the giants of the Trollclaw Range in the north, and the ogres and orcs of the Orcskill Mountains in the south.

The Ffolk of Moray are loyal to the High King. They hope for a return to a unified Moonshaes under the

and have fought occasional wars with the Ffolk in the centuries that the two groups have uneasily shared the islands.

ALARON

The largest and most populous isle of the Moonshaes is Alaron. The Ffolk stronghold of Caer Callidyr overlooks a bay south of the Fairheight Mountains, at the northern edge of Dornall Forest. The forest is a perilous place, filled with goblins, worgs, and their ilk. The deeper one goes, the more otherworldly the woods become, with fey creatures leading travelers astray—or to their doom. Even the High King's rangers walk the forest with care.

Rumor has it the Rookoath dwarves of the Fairheight range—bolstered by Clan Rustfire of the isle of Gwynneth, and adventurers out of Callidyr—have won victories against the local orcs and their shadow dragon master. High King Derid hopes to forge an alliance with the dwarves, but thus far they have spurned the aid of the crown.

Meanwhile, Kythyss, a port town on the Great South Head of Alaron, has been hiring mercenaries to guard caravans running north to Callidyr. Caravan masters there are always looking for help, if you're willing to brave the road for a while.

> ### VALKUR, HERO-GOD OF THE NORTHLANDERS
>
> While Northlanders revere many other gods—Auril, Umberlee, Talos, and Tempus, in particular—they see mighty Valkur as the most important. This hero-god is unique to the Northlanders and embodies the qualities that Northlanders most admire: fierceness, cunning, courage, strength, and sailing skill.

Kendrick banner and are determined to hold on long enough to see it.

NORLAND

North of Moray lies Norland, the stronghold of the Northlanders of the Isles. Much has happened among the Norls of late, weakening their grip on the Moonshaes, but I fear High King Kendrick lacks power to capitalize on it.

In recent years, a Northlander woman calling herself the Storm Maiden arose as a battle leader among them, which was unusual because Northlanders don't allow women to raid or fish. Said to blessed by both Valkur and Umberlee at her birth, the Storm Maiden gathered great numbers of Norls to her banner, and it seemed she might contest the king for control of Norland. However, a decade ago, she seemed to be consumed by the power of Umberlee, and she drove her followers on a mad quest to control the Sea of Swords. When at last she was defeated at sea, she and her ship vanished into the waves. She is known to be unable to drown, and many people fear her return.

Rault the Wise, king of the Norls, lost both his elderly son Olfgaut and grandson in battles against the Storm Maiden, leaving succession in question. He has a granddaughter of great spirit and wisdom, but in the male-dominated Northlander society—and so soon after the disastrous rise to power of the Storm Maiden—it is unthinkable that rule should fall to her.

OMAN'S ISLE

The last time I set foot on Oman's Isle was just after the Moonshaes had unified, and it was a peaceful, lovely place. It had sheep, farms, and fishing boats, and plenty of folk willing to trade the gold from their mines for goods from the mainland or other islands. Now, Oman's Isle is a blasted place is controlled by giants, especially fomorians, that hurl huge stones at any ship that comes too near the coast. If you do make it to shore, bring friends, and plenty of weapons—it's a dangerous place, but might be worth the risk. I can scarcely imagine the reward Jarl Rault or High King Derid would offer to the adventurers who reclaimed the ruins of Iron Keep, once home to the isle's rulers.

SNOWDOWN

The little isle of Snowdown, south of Alaron, is a possession of Amn, where Lady Erliza rules from Caer Westphal. She is the second of her name, noted for her striking resemblance to her great-grandmother, the first Amnian ruler of the isle.

Since taking possession of the place, Snowdown's occupiers have cut down its woods, stripped its mines, and choked its waterways with the refuse of the overworked Ffolk under their rule. Lady Erliza and her soldiers have ruthlessly put down several rebellions, and the Ffolk here refer to her as "Bloody Erliza." Some Amnians believe the isle is becoming more trouble to hold on to than its diminishing exports are worth, and further uprisings are almost certainly brewing amongst the Ffolk, quietly supported by Alaron.

NORTHLANDER ISLES

Well to the north of the Moonshaes and west of Faerûn are the home islands of the Northlanders, which exist as they have for centuries. The greatest of these islands, Ruathym, holds the oldest settlements the Northlanders claim, and from there, all manner of northern kingdoms and legends have sprung.

The Northlander Isles are scoured by strong winds and powerful waves, and also suffer biting, bone-chilling cold for most of the year. In deepest winter, the inlets are choked with ice, and fog lingers late into the day, if it breaks at all. Most wear furs to keep out the cold, and those going to war supplement their protection with thicker hides, and helms lined with wool or fur. They disdain magic and glorify battle, to the point that most communities grow restless when they don't have an enemy to fight.

Because the Northlanders are good at fighting and sailing, and perfectly willing to attack ships close to their shores, best to be cautious around any Northlander Isles, especially if you haven't been assured of safe passage, and often even then.

Northlanders pay homage to several deities, but they most honor Valkur, a hero-god of their own who exemplifies the qualities their warriors hold most dear. Take care not to question or insult this veneration in their presence.

GUNDARLUN

The fisherfolk and merchants of Gundarlun are more like their mainland cousins than most island folk. Unlike other Northlanders, they are less apt to start a fight with folk they don't recognize. Because of their more peaceful bent, you're more likely to be able to safely get fresh water and supplies in Gundarlun, though you should be prepared to trade generously during your stop.

More than a dozen settlements pay homage to the king in Gundbarg. They profit from the island's reputation as a safe stopover. Though Gundarlun might not provide the best seaworthy warriors, nevertheless ships that are looking to make repairs, take on sailors or sail-menders, or store large cargoes are likely to find their needs met here.

PURPLE ROCKS

If you seek shelter during a storm, you might find it in the many islands of the Purple Rocks. It was once my great fortune to find safe harbor at the port village known as Ulf of Thuger. The welcome I received was nearly as warm as I might have found among the Gunds, and I found the Rocklanders to be a fine audience for my tales of travel and adventure. However, something makes me think I shouldn't return.

On the day that the storm broke, I emerged from the longhouse in which I had been hosted and beheld a well-tended and organized settlement with green pastures and full fishing nets. The ship's crew and I were dealt with cordially by everyone, and the ship was already repaired and prepared for our leaving, the Rocklanders having apparently worked through the night to make it ready.

We left on good terms, and it wasn't until we were well away that we realized we all shared a strange apprehension. We had not seen much of women while we were on the island, which was to be expected since Northlanders typically house guests well away from the homes, farms, and forges that are the Northlander women's domain. But we also neither saw nor heard any children or young men, and never once did we see any old men or women. Indeed, I hesitate to say that any man among the Northlanders we met had a single gray hair on his head or in his beard. This strange fact, and the Rocklanders' weird custom of giving any human figure in their art the arms of their totem—a many-tentacled squid—makes me leery of a return.

RUATHYM

The island of Ruathym is the ancestral homeland of all the Northlanders who live on the islands of the Sea of Swords and the humans who would go on to found old Illusk, now Luskan, and spread out as the Illuskan people. The warlike folk of Ruathym know they have this legacy, and they consider rule over other Northlanders and the cities of the coast to be their birthright.

Merchants can occasionally trade with Rauthym at its capital city, also called Ruathym, but I don't risk such a stopover if I can help it. One never knows when Ruathym is going to be at war, and any ship within sight of the island when it is will be fair prey.

TUERN

Well to the west of its nearest neighbor, the remote island of Tuern is host to violent folk who raid and pillage at will and seek to enslave any outlanders they capture on or near their island. They trust no magic of any kind, and offer tribute to the red dragons and giants that dwell in the high mountain caves of this place. They have five kings, with a High King supposedly enthroned in their capital of Uttersea, but like any sailor with sense, I've avoided the island by a great distance, so I can't tell you which bloodthirsty knave currently rules the roost.

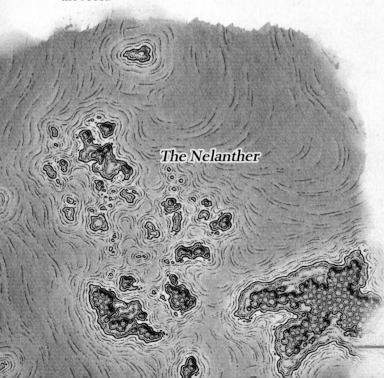

The Nelanther

THE WHALEBONES

The tiny outcrops that make up the Whalebones are so numerous it's impossible to accurately chart them all. Each has its own legends and its own (often self-proclaimed) king, and they battle one another incessantly in skirmishes where the casualties number in the dozens, at most.

The Whalebones are so called because of the scattered skeletons of those great sea creatures that litter the beaches of most of the islands. These bones are the only real commodity of worth these isles have—which means that anyone thinking to simply sail up and pluck ivory from the shores of the Whalebones is sorely underestimating how furiously its inhabitants defend their property.

ORLUMBOR

If you're looking to purchase or repair a ship, there is no better place to do it along the Sword Coast than in Orlumbor. The finest shipwrights in the world live here, and their joining work is among the reasons Waterdeep remained so strong for so many years. Even when much of the city's navy lay disabled in its harbor, the strong ships of Orlumbor proved sturdy enough that folk could live on and in them while the city recovered.

Orlumbor was once a simple shipwright island, supplying the city-states of the Sword Coast with vessels for their navies. Waterdeep in particular relied on Orlumbor to supply ships for its defense, making the island a wealthy and well-protected place in return. When Lord Neverember sank Waterdeep's navy in his fight against pirates, he arranged to hire mercenary ships to replace the force, funneling ill-gotten proceeds into his own pockets, and leaving both the coffers and the shipyards of Orlumbor high and dry. After Neverember's ouster, Waterdeep's business returned, and with it much of the isle's prosperity.

Reaching Orlumbor by ship is tricky because of the rocky, cavernous approach to the harbor. Once a ship navigates the route properly, it can find a wider berth, and any minor damage to the new visitor is happily (and cheaply) repaired by the Orlumbor dockworkers. These are folk born and bred to work on ships. The homes on Orlumbor are built into the caverns of the island, and just as well defended as the docks that are its life's blood.

More than once down the years, Waterdeep's protection has kept Orlumbor from falling to Mintarn, Luskan, Amn, or Baldur's Gate, all of which have sought to claim the islands and its shipyards for their own. None of these other places ever considered that Orlumbor might simply choose not to build ships for them, but thankfully, it's never come to that. Now, Orlumbor once again serves Waterdeep, in exchange for coin, foodstuffs, and other goods from Faerûn.

SOUTHERN ISLES

Off the coast of the southern realms of Faerûn, even south of the Moonshae Isles, are some smaller, less influential island nations. The Nelanther, just across

Asavir's Channel from Tethyr, is a land of raiding pirates. Farther south, some three hundred miles from the Moonshaes, is the fabled island of Lantan, birthplace of many odd inventions. Well south of there, beyond the jungles of Chult, is the mysterious island of Nimbral.

LANTAN

I had not visited Lantan for over a year when it happened, but the way most tell it, when magic failed utterly in this place, all the stored smokepowder and magical gewgaws in Lantan exploded, one by one, just as great waves washed over the island. Within a terrifyingly short time, Lantan was no more.

Or so the stories of survivors went. It appears now that Lantan was transferred to another world, much like Halruaa. Halruua, though, had foreseen the calamity and taken time to prepare. Lantan was not so lucky.

The Lantanese were fascinated—some say obsessed—with building mechanical wonders. Though they employed magic from time to time, the whole island smelled like sawdust, grease, and freshly scraped metal, as shop after shop worked on refining its latest and greatest invention. The new creation might have been little metal knights that walk and fight and knock each other over, elaborate coffers with locks that latch themselves, or mechanical arms that copy what a scribe is writing onto a second sheet of parchment. During my past visits there, I'd seen all of those and more with my own eyes.

Were these gewgaws and trifles of help to the Lantanese when the whole world was ripped from under them? To whom did they turn when in that other world their prayers to their favored god, Gond, went unanswered? What happened in their century away, and now that they are returned, are they happy to be here, or does it seem like their world has once more been ripped away?

Some ships claiming to be from returned Lantan have appeared in ports along the Sword Coast, but from what I hear, the Lantanese who emerge from them are guarded and say little about their homeland. These traders seek to attain large quantities of raw materials such as various types of woods and metals, trading unusual gems and strange gold coins in return. Of their inventions, folks have seen little, but the few glimpses attained have fueled much speculation about Lantan's development of smokepowder weapons and greater willingness to blend magic with machinery. Indeed, Lantanese traders have reportedly offered many shield guardians in private auctions up and down the Sword Coast, and such golem-like constructs are usually the province of wizards, not tinkerers.

NELANTHER

Take an old salt's advice and beware the Pirate Isles of the Sea of Swords, the Nelanther. Here, all manner of seafaring or sea-dwelling creatures live, from lizardfolk and minotaurs to orcs and ogres, with a smattering of humans and others thrown in for variety. Where some pirates hold to their own code of conduct, the folk of Nelanther care nothing for rules, honor, or even good, neighborly sense: they attack each another as often

BANNER OF THE
KNIGHTS OF NIMBRAL

and as viciously as they do any passing ship or convoy. Simply put, the Nelanther Isles are a chain of reavers and raiders, who eke out a living fighting whomever they can find.

No one's ever bothered to count or name all the tribes of these islands, and I doubt anyone's going to start now. For one thing, it's a fool's errand: tribes split up or are destroyed at such a rapid pace that by the time you finished counting, you'd have to start over anyway. For another, it's dirty, dangerous work, and dealing with pirates is a task best left to swift ships, well-armed navies, and the kinds of fools that would want to count them in the first place.

If you do find out the name of a tribe in the Nelanther, be careful about mentioning it to another Nelanther ship unless you can confirm that the ship belongs to a friendly tribe. Even so, be advised that alliances are short as summer storms in these isles, and it's not likely you'll be around long enough to witness a new one being forged. Proclaiming your allegiance to a certain tribe might anger the one you're talking to.

Still, if you're looking for cheap, strong hands, Nelanther may be the place for you, but don't expect much in the way of loyalty or cleverness out of them. Hiring too many Nelanther sailors on a ship is just asking for your ship to be taken from you, sailed back to the islands, and given new life as a pirate vessel.

NIMBRAL

Ever seen an island simply disappear? That is, supposedly, what happened to Nimbral at about the time

Lantan drowned, or so they say. Four ship captains of my acquaintance claim to have seen it one moment, and then not seen it the next, and sailed straight through its former location as though it was never there.

Some claim that powerful magic moved or hid the island in a vast illusion. That I find believable, because the Lords of Nimbral have long been known for illusion and trickery. If any isle were to vanish into thin air, it would be theirs. Likewise, Nimbral's return is certainly within their capabilities, and perhaps this event is the climax of a trick so long and complex that even a gnome can envy its scope.

Nimbral today is much as it has always been: far-flung and secretive. Where the island went, what it did while gone, and why it came back all seem to be facts the Lords of Nimbral prefer to keep to themselves.

Nimbral is still ruled by its mysterious lords, a closely related family of archmages, master illusionists all. They in turn appoint the heralds, who proclaim the laws, and the Knights of Nimbral, fabled hippogriff riders clad in armor clear as glass but strong as steel. Don't let the fact that they are called knights fool you. The Knights of Nimbral have always acted as pirates when out on patrol over the seas, preying on ships that strayed close to their island.

What my captain friends were doing in waters so close to Nimbral they did not disclose. "Business" was all they'd say, but no one has business so far south as Nimbral, unless they expect to dock at the island. Alas, in the time since we last spoke, all those captains have died, and I can't question them further about what they know of the place.

If you have cause to sail south by Chult, keep a wary eye on the skies. It might not help, since the Knight of Nimbral have been known to appear out of nowhere, apparently invisible before they attacked, but it pays to be cautious when you're doing something foolish.

Evermeet

What I tell you now is truth as pure as Garl's nugget, and the only reason I've written it in a book for all to see is that no one else shall ever achieve the feat: I stowed away on a ship bound for Evermeet, and my feet touched its blessed ground!

Any who're knowledgeable about the place might scoff at my claim, and those ignorant of it like as not think the deed not the feat of legend it was, so let me explain to those doubters among you what Evermeet is and why, by the end of my tale, you'll envy my boots.

A Little Piece of Heaven

Legend has it—and so believes every elf I've ever met—that the island of Evermeet is not of this world, and that it never was. In ancient days, so long ago that even elves think of it as their mythic past, the elves of many nations sought a perfect homeland for their people. (That was the problem there, of course. You'll miss out on a wealth of beauty if you're always looking for the perfect gem.) Not finding it in the world, some elves (sun elves, I'd wager) looked beyond the world to create one. These High Mages gathered together to perform a mighty work of magic that would bring Toril into

contact with Arvandor—that's right, the mad fools actually wanted to bring into our world some of the lands in which their gods dwelt!

Tales differ on whether Corellon allowed this or was powerless to prevent it, but it happened, and calamity gripped Toril as a result. This was the first Sundering, and elves have always said it echoed through time. Recent calamities would seem to prove them right.

When things settled down, the elves realized their folly. For thousands of years, no elf dared set foot on Evermeet. But eventually Corellon must have forgiven his wayward children, for the oldest elves began to feel the call to the west.

Perhaps you've seen a moonbow hang over Selûne and heard the idea that it means an elf is being called to Evermeet. Well, that is no children's story. Ever met an elderly elf? How would you know, right? Well if you're ever honored to meet an elderly elf at such a time, you'll see a similar arc in each of the elf's eyes above the pupil. This is Sehanine Moonbow's way of guiding the elf to the afterlife. The arcs can blind the elf to this world, but they vanish when the elf enters the next, allowing sight of the elven heaven. Well that's exactly what happens in Evermeet, and the elf need not be dead to achieve it. Don't believe me? Well, I saw what I saw.

Some elves followed their aged kin to Evermeet, and soon a kingdom of elves dwelt in a heaven on Toril. For ages Evermeet was protected by mighty beasts, mighty magic, and the might of the Seldarine themselves. Elves of all types from all over the world journeyed to Evermeet seeking solace. And when the elves declared their Retreat from the world, where do you think they went?

Then the Spellplague struck, and some of that old elven High Magic must have unraveled. Evermeet became unmoored from the world and found itself instead in a sea of the Feywild, that strange realm of faerie that touches the world in mystical places. For a century, it seemed Evermeet was lost to the world. Venerable elves tried to hold on, hoping that this echo of the first Sundering might echo Evermeet's connection to the world once the period of calamity ended.

Their patience (who but an elf could have such patience?) was at last rewarded, when ships from Evermeet docked once more in Sword Coast ports.

Sailing to the West

Knowing all this and having just met a venerable elf who was preparing for the journey, how could I not take the opportunity to tag along? I felt a little bad about taking advantage of the elf's blindness and forcing him to leave behind some of his baggage, but it was the opportunity of a lifetime!

I overheard it said by the captain of the ship that Evermeet now somehow straddles all three planes: our world, the Feywild, and Arvandor. It touches them all, but exists fully in none of them. To find it, you must follow a pattern of stars until the stars change and then follow new stars. (I swear by Garl's nugget that's what he said!) Those who stray from the path are lost. How

I wish I could have asked the captain where the lost ships went! But I couldn't give myself away.

I had brought some food with me, since I didn't know how long I'd have to remain hidden aboard the ship. At the start of the journey, I pricked my ears up at every creak of the boards and at each elven voice, but after a time, lulled by the rocking of the sea, I fell asleep. The journey after that has a dreamlike quality. I know I must have awoken, eaten, slept, and taken care of other necessities—at least my food was all eaten by journey's end—but I don't recall the specifics. I only know that at some point the ship stopped, and someone took the basket in which I was hidden and placed it on a sandy beach.

WHAT I SAW

I felt it before I saw it. With the barest glimmer of golden light through the basket weave all that I could see, Evermeet took my breath way. Coiled in the basket like a snake, with cramps in every limb, I was desperate not to give myself away, yet I could feel the magic of Evermeet seep through my body, soothing aching limbs and easing guilty conscience. When I could breathe again, I gasped. And that was how the elf discovered me.

The blind elf, whose beloved treasures I'd displaced to take my journey, pulled me from his basket, and when he did so, his eyes were clear as diamonds and just as hard. I thought for sure that I was dead, and on seeing my surroundings, I can say with all my heart that I didn't care. Had the elf killed me on the spot, my soul would have gone to Garl and demanded a ship so that I could sail right back to Evermeet. My dumb wonderment caused the elf to turn and look, and he too was enraptured.

As to what we beheld, well, imagine a place of staggering natural beauty and impossible elven artifice, an alien realm as distant and beautiful as the stars, but as much a part of you as your own dreams—part heaven, part home.

I'd like to say we shared a moment there, the elf and I. Perhaps in recognition of that, he didn't kill me.

It was over all too soon. I was put back on the boat, returned to the world, and warned never to try anything so foolish again—on pain of death. And I don't think I will—at least not until I'm getting up there in years. Then I'll keep my eyes peeled for elves with cloudy eyes looking west!

Now, see? Wouldn't you have liked to have been a gnome's boots and touched Evermeet, even for just a few beats of the heart?

TOME OF
FEYWILD LORE

INDEPENDENT REALMS

I HAVE WANDERED THESE LANDS FOR LONGER THAN *you've been alive, caravan master. I say this not to somehow lord these years over you, but so that you understand that when I say your proposed "short cut" leads only to the bloody demise of yourself and your work hands, you will believe me, because I have seen others make the same assumption, and die the same deaths.*

—Aedyn Graymantle,
to Wundrith Parr, Waterdhavian caravan master

Though there are myriad nations, kingdoms, and city-states scattered across the length and breadth of Faerûn, it would be a dangerous mistake to assume that all of the lands in and between those places are tamed. Travel a short way beyond most civilized places, and one finds oneself in the midst of wilderness haunted by creatures deadly and foul.

The information below is excerpted from *Far from the Misty Hills*, a treatise on far-flung places in the North, composed by one Aedyn Graymantle, a moon elf ranger who hails from Evereska. In her years of braving the wilds, Aedyn has acted as guide, caravan guard, bodyguard, and trailblazer.

BOARESKYR BRIDGE

Boareskyr Bridge stands on the Trade Way and is the only consistently safe crossing over the Winding Water for more than a hundred miles in either direction. This alone makes it remarkable, but there, in the midst of a wilderness with nothing to set it apart for greatness, a mortal man murdered Bhaal, the god of murder. This is no tall tale. Even a century after Bhaal's blood was shed there, the river's waters run black and foul for miles west of the bridge.

Adding to the location's sacred nature, Cyric, the man who killed Bhaal, was himself elevated to godhood. Although he proved to be a malign power, statues of both Cyric and Bhaal were erected on the ends of the bridge, the two gods facing each other (though it is said Cyric stabbed Bhaal in the back). About a century ago, fanatics of Mystra tore down the statues and flung their stones in the river, but fearing retribution for such sacrilege, the merchants who use the bridge pooled funds to have them rebuilt in grander style than before. Now each god stands atop his own decorated archway that serves as entrance to the bridge.

Boareskyr Bridge is named for a long-ago adventurer who built the original bridge and used it as the center of a small kingdom, which also bore his name, north and east of the Trade Way, though it lasted only a few decades before falling to threats from the Fields of the Dead. The bridge serves as a connection between the lands of the North and the Western Heartlands.

The enormous black granite bridge is wide enough that two wagons can pass one another going opposite directions, and its waist-high ramparts are thicker than some castle walls. On most days of the summer and even during seasons less suitable for travel, merchant caravans cross the bridge and pilgrims come to pay homage, all beneath the protective gaze of the paladins of Elturgard stationed at nearby Fort Tamal.

Fort Tamal

For many years, a ruined keep on the southern bank dubbed Bridgefort served as the campground for caravans passing over the bridge. Whether going north or south, caravan masters could anticipate a safe rest within the grassy space enclosed by the ruined walls, sharing the duties of keeping watch with other travelers.

Then in the midst of a crisis of leadership in distant Elturel, one of the heirs apparent for the post of High Observer, a paladin named Tamal Thent, went missing with her entire retinue near the bridge. Although an investigation was undertaken, no sign of Tamal or any of the others was discovered. Thavus Kreeg, Tamal's rival for the post, was elevated to the post of High Observer soon after, and one of his first declarations was that Bridgefort be rebuilt and given a new name in honor of lost Tamal.

A flurry of activity occurred around Boareskyr Bridge at that time, with the soldiers of Elturgard making frequent patrols of the road and surrounding lands while Fort Tamal was being constructed. Today things are fairly quiet at the bridge. The tradition of caravans camping at the bridge and pilgrims visiting it continues, but now people stay in a caravan ground around a small village that has grown up outside the fort.

Activity around the area is overseen by a curious mix of Companions of Elturgard. The Companions—all paladins of gods such as Tyr, Torm, Helm, and Amaunator—tend to be either young firebrands or grizzled veterans content to sit by a fire. Many of the veterans have been stationed at Fort Tamal since it was constructed, and they have families that live in the village outside its walls. Their more youthful counterparts come from all over Elturgard, but all seem to have been assigned to Fort Tamal after some act of insubordination. Perhaps it is hoped that time out on the frontier with their more experienced counterparts will cool some of the young Companions' zeal.

Certainly some of the young Companions I've spoken with see their post as a punishment. Boareskyr Bridge is far from the rest of Elturgard, and the caravans that camp at Fort Tamal never seemed to need such a robust guard before. Even the relative nearness of Najara seems to provide little reason for so many of Elturgard's mightiest defenders to be squandered on such a trivial task. For their part, the elder Companions talk of fulfilling duties and following orders, but to me they seemed too content.

A paladin should have drive. They have been granted the power of the gods for a reason, and surely that reason can't be to stand guard while merchants sleep. Then again, the High Observer is, by all reports, a wise and effective ruler. Perhaps he perceives threats at Boareskyr Bridge that I can't. Najara has been more active of late, despite its quiet exterior, I assure you. Dragonspear Castle to the north was once again the source of an infernal incursion. And maybe there is something sinister about this place where a god of murder died and a god of lies is honored.

For my part, I sympathize with the young firebrands, and I counseled those to whom I spoke to look to the skies. In the time of Cyric's legendary battle with Bhaal, pegasi dwelt nearby. The magical creatures are said to favor those of pure heart and even allow themselves to be ridden by such folk when the cause is just. That favor might never be bestowed on the young paladins, but I'm sure the thought will provide them with some pleasant daydreams.

Candlekeep

The great keep never fails to take my breath away: it stands on a volcanic crag a hundred or so feet from the coastline, a flat-topped spur of rough stone out in the midst of the surging sea. Imagine, if you can, the top of this crag hemmed in entirely by a tall wall. This wall is interrupted by several towers all the way around, and it encloses a large space from which even more of these same towers rise. Those who have seen this vista from above have said that it looks like nothing so much as a cake decorated with too many candles. The mist of sea-spray fills the air nearest the western walls, and in winter, this moisture can cause treacherous build-ups of ice. Sometimes entire towers along the western edge of the keep have to be abandoned for the season, they become so overtaken by frost.

From the center rises the largest and thickest tower of Candlekeep. If the other towers are well-wrought branches and blossoms, then this surely is the bole of the tree: strong, massive, and rising well above the perimeter structures. About the central keep a garden spirals in rising steps, and those lucky enough to enter the library proper do so by passing around and up through this green space to the keep's main door. However, most folk who visit Candlekeep see this structure only from the courtyard east of it, where the facilities for arriving scholars lie.

The only gate into Candlekeep stands at the end of the Way of the Lion, which is the only road that provides access to and from the outside world. The route extends from Beregost, leagues away, and winds a lonely path out on the peninsula where Candlekeep stands.

The Great Library

Candlekeep is the largest repository of lore and writings in all the Realms (although my scholarly kin in Evereska don't like being reminded of that). It was once the home of the great prophet Alaundo the Seer, and within its walls were written the Prophecies of Alaundo. Its vaults, it is said, contain hidden knowledge enough to make any person with the ability to discover and absorb it all powerful beyond compare. The problem with doing that, of course, is the same as with secrets in any other location: one must know that a secret exists before its details can be sussed out.

To that end, Candlekeep's vast library is something of a defense in and of itself: for every bit of hidden lore of potentially great power that lies within, there are thousands of inconsequential recipes, old songs, bits of history, journals of long-dead folk, and myriad other pieces of writing of no lasting importance save to the monks of this place, and the sages who come seeking such trifles.

Of course, before this treasure trove can be plumbed, one must gain entry to its hallowed halls. The cloistered scholar-monks of Candlekeep, who are called the Avowed, guard this place and work tirelessly to ensure the library's protection and preservation. Though they are friendly enough in a workaday fashion, they are also suspicious of all visitors to the library.

GAINING ENTRANCE

I have assisted more than one visitor with entry into the library, so I know the process well. The price of admission is the donation of a work of writing not already in the possession of Candlekeep. Though the monks refer to this offering as the "entrance-gift," it is a toll to be paid, and often a quite high one.

To most, this requirement might seem difficult or even impossible to fulfill. After all, how is the would-be visitor to know exactly what Candlekeep does and does not have in its labyrinthine stacks? To this end, most visitors come to Candlekeep with multiple books they suspect might meet with approval.

Fortunately for some, the donation need not be utterly unique. Some tome or treatise the library doesn't have in its archives is preferable, but the monks are open to a few other possibilities: rare editions, books with a great deal of history tied to them, even tomes with insightful (or just interesting) notes scribbled in the margins have all been accepted, as have the journals of folk who are well traveled or highly learned.

Most of those who come as petitioners to the gates of Candlekeep already know the cost of entry; those who don't are told of it at the gates, and turned away kindly if they have no such gift. Heralds; priests of the gods Oghma, Gond, Deneir, and Milil; certain archmages; and others acknowledged as "friends of Candlekeep" are permitted to enter without making such a donation (though such folk often contribute to the library's vaults as a matter of course anyway).

The great double gates of Candlekeep are as three times the height of a human, and wrought of strange black metal that seems to repel lightning and to be immune to magical divinations, according to at least one wizard I've accompanied here. Both of these panels are emblazoned with the castle-and-flame sigil of Candlekeep in their upper reaches. One of the two gates stands open far enough to admit visitors during the day, with the other kept shut.

Five purple-vestmented monks tend this entrance. One of them steps forward to greet those seeking admission, discussing with new arrivals their intentions and examining what gifts they have brought. As the first monk examines an offered gift, determining its title and provenance, a second gate guard performs a casting of the *message* spell. The Waterdhavian sage Waldrop tells me that the recipient of this spell is an Avowed in a room nearby with a massive tome that notes the books in Candlekeep's vaults. Apparently aided by magic of some kind, that tome-keeper determines if the library has the book being offered, and responds concerning whether the gift is accepted or not.

One of the priests of Deneir whom I regularly accompany to Candlekeep has mentioned truth-seeking

magics being at work on this threshold. The door-guard's fellows watch closely for any trouble, and other monks peer from the high towers that flank the gates, ready to summon help or lend magical support in case of attack.

Those who are admitted are referred to as "seeker," but also addressed by name if the monk knows it, or by "goodsir" or "goodlady" otherwise. Once a visitor is admitted, the monks at the gate part ranks to allow the seeker inside to the Court of Air. Visitors are instructed to cross that area and stand before the Emerald Door, where another monk receives them, offers them food, bath, and sleeping quarters, and arranges for each to meet a monk who will help to plan and then supervise the seeker's visit to the library.

THE COURT OF AIR

The Court of Air is aptly named. This cobbled courtyard is empty, containing neither tree nor well. Its southern wall is the southern wall of Candlekeep itself, with a number of fieldstone-wrought buildings intended for visitors' use built along it. Nearest the western wall of the courtyard stand two buildings: the House of the Binder, a large temple of Oghma with plenty of space to allow his faithful to camp and socialize, and the Baths, a public facility that draws water from the natural spring beneath the keep.

On the other side of the baths is the Hearth, a great eating-place and social hall for seekers, which has shrines to Deneir, Gond, and Milil built into it. The Hearth connects to the House of Rest, a structure with four-bunk rooms where seekers are assigned quarters upon their acceptance. Finally, next to the House of Rest, and built up against the eastern wall of the courtyard, are the stables, where mounts are housed and provisioned for the length of a seeker's stay, and the granary.

The northern edge of the Court of Air is made up of a wall into which are set twelve towers. These are the towers within which visitors are allowed to study.

The famous Emerald Door stands in the western wall. Here a Keeper of the Emerald Door stands at all times, assisted by a small group of under-monks who act as messengers and runners. It is the Keeper who officially welcomes newly arrived seekers, and makes arrangements for their stay. Only this door leads deeper into the inner ward; the other towers have entrances onto the Court of Air, but don't have points of egress into the inner ward and thus the rest of the library.

These court-facing towers in the north wall, called the "necessariums" by the monks, are the main places in which visitors interact with the treasures of Candlekeep. They are honeycombed with reading rooms and small gathering chambers, where monks may bring individual tomes to seekers to be read, and where seekers may consult with monks on further materials to enable their research. Despite being adjacent to other towers and having bridges to more distant ones, the chambers that guests can reach in the necessariums don't allow access to the rest of the keep.

WITHIN THE KEEP

Unfortunately, the foregoing is the extent of the information I have about the interior of Candlekeep. My personal experience is limited (as is the case with most visitors) to the Court of Air. Though the stories fly fast and thick in the Hearth about what lies beyond the necessariums, it is almost all conjecture and hearsay, with a heavy dose of fable, you can wager safely.

From the Court of Air, one can see that the tall towers that rise up above the northern court wall are interconnected by covered walkways. Many of these are roofed, but not walled, and monks—some of them under quite prodigious burdens of books—scramble to and fro along them. The passages are sometimes interrupted by small spiral staircases that provide access to higher and lower levels, and some of the larger walkways slope gently from one floor in a given tower to the different level in another.

The only other fact I know about Candlekeep's interior is that it extends even beneath the level of the courtyards, with staircases in the cellars of certain of the towers that lead down into the very bedrock of the pillar upon which the keep is built. A monk once confided to me that these caverns store emergency supplies and provide access to great wells, all of which would enable the great fortification to survive entire seasons—if not years—of siege.

THE AVOWED

The monks of Candlekeep are all cloistered scholars. Most of them have no magical power to speak of (though many of them are trained to know about such things); a notable handful, though, are spellcasters—either clerics of gods that represent the pursuit of knowledge or wizards. Even warrior-monks and paladins have been known among the Avowed, though never many at once.

The Avowed are the sworn servants of the great keep, each rigorously tested to weed out any deceit before being permitted to take the oaths of the order. The monks' first priority is the defense of the library's knowledge against those who would steal or destroy it, but also against natural effects that might do likewise, such as mold, wet, and decay. Many of the monks wield various kinds of magic items to aid in these endeavors, and Candlekeep's facilities include more than a few scriptoria to facilitate the copying of books becoming worn, binderies to repair the same, and even magical storage that preserve rare books from any further decay or damage.

I've never made a detailed study of the Avowed, as it's never been terribly needful for me to do so, but from my time spent in Candlekeep's Court of Air, as well as my conversations with Waldrop, I've picked up a few things.

The rank-and-file of the Avowed are divided into acolytes, who are newcomers to the order, and scribes, who tend to the majority of the work in the keep. Acolytes provide labor, doing the cleaning, lifting, and general sweating that a place of such size requires, and work at their studies, hoping to prove themselves and be accepted into the ranks of the scribes. The scribes do most of the archival labor required of the Avowed, and often pitch in with hands-on efforts when a particularly large chore needs doing.

The master readers are the sages and elder monks who oversee the scribes and teach the acolytes. All are possessed of significant experience and dedicated to the great library, and it is from this group that individuals are chosen to fill in the upper ranks when positions open up.

Above the master readers are other high-ranking posts, each with specialized duty, from the Gatewarden who tends to the security of the keep to the Guide who instructs and educates the Avowed. Of particular note is the Chanter, who is responsible for continuing the ongoing recitation of the prophecies of the great seer Alaundo, who once made his home here.

I remember the first time I came upon the Endless Chant. It starts at the edge of one's hearing (I was one of the first in the courtyard to sense it), and slowly grows closer and louder. As it does so, everything else falls silent around you. In short order, a procession of Avowed arrive on the scene, and the only sound anyone can perceive is their echoing, sonorous chant. The Chanter or one of his subordinates (called "voices") leads this procession, and each of the Avowed is expected to lend his voice to the procession occasionally.

It was through my friendship with Waldrop that I met one of the eight Great Readers, the council of elder Avowed who oversee the operation of Candlekeep. She was tall, and I remember thinking that she was one of the most erudite folk I'd ever spoken with. Each of the Great Readers is given an arena of responsibility within the Avowed, usually a topic of scholarly importance, and acknowledged and treated as the foremost expert in that field.

Finally, above them all are two others: the Keeper of Tomes and the First Reader. Where the First Reader's focus is maintaining the integrity of Candlekeep's scholarship, and ever expanding its literary resources and base of knowledge, the Keeper governs the great library. The Keeper's word is law, quite literally—each Keeper's edicts are recorded for the edification of future Keepers, and all are maintained as ongoing traditions until changed by the word of a future Keeper. Waldrop tells me that traditionally the Keeper and the First Reader are supposed to have an antagonistic relationship, one focused on the cloistered monks and the enlightened goals of the library and the other on the mundane aspects of scholarship and Candlekeep's interactions with the outside world.

Although these high-ranking monks keep most visitors at arm's length, it isn't unknown for them to deal with adventurers directly when they need such services. While these scholars rarely have much coin to pay for the services of a company of venturers, they do possess the precious currency of Candlekeep: knowledge. I know of many companies who have been shown lore concerning lost ruins, then asked to brave some dangerous place and return with prizes that can be found only in that location. If the treasure that might be found in such places isn't enough of a reward, some Avowed are empowered to offer inducements such as procedures for creating magic items and written copies of rare spells to sweeten the deal.

SERVICES

Those who come to Candlekeep are permitted to remain for one tenday before departing, and must remain away for at least a full month before returning. During this tenday, they may ask to read specific tomes known to be in the possession of the library, or they may ask the monks to find them tomes concerning certain topics. These works are brought to the reading rooms in the towers that face the Court of Air. Guests are permitted to ascend into those towers and read (but not copy) the tomes there, always in the company of one of the monks.

One of Candlekeep's main sources of income is the sale of books. Three kinds of such books exist: copies of tomes of nonmagical lore, copies of spellbooks and other magical formulae, and works of the Avowed.

Copied Lore. The copying and binding of a work of nonmagical lore in Candlekeep's library is generally performed at a cost of 100 gp or so (though quite large books are always more). This manufacture may take several weeks, particularly for large tomes, so it isn't uncommon for those who desire such a work to commission it in writing, along with advance payment, and then come to the gate to pick up the book, or pay an additional price to have it delivered.

Spellbooks. In contrast, magical books of spells and formulae cost much, much more—a spellbook might be priced at thousands or even tens of thousands of gold pieces. Each simple spell or cantrip in such a tome costs 25 gp or so, with the more complex and powerful spells fetching 150 gp or more each.

Works of the Avowed. Each year, the monks of Candlekeep release a small book stamped with the sigil of the keep, and credited to "The Avowed of Candlekeep." These books are always focused on singular topics, and contain short essays, excerpts, and other writings germane to the topic. They are sold at Candlekeep and by representatives in large cities for between 50 gp and 100 gp per book, though some are often resold for a great deal more.

Candlekeep also buys books and even sponsors adventurers on expeditions to seek out lost sources of lore across the Realms. The exchange of coin in such undertakings is, of course, open to the usual sort of negotiation.

DARKHOLD

I don't suppose you've heard of Darkhold. It's been many years since folk whispered the name of the place in fear. After all, the Zhentarim, the organization that gave Darkhold its evil reputation, are by all accounts no longer the cadre of thieves, assassins, and evil wizards they once were. And strangely enough, according to my source among the Zhentarim, that change in character can be traced right back to Darkhold. As it was told to me, it came about like this ...

Zhentil Keep was burning. The Citadel of the Ravens lay in ruins. The leadership of the Zhentarim died, were captured by the Shadovar of returned Netheril, or were in flight. The vaunted Black Network was shredded.

Northdark
Wood

Hardbuckler

Sunset Mountains

Darkhold

The Storm Horns

The Reaching
Woods

The Far
Hills

Scornubel

Sunset Mountains

DARKHOLD VALE

I was curious about my source's tale, and so when I had cause to be in the region, I made my way toward Darkhold. An enormous mountain peak called the Gray Watcher of the Morning looms behind Darkhold to the east, casting a great shadow over the keep from sunrise until nearly midday. Darkhold sits in a cleft in the side of the Gray Watcher, the highest point of permanent occupation in a relatively flat and defensible valley called Darkhold Vale.

Darkhold Vale contains a small settlement of the same name, consisting mostly of shepherds who tend their flocks in the high meadows of the Sunset Mountains, and a few farmers who coax fine crops from the soils that cling to the vale's fields. The settlement's main source of prosperity is the black stone quarry at the southeastern edge of the vale; the heavy carts groaning with slabs of stone for sale and the large, muscled workhorses that pull them are common sights here. The common folk of Darkhold Vale tend to be surly and suspicious of outsiders, though they are careful to avoid offense.

This settlement of about a hundred or so is utterly under the dominion of Darkhold and has seen some benefit from the situation: the vale folk see a great deal more traffic and trade than the little hamlet would ever expect otherwise. Until recently, all the caravans bound for Darkhold could seek sanctuary only in the shadow of the keep itself. Now the people of the vale have recently built both an inn, called the Wyvern's Rest, and a separate tavern, called the Rookery.

Some of the locals send to market bales of the thick, rich wool they shear from their sheep. Others make a living hawking the dandelion wine that Darkhold Vale has always produced, but only recently begun to sell abroad. The vale has a small militia, technically under the command of the Pereghost, but which answers to a local captain named Sulvarn.

To those who've come into conflict with the Zhentarim, living in a place so firmly in their power seems unthinkable, but the reality is that life is sedate here. Certainly, the soldiers in the castle aren't to be trifled with, but they hardly ever engage in the acts of petty cruelty that one expects from warriors serving a local lord. Those who misunderstand the Zhentarim often do so because they imagine them to be cackling villains in the vein of the Zhents of yore. In reality, they are pragmatic, willing to do whatever necessary to achieve their ends. But they have no need to terrorize the folk of Darkhold Vale, for one simple reason: they already control them.

In years past, these folk lived in fear and suspicion, with a hearty helping of racial prejudice; my first visit to Darkhold nearly a century ago was occasion for me to hear some of the vilest epithets attached to my kind that I've ever heard—even worse than those that fall from the foul lips of orc raiders in the North. The attitudes of the vale folk have changed over the years, however, no doubt due in part to the orders of the Pereghost when he reengaged the Zhentarim with the wider world.

Cells of Zhentarim agents were cut loose, and without connections or direction, they dissolved or were crushed by rivals. The Zhentarim was no more.

Or so it seemed. There was one stronghold of the Zhents that had not fallen and whose leader never wavered in his dedication to the organization. Darkhold stands deep in the mountains of the Western Heartlands, and there the remnants of the Zhentarim quietly gathered. There they swore allegiance anew to the leader who promised to reforge the organization into something stronger than before.

The man to whom this new Zhentarim owed fealty was a dark knight known only as the Pereghost. The Pereghost had long led the armed forces of the Zhentarim at Darkhold, and his vision for the revival of the organization was along military lines. After a time of recruitment and training, the Zhentarim emerged from Darkhold not as conquerers or as bullying capitalists but as mercenaries willing to serve others instead of forcing them to serve.

In the years that followed, the transformation served the Zhentarim well. They earned a reputation for sterling service, and their ranks swelled. Those who knew of Darkhold thought of it as the headquarters of this new version of the Zhentarim.

Membership in the Zhentarim is difficult to assess, but my source told me they might have greater numbers now than before their organization's fall. New leadership for this larger group has led to a shift in focus. While still a source of capable mercenaries, the Zhentarim have diversified into mercantile pursuits. Zhent guards now ride alongside caravans of their own. And whereas a military organization served it well in the chaotic period after its fall, my source frequently described the Zhentarim as a "family" and leaders as "my good friend."

My source also spoke in awed tones of the Pereghost, as though that figure were still alive and a leader of Darkhold. The Pereghost is never seen without his full armor and a face-covering helm. If it isn't an elf behind the mask, then I suspect a series of humans might have masqueraded as the Pereghost during the past century.

Darkhold Castle

When I first beheld the great black walls of Darkhold, I thought all the legends about it must be true. On my second visit, I thought I'd try to confirm my suspicions.

According to legend, Darkhold's story began more then a millennium ago, when it was known as the Keep of the Far Hills. It was built as a summer capitol for the so-called "giant empires." Situated in the Far Hills, the castle was in a position to dominate trade routes north out of the Iriaebor Valley. It could also dominate river trade down the Yellow Snake Gorge.

The role of the so-called Giant Emperors is still a matter of conjecture and discussion today. However, there are some, scattered among the giant tribes of the North, who claim to be heirs to the ancient thrones. Whatever the truth of the empires might be, the castle itself was definitely built for giants. Its size and construction support no other explanation.

Legend has it that Darkhold was lost to the giants due to internal strife—a pair of brothers quarreling over their inheritance. Through poison, magic, and mercenaries, the brothers thinned the castle's population until only the brothers themselves were left. The two fought and mortally wounded each other, and each dragged himself off to die alone. The brothers' spirits are still said to stalk the castle, each still seeking his brother's destruction.

The keep was then occupied by a succession of owners, including a dragon of some repute, but it was not until a lich claimed it that the castle came to be known as Darkhold. The lich was called Varalla, and supposedly she conjured all manner of evil creatures to serve her, sending them out to dominate the lands beyond and establish an empire of evil. Varalla ruled Darkhold until the infamous leaders of the old Zhentarim—Manshoon and Fzoul—heard tales of her wealth in magic and gold. Lured by the promise of such rich rewards, the pair defeated her and claimed the castle for themselves.

Upon my arrival at the great gates to the fortress, I found that I was expected, as I must have been watched since entering Darkhold Vale—perhaps even before then. After a short wait, I was met by a seneschal, a forthright woman with a strong handshake, who warmly referred to the person who secretly supplied me with the history of the Zhentarim. I found myself taken aback by this because I had thought my source and I had spoken in confidence. As you no doubt have noticed, I've avoided mentioning the name, gender, or physical description of my source, for I swore an oath of secrecy. Besides my initial shock, my exchange with the seneschal was pleasant, and I was given a tour of some of the mighty castle.

When I asked about the legends of Darkhold's creation and occupation, she told much the same story as I have told, adding a few characters from its history that I hadn't heard of before. When asked about castle hauntings, the seneschal only smiled in reply. Although it seemed a genuine smile, I could wring no truth from it.

Of the castle's defenses, I can say little. My tour was limited. But I did note that, while some things on the giants' scale have been modified to suit humans (such as stairs and most doors), other things remain titanic. For instance, I have no idea how they managed to open the gates for my entrance without the use of magic.

Denizens of Darkhold

I didn't see the Pereghost during my visit, so I can't confirm anything about the man. But the seneschal and everyone else with whom I conversed spoke of the Pereghost in awed tones. Whatever the truth of this savior of the Zhentarim, he is apparently too busy to entertain curious visitors. While at Darkhold, I heard the name of another leader of some importance, Manxam, but my queries about this figure were redirected to other topics, and I didn't feel comfortable pressing the seneschal on the matter.

Of the rest of Darkhold I can relate only a little more. The Zhentarim maintain two war units within Darkhold: the Storm Watch, a cadre of veteran Zhentarim soldiers who act as heavy infantry, and the Gray Feathers, archers primarily responsible for the defense of the fortress.

These aren't the only forces Darkhold can bring to bear, however. The years when a contingent of giants lived in Darkhold are long gone, but in their place is an aerie of wyverns, bred and trained to defend Darkhold and to obey the Pereghost. Their trainer is a ranger named Grigarr, whose body is pocked with myriad scars from wyvern stings. The man is a greedy wretch who claims he is now immune to the wyverns' venom, after having been stung so many times. He loves telling stories in the Rookery about how he got his many stings, and thinks himself an entertaining storyteller because people listen and applaud. The truth is that the locals are terrified of him, so they humor him while he is in his cups.

ELTURGARD

Ah Elturgard! If any place in the world exemplifies humanity's potential for greatness, it is this nascent nation. Who could forget the shining sight of a host of its Companions, paladins all, riding out on the field, banners taught and snapping, breastplates and shields agleam with the symbol of Elturgard, and each bearing a holy symbol of his or her god—armor for the soul. We have no shortage of the good and the just among my people, but the sheer zeal and genuine bravado the Companions have in pursuit of righteousness seems to me something uniquely human. And it's not just those few touched by the gods who seek these high ideals; Elturgard's armed forces swell with men and women who aspire to join the Companions. They are the Hellriders, so named because long ago warriors of Elturel literally rode through a gate into the Nine Hells to pursue and destroy devils that had been plaguing their people. With these bright examples to look up to, is it any wonder that the common people of Elturgard also tend to be devout in their pursuit of justice and worship of the gods?

Oh how bright Elturgard's light burns! If only it could last. Humans are, after all, short-lived creatures, and fickle in their faith and attentions. Elturgard is the product of just a generation or two of humans, and it seems implausible that it will last many more. Sadly, I think I shall witness Elturgard diminish. But it was a miracle

THE CREST
OF ELTURGARD

that brought about the nation of Elturgard, and perhaps that divine provenance will preserve it.

It began, as all the great stories do, in darkness. Half a century ago, the city of Elturel was a petty power. It had claimed its neighbors' territory under various excuses, putting them under "Elturel's Guard." Then, the city's leader, its High Rider, was revealed to be a vampire. The extent of the vampire's network of charmed servants, undead allies, and willing sycophants took the Hellriders by surprise. An undead plague swamped Elturel, and although its Hellriders made some gains by day, in darkness the vampire and its minions inflicted cruel losses. Each night the good people of Elturel prayed to the gods that dawn might come more swiftly.

Then, on a particularly disastrous night when all seemed lost, dawn did come. A warm golden light suffused the city and surrounding lands, cast down from a golden orb that hung unwavering in the sky, so bright that it seemed a new day had dawned. Caught outside when this miracle appeared, the High Rider and his vampire spawn burned away to dust, and the other undead quailed in its illumination. In short order, Elturel was free.

When the true dawn came, the new sun remained. And it stayed in the sky through the next night, and the night after, and each night from then until now. While some called it Amaunator's Gift, none could say what god granted them this boon. Most saw it as a companion to the sun and to themselves, and so it is known as the Companion. This holy wonder brought pilgrims of all kinds to Elturel. The devout, the curious, the afflicted—all came to bathe in its warmth and see its blessed light

by night. Paladins had always been small in number among the Hellriders, but the Companion drew many to Elturgard, and the best among them was named High Observer to rule in the High Rider's place.

To maintain order among the many faiths of the paladins, a special knighthood was created, named after the Companion sun. These paladins swore to uphold the Creed Resolute, an oath of service to Elturgard and all good people. And thus Elturgard now has both the Companions and the Hellriders.

The post of High Observer is no longer occupied by a paladin, but by a priest of Torm named Thavus Kreeg, and this to me seems fitting. Paladins should be out in the world, using their divine gifts for the good of all, not signing documents behind some desk or dithering with dignitaries. High Observer Kreeg has ruled wisely and well these past forty years or so, but as a short-lived human, he is nearing the end of his years. When he passes or can no longer cope with the demands of his office, I hope that Elturgard can make a smooth transition to equally strong leadership. It is during such change and the struggles for power that result that humans often stray from the righteous path. Perhaps the light of the Companion will show them the way.

ELTUREL'S GUARD

Sometimes called the Kingdom of Two Suns, Elturgard encompasses Elturel, Triel, Scornubel, Soubar, and Berdusk. It also claims and protects many small villages and farms strung along the roads and rivers in the Western Heartlands.

The heraldry of Elturgard—the sun and a smaller companion sun surrounded in a blaze—is familiar to many of us along the roads that lead to and through Elturgard, for it also blazons the armor and flags of its two groups of guardians, the Hellriders and the Companions.

It might be fairly said that the only reason Elturgard can exist as a nation is because of these knights, for it faces threats from all around. The wilderness to the south is home to ravenous monsters, and the serpent kingdom of Najara to the north routinely sends agents—both raiders and spies—to test the strength of Elturgard. The knights can't afford to be anything but vigilant, and fortunately for the folk of Elturgard, they are just that.

I regard crossing the border into Elturgard as a relief, for it usually means the beginning of a safe haven, with a need to set fewer guards at night. Many adventurers find good cause to visit Elturgard, whether pursuing personal goals or seeking sanctuary from the dangers that surround the small nation. Additionally, the High

FORT MORNINGLORD

Several years ago, the entire complement of paladins at Fort Morninglord simply disappeared in a calamitous event that blackened every stone and sealed its doors and windows. The High Observer at the time ordered the fort, a day's ride west of Elturel, to be bricked up, and the curious forbidden entrance, for fear of what evil they might release into the world. The fort remains sealed today, and guards occupy a fortified encampment nearby to patrol this area and serve as a deterrent to adventurers and other ne'er-do-wells who might otherwise try to find whatever is trapped in the fort's depths.

Observer is known to employ groups of adventurers in matters of importance to the nation. Though it has many paladins and clerics in its ranks, outside assistance is essential to the continued defense of the realm.

THE COMPANION

The second sun that sits directly above Elturel burns night and day. This orb is commonly called the Companion, but some ascribe it to one deity or another. Where the natural sun journeys across the sky and disappears at night, the Companion is steady and loyal, ever preventing creatures of darkness from assaulting the city.

This second sun provides daytime illumination to the people of Elturel at all hours, and its illumination is as harmful to creatures vulnerable to sunlight as the sun is. This constant daylight lessens the farther one travels from Elturel, casting a sort of wan dawn light for fifty or so miles around the city. Beyond that, the orb is visible as a bright beacon in the sky. It can be seen clearly at night from as far away as Boareskyr Bridge and Berdusk, looking like an unmoving star low on the horizon. It might be fairly said that every land touched by its light is now under "Elturel's Shield," but such claims raise hackles among Elturgard's neighbors.

THE CREED RESOLUTE

With no clear sign of the source of the Companion and so many faithful arriving in Elturel each day, the first High Observer brought together a cadre of paladins and devised the Creed Resolute. This series of oaths and maxims outlines, among other things, that those who swear by it will not ascribe the Companion to any one god, nor allow religious differences to come between themselves and others. Those who swear the Creed Resolute also promise to serve the High Observer and uphold the laws of Elturgard, and always be in service to the greater good. While originally the Creed Resolute was intended to forge the fractious paladins of Elturgard into the Companions, the oath has since been taken by all among the Hellriders as well. If a Hellrider or Companion oversteps the bounds of the law or good conduct, often a fellow will say "recall the Creed," and soon things are set right.

Though some of the Creed's agents seem unnecessarily stern, the people of Elturgard hold the Hellriders and Companions in the highest esteem. The Companions are without a doubt the champions of the people first and foremost, and the folk of Elturgard love them for it. Though it might be hard to get the Companions to crack a smile, I've found even the lowliest of the guards here willing, without a second thought, to lay down their lives in defense of their people, and the folk of Elturgard know it. Disrespect the Creed, and it isn't the Creed's wrath you face, but that of the local citizenry.

ELTUREL

Elturel is a city on a hill. It stands overlooking the River Chionthar, constantly illuminated by the Companion. A major location along the trade route through the Western Heartlands, Elturel and its environs for many miles around are a safe haven for visitors and citizens alike. Much of this safety comes from the efforts of the

Hellriders, whose cavalry patrol the roads that lead into Elturgard, as well as the paths along the river.

In the city's center, directly beneath the Companion, is a cliff-sided tor that holds aloft the High Hall. This castle, whose walls surround the summit of the mount, is home to the High Observer, and to a great deal of the bureaucracy of Elturgard. A stream runs out of the center of the castle, spawned by the powerful springs in its cellars. It flows north across the tor's top and then down one of its cliffs in a series of waterfalls called the Maidens' Leap. By canal it forms a moat for the eastern Dock District, before it joins the Chionthar. Along the stream across the tor lies the long, narrow garden, an open place of flowers, wooded paths, and arched bridges. The garden is a favorite meeting place for citizens of Elturel and retains a wild beauty in winter. The rich folk of the city dwell nearest the garden atop the tor, while folk in the town below live mostly in tall, narrow homes that are rich in balconies and windows.

Its benefits notwithstanding, the constant illumination that bathes Elturel can be difficult for newcomers to adjust to. Inns and boarding halls usually swathe the windows of their guest rooms in thick cloth to block out the light so that visitors can get some sleep. Without the onset of dawn or dusk to frame the day's labors, citizens rely on the tolling of the bells from the High Hall to denote the start and end of the workday. The lack of natural darkness means the city sees less of the sorts of activities that city folk in other places often undertake at night. Elturel has a low incidence of brawling and ambushes in the alleys around its inns and taverns, and those who would engage in thievery must be especially careful and shrewd to succeed.

OTHER COMMUNITIES

A few other major settlements of note are located within the borders of Elturgard. I describe three of them briefly here.

Berdusk. A large population of artisans drives the activity in the city of Berdusk. Its native nobility, the so-called "First Folk of Berdusk," have made a great show of their piety since the founding of Elturgard, and a great many of the high-ranking priests hail from their families. Over the years a few bad apples in their midst have given Berduskans a reputation for the sin of "false piety"—pretending to a stronger faith than one actually possesses. Though this attitude is disapproved of by the Creed, it has given rise in other parts of Elturgard to the expression "as holy as a Berduskan priest"—which is to say, not very.

Scornubel. Known far and wide as the City of Caravans, Scornubel is the great trading nexus of the Kingdom of Two Suns, and the Elturgard city I am most familiar with. Though responsible for a great deal of the nation's prosperity, it is also the source of plenty of its trouble; Scornubel is a haven for outlanders, many of whom are either troublemakers or folk whom trouble is pursuing. Add to this the machinations of Scornubel's native merchant-princes and the rumors of a thieves' guild somewhere in its walls, and it can be understood why the saying "The High Observer's headache is named Scornubel" has some merit.

Marsh of Chelimber Greycloak Hills

Evereska

Ss'thar tiss'ssun

Soubar. Soubar is a small walled town with supporting farmsteads strung along the road to the north and south. It is a waypoint settlement much like any other except for the existence of the Black Abbey. This dark stone structure once served as a monastery to Bane and lay in ruins for many years. Now priests of Bane have begun rebuilding it, bringing an influx of wealth and trade, along with the many skilled masons and laborers necessary for such a project. Some people question the desirability of a temple to Bane in Elturgard, but those who do are encouraged to recall the Creed. For their part, the priests of Bane have pledged to aid in Soubar's defense against raiding goblinoids and other threats, a promise that gives some solace to the suspicious.

EVERESKA

I would be remiss if I didn't mention Evereska, but I will be brief for I have no desire to publish all its secrets. I shall endeavor to describe my own homeland in as unbiased a way as I might, but I must warn: I am a daughter of the Greycloak Hills, and its mists yet roil through my soul as surely as elven blood does through my veins. Ere I make mention of my home, though, I will discuss the meeting-ground that is the closest most outsiders will ever get to fair Evereska: the Halfway Inn.

THE HALFWAY INN
Evereska lies hidden in the Greycloaks. Our paths to it are secret, cloaked by natural features and magical guise. No significant human settlement stands within a hundred miles west of it, and to the east lies the hungry desert sands of Anauroch.

Strange, then, that the Halfway Inn should stand where it does. Perhaps it is there because, as humans put it, "It is halfway to everywhere." A small village surrounds the titular inn, which is itself not a single building, but a small compound that includes stables and other outbuildings. The folk who live here year-round are hunters, trappers, gold prospectors, gem seekers, smallholders and their families, and it is they who staff the inn when traders come to see what goods can be reaped from the region.

Evereska is self-sufficient, but its citizens in their travels sometimes stop at the Halfway Inn and, if traders are present, exchange goods with them. Whenever I return home, I make it a point to spend at least a night at the inn to see old friends (often much older since last I saw them) and learn what has passed since my last visit.

Elf artisans sometimes come out of the Greycloak Hills to sell their goods here, and some of the best-known can sometimes spark impromptu bidding wars over the right to purchase their wares. My kin don't do anything so pedestrian as set up booths or tables for themselves, but instead deal with a few traders who might be at the inn at the time. These agents then travel out and sell the elven crafts to others, which has given the Halfway Inn an undeserved reputation as Evereska's trading post.

Permit me to state this in as clear a fashion as writing allows: don't venture into the mountains seeking Evereska unless you are in the company of a citizen of Evereska. You will not find such accompaniment easily, for we are determined over the whole of our lives that no outsiders may gaze upon our homes without invitation from the eldest among us. If strangers need to meet with any of us, that is the purpose the Halfway Inn fulfills.

THE REFUGE IN THE HILLS
When I rest at the end of the day and retreat into reverie, I do not revisit the wonders of ancient ruins and majestic creatures I have seen on my wanderings. At those times, I recall the Evereska I wandered as a youth, when I followed a haunting song or a wisp of light among the roiling fogs of the Greycloaks, picked sweet berries in the hollows of the hills, and swam in the cold streams that flowed out of their heights.

Evereska nestles in a sunny canyon, high in the mountains. The surrounding peaks hide it from all but the most powerful fliers who can stand the chill and high winds of their towering heights. Yet should such approach Evereska, its guardians mounted on giant eagles would ensure no ill befell the vale.

Unlike cramped and crowded human cities, Evereska is composed of clusters of buildings throughout the many levels of the great valley, with many a footpath between them. These clusters are separated by clearings, meadows, and small woodland groves—natural spaces just as much a part of the city as the buildings are, their presence essential to our way of life.

With the recent tragedy of Myth Drannor's second fall, Evereska has seen the largest influx of new citizens in many centuries, in the form of our Cormanthan brethren. They have been warmly welcomed into Evereska, but some of our people are concerned that so many new residents will disrupt the peace and balance we've thus far been able to maintain. At the same time, some of the newcomers have reacted unpleasantly to Evereska's reclusiveness, which they see as a form of prejudice or cowardice, and a few of their younger folk have taken it upon themselves to speak on such topics rather heatedly. I'm hopeful that the coming decades will smooth over these differences and sooth the contentions. Evereska is a beautiful place, and I see no reason to mar that beauty with an argument among friends.

FIELDS OF THE DEAD

The expanse known as the Fields of the Dead has been the battleground for myriad wars and skirmishes over the centuries. It is said that the hills that dot the countryside here all hold the dead, and there is some measure of truth to that—many of the hillocks are indeed barrows, raised to house the fallen dead of one faction or nation on either side of a war. I have seen more than one such barrow, either broken open from the outside by those seeking lost treasures, or somehow broken from within.

The Fields of the Dead is a vast, rolling plain of windswept grasses that seems to go on to the horizon in every direction. Regular travelers through the area speak of the "whispers of the dead," the popular term for the sound that results when a breeze rustles the grass. The wind almost always blows here, and it isn't uncommon to smell salt in the air even dozens of leagues inland.

Though this land is uncivilized, it isn't barren. Even if many monsters hide in the tall grass or build burrows in the sides of the hills, the fields represent an opportunity for shepherds and free folk to claim a plot that no one else has yet occupied. Small, stout farmhouses and even a few walled enclosures that contain several such dwellings can occasionally be found a short distance away from the roads and rivers that run through or near the Fields.

The folk of this land are kind but wary, usually willing to share their wells or cisterns, and part with the goods they store away in return for goods in trade. I have met a few who show greater hospitality, letting strangers make camp within the shelter of the low stone walls that surround their steadings. They are a good and honest people, by and large.

Away from the vicinity of these settlements, there are threats aplenty. Small bands of nomadic humanoids traverse these grasslands, as do monsters from out of the Wood of Sharp Teeth to the south, the Trollclaws to the north, or the serpent kingdom of Najara to the east. Occasionally, one of the barrows bulges and vomits forth undead, wakened by some instinct known only to them, or a patch of terrain buckles and collapses in on itself, revealing a sinkhole to warrens beneath.

DRAGONSPEAR CASTLE

Though the structure is crumbled and perpetually shrouded in mist, more than one of the caravans I've guided through these lands have seen Dragonspear Castle from afar and expressed a desire to seek shelter there. As I tell them at such times, it is better to seek shelter inside an opened tomb in these lands, and crawl in to huddle among the warrior dead within, than to seek anything like sanctuary from Dragonspear.

Built by an adventurer named Daeros after he found a wealth of gems in a sunken dwarven settlement, Dragonspear Castle was erected above the very caverns where that settlement—fallen Kanaglym—was interred. Two hundred years ago, sorcerous machinations brought about the fall of Daeros and the opening of an infernal portal in the depths of the castle.

After that event, Dragonspear's ruins were occupied by hobgoblins and myriad bands of bandits, until Waterdeep and Baldur's Gate sent troops to root them out. Discovering that the portal yet existed, but unable to destroy it, they established the Hold of Battle Lions, a fortified temple of Tempus, in an attempt to prevent anything from coming through. In time, though, devils broke through new portals inside the castle's walls and overran the defenders.

Then came the Second Dragonspear War, more than a century ago, during which a strange cloak of mist settled over the castle, and the forces of Waterdeep and Baldur's Gate once more attacked. This time, they defeated the devils, leaving the castle ruined and still cloaked in mists. At least one other time since then, the devils have punched back through, amassing other fell creatures to attack the nearby settlements (notably Daggerford), but they have been fought off by adventurers each time. The most recent stories tell of heroes confronting Red Wizards of Thay and other devilry. I pray that this will be the last time such efforts are necessary, but somehow, I think not.

Today, Dragonspear remains crumbled and mist-shrouded. Rumors say that the castle—seemingly quiescent—has become home to undead horrors of some sort, but no one seems terribly inclined to investigate such claims, so long as they don't threaten the folk who live nearby. Some interested parties out of Baldur's Gate offered me more than a fair amount of coin to investigate the truth of these rumors, though I demurred. I don't fancy myself an investigator or a spy, and I know better than to seek out whatever foulness might have taken hold in this place.

TROLLCLAWS

A tangled landscape of rough hills along the northern edge of the Fields of the Dead, the Trollclaws are home to a great many of the regenerating, bloodthirsty beasts. Exactly what makes these hills such prime ground for trolls is unknown (and a favorite topic of conversation around many of the campfires I've sat at while passing through or near this place), but there's no doubt that they dwell here in great numbers.

Those traveling south to Baldur's Gate or north out of the Fields of the Dead typically travel through the Trollclaws. The Trollclaw Ford, so named for obvious reasons, is the only place for leagues that wagons can safely cross the Winding Water. Important as it is, the site has been occupied by several forces over the years, as evidenced by the ruined remnants of forts and similar buildings nearby. But those claimants have always fallen eventually to prolonged assaults by trolls. My advice is to avoid the region entirely, but if you can't, keep a lit torch handy at all times.

HARTSVALE

I have been to Hartsvale only once, and found it surpassingly beautiful each time. Its wonders are wild and untamed, with even the so-called civilization of the place exuding a kind of primal beauty that is found nowhere else that I know of.

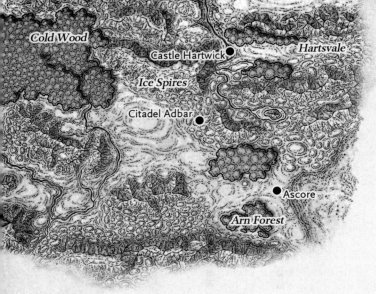

Cold Wood

Castle Hartwick

Hartsvale

Ice Spires

Citadel Adbar

Ascore

Arn Forest

Hartsvale is far in the windswept north, a fertile mountain valley where the Ice Spire Mountains abut the High Ice. The Clear Whirl River, easily the cleanest and coldest I have ever bathed in, flows south into the valley out of the lands of the Endless Blizzard, feeding the rich soil tucked between the northern and southern arms of the Ice Spires. The river splits as it runs through the hilly lands, eventually draining into a series of lakes along the southern edge of the vale. Two small woods also grow in the vale, one along its northern edge, between the vale proper and the northern Ice Spires, and another fed by the lakes on its southern edge.

Originally the home of giant clans and ragtag barbarian tribespeople related to the Uthgardt, Hartsvale was conquered by the hero Hartkiller. He was a giant who had ventured into the lands to the south and learned of their ways. When he came to Hartsvale, he rallied the human tribes, uniting them into a fighting force capable of defeating the giants who tyrannized them, and they threw the giants down, claiming the vale between the mountains for their descendants.

Giants aplenty still dwell in Hartsvale's mountains and forested hills, but they've reached an accord with the humans of the vale. So far as I know, they live peaceably distant from the human lands, and taboos exist among both humans and giants that keep them separate. In my time in Hartsvale, I saw no giants, but surely I saw their works. At the boundaries of lands where humans (and other folk smaller than giants) may not go stand titanic menhirs, likely erected by stone giants.

The folk of Hartsvale are ruled by House Hartwick, a line of royals supposedly descended from Hartkiller. Though human, House Hartwick's scions are all very tall and strong, most standing seven feet in height. The king of Hartsvale sits on the Alabaster Throne in Castle Hartwick, and the many earls of the vale's duchies owe their fealty to him.

Peace has reigned for many years in Hartsvale. Grauman, called the Good King by his people, sits the Alabaster Throne, though his years are advanced. His eldest son and heir, Taumarik, is a young ranger who has recently returned from a three-year journey to explore the North. He came back with a wife, the sorceress Ylienna of Silverymoon, and has begun to take on more of his father's onerous responsibilities. There is some strife in the court, however, for the earls don't seem to trust his "out-vale witch-bride" (a phrase that infuriates Taumarik, but seems to gently amuse Ylienna). For myself, I found the lady Ylienna a delight on the one occasion when I was in her company.

The vale is well guarded, as all jewels should be—in this case by the perils of the mountains and giant-steads that surround it. Nonetheless, a certain strong breed of merchant travels the narrow mountain passes leading into Hartsvale. The dwarves of Citadel Adbar jestingly refer to these people as "goats of coin," for they will cling like such animals to the most precarious of mountain ridges while seeking the opportunities that wait beyond. My own journeys with the goats of coin have impressed upon me the skill of these folk, who brave crumbling paths, avalanche-ridden passes, terrible howling blizzards, and monsters of all sorts to reach Hartsvale and get safely out of the vale again.

It isn't merely the high mountains around the vale that hold dangers. Though the valley has scattered settlements, all of Hartsvale can hardly be considered civilized. In my time traveling these lands (with one of the few goats of coin that refused to be daunted by the fens around Castle Hartwick), I've found these lands to be still frontier-like, similar to some of the wilder portions of the North, particularly in the days before the founding of Luruar and the resettlement of Mithral Hall. Fell beasts aplenty make their lairs in out-of-the-way places across the valley, and raiding bands of ogres often come down out of the mountains.

CASTLE HARTWICK AND STAGWICK

Between two branches of the Clear Whirl River lies a great island on which Hartkiller built his castle. Stagwick, on the east bank of the river, is a small community of folk who work as farmers, fishers, herders, and artisans. These folk do a brisk business, as most outland merchants choose not to journey beyond Stagwick and instead sell their wares to the Hartsvale merchants. Perhaps a third of the merchants who journey to Hartsvale choose to undertake the trip out to the fiefdoms of the earls, who pay more to encourage this behavior.

THE OGRES

For reasons I can't fathom, Harstvale and its surrounding mountain ranges host many tribes of ogres—indeed, not mere family groups, but whole tribes of them! Whereas elsewhere ogres seem to live like bears, near Hartsvale they act more like orcs. Thankfully the brutes are still too stupid for such complex tasks as working metal, but from what I heard in my time in the vale their culture is surprisingly sophisticated. Different tribes worship different gods, Vaprak being the one I heard most about, and these differences in religion apparently set the tribes against each other. From what I heard, both the giants and the people of Hartsvale hate the ogres, a fact for which I'm sure many are grateful. If one or more giants decided to organize the ogres, I don't know if any in Hartsvale could stand against them.

Helm's Hold

Helm's Hold has stood as a place of watchfulness and protection for generations. Ever since its foundation by the Company of Crazed Venturers, travelers have used it as a safe place to rest and recuperate on their journeys. Even during the dark times when Helm ceased showing signs to his faithful, the priests and people at Helm's Hold kept their doors open and their eyes on the road, providing refuge to any who came in peace. This outlook was recently sorely tested, and I'm uncertain if Helm's Hold passed or failed the test.

Even though the Watcher was destroyed just prior to the Spellplague, the faithful toiled on through terrible times to complete a grand central temple for the good of the community and the glory of their god. The kindly clergy of this temple, dubbed the Cathedral of Helm, took in those who had been touched by the plague or rendered insane by the destruction of Mystra's Weave. Sadly, as all too often occurs, corruption crept into the settlement, in the form of predatory creatures and malefactors who sought to experiment on the unfortunates in the care of the temple

In time the leadership of Helm's Hold was itself corrupted, falling into the hands of a shapeshifting succubus, who turned many monks into willing servitors. When her machinations were at last revealed and the battle for Helm's Hold began, other otherworldly forces came to the fore: summoned devils, undead raised from the very crypts of the temple, and tentacled, jelly-skinned things whose origin I dare not consider. With the aid of adventurers from nearby Neverwinter, all were defeated and Helm's Hold at last cleansed.

Order of the Gilded Eye

Among those stalwarts who saved Helm's Hold was a member of the Order of the Gauntlet. This man was Javen Tarmikos, and seeing the horrors unleashed on the world in Helm's Hold, he found his own order at fault. The Order of the Gauntlet doesn't punish the criminal before the crime is committed. When evil arises, members of the order strike and strike hard, but they leave the orcs alone in their mountains and don't disturb dragons in their slumber. After Helm's Hold, Javen found this philosophy flawed. Evils unlooked for can breed in the shadows, growing stronger until they attack. This seemed particularly true of otherworldly threats, such as portals to fiendish realms, evil spirits that seek to possess the living, and the corrupting influences of alien planes.

Javen says he was ruminating on this when he received a sign of Helm's return. In the main chapel, the faithful had erected a new symbol of Helm after the last had been desecrated. Javen says he was gazing at this symbol and meditating on his order's failure when Helm's unblinking eye wept tears of gold. Soon after, uncorrupted priests of Helm's Hold, men and women who had remained ever watchful for Helm's return, experienced their own divine signs. In response to prayers, some were even rewarded with spells. Javen

took those priests and followers from the Order of the Gauntlet loyal to him and formed a new order, swearing them in under the watchful gaze of Helm's still-weeping eye.

The Order of the Gilded Eye is dedicated to protecting the world and good people by rooting out hidden evils and severing connections with other planes. According to their members, it's not enough to fight threats that arise. Many lives can be saved if the signs of evil and those who dabble in darkness are actively sought out and destroyed before they open the gateways to larger threats. Since its founding, the Order of the Gilded Eye has grown in number and its capacity to deal with threats, welcoming exorcists, abjurers, and spies, as well as paladins and clerics of Helm. I've even heard that assassins bear the order's symbol—Helm's eye upon a golden gauntlet curled into a fist—and it is a claim I can't disregard. The Order of the Gilded Eye can be brutal in their pursuit of evil.

Did Helm's symbol weep as Javen Tarmikos and others have said? If it did, was Javen's creation of this order Helm's intention? Is the Helm that has returned from death different from the god whose worship was familiar to me in my youth? How can we mortals know? Helm was ever a god of watchfulness and protection, but that didn't make him a just god, nor a kindly one.

Whatever the truth may be, know this: The Order of the Gilded Eye controls Helm's Hold now. If you hide evil in your heart, or if there is the whiff of something otherworldly about you, ride on. You'll find no sanctuary there.

Places and People of the Hold

Helm's Hold is still a relatively small settlement: a handful of streets that encircle a central marketplace, with sturdy stone-and-timber embankment walls all the way around. In the center of town sits the Heartward, a large marketplace with several rows of stalls radiating out from its central feature, an old gallows that doesn't see much use these days. The market is so named for the shrine to Sune that once stood along its edge. That shrine has since been replaced by a recently constructed temple to Lady Firehair, called the Heartward Hall.

Not far from Heartward lies the town hall, a former inn that has been turned into the council building where the Speakers of Helm's Hold meet. The Speakers are the duly elected representatives of the hold, numbering eight in all, plus the Chief Speaker. The current Chief Speaker is Amarandine Wanderfoot, an older halfling matron who was an adventurer in her day. The Speakers work closely with the Holy Watcher to see to the proper governance of the hold.

A short distance from the town hall lies the Venturer's Rest, a favorite stopping-off point of adventurers in the area, and of the locals who like to sit at the bar and listen to the tales such folk bring with them. The Rest was until recently called the Old Dirty Dwarf, but was rechristened by its new owner, a winsome Chauntean paladin by the name of Kharissa Anuvien. Dame Kharissa claims that one of her ancestors was in the Company of Crazed Venturers, associated with the founding of Helm's Hold, and her quick-rising popularity among the people has won her a seat as a Speaker.

Dominating the skyline of the hold is the great edifice: the Cathedral of Helm. As much a fortification as it is a temple, the cathedral has a small building on its grounds that serves as an orphanage, wards for caring for the sick and injured, as well as a newer addition that houses the mad and deformed who have been brought up from the catacombs.

The settlement enjoys prosperity today, but such benefit was hard-won and requires vigilance to retain. Helm's Hold is vulnerable on many fronts, in large part because of its proximity to Neverwinter Wood—which, if anything, has become more dangerous in recent times. Rumors of maddened treants abound, as well as stories of Uthgardt barbarians once again raiding the trails that lead to the hold.

Worse still, the Holy Watcher has seen premonitions of something unspeakable rising from the depths beneath the hold, bringing down the lowest vaults of the cathedral in its bloody ascension. As a result, the temple has dramatically increased guard patrols in the tunnels, perhaps as a prelude to hiring adventurers to explore the tunnels deep under Helm's Hold for some clue of what those visions might portend.

High Forest

Anyone with even a hint of elven blood can't help but feel it stir upon setting foot in the High Forest. The sheer age and the power of the trees, the depth of their roots, and the wind whispering through their leaves—all these things call to us.

A vast green cloak in the midst of the North, the High Forest is a reminder of ages past, when thick woods blanketed much of Faerûn, and sylvan creatures of all types lived among the trees. Even today the High Forest has barely known the tread and touch of humans, and old growth dominates its flora.

Elven communities in the forest are typically small and often nomadic. In part, this is a reflection of the desire to keep the woods untouched, but there are ruins here, such as those of Ascalhorn—now called Hellgate Dell—that remind us of the fallen cities and empires of the past.

The High Forest once sheltered three great elven realms beneath its boughs, and the bones of those empires still lie tangled in its roots. Many tribes of wood elves—and a few moon elf tribes—still roam the wood protecting these ruins, the monuments to their golden age. Few beyond the borders of the High Forest know much about these elves, who have no single leader and make little contact with the outside world. Travelers in the High Forest must always be wary of elves they meet for they can never be sure of their welcome, and any promises of safe passage might not be honored by the next band of elves.

One elf is leading the effort to change this situation. Known as the Red Lady, or simply the Lady of the Wood, Morgwais is a wood elf who seeks to unite the disparate tribes. She leads the Caerilcarn, the "Council of the Wood," which periodically gathers many tribal leaders together to share information, consult, and deliberate.

Her stated aim is to resurrect the kingdom of Eaerlann, and she has made bold steps in that direction by allying the settlements of Nordahaeril, Reitheillaethor, and Teuveamanthaar (which most know as Tall Trees). As yet though, the elves who believe in this vision are small in number and spread far apart over the eastern reaches of the High Forest.

Fey and sylvan creatures of all sorts—including satyrs, dryads, and treants—inhabit the High Forest. Small wonder that one almost immediately feels the presence of unseen watchers upon entering the woods.

Nowhere in the forest is this feeling more palpable than near the Grandfather Tree, an oak larger than you might imagine possible, which serves as a holy site for the Treeghost tribe of the Uthgardt. Four smaller oaks—enormous indeed, though still smaller than the Grandfather—mark the boundaries of the site, protecting the tree and aiding those whom its spirits determine are worthy, speeding their natural healing. Teleportation magic often goes awry here, and the caverns deep beneath the site are rumored to contain all manner of magical portals.

If it isn't the elves, the fey, or the trees themselves watching visitors, it might be the centaurs who make the High Forest their home, claiming the plateaus near the head of the Unicorn Run. For decades, the centaurs have been growing in number, enough so that they may soon divide their tribes and claim additional lands as their territory. Pegasi and unicorns can be found here, and even some of the fabled aarakocra, the winged birdfolk, live among the peaks at the heart of the wood.

Within the depths of the forest is an entire mountain range known as the Star Mounts. Constant strong winds keep weaker flying creatures from approaching the peaks of the mountains, with the strange exception of the aarakocra, who had an ancestral homeland there before being chased out by a dragon. Most the peaks may be viewed only from afar, and at a distance they seem to glitter from the strange, massive crystals dotting their slopes. They are also known to hold rich deposits of iron and nickel, but no one has mined these mountains in hundreds of years.

The Star Mounts are the source of the waters of the Unicorn Run, which cuts through the rocks of the lower range to form a series of gorges and cliffs known as the Sisters. The sight of the tiered waterfalls is positively breathtaking, well worth the challenge of reaching them. Mist shrouds the Sisters, and feeds the vegetation on the small plateaus of the area. To the north, the headwaters of the Dessarin River flow down from a smaller pair of mountains called the Lost Peaks.

Far less idyllic are the cursed ruins of Karse. Here are the remains of the great heresy of the Netherese wizard Karsus, who sought to claim godhood, slew the goddess of magic, and brought about the end of an age and untold destruction across the entire world.

High Moor

The High Moor was once a place much like the High Forest or the nearby Misty Forest, but during the Crown Wars, thousands of years ago, powerful magic burned

the land such that all that remained was a blasted moor. It is a rocky wilderness infested with trolls and goblinoids and all manner of other dangers for anyone who treks across it instead of going around.

As the name suggests, the High Moor is a raised area extending for many miles of heath, lichen-covered outcroppings, and hidden gullies. Herd animals wander the land, from sheep to rock ponies to the occasional rothé. These beasts graze without great risk, because wolves and other predators that would thin the herds are themselves the prey of the trolls and goblinoids that otherwise rule the moor. These two-legged threats sometimes seed the High Moor with traps, but are normally occupied with fighting and killing their prey and each other. There is something of a cycle to the hunts of the High Moor: wolves are killed off by the hobgoblins one year, leading to more sheep grazing, which brings the trolls out (the local trolls enjoy mutton, it seems), which brings intrepid adventurers to deal with the growing menace, enabling just enough of the wolves to survive that they aren't wiped out completely.

Human barbarians also inhabit the High Moor, living mostly on its western fringes with large herds of sheep and goats, the soil being too thin and too poor for farming. They aren't Uthgardt or related to them, but they might have some distant ties to the Northlanders, as they seem to be of Illuskan stock. They speak a dialect of Illuskan I'd not heard before, and my first meetings with them were quite tense and filled with misapprehension. However, I came to know people from both the Girondi and Belcondi tribes, all of whom acted with bravery, honor, and good humor in my presence. Travelers in this region should note that the human tribes share the suspicion of magic common among many Northlanders, but thankfully it isn't the fanatic hatred shown by the Uthgardt.

There are also some small orc tribes, Redclaw and Blue Feather, among them. The humans and goblinoids both despise the orcs, and my hosts said they allied with one another in the past when the orcs grew great in number.

Orogoth

For such a large expanse, the High Moor contains few known ruins. One such is Orogoth, the former villa of a noble family of old Netheril. Local legends say the family dabbled in dragon magic, attempting to capture those powerful wyrms and acquire their powers. The tales differ as to what folly led to the family becoming immolated in its home, but most agree the culprit was a dracolich, of all things, residing in the ruin and defending the family's wealth. The gods only know what led to the creation of such a creature or what binds it to this place. The answers—if any there be—lie within its lair.

MISTY FOREST

West of the High Moor but heavily influenced by it, the Misty Forest draws its name from the fog that rolls off the heights of the moor to shroud its trees. Melandrach, King of the Woods, rules here and holds the forest as the exclusive domain of the elves. Though game animals roam in plenty, the local humans know well that the elves protect them and punish trespassers who poach in the forest. Even barbarians know better than to hunt here, as they don't wish to draw Melandrach's attention or ire.

Travelers who leave the inhabitants of the Misty Forest alone, and who build their campfires small and solely of fallen branches, are usually permitted to pass, so long as the folk of the forest aren't in a foul mood or stirred up against outsiders for some other reason.

SECOMBER

Just off the High Moor, on the north bank of the Delimbiyr near the Unicorn Run, is the small town of Secomber, on the border between the North and the settlements of the Western Heartlands. Built over the ruins of Hastarl, capital of the ancient kingdom of Athalantar, Secomber is a quiet place where fishers and farmers go about their work, and local folk hire out to hunt or fish, or guide travelers through the area. Skilled guides who know the High Moor well, and can navigate its many dangers and its local tribes, are common—or appear to be, given how often their services are offered. Local stonecutters, primarily from a small clan of dwarves, excavate pink granite from the rock walls on northern edge of the moor.

RHYMANTHIIN: HIDDEN CITY OF HOPE

Stories persist that Faer'tel'miir, an ancient city of Miyeritar, was restored by High Magic sometime in the last century—perhaps even before the Spellplague—up on the High Moor. The restored city of dark, smooth stone, called Rhymanthiin, or "The Hidden City of Hope," appears on no maps, and is reputedly concealed by magic or some other artifice. Supposedly only those who are worthy, without malice in their hearts, may reach it, while others (as the tales have it) "shall not find their way there." Such tale-tellers must be few and far between, as I know of no one who can rightly claim to have seen it, but still the stories seem to have a life of their own.

NAJARA

Gone are the days when the tales of a kingdom of serpents were rumor and hearsay, stories concocted by adventurers and travelers who strayed far off the path and somehow managed to escape. It was once easy to doubt their veracity, for what nation didn't patrol its borders or establish communication (amicable or otherwise) with other nations? The stories of naga and yuan-ti were easy enough to believe, for this area had always hosted such things. But a nation of such creatures?

As we now know, the kingdom of Najara, as proclaimed by the serpents that live within, lies along the northern edge of the Trade Way, northeast of Boareskyr Bridge and southeast of the High Moor. The Winding Water flows through these lands, and its other main geographical features are the Serpent Hills, the Marsh of Chelimber, and the Forest of Wyrms.

I discovered for myself the truth of Najara, the Kingdom of Serpents, when a sage in Baldur's Gate hired me to guide him, his apprentices, and a handful of adventurers to some ruins in the eastern edges of the High Moor. I will forever regret accepting that commission, for not only did half the adventurers turn out to be greedy swine intent on plundering the ruins rather than allowing the sage his study, but their idiocy awoke an ancient spirit that caused most of the group to drop off into a deathly sleep while it consumed their souls. Since I am unaffected by magics that force slumber, I escaped, along with a half-elf among the apprentices to the sage. The spirit chased us across the moors relentlessly, forcing us into the tunnels beneath the Serpent Hills, where we were taken prisoner by yuan-ti patrolling the borders of their domain. The half-elf was hauled away in slaver's chains, but for some reason I was taken to the court of Jarant, the Serpent King. A brief account of that experience follows.

Ancient and evil, the spirit naga Jarant rules the kingdom by virtue of his personal power and thanks to the aid of the *Marlspire of Najara*, a thin silver crown that has protective and other magical abilities. Though he still preferred to remain utterly isolated from the outside world at the time when I met him, ten years ago the Dark Serpent began sending ambassadors to neighboring kingdoms to warn them about the consequences of interfering in Najaran matters. Though I saw the king for but a moment, Jarant's influence in his realm is undeniable, for his name is spoken reverently by all his subjects. A guard might swear "by Jarant's crown" to emphasize an edict, and the yuan-ti who owned the keys to my shackles referred to Najara's laws as "Jarant's will."

No one knows why Jarant chose the time he did to make public his kingdom's sovereignty, or what he hoped to gain by such an act. The yuan-ti ambassadors he sent forth made their king's wishes clear to the nations they visited: leave Najaran prosperity alone, and discourage intruders (such as adventuring types) from violating Najaran borders to steal the fortunes of the serpentfolk. In return, the serpents promised that any caravans and other legitimate travelers passing through Najara's dominion would be unharmed and unhindered—as long as they don't stray from the main route.

Reaction among the places approached raged from one extreme to the other. Darkhold reportedly feted the ambassadors well, and the serpentfolk left with not only an agreement from the Zhentish lords, but also an offer of a possible future military alliance. Not surprisingly, Elturgard refused the edict outright—and in the process of expressing that refusal, bloodshed erupted. The paladins slew all but one of the ambassadors, and sent the survivor back to Jarant's court to communicate their answer.

The other responses to the Najaran ambassadors fell somewhere in between. Acceptances and refusals to cooperate, usually polite, trickled in, but regardless of their substance, Jarant's goal had been accomplished: Najara's neighbors now saw the realm as a nation, no matter whether they viewed it as a potential ally or foe.

The economy of Najara, such as it is, depends on slaves to exist. Slavery is arguably the only actual trade conducted in Najara, with the ruins of Thlohtzin in the Forest of Wyrms serving as a gathering place for those who would stoop so low as to sell slaves to the yuan-ti. Different factions among the Najarans have agents waiting near Thlohtzin, each hoping to strike a bargain with slavers before others arrive. Slaves with unusual abilities or specialized knowledge sometimes set off bidding wars among the yuan-ti. I fear that such was the fate of that apprentice who accompanied me out of the High Moor.

To everyone of any influence who might read this, heed my words: do not be misled. The serpents do not intend to coexist peacefully—they merely wish to use their strange diplomacy as a cloak and a shield, to protect them against the vigilance of others until they are ready to put their plans, whatever they may be, into fruition.

THE COURT OF THE SERPENT KING
I was imprisoned in Ss'khanaja, a mostly subterranean city on the Winding Water, where gathers the court of King Jarant.

During my time in the custody of the Najarans, I learned much about—and from—Dhosun Silverscale. A yuan-ti pureblood in Najara, Dhosun acts as a councilor to the king and often seeks to mitigate Jarant's excesses. I believe that the sending out of the ambassadors was Dhosun's idea, for while I was imprisoned, he visited me several times, asking what I knew of the arts of embassy and ambassadorship. From the talk at court, Dhosun makes no secret of his desire to help his king build a nation whose status equals or outmatches other realms across the face of Faerûn. Jarant keeps him near, it is said, because of all the king's courtiers, Dhosun is the likeliest to attempt to steal away the *Marlspire*. Whether or not he is capable of such an act, I found the yuan-ti naga to be honorable—it was he who secretly arranged the opportunity I needed to escape, and I know he has done likewise for others in the past. I owe him a debt I intend to repay one day.

Another figure of note in the court is the cunning green dragon Emikaiwufeg, often called the Emerald Daughter. She is young for a dragon and still small enough to fit in tunnels leading down to Jarant's audience chamber. Jarant is said to appreciate the twists and turns of her wit. Some courtiers believe that she is frequently kept to hand as a foil to Dhosun, as her slickly vicious nature offsets the Dhosun's more honorable tendencies. For my part, I believe she's biding her time. A great many metallic dragons dwell in the Serpent Hills, and a clear rival for mates, wealth, and power—the green dragon known as Ralionate—lives in the nearby forest of Wyrms.

A variety of advisors and hangers-on can be found within Jarant's court, which is a dangerous place. A trio of yuan-ti warlocks, who claim to have tapped into the vestiges of the ancient serpent deity once worshiped at Ss'thar'tiss'ssun, leads the yuan-ti of Najara, though at court they frequently lurk in the background, simply watching.

SERPENT HILLS
The Serpent Hills is a desolate region of red clay hills and deep, treacherous ravines, featuring stretches of rough, ridged land surrounding tall mesas. Only scrub can manage to grow here, tenaciously clinging to the dry clay. Beneath this perilous territory—filled with serpents and poisonous creatures of all manner—lie the Serpent Ways, a series of intricate, well-guarded tunnels interspersed with caverns and chambers. The passages serve as the main pathways for the folk of Najara through these lands; indeed, it was while resting within such a cavern that the half-elf apprentice and I were captured by yuan-ti. I have since learned that in general, the serpents don't care who tromps *over* the hills, so long as they stay out of the places *under* them. The Najaran capital city, Ss'khanaja, is found in the northwest of the Serpent Hills, but an even larger population of snakefolk live beneath the surface. It is common to find settlements inside the large underground chambers connected by the tunnels, excavations many centuries in age.

MARSH OF CHELIMBER
I didn't have occasion to travel to Chelimber before my "sojourn" with the Narajan court, but I did ask Dhosun about the place. It was through those questions that he divined my intention to escape, in fact, and offered his aid. A vast marshland pocked with sulfurous pools that often gout their steaming contents high into the air, the marsh is inhospitable even to most serpents;

the majority of the denizens in these lands are lizard-folk. Once a Netherese principality, ruled by vampires, and then a holding of the Zhentarim, the Marsh of Chelimber is solidly within the grasp of Najara today. Though each tribe of lizardfolk is dominated by a chief-tain from among their kind, each of those leaders has sworn fealty to the King of Najara.

FOREST OF WYRMS

In the end, it was through the Forest of Wyrms that I fled Najara, though Dhosun advised me against doing so. Ultimately, I chose it for the same reason he tried to discourage me: because only a fool would enter this wood intentionally. The forest is infested with a great many serpents of both normal and monstrous varieties.

Sages who have studied the serpent-life of the forest claim that some force seems to draw ophidian creatures here and then changes them—varieties of snake that ought not be poisonous bite with envenomed fang in this forest, and most breeds of snake grow to nearly double their size here. Ralionate, an ancient green dragon apparently not aligned with the yuan-ti, makes this forest her lair. It is good terrain for her; tall redwoods and coarse pines create a dense, dark canopy.

Dhosun warned me that the ruins of Ss'thar'tiss'ssun, an ancient temple-city, lie in the northern fringes of the forest. At some point in the distant past, humans built a small settlement, once called Serpent's Cowl, above these ruins, but it now stands empty, likely due to the depredations of yuan-ti. Though discernible as little

more than low hills in the forest today, Dhosun told me that deep inside the ruins lies the Shrine of the Cowled Serpents, a site of pilgrimage for the serpent-folk.

A place of great danger within the forest is Thlohtzin, once the citadel of a lich and now an important site in Najara's slave trade. Slavers from around the region know that the serpent-folk pay good coin for slaves brought here. They are then usually transported to other places in Najara for service.

I chose to make my escape from Najara through the Forest of Wyrms because, though serpent-infested, it is a woodland yet, and I am at home in such places. I moved through its shadows, remaining deep enough within the forest to avoid notice but not so far as to come near its heart, and then skirted its edges until I could see the hills of Trielta in the distance.

TRIELTA HILLS

In the rolling terrain of the Trielta Hills, scattered with small settlements of gnomes and halflings, life seems pastoral and idyllic. Halfling farmers tend to their plots, and gnome miners scrape out the interior of the hills seeking the bits of gold and silver they may find waiting there. No warlords threaten this land, no liches or drag-ons plot to seize it for themselves. There are no great castles to covet here, nor ruins to pillage. All told, the place seems dull and unremarkable.

That, of course, is just the way its residents like it. They enjoy their solitude, which is broken only rarely.

The hills of Trielta do occasionally offer up some impressive bounty, in the form of heretofore-undiscovered gold and silver. While such finds are usually small lodes that are played out almost before others become aware of them, Trielta has played host to full-on gold rushes from time to time. Someone stumbles on a particularly large vein of ore, and prospectors and fortune-seekers come pouring in by the dozens. Trieltan folk tend to see these occasional influxes of gold-hungry seekers the way other settlements look upon periodic plagues of locusts: aggravating, inevitable, and thoroughly disruptive, but also part of the natural order, and so nothing to get bothered about.

Indeed, even the largest of these discoveries isn't so lucrative as to be worth the construction of the full-scale mining operations that can be found in other lands. No large nations or trading consortiums are waiting in the wings to invade and take over the mines of Trielta. They are what a dwarf acquaintance of mine once referred to as "scratch mines"—close-to-the-surface operations, with decent yield for a small amount of digging, but not worth the construction of "proper" (by which he of course meant dwarven) mines.

I was in Trielta resting after my escape from Najara when just such an outbreak of "gold on the brain" (as the locals term it) occurred. Though most of those who come at such times are honest prospectors seeking to make their fortunes, the sudden opportunity for wealth does attract less scrupulous sorts, including all manner of thieves, swindlers, and claims-jumpers—not to mention monsters that prey on unlucky or ill-prepared miners who unknowingly invade their territory.

The most intense traveling I've done through these hills was in pursuit of a band of marauding lizardfolk. The head of the kindly gnome family I was staying with was taken prisoner, along with his oldest son. I helped the local halfling sheriff and the small band of militia he put together to track the band, and to do so quickly, rescuing the captives. I've been welcomed in this area ever since, and have gotten to know the goodly folk here well.

HARDBUCKLER

At the southern edge of the hills lies the walled settlement of Hardbuckler. It is a town of mostly gnomes, with the occasional human, halfling, or half-elf among their number. It is one of the best-defended towns I've visited, with a several batteries of ballistae on impressive cog-run cranking mounts that allow for a nearly constant cycle of firing and reloading from any of the wall emplacements. Though the folk of Hardbuckler don't have cause to use them very often, these weapons usually discourage the bandits, raiders, and occasional orc bands that would lay claim to Hardbuckler's wealth.

The town eschews the sort of street network that tends to delineate most large settlements; instead it has a single street running inside the circular town wall, and another pair of straight roads crossing the town north-to-south and east-to-west that meet in the center of town in a crossroads marketplace. Many buildings structured for larger folk line these streets, for taller folk tend to prefer the comfortable familiarity they provide, but the rest of the town is made up of a series of narrow paths between the smaller-proportioned buildings that are the homes of the city's gnomes.

The first time I walked along these tight lanes, I felt as though I was only seeing a small portion of the actual settlement, and I was right. Later I discovered that beneath the slate-roofed houses, with their modest little adjoining gardens behind plank fences or fieldstone walls are the tunnels that constitute the true thoroughfares of Hardbuckler.

Beneath each small dwelling is an extensive cellar, often three or more levels in depth. These spaces are where the industrious folk of Hardbuckler engage in their livelihoods. Some of the cellar spaces are shops or workspaces for artisans who sleep in the house above. Other of these croftholds rent out their extra space to travelers, setting aside a few rooms for rent, and using a single large space as an open taproom, serving the sort of fare one might find in an inn. The food in such an establishment is odd—a great deal of mushrooms, potatoes, turnips, dense lichens, and stews made of shrews and voles—but filling and tasty in its own way.

The chambers in these underground inns are well heated by generous hearths, and thus provide for very comfortable accommodations. More than a few merchants arrange their travels so as to be in Hardbuckler ere winter arrives, so that they can spend the cold months beside a hearth, with a slice of fried pie in one hand, and a tankard of bitter gnomish stout in the other.

Any cellar space not devoted to another purpose is used for storage rather than being left vacant. Almost every family in the town has some space that it uses for its own needs or rents out for use by others. Those who buy storage from a Hardbuckler must purchase their storage crates and other necessary goods from local artisans, who also make locks, latches, waxy sealants for waterproofing crates and boxes, and the like. The crates are all built to specific sizes, with shelving and space in the cellars measured so that each container fits snugly and exactly.

Hardbuckler has a well-paid wizard who provides magical security for stored items, for those who wish it. Outlander wizards aren't permitted to lay wards or protections on goods destined for the cellars—such must be applied by Daelia Inchtarwurn, the latest wizard in a long line of folk who have worked in Hardbuckler over the generations. She wears a set of magical bracers passed to her by her father.

RURAL SETTLEMENTS

Most of the outlying settlements in the Trielta Hills consist of a dozen or two dozen halfling or gnome families, living in homes molded gently into rolling hills. Relatively shallow valleys serve as agricultural land, while the slopes are used for growing vine crops (such as pumpkins and strawberries) or grazing small herds of the large-horned sheep many of the halfling families keep, or the ornery braid-bearded goats favored by gnome goatherds.

Most of these small communities aren't exclusively populated by halflings or gnomes, since such groups seem to prosper better when members of both races

Forest of Wyrms

Boareskyr
Bridge

Trade Way

Trielta Hills

Northdark
Wood

Hardbuckler

The
Reaching
Woods

Triel

are in residence. Halfling families often focus on agricultural endeavors (aside from the small fungi gardens many gnomish households maintain in their cellars), while the area's miners are almost exclusively gnomes. Both folk work as herders, with halflings favoring sheep, and gnomes goats, as well as artisans of all sorts. Each community has a sheriff who maintains peace and leads defense—a role most often fulfilled by a halfling, I've found, though gnomes will certainly rise up in defense of their homes and neighbors when called upon.

Some of the rural settlements mark the former locations of mines that have been played out. It isn't uncommon for halflings to move in where a gnomish mine have been abandoned, fixing up the surface entrances into acceptable, comfortable homes, with built-in tunnels that worm through the settlement. These passages might be helpful for defense or escape, but they are most often used when it's raining out to reach a neighbor's door and borrow a cup of honey, so as not to get oneself wet or track mud everywhere.

On occasion, a community that sports large dwelling-tunnels, with ample space for larger folk (or "big'uns," as the local gnomes say), turns its settlement into an establishment that caters to such clientele. The inns I know of are the Merry Mine-Lass, the Pipe and Hearthstone, and the Giants' Respite, my favorite.

Each of these settlements is impressively self-sustaining. When official leadership is needed, the eldest halflings and gnomes are called upon to act in that capacity, but amity is the heart of community life in these hills. It is a shameful act among the Trieltans to refuse to reach a peaceable accord with one's fellows over some dispute. The folk here enjoy their simple lives, although I've come across a half-dozen or so young adventurers who hail from here, seeking out the newness of the world as a contrast to the familiarity of their homeland.

Few dangerous creatures lurk in the hills—they are so densely settled (on and beneath the surface) that there is little space for monsters to lair. Cruel or ravenous creatures do occasionally creep into Trielta, mainly from the Forest of Wyrms, but such incursions don't last long—after a few sheep (and possibly a shepherd or two) are eaten, the sheriffs waste no time in forming a posse to hunt down or chase off the predators before they can do more harm.

Now, sad to say, this situation might be changing for the worse. According to recent letters I have received from friends in these hills, parties of Najaran raiders have become more common and numerous. My friends fear that the threat from the Serpent Kingdom to the north will force Trieltans to seriously consider putting up an active defense of their lands for the first time in generations.

UTHGARDT LANDS

When I was newly departed from my homeland and first found my way to the North, I encountered a band of Uthgardt nomads on the trail—a part of the Elk tribe, led by a warrior named Gyrt. It was a tense meeting.

I think the only reason I was not killed on sight is that I was an elf traveling alone. I think they feared I was a wizard. Uthgardt hate all magic but that of their shamans and any enchanted weapons and armor they find, but a wizard willing to walk the wilds alone could be a powerful one. Traveling as we were on a grassy plain, we could see one another for some distance. Since I didn't strike them down with lightning from afar, they were willing to approach peaceably.

Still, they stopped when they were within bowshot and seemed to be arguing about whether to shoot me. I waited as patiently as I could until one who seemed to be their leader addressed me in heavily accented Common. I replied a greeting in Bothii, their own ancient language, which again set the group to argument. At last, the leader dismounted and approached me, giving her name as Gyrt. Glad was I then that I took the time to learn the language from a learned friend in Evereska!

In anticipation of any demand, I offered Gyrt a fine dagger from Evereska, as well as a necklace I wore. For her band I offered a bag of baubles I'd brought for such an occasion. Pleased with my gifts and assured that I was no wizard, Gyrt and I sat down to talk. I asked to share her campfire for the night, and Gyrt made space for me. That was my first meeting with Gyrt, but it wouldn't be my last, nor my last encounter with Uthgardt. I'm grateful to my friend Gyrt for teaching me so much about her people, for it has allowed me and many fellow travelers to see Uthgardt and live to tell the tale.

Over the years, as I earned Gyrt's respect and she mine, we became friends, and I came to know her three sons as well. Though Gyrt died some decades ago, I still visit her children, whom I played with when they were young. They now have children of their own, and all call me auntie.

During my time with Gyrt and her kin, the people of the Elk explained much to me about the workings of their tribe—their view of the world and their place in it, their traditions and the laws they live by. I came to realize, as I came across other Uthgardt tribes in my travels, that much of what is true for the Elk tribe is true for other Uthgardt. Though they comport themselves in seemingly disparate groups honoring different totems, Uthgardt have much in common. What follows is what I have learned of the people who call themselves "children of Uthgar."

Though the Uthgardt each belong to a given tribe, these are markers of identity, rather than coherent populations. In my experience, it is rare outside of occasional large events (such as the ascension of a new chieftain, or certain religious gatherings) for all members of a single tribe to come together in one place. Instead, the Uthgardt tend to travel in bands, groups of tribesfolk that number between a dozen and a hundred, usually twenty to fifty. These bands generally consist of several family groups, each led by a matriarch or patriarch. In many ways, these folk are similar to nomadic *Tel'Quessir*, in that they make their decisions by consensus among the heads of the families, and disagreements are handled efficiently: those who don't like the decision of the majority go their own way, forming a new band or joining a different one.

The Uthgardt are spread across the North, rarely found farther south than the High Forest. There is no nation of Uthgardt to which they belong; instead, each tribe has a central ancestral mound, regarded as a holy site. Gyrt told me that the holy site of the Elk tribe is at a place called Flint Rock, somewhere in the Evermoors. She, understandably, never offered to take me there, and I was never foolish enough to ask.

By and large, the Uthgardt are a hunting people who rely on game for much of their sustenance, favoring large herd animals such as elk, rothé, and deer. Young men and women looking to make a name for themselves sometimes build their reputations by hunting dangerous predators and great beasts: bears, great cats, large boar, and even monsters such as wyverns, owlbears, and displacer beasts.

Some tribes put the prowess they demonstrate in hunting to good use in another endeavor, for which the Uthgardt are well known: raiding. As a rule, the Uthgardt engage in raiding only in remote areas—meaning that the closer a potential target is to civilization, the less likely it will be set upon. The raiders prefer to strike against wealthy merchant caravans and nobles' baggage trains, which offer the likelihood of fine foods, alcohol, and jewelry that Uthgardt wear as trophies and trade among themselves. For the most part, Uthgardt have little use for coin, so travelers hoping to buy their way out of a confrontation are advised to offer something else.

Uthgardt don't see national boundaries or the bonds of civilization that tie a merchant to a farmer whose house the merchant passes on the road. To them each interaction with us—meaning we who aren't Uthgart—is different. Thus, an Uthgardt band that raids in one season might come to trade during the next. They do understand the concept of belonging to a larger group, and that those groups might be in conflict. After all, each tribe of Uthgardt has its ancestral enemies among the other Uthgardt tribes. Yet when I attempted to explain how I, and elf from Evereska, was connected to folk in Waterdeep or Silverymoon, Gyrt just laughed. She had not seen these cities, so I might as well have said I knew folk who lived on the moon. When I mentioned Yartar and Red Larch, places that I knew Gyrt's band had passed near, she laughed still harder. To her I was too great, too "strong" as she put it, to have any

THE UTHGARDT TRIBES AND THEIR TERRITORIES

For most Uthgardt tribes, the only stability in their history is the site of their ancestral mound. Most of the Uthgardt holy sites have existed since antiquity, but the fortunes of the tribes that revere them have hardly been static. Following are brief descriptions of the Uthgardt tribes today.

Blue Bear. The easternmost of the Uthgardt are the Blue Bear—thought destroyed more than a century ago—who have recently emerged from inside the High Forest and reclaimed their ancestral mound at Stone Stand, just south of the Moon Pass and north of the forest. The Blue Bears have reoccupied much of their old territory in the time since they returned to prominence, though they don't venture near Hellgate Keep, considering it a taboo place.

Black Lion and Red Tiger. North of Blue Bear territory, in the Glimmering Wood, is Beorunna's Well, a settlement of some size that near the ancient ancestral mound of the Red Tiger tribe. The settlement was founded some time ago by members of the Black Lion tribe, who put down roots here rather than continuing to live as nomads.

Though the Red Tigers are less than comfortable with the present situation, they consider Beorunna's Well their holy site, so they make the best of things. Bands of Red Tiger tribespeople often winter in Beorunna's Well, and many of its hunters and trappers use the settlement as a place to sell the leather and furs they acquire in nearby forests.

Sky Pony. In a part of the Glimmerwood called the Moonwood stands the One Stone, the ancestral mound of the Sky Pony tribe. These are a people divided; half of the tribe has settled and built a sizable steading around the One Stone, similar to what Black Lion has done at Beorunna's Well. The other half of the tribe considers this act an insult to their totem, so they launch raids on the settlement, burning as much of it as they can and then escaping.

Tree Ghost. In the depths of the High Forest stands the Grandfather Tree, the ancestral mound of the Tree Ghost tribe. The Tree Ghosts split off from the Blue Bears long ago and all but disappeared into the forest, although occasional reports reach civilization that they are still alive and can sometimes be seen clustered around the Grandfather Tree. Some sages postulate that the newly reborn Blue Bear tribe might well be Tree Ghost Uthgardt who are following a call from a revived Blue Bear totem.

Great Worm. The Frost Hills, a small southern spike of the Spine of the World Mountains just north of the Evermoors, is the site of Great Worm Cavern, the ancestral mound of the Great Worm tribe. These Uthgardt are notoriously reclusive; it has been twenty years since the tribe has sent raiding parties out anywhere but against the orcs of the Spine Mountains.

Black Raven. As forbidding as the Spine of the World Mountains they roam, the Black Ravens are fanatical in their adherence to the old Uthgardt ways. Ranging out from Raven Rock, their ancestral mound deep inside the mountains, they have been known to send raiding parties as far south as Silverymoon, but their most frequent targets are the caravans that come in and out of Mithral Hall.

Elk. The Elk are fierce raiders and savage killers throughout their nomadic range: the Evermoors and the plains east of the Dessarin and lower Surbrin river valleys. Of the Uthgardt tribes, they are the most arrogant, surly, and self-indulgent. Considered by many to be little more than bandits, they often raid other tribal settlements for food, plunder, and sport.

connection to places she saw as providing prey for her tribe.

If a band of Uthgardt come upon your campsite, my advice is this. First, do what you can to hide all signs of magic or spellcasting. Then show them hospitality and invite them to warm themselves. If you have jewelry or a fine weapon, offer these gifts to the one who seems like the leader. Ask how their hunting goes, and give them a chance to brag. Be appreciative, but not obsequious. Tell them you have heard of the prowess of the Uthgardt people—their hunting skills and strength first and foremost—but attribute these claims to a tribe other than their own. The strongest among the band will insist on the chance to prove him- or herself better than the stories you've heard, and will want you to bear away tales of about his or her tribe instead.

You or one of your companions might need to agree to a challenge of some kind, a feat of strength or a bout of fisticuffs, by which the band may measure your prowess. It doesn't greatly matter if you win or lose, though. Simply express a desire or a willingness to compete, and you will earn some measure of respect. If you win the challenge, be gracious, and express gratitude that you finally found someone of great status to test yourself against. If you lose, be self-effacing and rueful, and give the victor the best part of the meal at hand.

This advice will not always work, of course. Some bands aren't so easily assuaged, particularly if they are out deliberately hunting you or folk like you. At all times, remember that these are a proud and strong people with a fierce love of life and its simple pleasures. Demonstrate an outlook complementary to theirs, and they might make of you a comrade. Show fear or contempt, and they will respond with quick violence.

THE PEOPLE OF UTHGAR

The Uthgardt trace their origins back to the mighty hero Uthgar, a warrior without compare. During my time with his tribe, Gyrt spoke freely of the tales of Uthgar that have been passed down among his people. The saga begins in the distant past when the humans of the North lived in fear and isolation. Great spirits roamed the forests of the North, preventing humans from banding together to rise up against them. Into this turmoil came Uthgar, who challenged each of the great spirits, one at a time, besting them and subjugating them to his rule. Each of the defeated spirits became embodied in the totem of one of the groups of humans who followed and revered Uthgar. Thus were born the tribes of the Uthgardt, each taking the name of their totem spirit.

The sites of Uthgar's victories are marked even today with the great ancestor-mounds of the Uthgardt. Each is said to have been built over the remains of a tribe's totem spirit, along with the tribesfolk who died while helping Uthgar to fight the creature.

A tribe lays claim to the territory around its ancestral mound for many leagues, declaring it as the grounds in which the tribe hunts and sets up camps. Generally speaking, Uthgardt bands of a given tribe will range as far as two to three weeks' travel away from the tribe's ancestral mound, with raiding parties going much farther afield. These holy sites are scattered through the North; in almost all cases, the exact location of one is known to few people other than members of that tribe.

Almost all of the original tribes of the Uthgardt are active in the North today. Even a tribe thought to be lost or destroyed might be represented somewhere by a small number of humans who claim to be descended from the one of the tribes of old, but such people, where they exist, aren't numerous by any means, and their claims are often spurious.

The Uthgardt take their ritual practices and taboos very seriously. Most taboos and traditions vary from tribe to tribe, but at least one stricture is universal among the Uthgardt: magic other than that of the shamans or the magic of weapons and armor is forbidden.

The priests of the Uthgardt revere their ancestor-god and also invoke the names of their totems as intercessors with the Father of the Tribes. Their ethos is simple: strength is rewarded with more strength, and when strength fails, it is because a person is not worthy.

WARLOCK'S CRYPT

On the western edge of the Troll Hills lies an area of bizarre terrain: shattered rubble is strewn across the landscape, between and among mounds of upturned earth and deep furrows of the sort one commonly sees in the wake of trebuchet blows that miss their mark. Farther in from the perimeter of this blasted land lies a scattered mess of buildings, some relatively intact, others half-collapsed and leaning on their neighbors.

In the center, rising above it all, is a handful of twisted towers looking for all the world like talons clawing at the sky. These towers can be seen from a good distance, seemingly unharmed by the cataclysm that produced the damage around them. Indeed, because of their pristine condition, some folk conjecture that these towers must have been built after that event.

The truth of the place now called Warlock's Crypt is something different altogether. All of the structures visible here, from the now-shattered outbuildings to the central towers, comprised a city that floated atop a disc of stone during the time of ancient Netheril. When the ancient and wicked magics of the Netherese failed, this city plummeted from the sky; the chunks and slabs of stone scattered about the site are not natural terrain, but are the shards of that disc.

My Only Visit

I have been to the Warlock's Crypt but once, in the days of my youth before I knew better. I was hired by Daerismun Aerath, one of the Avowed—the esteemed scholar-monks of Candlekeep—to guide him there. He was writing a treatise on the place and desired firsthand experience of the locale. Fresh as I was from Evereska, I'd never heard the warnings of the wise regarding this site. I am either extraordinarily beloved of Solonor, or stupidly lucky, to have made it back out alive. Tragically, Daerismun was not so fortunate.

As we approached, this ruined cityscape seemed uninhabited. Its expanse is fairly limited, and consists almost entirely of a mess of destroyed buildings and massive boulders.

The central towers were apparently preserved by some aspect of their magical construction—which isn't to say that they were entirely unaffected by the crash. Upon closer inspection, one of the central towers has a great crack running along its western edge, and several of the others display a degree of damage.

As we came even closer to the towers, they appeared to be anything but abandoned. In their windows flickered occasional eldritch lights, and on their sides we could see indistinct shapes scampering across the surface. These buildings were crafted to appear as though clad in black mail, made of overlapping plates and slightly discordant, off-center architecture creating the impression of joints that might bend at any moment.

The towers, joined in a rough circle by walls of smooth black stone, form a perimeter around the heart of the Crypt—which can be seen only from a terrifyingly close vantage. Obscured and protected by the towers are several strange plots of land: some barren, others overrun with twisted, thorny flora not found in nature. Rail-less bridges connect these towers at various points, and all of them spiral around the heart: that which is reputedly the demesne of the lich-king Larloch himself, who has also been called the Shadow King.

Threats and Defenses

I warn you: do not come to this place. And if you must, do not tarry, for its defenders are brutal and bloodthirsty, as inimical to life as any plague or poison, and they take delight in the suffering of those who come into their reach.

This place is rife with undead, of all varieties. In addition to the Shadow King, the Crypt houses several other liches, undead sorcerous vassals to Larloch. He calls upon their power when he has need, but otherwise leaves them alone to conduct the experiments and plots he demands of them. Though he once bound their influence tightly, reports suggest he has begun giving them a greater lead on their leashes, for magical horrors that could well be the result of their experiments have been seen unleashed in the Troll Hills and Troll Forest around the ruins.

Such monstrosities are also common prowling the ruins of the Crypt itself. During my brief sojourn into this place, I identified several creatures that likely began their lives as griffons, owlbears, trolls, and even a beholder, but they had become twisted and nearly unrecognizable. What it is these liches do to these creatures is a question for minds far more wise than mine—I know only that the first such abomination I fought nearly killed me, and I barely escaped from the others we sighted.

The Crypt has defenses other than monsters, as well. My companion Daerismun asserted that it was protected with layers of "spell webs," constructions of magical energy waiting to unleash spells against those who stumbled into them. I had the terrible opportunity to see one of them in action, when the Avowed scholar unknowingly breached one of those so-called webs and set off a ball of fire, which ignited with himself at its center.

As one might imagine, this blast drew the attention of all manner of twisted predators and hungry undead, which came forth to investigate. I don't know how these creatures kept from being caught in these traps, or if they had simply dwelt here long enough to know how to avoid them. Before I could give the matter any thought, I was forced to flee, and I don't intend to ever return.

Luskan

Anyone who goes to Luskan should know about its ruling Ships and the Arcane Brotherhood. The Ships of Luskan have been described as bands of pirates, but that characterization misses how deeply ingrained the Ships are to the society of Luskan and the mentality of its citizens. Attack a Ship member and you might incur not just the wrath of the Ship, but of much of the city as well. As for the Arcane Brotherhood, one member of it may or may not come to another's aid, but know that each of these egotistical mages is eager to prove his or her magical prowess, and none can afford to show weakness before the folk of Luskan.

Luskan, the City of Sails, spans the icy River Mirar, which tumbles from the Spine of the World, races past Mirabar, and then plunges toward the sea. The swift river has cut deep here, and Luskan rests atop two escarpments on either side, with sheer, forty-foot bluffs of gray stone rising above the water. Around the city's perimeter, thick stone walls with squat towers provide defense. The southern gate, called the Twin Teeth, boasts the most impressive towers, standing twice as tall as the city walls, and bedecked with crenellations and arrow slits enough for numerous defenders, in a show of strength toward the southern approach.

The Ships

Within the city walls and on the nearby waters, Luskan is ruled by its Ships and their five High Captains:

- First High Captain Beniago Kurth
- Second High Captain Barri Baram
- Third High Captain Dagmaer Suljack
- Fourth High Captain Throa Taerl
- Fifth High Captain Hartouchen Rethnor

The five High Captains take the names of their Ships when they ascend to leadership. The captains are the highest authorities in Luskan; they and the members of their Ships conduct themselves as a sort of nobility, albeit one that isn't hereditary.

Despite the name, each Ship is not a single vessel, but an organization of stalwarts owing allegiance to one another and to their captain, whom they elect for life. To be a member of a Ship is a select privilege, one that only one in ten of Luskan's residents can claim.

The five Ships of Luskan are more than gangs of pirates. They are fellowships of people who live, train, work, make love, and go to war with each other. To join one is a mark of honor and continues a grand tradition that Luskar associate with democracy, self-determination, and individuality.

Each Ship has its own symbol and colors. Members of a Ship often wear their colors, decorate their round shields with the symbol and colors, and tattoo themselves with the symbol. Like their Northlander relations, Luskar Ship members regularly tattoo their faces, but instead of representing their island, the tattoos are either personal marks or tattoos of their allegiance to their Ship.

Membership in a Ship is voluntary, but once undertaken it is until death. To join a Ship, a Luskar must be of fighting age (fourteen or so, for humans), and possess at least one sword or axe, one spear, and three of the sturdy, bossed shields the Northlanders prefer. Each Ship accepts new candidates from time to time to fill vacancies caused by death, but as a rule, the Ships don't expand their ranks by taking on a large number of new members at one time.

Each Ship has some number of sailing vessels, the size, crew, and type of which help to determine the influence of the Ship's High Captain and its rank within the city. The current First Ship, Kurth, has so many vessels that it nearly outnumbers the next two Ships combined, and its membership is so numerous that Ships Suljack, Taerl, and Rethnor could merge and still not equal it.

The laws of the city govern the behavior of the Ships and their captains, decreeing the Ships responsible for the city's defense, its administration, and the management of its resources. Beyond these universal tasks, each captain takes on other duties as desired in order of that Ship's standing in the hierarchy, leaving less

glamorous and less lucrative tasks to the captains and Ships of lower rank.

Since each of the Ships has the ability to take what it likes and leave what it doesn't want to the lesser Ships, a strict division of duties has arisen among them.

Ship Kurth controls the city's docks and activity occurring thereupon. Among the most profitable of the merchandise that passes through the port are weapons and tools from Ironmaster, and ambergris for the perfume trade.

Ship Baram operates Luskan's fishing industry. The food it provides is so vital to the city's welfare nowadays that Baram has risen to Second Ship on the strength of its successful forays out to sea.

Ship Suljack holds sway over, and conducts most of, the piracy and raiding that originates out of Luskan. It occasionally passes the more meager opportunities down to Taerl.

Ship Taerl, recently elevated from Fifth Ship, had been accustomed to taking the hindmost. Now its workers and sailors happily accept chances for profit handed down from above, and just as happily delegate the most menial and undesirable chores to Rethnor.

Ship Rethnor engages in few worthwhile activities aside from guard duty, which is a poor source of income. Rethnor toughs sometimes roam the streets of Luskan, looking for a quick and perhaps violent way to grab some coin.

PEOPLE AND LAWS

Without question, the people of Luskan show their Northlander heritage. They raid ships and coastal settlements, engage in interdiction and piracy, and value strength of arms above most other qualities. During Luskan's long history on the Sword Coast, however, the city has adopted many of the attitudes of mainland folk. Luskar don't kidnap people from other settlements or tribes, and they hold that women have social standing equal to men (two of the High Captains, Suljack and Taerl, are women). They don't distrust magic, as their island brethren do. Slavery is, at least nominally, illegal in Luskan, though a slave taken and sold at sea is usually overlooked by authorities.

The law in Luskan is supposed to be upheld by soldiers of the Ships, who are empowered to arrest criminals and bring them before the Magistrates of the city. In practice, arrests are as often made by mobs, but the result is the same: an appearance before the Magistrates. Each of the five Magistrates is chosen by a High Captain, but need not be a member of that captain's Ship. The Magistrates are, at least officially, neutral. Most citizens have their cases decided by a single one of these judges, but a dispute involving a Ship member is heard by all five.

TRADE AND COMMERCE

Luskan doesn't officially tax its citizens; the city makes its money through trade, fishing, piracy, and raiding. The defense of the city comes at the expense of the Ships, paid for by the profits of those activities as well as the protection money the Ships extort from businesses and homes to keep the thieves and gangs at bay. Bribery

Raven Rock

Mirabar

Fireshear

BlackfordRoad

River Mirar

Luskan

Blackford Crossing

Morgur's Mound

Gauntlgrym

Mount Hotenow

is a common practice, a seemingly accepted means of gaining the favor of one of the High Captains to obtain fishing rights, earning an advantageous decision from the Magistrates, or having a business rival or undesired suitor arrested, accosted, or roughed up.

Given its status as the harbor that feeds the goods of Mirabar to the Sword Coast, bridging the coast with the utter north, and offers the only convenient crossing of the River Mirar for many miles, Luskan makes considerable coin as a crossroads. Merchants wishing to avoid Luskan can choose to use the Blackford Crossing, some thirty miles upstream, eventually connecting with the Blackford Road on the northern bank, but the savvy know that Luskan's Ships control the cable-guided ferries at the crossing, and demand tolls based on the size and contents of the goods being ferried across. The Blackford Road still bears the ancient marks of the dwarven realm of Gharraghaur, reminding travelers of whose wealth sustains the region.

North of the city, the Northern Means heads up toward Icewind Dale. Not many take this route without purpose, but scrimshaw from the dale finds its way into Luskan, where those who would purchase it can do so without going any farther into the frozen terrain.

The north side of the city, known as North Bank, is devoted almost entirely to warehouses, caravan yards, and workspace. It includes the Mirabar Shield, the fortified compound that represents Mirabar's trading interest in Luskan. Mirabar uses it as a base to trade with the Sword Coast and the islands of the Trackless Sea.

The main city stands on the southern side of the River Mirar. North of Reaver's Run is the Reach, where most of the homes and smaller businesses are located. South of the Run are the slums, the "bad" area of town. Near the slums is the Captain's Close, where the residences of High Captains Taerl and Suljack stand, but the area is otherwise quite poor.

The Islands

Five islands stand in the bay formed by the River Mirar and are claimed by Luskan:

• Blood Island is filled with Ships' soldiers tasked with guarding the city; it holds a guard tower, barracks, an armory, and little else of interest.
• Closeguard Island is the home of High Captain Kurth.
• Cutlass Island has two rocky heights split by a pebble-strewn beach. The southern peak is surmounted

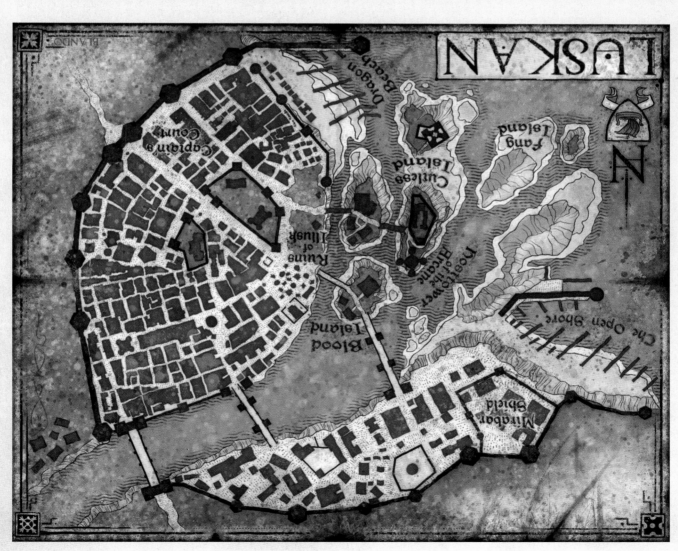

by the Sea Tower, where Luskan's first pirates built their stronghold, while the northern one is home to the Hosttower of the Arcane and the stables it shares with Ship Kurth.

- Fang Island has no inhabitants, and is named for its propensity for destroying vessels swept down the River Mirar.
- Harbor Arm Island is a tall spire sheltering Whitesails Harbor from the worst of the storms and waves that wash in from the south.

THE BRIDGES

The North and South Banks are spanned by three bridges: the Upstream Span, from the South Bank straight to the North Gate; Dalath's Span, the middle bridge with a name none can place in legend, and Harbor Cross, split between the Short Span that runs from the South Bank to Blood Island, and the Long Span that continues on to North Bank. Only Ship members and those authorized by a High Captain may traverse Harbor Cross.

Dark Arch connects South Bank with Closeguard Island, and only members of Ship Kurth and the Arcane Brotherhood may cross that span unchallenged. The same is true of Sword Bridge, which crosses from Closeguard Island to Cutlass Island. Although Closeguard Island is officially unguarded, it's still true that only members of the Arcane Brotherhood or Ship Kurth are expected to be there, so anyone out of place is aggressively questioned about their presence.

THE ARCANE BROTHERHOOD

In the last decade or so, two great changes have come over Luskan. The first was the plague that crippled the gangs that had controlled the city, allowing the High Captains to reclaim the power they had long held in

THE SYMBOL
OF THE ARCANE
BROTHERHOOD

Luskan. The other, far more sudden, was the return of the Arcane Brotherhood and its five-spired tower. A few years ago, the ruined Hosttower of the Arcane began regenerating its damaged stone, climbing into the sky once more. Shortly thereafter, mages of the Arcane Brotherhood emerged, almost immediately began cleansing the Luskar ruins of undead, and fought off a dragon menacing the city. Cheered by the citizens, they swore to keep themselves out of the politics of the High Captains and the city at large, but the notion that powerful wizards closely aligned with one another can truly remain neutral is laughable to anyone familiar with such things.

Now, the Arcane Brotherhood again walks the streets of Luskan, marked by the distinctive colors and patterns of their cloaks. From a distance, these cloaks all bear the same cut and silhouette, but each wizard of the Hosttower chooses a color or a design, and a moniker to match it. The leadership of the Arcane Brotherhood is the archmage and the four overwizards of the other spires of the Hosttower:

- Cashaan the Red, Archmage Arcane
- Zelenn the White, Overwizard of the West
- Jendrick the Blue, Overwizard of the South
- Teyva the Gray, Overwizard of the East
- Druette the Raven, Overwizard of the North

Other notable members of the Brotherhood include Vaelish the Brown and Maccath the Crimson.

ICEWIND DALE

Go far enough north, and you will come to the mountains rightly called the Spine of the World. Turn west and go toward the Sea of Moving Ice, and you might eventually come upon one of the scattered communities of Icewind Dale. You can also travel up the ever-narrowing road from Luskan called the Northern Means, and eventually come upon the frozen tundra beyond.

Why travel so far? Well, if you're like many who've drifted up there from the south, it is because an easier life doesn't suit you, you're running from something, or you just don't fit in anywhere else.

TEN-TOWNS

Coming up the hard road from the south, the first thing you'll see is Kelvin's Cairn, a great mountain scarred by a crack down its southwestern face. Even in high summer, its peak is capped in snow and ice. In the mountain's southern shadow is Bryn Shander, the largest, most populous, and most fortified of the Ten-Towns of Icewind Dale. Ten-Towns is a grouping of communities clustered around the three lakes of the area: Maer Dualdon, from which the Shaengarne River flows down toward Ironmaster; Lac Dinneshere to the east, whose waters are nearly always cold enough to kill; and Red-waters, named for an old battle between rival fisherfolk that left the waters bloody.

Ten-Towns thrives on fishing and trade, both endeavors reliant on the knucklehead trout of Icewind Dale's lakes. Without these fish, the people of Ten-Towns would starve, but there would also be little for them to barter or sell. The ivory-like bones of these fish are the

DO YOU KNOW WHAT IT IS TO BE A SLAVE? TO FEEL THE crack of a whip, the venom of a drow priestess's snake-headed lash, the weight of a burden you can't possibly lift after so much toil? No, you don't. So close your mouth and open your eyes and ears, and dip your quill.

—Oshgir the half-orc, to Kimitar Thaeless, glyphscribe of Denir

THE UNDERDARK

Known by many as the Realms Below, the vast, miles-deep network of caverns, caves, and underground waterways called the Underdark is home to many strange creatures and even stranger societies. No one is quite sure the extent of this massive ecosystem, except to say that it reaches at least the breadth of the continent, and that most creatures are fully capable of surviving their entire lives within it, provided they can find enough food and safety to do so. Breathable air is plentiful, and clean water can be found. Beyond that, most surface folk only have the tales of adventurers, the survivors of attacks, and the occasional escaped captive to describe the horrors lurking below the surface.

What follows are portions of the tale told by Oshgir, a half-orc warrior who was captured by a duergar raiding party, sold to a Zhentarim agent, captured by drow, and then escaped his captivity by killing an overseer and fleeing to Blingdenstone. This account was recorded by a traveling scribe of Denir named Kimitar Thaeless and submitted to the library at Candlekeep. Most don't believe that a half-orc was quite so eloquent in his telling, and thus contend that the scribe embellished the tale somewhat.

CAPTURE

It's impossible to describe the shame of a hardened warrior driven to his knees by a half-dozen duergar that have just slain his fellows. Never mind that we were asleep and unarmored at the time, or that I was able to take four of them down before an axe cut the strength from my leg. I was shackled and gagged, my wound wrapped in a bandage tight enough to stop the bleeding and numb my leg, as the gray pests laughed and spouted jokes at me, and then forced me to walk until I lost consciousness. When next I awoke, there was no longer a sky overhead.

GRACKLSTUGH

After days of walking in the deep, dark places beneath the surface, I was led, in heavy chains, to Gracklstugh, on the shores of the Darklake. I was set to work almost immediately at a forge, to pump bellows, heft ingots, and carry barrels of quenching oil. The place is called the City of Blades, for good reason: the fine steel of the duergar is impressive, considering the quality of the iron they were starting with. Hammering, refining, and careful polishing gave the metal the strength and sleekness necessary, and diligent sharpening added wicked edges to many of the blades I handled.

basis of the famous scrimshaw that is sold as far south as Calimshan and farther east than I care to consider. The bones are also used to make all manner of small, sturdy tools: fish hooks, arrowheads, sewing needles, buttons, and more. Each town on the lakes has its own fleet of fishing boats, and the towns carefully divide the lakes to protect the population and the delicate balance between the communities.

Independent-minded folk who come to Ten-Towns are discouraged from striking out on their own, and when they do, they often fail, either due to the dangers of the waters, being blocked out of the best fishing areas, or simply being refused trade by the scrimshanders, whose wares are expensive. Icewind Dale is a place where cooperation is essential for survival, and ignoring that fact can leave one quite alone in a time of need.

Where nine of the Ten-Towns survive primarily on fishing, Bryn Shander lives on trade, making it the place to visit when you come here. The walls keep the town safe from barbarians who raid the area and the beasts of the tundra, and the packing in of its people means Bryn Shander is also warmer than the other towns, both literally and in terms of the welcome you receive. I have visited only a few of the other towns, and while they have their quirks and charms, they are mostly what you might expect: fishing villages at the edge of frigid waters in a frozen waste. Certainly, there is trade to be done, coin to be made, and intrigue to be investigated in even in the smallest of these communities (which can number as few as a hundred souls). The only other point of interest is the town of Targos, on Maer Dualdon, which has grown rapidly and is threatening to burst the bounds of its protective wall, and thus has a hum of opportunity about it.

REGHED BARBARIANS

Ten-Towns isn't the only community in Icewind Dale. Tribes of human barbarians called Reghed also operate in the area. Hunters and raiders who value strength and devotion to their ancestral heroes, they claim a great many heroes among their honored dead, including some who were responsible for the safety of Ten-Towns, Icewind Dale, and beyond. A Reghed camp is made up of a large ring of hide tents, able to be broken down and transported as the Reghed move to keep up with the herds of reindeer they depend on for food and clothing.

THE DWARVES

Dwarves still live in the mines of Kelvin's Cairn, but in fewer numbers than they once did, and with less influence than they had on the rest of Icewind Dale a century or two ago. The dwarves here claim their continued allegiance to Clan Battlehammer of Mithral Hall, even though they returned to the colder north when they discovered their ancient home no longer suited them. Bryn Shander serves them as a trading post, allowing them to keep humans and other strangers away from their mines, which are some distance away in the shadow of the Cairn. The dwarves send a representative to the council of speakers that governs Ten-Towns, but have no say in their proceedings except to declare acceptance or refusal of the decisions of the human gathering.

The duergar make their homes mainly beyond a great wall, which I never passed through. To the north, the floor of the cavern that contains the Darklake hovers dangerously low, such that in some places it is barely ten feet above the water's surface. The whole of the great cavern glows, and the continuous flow of hot iron through the city gives the illumination a yellow cast at all times. It is frightening, if you forget where you are. More than that, it is hot.

After a month or so of working under a minor smith, I quarreled with the apprentice set to supervise me, and he dared me to test the strength of his new blade. It broke, as I expected, but did the job well enough. The duergar didn't seem to be angry that the apprentice lay dead at my feet, but it was only a short time thereafter that I was dragged off to the market to be sold. As it happened, a human was in the city on some diplomatic mission. I caught his eye, and he purchased me.

MANTOL-DERITH

I soon learned that I was not bought entirely for my brute strength, but also for what knowledge I had of the duergar. My new owner was a member of some group he called the Zhentarim, and when I told him all I knew, he offered me my freedom and a place among his agents. Together we would journey to a place called Mantol-Derith, where I would serve as his bodyguard. From there we would go to the surface, and I could remain in his employ if I wished. Freedom and a job? How could I refuse?

Mantol-Derith is a hidden place accessed by secret ways. Slaves, such as I had been, are typically not permitted to go there. Once in the cavern, I had to remain near my employer, but by keeping my eyes and ears open, I learned a lot about this place.

Mantol-Derith is where duergar, drow, and svirfneblin come to trade with each other and with surface-dwellers interested in conducting business with the deep places. Its location is kept secret—I only know that it is fairly close to the Darklake. The drow sell weapons, armor, magic scrolls and potions, and fine works of art. The duergar trade mainly in fine steel, and demand high prices to do so. Deep gnomes come to market with gems, certain fungi only they are capable of growing, and salt, which much of the Underdark has little ready supply of. The surface folk bring wines, ales, and spirits, cloth, wood, paper, and a great many other goods.

The laws of Mantol-Derith don't seem to care about anything other than commerce. There must be no prohibition on what sorts of creatures can visit here—among other things, I saw a pair of mind flayer envoys doing business in the market. The most serious of crimes are theft, the use of magic to influence negotiations, and the counterfeiting of goods by mundane or magical means. Anyone discovered to be in violation is sentenced on the spot, wrapped in heavy chains, and carted off to be tossed to the bottom of the Darklake.

When my employer's business was concluded, he was true to his word, and we left for the surface. If only the drow with whom he did business were so trustworthy. We were ambushed, he was killed, and I was again put in chains.

MENZOBERRANZAN

I eventually got away from the place, but not before I had learned more about Menzoberranzan than any sane person would care to know. Although the life of a slave can be brutally short in the City of Spiders, the drow aren't so extravagant that they do away with every captive they take. At the same time, they are masters of punishment—it is fear of pain, not fear of death, that motivates the slaves of drow. If you're lucky, you'll only feel normal shackles and the occasional whip or light spell-blast. A bit less luck or more malice, and the serpent-headed whips of the priestesses come out.

If you aren't a drow in the City of Spiders, you aren't worth a name. All manner of surface-dwellers—orcs and elves, humans and halflings—are brought here to serve as slaves to the drow in their refuge. The constant fear of punishment, from one's mistress or another, more powerful drow, keeps most slaves obedient, even when they aren't directly supervised.

The great cavern of the city is filled with tall spires, and homes both great and small are carved into the stalagmites and stalactites that pierce the darkness. Gentle illumination from magic or glowing fungus decorates some homes and businesses, as well as the mansions of the high houses of the city, eight of which have positioned themselves above all others. While the lesser houses dance and fight and scheme for advantages over each other, they all live under the heel of House Baenre and the Matron Mother, who rules the city in Lolth's name.

On a large plateau high above the cavern floor is Tier Breche, also called the Academy, where the city trains its priestesses, mages, and noble warriors. The city's market is centrally located, and rothé are raised on an isle toward the eastern edge of the city.

If you are ever so unfortunate as to be enslaved by the drow of Menzoberranzan, my advice to you is simple and stern: do as you are commanded, avoid insulting their goddess (which means don't even brush off a spider crawling on you), and attempt escape only if you are desperate or sure of your survival. If you are given the proper opportunity, as I was, you might discover that the neck of a drow snaps with surprising ease.

ESCAPE

One day, well after I had lost count of how many days I'd been a captive, I was in a small outlying cavern with a few other slaves harvesting a mushroom patch. I was given leave to answer nature's call away from the mushrooms, and I lingered long enough in a side tunnel to force my watcher to come and find me. I took the first lash he offered me with his whip, then grabbed the weapon and pulled the skinny fool toward me before he could sound an alarm or get his blade out. It took me but a second to get both hands around his throat. When he lay dead at my feet, I took his sword and ran as fast and far as I could. I knew the gnomish city of Blingdenstone was nearby, and I came upon it eventually, but the journey took days as I wound through convoluted passageways and tried to avoid notice.

BLINGDENSTONE

My initial joy at reaching Blingdenstone was quickly tempered. The deep gnomes don't seem to like visitors they can't recognize or identify, and being a half-orc didn't help matters in the least for me. After dodging arrows loosed from the high walls of the city, I gave up on going through the gate and snuck in through a small cart tunnel, emptying out part of a load of ore to make room for myself.

I managed to avoid conflict with the guards that discovered me in the cart. When they ordered me to stand, I did so with my weapon held at my side, and I turned to display my back to them. When they saw that it was covered in lashes and the scars of the priestesses' fanged whips, and they realized that my blade was of drow manufacture (though I clearly was not), they were willing to believe my story.

Though the gnomes kept me under watch, I was allowed to regain my strength for a few days, and I saw a bit of their community in the meantime. Once I was inside the city, I could tell that it's not much of a city at all. The svirfneblin all live in close contact with one another, and this togetherness can be disconcerting, especially for someone accustomed to small luxuries like shutters on windows and doors on privies. The homes are all smoothed-over natural stone, with little evidence of hard corners.

Each industry has a portion of the city to itself: trading, smithing, mining, and the growing of a special fungus crop. Still many of the old tunnels and caverns remain unclaimed and sealed off, whether to guard against invasion or perhaps because of what now dwells there, I don't know.

If you're welcomed long enough to the city, you can trade for fine goods and armor here; the gnomes' chain mail and mining picks seem most worth acquiring. Before sending me on my way, the gnomes were kind enough to give me a pick, a dagger, and some of their trillimac, an odd fungus that can be made into something like bread. It's a bit spongy, but it doesn't spoil quickly, and it got me to the surface before I starved to death.

THE CAVERN OF MENZOBERRANZAN

Menzoberranzan fills a large vault that was formerly a lair of giant spiders and beholders. The vault is known by its dwarven name, Araurilcaurak ("Great Pillar Cavern"), because of Narbondel, the giant rock pillar at the vault's center that joins floor and ceiling. The cavern is roughly shaped like an arrowhead, with the pool of Donigarten at its tip, and stretching two miles across at its widest point. The ceiling rises a thousand feet high, and the floor is studded with stalagmites.

Two areas rise above the rest of the city: Tier Breche, the side cavern occupied by the Academy where most drow citizens are trained for adulthood; and the larger Qu'ellarz'orl (or House-Loft), a plateau that is home to many of the city's mightiest noble houses, separated from the lower city by a forest of giant mushrooms. From either of these heights, a surveyor can view the city. The view shows rows of spired stone castles, their sculpted highlights lit by the soft, tinted flows of permanent *faerie fire* lights.

Chapter 3: Races of the Realms

AERÛN IS HOME TO MANY RACES, SOME OF them immigrants from other worlds who found their way here in ancient times when gates and portals were more plentiful, and easier to traverse. Others are relative newcomers to the world, still finding a place for themselves among the long-established races. The civilizations of the elder races have declined, while those of the younger races are flourishing and spreading ever outward.

The character races described in the *Player's Handbook* are all found in the Realms, along with some subraces unique to Faerûn. Each character race has all the traits of the primary race, as given in the *Player's Handbook*, plus traits for each subrace that are unique to those individuals. This chapter provides racial traits for a subrace only when they differ from or replace those given in the *Player's Handbook*. The information in this chapter is specific to the Realms, so if something stated here differs from what's presented in the *Player's Handbook,* this material takes precedence.

Dwarves

The Stout Folk are deliberate and steadfast, with a proud history as great artisans, builders, and warriors. Although the glory of their empires faded long ago, the dwarves still hold to their ancient ways and traditions. They stubbornly defend what remains of their old domains beneath hill and mountain, and some seek to reclaim what they have lost to the depredations of orcs, goblins, and the inexorable march of time.

According to their own legends, dwarves were formed from iron, mithral, earth, and stone on the Soulforge of Moradin. After the All-Father breathed life into them in the heart of the world, dwarves found their way to the surface and, from there, spread across each continent.

Thousands of years of settlement and separation divided the dwarves into distinct subraces: the shield dwarves, most common in the North and the Sword Coast; the gold dwarves of the southern lands; and the gray dwarves, or duergar, of the Underdark.

The Dwarvish language of Faerûn uses a runic alphabet called Dethek, whose characters are easy to etch into stone and metal, as evidenced by the runestones and way-markers found in ancient dwarven tunnels and mines.

Shield Dwarves

The ancestral home of the shield dwarves is in northern Faerûn, where ancient dwarfholds exist in the North, Damara, Impiltur, Vaasa, the Vast, and the Western Heartlands. The most famous of the old shield dwarf cities is Citadel Adbar, north and east of Silverymoon. Many of these dwarfholds have changed hands over the centuries in a cycle of invasion by enemies, followed by reconquest by the dwarves.

Living in a near-constant state of war for generations, shield dwarves are a hardy people, slow to trust, with long memories and often an equally long list of grievances against their ancient enemies. The more conservative among them want to maintain the traditions and remaining holdings of their people, isolated from the influence of outsiders and safe from invaders behind thick walls of stone. Shield dwarves of a more adventurous bent are interested in exploring the world and seeing what lies beyond the bounds of their ancient dwarfholds.

Shield dwarves have the racial traits of mountain dwarves in the Player's Handbook. Their skin is usually fair, eyes green, hazel, or silver-blue, and they have brown, blond, or red hair. Full beards and mustaches are commonly seen on male shield dwarves.

Shield dwarves are renowned artisans, particularly in metal and stone. They tend to focus more on sturdiness in their craft than on the artistic flourishes and gilding favored by their gold dwarf cousins. Shield dwarf crafters build to last, and each one's signature mark placed upon an enduring masterpiece serves as a way of gaining immortality.

Gold Dwarves

Gold dwarves are common in the lands to the south and east. They are formidable warriors, proud of their long traditions, with strong ties to clan. They are gruff and haughty and have a love of fine craftsmanship and an eagerness to trade.

Significant settlements of gold dwarves exist in the Great Rift, the area surrounding the Dragon Coast, as well as in the Old Empires of eastern Faerûn. Smaller communities are found in the Smoking Mountains, in the Giant's Run Mountains, and the Western Heartlands.

Because they have not endured the same cycle of invasion and displacement, gold dwarves tend to be more optimistic than their shield dwarf cousins, but they're still standoffish and prideful as only a dwarf can be. They believe their race's stable history is the result of their attentiveness to tradition, and have little doubt that the future of the gold dwarves will be just as peaceful, if they remain true to their customs and principles.

Dwarf Clans of the North

All dwarves count their clan heritage as an important part of their lineage and identity. While in some cities a single clan dominates (or is the only one in residence), in other dwarven communities there is a complex relationship between family, clan, and the larger society.

Some of the dwarf clans in the North are Arnskull, Battlehammer, Blackbanner, Blackhammer, Bucklebar, Darkfell, Deepaxe, Deepdelve, Eaglecleft, Foehammer, Gallowglar, Hillsafar, Horn, Ironshield, Jundeth, Narlagh, Orothiar, Quarrymaster, Rockfist, Sstar, Stoneshaft, Stoneshield, Stoneshoulder, Trueforger, Watchever, Worldthrone, Wyrmslayer, and Yund.

Some dwarves hail from the family that founded or rules a given clan, and so they use the clan name as their family name. Others are simply "of" the clan, but bear the clan name with as much pride as their own surnames.

Gold dwarves have the racial traits of hill dwarves in the *Player's Handbook*. They are stocky and muscular, averaging about 4 feet tall, with brown skin, black or brown hair, and brown or hazel eyes, with green eyes rare (and considered lucky). Males grow full beards that they keep oiled and well groomed, and both genders wear their hair long and often elaborately braided.

Gold dwarves are best known for crafting beautiful objects. According to them, all the natural resources of the world exist for mortals to turn them into objects of great beauty. Gold dwarves don't want the most of everything; they want the best. Their artisans toil over items for years, getting their etchings and fine details just right before being satisfied with their efforts.

That deliberate, perfectionist approach is a reflection of gold dwarf culture, in which there is a right and proper way to do everything. Tradition dictates every aspect of a gold dwarf's life, from one's place in society, to prospects for marriage, to what careers are acceptable. Gold dwarves who take up a life of adventuring, away from the clan, rarely forsake their traditions when doing so. Even though they might have to live as outsiders for a time, they hope to ultimately improve their standing in their society.

Gray Dwarves (Duergar)

The gray dwarves, or duergar, live deep in the Underdark. After delving deeper than any other dwarves, they were enslaved by mind flayers for eons. Although they eventually won their freedom, these grim, ashen-skinned dwarves now take slaves of their own and are as tyrannical as their former masters.

Physically similar to other dwarves in some ways, duergar are wiry and lean, with black eyes and bald heads, with the males growing long, unkempt, gray beards.

Duergar value toil above all else. Showing emotions other than grim determination or wrath is frowned on in their culture, but they can sometimes seem joyful when at work. They have the typical dwarven appreciation for order, tradition, and impeccable craftsmanship, but their goods are purely utilitarian, disdaining aesthetic or artistic value.

Few duergar become adventurers, fewer still on the surface world, because they are a hidebound and suspicious race. Those who leave their subterranean cities are usually exiles. Check with your Dungeon Master to see if you can play a gray dwarf character.

Duergar Subrace Traits

The duergar subrace has the dwarf traits in the *Player's Handbook*, plus the subrace traits below.

Ability Score Increase. Your Strength score increases by 1.

Superior Darkvision. Your darkvision has a radius of 120 feet.

Extra Language. You can speak, read, and write Undercommon.

Duergar Resilience. You have advantage on saving throws against illusions and against being charmed or paralyzed.

Duergar Magic. When you reach 3rd level, you can cast the *enlarge/reduce* spell on yourself once with this trait, using only the spell's enlarge option. When you reach 5th level, you can cast the *invisibility* spell on yourself once with this trait. You don't need material components for either spell, and you can't cast them while you're in direct sunlight, although sunlight has no effect on them once cast. You regain the ability to cast these spells with this trait when you finish a long rest. Intelligence is your spellcasting ability for these spells.

Sunlight Sensitivity. You have disadvantage on attack rolls and on Wisdom (Perception) checks that rely on sight when you, the target of your attack, or whatever you are trying to perceive is in direct sunlight.

Dwarven Deities

The gods of the dwarves are a pantheon, or clan, collectively known as the Morndinsamman.

Forge Father and Revered Mother

Moradin, the Soulforger, leads the dwarven gods. Known as Dwarf-father or All-Father, he is the god of the dwarf people as a whole, as well as the god of creation, "dwarf-crafts" (smithing and stonework), and protection. His wife is the Revered Mother, Berronar Truesilver, goddess of hearth and home, of honesty and faithfulness, and of oaths, loyalty, and honor.

Gods of Battle

Clangeddin Silverbeard is the dwarven god of war and valor. Gorm Gulthyn, also called Fire Eyes and the Lord of the Bronze Mask, is the god of defense and vigilance, the protector of dwarves. Haela Brightaxe is the goddess of luck in battle, and the patron of dwarf fighters.

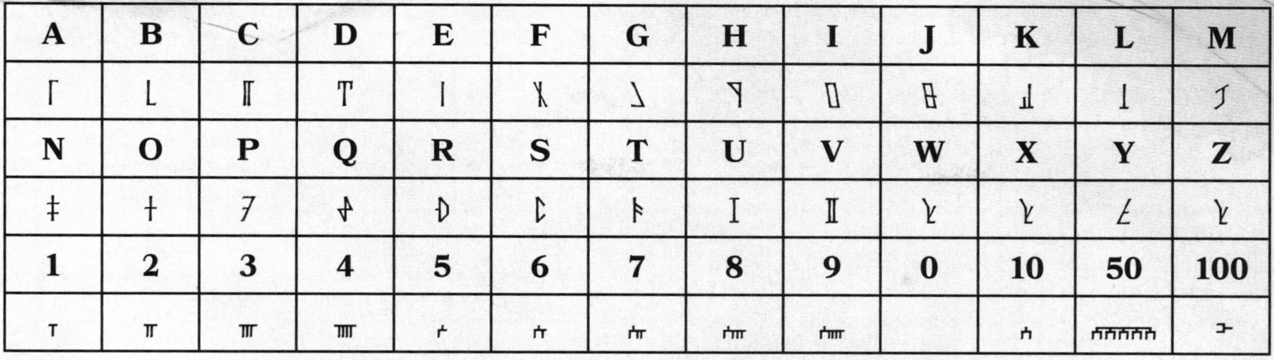
A B C D E F G H I J K L M
N O P Q R S T U V W X Y Z
1 2 3 4 5 6 7 8 9 0 10 50 100

Dethek, the Letters and Numerals of Dwarvish

Gods of Craft

Dumathoin, the Keeper of Secrets under the Mountain, is the patron of the shield dwarves, as well as the god of buried wealth, mining, gems, and exploration, and the guardian of the dead. Sharindlar, Lady of Life and Mercy, is the goddess of healing, romantic love, and fertility, often associated with the moon.

Gods of Far Places

The god of invention and discovery is Dugmaren Brightmantle, called the Wandering Tinker or the Gleam in the Eye. Marthammor Duin is the traveler's god, patron of expatriates and guides, and deity of lightning and roads.

Gods of Wealth

Vergadain, called the Merchant King, is the god of thieves (who commands his followers never to steal from other dwarves), luck, and chance, as well as commerce and negotiation. Abbathor is the god of greed, sometimes portrayed as a dragon filled with envy of the wealth of others, who jealously tends his own hoard.

Gods of Evil

Laduguer is the patron of the duergar, god of magic and those crafts not governed by Moradin. Also worshiped among the duergar is Deep Duerra, a goddess of conquest and of the powers of the mind.

Elves

Skilled in both magic and warfare, the *Tel'Quessir*—"the People," as they call themselves—came to Faerûn ages ago, building vast and powerful empires long before the rise of humans. The days of the great elven nations are now long past, and many elves have withdrawn from the world into isolated sylvan realms, or set sail across the Trackless Sea to the isle of Evermeet.

Unlike dwarves, who developed subraces in the world, elves brought their divisions with them, settling into separate kingdoms by type. Beings of immense power, the first elves explored and settled the world, bringing about a golden age of art, magic, and civilization. At the height of their power, the elves performed a High Magic ritual intended to create the ideal homeland. They succeeded, but the spell sundered the land in a terrible cataclysm at the same time that

it caused the distant isle of Evermeet to rise from beneath the sea.

Then came the Crown Wars, a series of conflicts between the great elven kingdoms lasting three thousand years. These battles devastated much of the world and resulted in the dark elves' flight into the Underdark.

Reeling from these calamities, the elven empires went into a long, slow decline, and many of their kind took part in the great Retreat to their refuge on Evermeet. As the elves increasingly withdrew from the world, other races and civilizations rose to prominence in Faerûn.

The Elvish language used across Faerûn—sometimes called the True Tongue by elves—is written in the graceful script of the Espruar alphabet. Seldruin, the ancient language of elven High Magic that uses the Hamarfae alphabet, is all but forgotten nowadays.

Moon Elves

Also called silver elves, or *Teu'Tel'Quessir*, moon elves are more tolerant and adventurous than elves of other sorts. In ancient times, the dissolution of their empires dispersed moon elves among other races, and since then they have traditionally gotten along well with their non-elf neighbors. They mingle with other people while their kin remain in hidden settlements and secluded strongholds.

Moon elves are sometimes seen as frivolous, especially by other elves. But it is the easygoing, fluid nature of their culture, philosophy, and personality that has enabled them to survive and flourish during and after tragic times in elven history. While communities of moon elves can be found in mainland Faerûn, many moon elves live in the settlements of other races, staying for a few seasons or several decades before moving on.

To a moon elf, home can be among the members of one's family, clan, or other friends and loved ones. Moon elves who temporarily take up residence in or near sun elf communities aren't shy about expressing the opinion that their kin need to be less serious. In turn, the sun elves pretend to be more annoyed by their moon elf neighbors than they truly are, provided that the moon elves' whims and adventuresome urges don't cause serious disruption. Given that the moon elves usually move on before wearing out their welcome, such unrest rarely occurs.

Moon elves have the racial traits of high elves in the *Player's Handbook*. They have pale skin with a bluish tint. Their hair runs the gamut of human colors, and some moon elves have hair of silvery white or various shades of blue. Their eyes are blue or green and have gold flecks.

Given the race's love of travel, exploration, and new experiences, many moon elves become adventurers, utilizing their talents for warfare, woodcraft, and wizardry in different measures.

SUN ELVES

Sun elves, also known as gold elves, or *Ar'Tel'Quessir*, have a reputation for being arrogant and self-important. Many of them believe they are Corellon's chosen people and that other races—even other elves—are subordinate to them in skill, significance, and sophistication. They claim the title of "high elves" with pride, and indeed their race is responsible for great, and sometimes terrible, achievements.

Recalling and emphasizing the glorious aspects of their history, sun elves subscribe to the principle of "elven excellence"— no matter how interesting, exceptional, heroic, or noteworthy other races' accomplishments might be, there is an inherent superiority to all things elven. This attitude colors sun elves' relations with other elves, whom they see as diluted or diminished representatives of elven culture. Some sun elves reject this way of thinking, but it is common enough that when most folk of Faerûn see a sun elf, they see arrogance personified. Their haughty attitude can overshadow the fact that most sun elves are also tirelessly compassionate and thoughtful champions of good.

Sun elves have the racial traits of high elves in the *Player's Handbook*. Sun elves have bronze skin. Their eyes are black, metallic gold, or metallic silver, and their hair is black, metallic copper, or golden blond.

Sun elf culture and civilization is highly magical in nature, thanks to the race's many accomplished wizards, sages, and crafters. Not every sun elf is a skilled practitioner of the Art, but each one has at least a bit of inherent magic. Many sun elves mix magic with other art forms, which produces the complex dance of the

RARE ELF SUBRACES

Other lines of descendants exist of the elves who originally came to Faerûn, but they are so rare as to be legendary, often considered mythical.

Avariel. The *Aril'Tel'Quessir*, or winged elves, were among the first to settle in Faerûn. They are famed for their feathered wings and ability to fly. Ancient conflicts with dragons nearly wiped them out, and today they are rarely, if ever, seen.

Lythari. The *Ly'Tel'Quessir* have the ability to polymorph into wolves. Unlike werewolves, lythari don't have a hybrid form and aren't afflicted by a curse. They dwell together in secretive packs, primarily in wolf form, living free in the deep wilds of the world.

Sea Elves. The *Alu'Tel'Quessir* ("water elves") are an aquatic subrace of elves found in the oceans of the world, especially off the shores of Faerûn and Evermeet. Sea elves live along the Sword Coast in close-knit nomadic clans, but elsewhere sea elves claim kingdoms in sun-lit shallows. They have been at war with the sahuagin throughout their history.

Star Elves. The star elves, or *Ruar'Tel'Quessir*, look much like tall moon elves. They dwell on the demiplane of Sildëyuir near the Feywild. A conflict with the nilshai, a race of wormlike sorcerers from the Ethereal Plane, forced some star elves to leave their home and come to Faerûn.

Wild Elves. The *Sy'Tel'Quessir* are considered by many elves to be the most strange of their race, having abandoned or lost much of their ancient culture.

bladesingers as well as the enchanting music of their bards and the meticulous craftwork of their artisans. Sun elf adventurers often bring a feeling of noblesse oblige to their profession: they venture out into the world to challenge its dangers because someone must, and who could be better suited?

WOOD ELVES

Also called copper elves, or *Sy'Tel'Quessir*, wood elves are the most common elves remaining in Faerûn. Their ancestors left behind the strife of the Crown Wars millennia ago to found strongholds and settlements deep in the forests. Today, most wood elves stand guard over the ruins of the past, believing it their duty to preserve their fallen glory as an object lesson of the dangers of hubris.

Wood elves tend to be hardier than other elves, more solid and grounded than their cousins. This attitude is reflected in their culture and traditions; wood elves tend more toward physical pursuits than do other elves, and they view ancient elven history with a more critical eye. To the wood elves, the "great" elven kingdoms were responsible for many equally great mistakes. They look upon the Sundering, the Crown Wars, the descent of the drow, and other calamities as the result of acts of arrogance on the part of their ancestors. Living around and amid the reminders of this arrogance, and standing witness to the rise and fall of many elven empires, wood elves see the place of elves in the world differently than moon or sun elves do. Wood elves seek a quiet harmony, not domination, with the wider world.

Sylvan counterparts of the sun elves and moon elves, wood elves eschew the cities and strongholds of their kin in favor of living close to nature. Wood elves have not claimed a large realm of their own since the kingdom of Eaerlann was destroyed millennia ago. Instead they maintain a number of smaller settlements, the better to keep those communities hidden or protected. Wood elves claim territory in the High Forest, the Great Dale, the Western Heartlands, and beyond. Some wood elves live in other elven communities and territories, where they serve as scouts, rangers, and hunters.

Despite seeing themselves as part of the world, wood elves don't commonly emerge from their homes to encounter non-elves. Likewise, in the deep woods and forests of the world, most wood elves don't come across members of other races. Adventurers, diplomats, couriers, and those who pursue similar professions are the exceptions, traveling far outside their sylvan domains and meeting a wide variety of folk.

Wood elves in Faerûn have the racial traits of wood elves in the *Player's Handbook*. They have tan or coppery skin, with hair of wood brown, golden blond, black, or a shining metallic copper, and eyes of green, brown, or hazel.

Skilled naturalists, wood elves often take up professions that allow them to remain close to the wild or to make use of their knowledge of woodcraft, wildlife, and forestry. Wood elves are more than capable in warfare, particularly archery. They are less magically inclined than their cousins, but have their fair share of practitioners of the Art, as well as clerics and many druids.

DARK ELVES (DROW)

The drow are descended from the dark elves who retreated into the Underdark after the Crown Wars. They are infamous for their cruelty, evilness, and drive to dominate.

For much of history, many believed that all drow were beings of inherent and irredeemable evil. In truth, most drow do align with evil, engaging in torture, slavery, murder, and other nefarious activities in the name of their demon-goddess. Almost always, dark elves who reject the ways of their people are exiled, or executed for being rebels, heretics, and insurrectionists who have turned against drow culture and the will of Lolth. But the existence of noble and self-sacrificing drow such as Liriel Baenre and Drizzt Do'Urden suggests that the evil of the drow isn't innate and can be overcome. The actions of these few heroic drow have tempered some people's opinions toward the race, although the appearance of a dark elf on the surface remains a rare event and a cause for alarm.

Many drow in Faerûn hail from Menzoberranzan, the infamous City of Spiders, or one of the other drow city-states in the Underdark, such as Jhachalkhyn or Ched Nasad. Dark elves encountered on the surface are usually found near entrances to the Underdark, because they are harmed by the light of day, which weakens them and their magic. Drow who become adventurers often do so after fleeing the oppressive, cruel theocracy of the city-states. Most of these individuals live as outcasts and wanderers, though a rare few find new homes with another race or culture.

Drow have the racial traits of dark elves in the *Player's Handbook*. Drow characters can come from any background, though most have a history that links to one of the drow city-states of the Underdark.

Inherent magical abilities and a preference for dark places make drow naturally adept as assassins, thieves, and spies. Traditionally, male drow are warriors and wizards, and female drow occupy leadership roles as warriors or priestesses of Lolth. Drow exiles tend to follow their own path regardless of gender.

ELVEN DEITIES

The gods of the *Tel'Quessir*, collectively known as the Seldarine, have embodied the ideals of the elf people since time immemorial. They are believed to dwell in the realm of Arvandor on the plane of Arborea.

GOD OF THE ELVES

Corellon Larethian is the wise leader of the Seldarine, the god of elves, magic, poetry, rulership, and warcraft. He is thought of as the father of the race, but he is depicted as female as often as he is depicted as male.

GODDESS OF WISDOM

Angharradh, triune goddess of wisdom and the fierce mother-protector of the elf people, is Corellon's consort. Her three aspects are: Aerdrie Faenya, wild goddess of the winds and weather, as well as patron of the avariel; Hanali Celanil, the Winsome Rose, goddess of love,

A	B	C	D	E	F	G	H	I	J	K	L	M
⟡	⟡	⟡	⟡	⟡	⟡	⟡	⟡	⟡	⟡	⟡	⟡	⟡
N	O	P	Q	R	S	T	U	V	W	X	Y	Z
⟡	⟡	⟡	⟡	⟡	⟡	⟡	⟡	⟡	⟡	⟡	⟡	⟡
1	2	3	4	5	6	7	8	9	0	10	50	100
⟡	⟡	⟡	⟡	⟡	⟡	⟡	⟡	⟡		⟡	⟡	⟡

ESPRUAR, THE LETTERS AND NUMERALS OF ELVISH

beauty, art, and enchantment; and the Moonlit Mystery, silver Sehanine Moonbow, goddess of all life's mysteries, including mysticism, prophecy, death, and dreams. In legends, these goddesses are often separate entities from Angharradh, and frequently depicted as Corellon's daughters or consorts.

Gods of Nature

Deep Sashelas is a sea god, lord of the sea elves and of dolphins. Labelas Enoreth is the philosopher god, deity of time and history, whose gift of trance is crucial to elven identity and survival. Rillifane Rallathil is god of the woodlands and the wild places, the father of wood elves and protector of druids. Closely allied with him is Solonor Thelandira, the god of hunting, archery, and woodcraft.

Gods of Shadow

Of somewhat darker bent, Erevan Ilesere is a deity of mischief, a trickster-god; and Fenmarel Mestarine is the moody and sullen god of outcasts and solitude, who has little to do with the rest of the Seldarine (except for Erevan, who uses Fenmarel as a scapegoat in his plots and pranks). And then there is Shevarash, a god thought of as embittered and obsessive, to whom elves turn when they seek vengeance.

Faerûnian Gods

Many elves worship deities in the Faerûnian pantheon, including Mielikki (and the unicorn goddess Lurue), Silvanus, and Sune. In recent years, some elves have found delight in the worship of Lathander, as well.

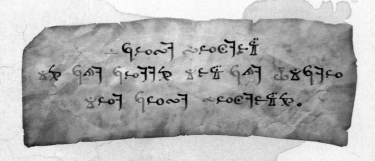

Drow Deities

The gods of the drow are fractious and treacherous as their worshipers.

The Spider Queen. Lolth, the Demon Queen of Spiders, reigns supreme as goddess of the drow, ruthlessly eliminating all who would threaten her position. Her priestesses do likewise with the cults of rival gods among their people.

Other Dark Powers. Selvetarm is god of warriors, and therefore patron of male drow, although perhaps not so much as Vhaeraun, the rogue god of thievery and of drow males who rebel against the matriarchy. Kiaransalee, drow goddess of the undead, is served by secretive cults of necromancers. Ghaunadaur, known as That Which Lurks, is a subversive power, the mad god of oozes, rebels, and outcasts, occasionally revered by drow.

The Dark Maiden. Some drow exiles have heard the song of Eilistraee, urging them out onto the surface to behold the moon as it rises. The drow goddess of song, beauty, swordwork, hunting, and moonlight, she is the patron of drow who reject the evils of their society, offering them light and hope.

Halflings

Folk think of elves as aloof and graceful, dwarves as fierce and hardy, and of gnomes—if they think of them at all—as clever and shy. Halflings, in contrast, have the reputation of being deft and plucky.

Halflings, or *hin* as they call themselves, exhibit a natural adroitness that often surprises larger folk. This nimbleness regularly comes in handy when their courage outruns their common sense, and tales about halflings abound with lucky breaks and narrow escapes.

Beyond these typical elements of the halfling character, halflings can be divided into two major subraces. Many aspects of the two groups' cultures make them distinct, but even without such trappings they are distinct due to a divergence in what seems to be a primal drive: to go or to stay. Lightfoot halflings are travelers as a rule, with tongues and hearts as nimble as their feet. Whereas if strongheart halflings are on the move, it always seems driven by a desire to return to home or find and settle in a new one. As the saying goes, "Lightfoot, light hearted. Strongheart, strong footing."

Although there are many halfling communities, particularly in the lands in and around Luiren, halflings frequently fit themselves into dwarven, gnomish, elven, and human societies. Lightfoots breeze into communities as they travel, make friends easily, and then move on as the wind or whimsy takes them. Stronghearts settle in, make themselves at home, and weave themselves so deftly into the fabric of a community that it becomes hard for folk to think of a time without them.

LIGHTFOOT HALFLINGS

For lightfoot halflings, neither the journey nor the destination matters more; the important thing is to keep moving. The life of a lightfoot is one long exploration with each new horizon, new town, or new face a chance to find something delightful.

Lightfoot halflings typically travel in small bands, using whatever conveyance is convenient but just as easily striking out on foot. Bands consist of loosely related individuals, and when bands meet, membership frequently shifts. Lightfoot halflings typically excel at tasks related to travel—be it navigation, handling pack animals, foraging, sailing, and cartwright work—having tried their hand at all such things before or learned from other lightfoots met during their journeys.

Lightfoot halflings are highly social, often as curious about other people as they are about what might lie around the next bend. They characteristically possess an easygoing and open attitude, curious about others and willing to share of themselves, which enables them to make friends easily. Their facile friendships and ease with partings can make lightfoot halflings seem disingenuous to others. Lightfoot halflings get stereotyped as flighty, easily distracted, fickle, and unreliable. But their friendships and courtships, if brief, tend to be genuine. The staid and stable life that most other people desire just isn't part of their character.

Lightfoot halflings have all the racial traits of lightfoot halflings in the *Player's Handbook*. They share the skin, hair, and eye tones of humans, but most lightfoot halflings have hazel or brown eyes and brown hair. Lightfoot halflings don't grow facial hair except that males and females typically grow short sideburns.

STRONGHEART HALFLINGS

Creatures of the earth who love a warm hearth and pleasant company, strongheart halflings are folks of few enemies and many friends. Stronghearts are sometimes referred to fondly by members of other races as "the good folk," for little upsets stronghearts or corrupts their spirit. To many of them, the greatest fear is to live in a world of poor company and mean intent, where one lacks freedom and the comfort of friendship.

When strongheart halflings settle into a place, they intend to stay. It's not unusual for a dynasty of stronghearts to live in the same place for a few centuries. Strongheart halflings don't develop these homes in seclusion. On the contrary, they do their best to fit into the local community and become an essential part of it. Their viewpoint stresses cooperation above all other

traits, and the ability to work well with others is the most valued behavior in their lands.

Pushed from their nests, strongheart halflings typically try to have as many comforts of home with them as possible. Non-stronghearts with a more practical bent can find strongheart travel habits maddening, but their lightfoot cousins typically enjoy the novelty of it—so long as the lightfoots don't have to carry any of the baggage.

While often stereotyped as fat and lazy due to their homebound mindset and obsession with fine food, strongheart halflings are typically quite industrious. Nimble hands, their patient mindset, and their emphasis on quality makes them excellent weavers, potters, wood carvers, basket makers, painters, and farmers.

Strongheart halflings have all the racial traits of stouts in the *Player's Handbook*. Strongheart halflings are shorter on average than their lightfoot kin, and tend to have rounder faces. They have the skin tones and hair colors of humans, with most having brown hair. Unlike their lightfoot cousins, strongheart halflings often have blond or black hair and blue or green eyes. Males don't grow beards or mustaches, but both males and females can grow sideburns down to mid-cheek, and both genders plait them into long braids.

HALFLING DEITIES

The *hin* have a small but intimate pantheon of deities, which are honored primarily at household altars, roadside shrines, and wooded groves.

THE BLESSED SISTERS

The *hin* mother-goddess and the head of the pantheon is Yondalla, the Blessed One, goddess of bounty and fertility, protector of hearth, home, and family. Sheela Peryroyl is the Green Sister of Yondalla. She is a nature goddess, the lady of fields, streams, and the wilds found in shire and glen, and the weather in such places. She is also a goddess of love, song, and dance.

GHOSTWISE HALFLINGS

Ghostwise halflings trace their ancestry back to a war among halfling tribes that sent their ancestors into flight from Luiren. Ghostwise halflings are the rarest of the *hin*, found only in the Chondalwood and a few other isolated forests, clustered in tight-knit clans.

Many ghostwise clans select a natural landmark as the center of their territory, and members carry a piece of that landmark with them at all times. Clan warriors known as nightgliders bond with and ride giant owls as mounts.

Because these folk are clannish and mistrustful of outsiders, ghostwise halfling adventurers are rare. Ask your DM if you can play a member of this subrace, which has the halfling traits in the *Player's Handbook*, plus the subrace traits below.

Ability Score Increase. Your Wisdom score increases by 1.

Silent Speech. You can speak telepathically to any creature within 30 feet of you. The creature understands you only if the two of you share a language. You can speak telepathically in this way to one creature at a time.

KEEPERS OF THE HOME

Cyrrollalee is goddess of the hearth and hospitality, as well as of trust and handicrafts. Arvoreen is a defender-god, a watchful protector who sacrifices personal comfort for the safety of others.

THE SHADOWED GODS

Brandobaris is the trickster-god of thievery and stealth, patron of many halfling adventurers. Urogalan is the silent, melancholy god of the earth and death. Accompanied everywhere by a great dark hound, he is saddened by his duties, and vigilant in ensuring that the dead are respected and protected.

LADY LUCK

Many halflings have taken to regular worship of Tymora, seeing her as a helping hand in their fortunes and a patron of the luckiness associated with the *hin*.

HUMANS

Humans dwell in every corner of Toril and encompass a full range of cultures and ethnicities. Along the Sword Coast and across the North, humans are the most pervasive of the races and in many places the most dominant. Their cultural and societal makeup runs the gamut, from the cosmopolitan folk who reside in great cities such as Baldur's Gate and Waterdeep to the barbarians who rage throughout the Savage Frontier.

Humans are famous for their adaptability. No other race lives in so many diverse lands or environments, from lush jungles to burning deserts, from the eternal cold of the Great Glacier to the fertile shores along rivers and seas. Humans find ways to survive and to thrive almost anywhere. In locations where elves and dwarves have withdrawn, humans often move in and build anew alongside or on top of an earlier community.

It follows, then, that the most common feature of humans is their lack of commonality. This diversity has enabled human civilizations to grow faster than those of other races, making humans one of the dominant races in much of the world today. It has also led to conflicts between communities of humans because of their cultural and political differences. If not for their penchant for infighting, humans would be even more populous and predominant than they already are.

HUMAN ETHNICITIES IN FAERÛN

Nine human ethnicities in Faerûn are detailed in the *Player's Handbook*. Several other noteworthy groups of humans are discussed here. Some are significant minorities in regions or nations that border the North, while others are prevalent in parts of the world far from the Sword Coast.

ARKAIUN

Short in stature with tan skin and dark hair, the Arkaiuns dwell primarily in Dambrath as well as Halruaa and the Shar. Many Arkaiuns lived under the yoke of drow slavery centuries ago after a failed military campaign against the dark elves, which led to the eventual destruction of the Arkaiun kingdom in Dambrath.

Arkaiun Names: (Male) Houn, Rhivaun, Umbril, Xaemar, Zeltaebar; (female) Glouris, Maeve, Sevaera, Xaemarra, Zraela; (surnames) Lharaendo, Mristar, Wyndael

BEDINE

Dark-skinned and dark-haired, the Bedine were warriors and nomads in southern Anauroch. Once divided into over a hundred tribes, the clannish Bedine mostly kept to their desert lands and interacted little with outsiders, except for trading. Over the generations, more

A	B	C	D	E	F	G	H	I	J	K	L	M
ϙ	✝	℮	⋀	h	⅃	♯	⅃	⊣	Ϸ	℣	○	⅗
N	**O**	**P**	**Q**	**R**	**S**	**T**	**U**	**V**	**W**	**X**	**Y**	**Z**
Ͼ	⋍	oᴏ	oᴏ	⊥	⅃	℩	⊓	⅌	∞	—	⊤	⅏
1	**2**	**3**	**4**	**5**	**6**	**7**	**8**	**9**	**0**	**10**	**50**	**100**
c	␣	␣	␣	℧	℧	℧	◡	℧	c	cc	cc	ccc

THORASS, THE LETTERS AND NUMERALS OF COMMON

Bedine have become city dwellers, leaving behind their nomadic ways, and reducing the number of tribes that still espouse their traditional way of life.

Bedine Names: (Male) Aali, Rashid, Tahnon, Tanzim, Whalide; (female) Aisha, Farah, Nura, Rashida, Zalebyeh; (tribe names) Alaii, Bordjia, Clelarra, Desai, Dakawa, Dursalai, Goldor, Iriphawa, Kellordrai, Lalajar, Qahtan, Yethtai, Zazalaar

FFOLK

The Ffolk of the Moonshae Isles are descended from Tethyrian settlers who came to the isles a thousand years ago. The Ffolk have a deep respect for nature, and are primarily farmers, worshiping the goddess they call the Earthmother and keeping to old druidic ways. Ffolk shipwrights are well regarded, having proven their ability to build sturdy ships that are capable of weathering the tumultuous seas around their home.

Ffolk Names: (Male) Artur, Bern, Colin, Manfred, Tristan; (female) Alicia, Gennifer, Meridith, Elaine, Olivia; (surnames) Archer, Gareth, Leed, Kendrick, Morgan, Waters

GUR

Related to the Rashemi, Gurs are stout, dusky-skinned, and dark-haired. They consider themselves "children of Selûne," and most of them revere the moon goddess. Gur communities live a nomadic existence wandering the Western Heartlands, leading others to refer to them as "the people of the highway."

Gur Names: (Male) Boriv, Gardar, Madevik, Vlad; (female) Varra, Ulmarra, Imza, Navarra, Yuldra; (surnames) Chergoba, Drazlad, Tazyara, Vargoba, Stayankina

HALRUAAN

The people of the mysterious and magical kingdom of Halruaa, the Halruaans are touched by magic, and many of them are talented in the Art. They and their land vanished during the Spellplague, but just as mysteriously returned after the second Sundering. Most Halruaans have blond or dark hair and olive complexions. Black, brown, and green eyes are the most common.

Halruaan Names: (Male) Aldym, Chand, Meleghost, Presmer, Sandrue, Uregaunt; (female) Aithe, Chalan, Oloma, Phaele, Sarade; (surnames) Avhoste, Darante, Maurmeril, Stamaraster

IMASKARI

An uprising of Mulan slaves brought about the ruin of Imaskar and its ruling wizards thousands of years ago, but some Imaskari survived and fled into the Underdark. There they changed, developing the pale, smooth skin and whitish hair now common among them. The Imaskari who dominated the region of Mulhorand have been forced into exile by a second uprising of those they dominated.

Imaskari Names: (Male) Charva, Duma, Hukir, Jama, Pradir, Sikhil; (female) Apret, Bask, Fanul, Mokat, Nismet, Ril; (surnames) Datharathi, Melpurvatta, Nalambar, Tiliputakas

NAR

More than a thousand years ago, the dark priests of Narfell amassed great power by treating with demons, but their actions eventually brought about a war that destroyed their civilization. The Nars abandoned their ruined and accursed cities and became nomads and traders. Nars have tanned skin, brown or black eyes, and black hair, often worn long and tied in a tail or topknot.

Nar Names: (Male) Avan, Ostaram, Petro, Stor, Taman, Thalaman, Urth; (female) Anva, Dasha, Dima, Olga, Westra, Zlatara; (surnames) Dashkev, Hargroth, Laboda, Lackman, Stonar, Stormwind, Sulyma

SHAARAN

Dark-haired and tan-skinned nomads from southern Faerûn, the Shaarans are skilled hunters, archers, and riders who revere various nature deities. They are organized into clans under the direction of elders and chieftains.

Shaaran Names: (Male) Awar, Cohis, Damota, Gewar, Hapah, Laskaw, Senesaw, Tokhis; (female) Anet, Bes, Idim, Lenet, Moqem, Neghet, Sihvet; (surnames) Cor Marak, Laumee Harr, Moq Qo Harr, Woraw Tarak

TUIGAN

A nomadic horde from the vast plains between Faerûn and Kara-Tur, the Tuigans once nearly conquered Faerûn under the great leader Yamun Khahan before being defeated by a coalition of armies. Since those days, Tuigans are sometimes seen on the Sword Coast and in other nearby regions, but not in great numbers.

The Tuigans resemble the Shou, with a bronze or golden cast to their skin and dark hair, but they tend to have darker skin and broader features. Each has only a single name (sometimes handed down from one's parent); Tuigans don't use surnames. No strangers to travel, Tuigan traders and adventurers are often familiar with many languages and cultures.

Tuigan Names: (Male) Atlan, Bayar, Chingis, Chinua, Mongke, Temur; (female) Bolormaa, Bortai, Erdene, Naran

ULUTIUN

The Ulutiuns are short, dark-haired, golden-skinned people who originated in northern Kara-Tur and migrated westward to Icewind Dale and other cold lands near the Endless Ice Sea. Hunters and gatherers, Ulutiuns live in small tribes that have managed to survive in one of the harshest environments in the world. Each has only a single name (sometimes handed down from one's parent); Ulutiuns don't use surnames.

Ulutiun Names: (Male) Amak, Chu, Imnek, Kanut, Siku; (female) Akna, Chena, Kaya, Sedna, Ublereak

HUMANS' DEITIES

The breadth and variety of the human race in Faerûn is never more evident than in the diverse collection of deities that humans worship. The Faerûnian pantheon (detailed in chapter 1) includes gods of every stripe, and a number of deities whose spheres of influence overlap and compete, which seems to be just how humans like it.

Along the Sword Coast, most human communities have temples and shrines tended by priests who are devoted to various Faerûnian gods. In some of these places, the faithful of deities revered by rulers and other powerful individuals play a greater role in local politics than those not so favored. In the extreme, worship that is deemed heretical or dangerous is outlawed—for example, in a region where followers of Shar hold authority and power, the worship of her good twin and nemesis Selûne might be against the law.

DRAGONBORN

Draconic humanoids from another world, the dragonborn of Faerûn are proud, honorable, and relatively rare. Slaves to dragons on their world of origin, they are now a free people looking for a place and purpose in their new world.

UNCERTAIN ORIGINS

As with all stories of the ancient past, tales of the origins of the dragonborn are hazy and sometimes contradictory. Each reveals something about the dragonborn in its telling, however.

One story relates that the dragonborn were shaped by the ancient dragon-god Io at the same time that Io created the dragons. In the beginning of days, Io fused brilliant astral spirits with the unchecked fury of the elements. The greater spirits became dragons—creatures so powerful, proud, and willful that they were lords of the newborn world. The lesser spirits became the dragonborn. Although smaller in stature, they were no less draconic in nature. This tale stresses the close kinship between dragons and dragonborn, while reinforcing the natural order of things—dragons rule and dragonborn serve, at least according to the dragonborn's former masters.

Another legend asserts that Io created the dragons at the birth of the world, but dragonborn did not yet exist. Then, during the Dawn War, Io was killed by the primordial known as Erek-Hus, the King of Terror. With a rough-hewn axe of adamantine, the behemoth split Io from head to tail, cleaving the dragon-god into two equal halves, which rose up as new gods—Bahamut and Tiamat. Droplets of Io's blood, spattered across the world, became the first dragonborn. For some who believe it, this origin story supports the view that dragonborn are clearly inferior to the dragons that were made by Io's loving hand, while others emphasize that the dragonborn arose from Io's own blood—just as two draconic deities arose from the god's severed body. So are the dragonborn not, therefore, like the gods themselves?

A third origin story posits that dragonborn were the firstborn of the world, created by Io before the existence of other humanoid races, which were pale imitations of dragonborn perfection. Io shaped the dragonborn and fired them with his breath, then spilled his own blood to give them life. The first dragonborn served Io as companions and allies, filling his astral court and singing his praises. The dragons he made only later, at the start of the Dawn War, to serve as engines of destruction. This view of dragonborn history is shared by those who believe that dragonborn are superior to other races and thus should be the masters of dragons and not the other way around.

Despite their differing conclusions, a common theme binds all these legends together: the dragonborn owe their existence to Io, the great dragon-god who created all of dragonkind. The dragonborn, all legends agree, are not the creations of Bahamut or Tiamat—and so they have no predetermined side in the conflict between those gods. Every individual dragonborn, regardless of one's particular draconic ancestry, makes a personal choice in matters of ethics and morality.

THE FIGHT FOR FREEDOM

Dragonborn hail from Abeir, the primordial twin of Toril. On that world most of the dragonborn are slaves to their dragon masters, though many won their freedom and formed nations of free dragonborn. During the Spellplague, the two worlds intersected and one of those free dragonborn nations, Tymanchebar, was transported to Faerûn. It displaced the nation of Unther, and out of the ashes of these two kingdoms, the surviving dragonborn formed Tymanther, a new dragonborn nation in Faerûn.

For a time, the dragonborn of Tymanther sought to integrate with their new world while maintaining their own traditions and culture. These efforts gave the nation and its people a reputation for being honorable and worthy of respect. Only a few generations later, however, the events of the Sundering returned Unther to Faerûn, and the formerly displaced land sought to reclaim all it had lost to Tymanther. Reeling from this disaster, the remaining dragonborn in Faerûn now find they must work even harder and with fewer resources to find their place among the people the world.

HONOR AND FAMILY

Every aspect of dragonborn life is dictated by the race's code of honor and strict adherence to tradition. Dragonborn society is highly ordered, with each member expected to do one's utmost for family and clan. This loyalty and sense of duty sustained the dragonborn during their long history of enslavement and also enabled them to form communities and nations of free dragonborn.

In dragonborn culture, the family is made up of one's direct relations, while a clan is a collection of families brought together by alliance, intermarriage, or shared history. Although they are rarely forced to choose one over the other, the clan's welfare is more important to most dragonborn than the family's. The promise of honor within the clan drives them to acts of heroism, daring, or excellence, all meant to bring glory to the clan first and the individual second.

The aftermath of the Sundering has tested these principles, leaving some clans fractured and decentralized. Some dragonborn in Faerûn seek to recapture the sort of connection they had with a now-lost clan or family by forging new relationships among their non-dragonborn allies and companions.

Dragonborn in Faerûn have the racial traits of dragonborn in the *Player's Handbook*.

PHILOSOPHY AND RELIGION

Their code of honorable behavior and unswerving loyalty serves the dragonborn as a kind of faith, and, according to the traditionalists among them, that outlook is all the religion they need. Because they were forced to worship their draconic masters in times past, dragonborn are generally skeptical about religion, seeing it as a form of servitude. The skeptics believe that no matter how their original god, Io, brought them into being, that ancient deity is either long dead or uncaring about their fate, and the dragon gods that supplanted Io seem primarily interested in amassing soldiers for their ages-old conflict.

Still, some dragonborn do hear the call of the gods of Faerûn and choose to serve them, and are as loyal in this faith as they are to any other cause. Bahamut and Tiamat have dragonborn worshipers, and both Torm and Tyr appeal to the dragonborn sense of honor and order. Similarly, Tempus and the Red Knight appeal to the warrior spirit in some dragonborn, and Kelemvor speaks to some of the inevitability of death and the need to live well in one's allotted time. Religious belief is an intensely personal thing the dragonborn who espouse it, some of whom are as devoted to their faith as they are to their family and clan.

GNOMES

Small of stature and dwelling in the corners of Faerûn away from prying eyes, gnomes are one of the least populous and influential races in the world, called the "Forgotten Folk" by some. This appellation doesn't bother the gnomes; they generally prefer their anonymity and the protection it affords them.

According to legend, the first gnomes in Faerûn sprang from mystic gems buried deep in the earth—an event that accounts for both the gnomes' love of gems and the cozy embrace of their underground warrens. It is said that mystic diamonds became the rock gnomes, emeralds birthed the forest gnomes, and rubies turned into the deep gnomes. Since the time of their creation, gnomes have settled in hidden places away from other races, concerned that their way of life couldn't survive wider exposure.

Gnomes gladly socialize and work with humans, elves, and dwarves, but they always keep in mind that, as a small and relatively insignificant race, their interests can become secondary even among their allies.

Indeed, members of other races sometimes thoughtlessly treat gnomes as second-class citizens, perhaps thinking highly of their gnome friends but rarely giving credit to gnomes as a people. Gnomes are regularly underestimated, and they use that lack of esteem as both a defense and an offense, when need be.

Like dwarves, gnomes have long battled for territory with kobolds, goblinoids, and orcs, but gnomes and kobolds share a special hatred for each other. Both races believe in a legend that, long ago, the deity Garl Glittergold tricked the kobold god Kurtulmak, collapsing the earth and trapping him in an endless underground maze and earning his everlasting enmity.

FOREST GNOMES

The reclusive forest gnomes live simply in hillside dwellings deep in the woods. A neighbor could live only a few miles from a forest gnome settlement for a lifetime and never know it. In these communities, anonymity and stealth help to ensure protection, peace, and survival. If they are discovered and treated well, forest gnomes make fine neighbors, but they usually avoid contact even with civilizations that seem friendly.

Forest gnomes use their affinity with small animals and their knack for illusions to help them remain hidden. When necessary, a forest gnome community defends itself with all the resources at its disposal. Many settlements, however, simply vanish if they are discovered, retreating to some uncharted corner of the forest to begin anew.

The rare forest gnomes who leave their people to become adventurers often draw upon their closeness to nature and their magical gifts to serve as guides, scouts, or mystics. Living close to nature also makes forest gnomes likely to take up roles as druids, who serve various forest spirits and deities.

Forest gnomes in Faerûn have the racial traits of forest gnomes in the *Player's Handbook*.

ROCK GNOMES

When most folk on the Sword Coast and in the North talk about gnomes, they mean rock gnomes. Unlike their shy forest cousins, the inquisitive and irrepressible rock gnomes interact regularly with individuals of other races, especially if those individuals have something to teach them. Rock gnomes prefer to live on the edges of other settlements in their own enclaves, though the occasional adventuresome rock gnome takes up residence in a human or dwarven city.

LADIES OF THE GOLDEN HILLS

A curious bit of gnomish lore is that the pantheon counts not a single female within its ranks. Legend has it that the mysterious Ladies of the Golden Hills went away together on some task in the most ancient days, and have not yet returned. The stories differ as to the Ladies' task, from seeking to gather examples of all of the beauty and riches of Toril, to a secret plan to thwart the evils of the world using their anonymity as a shield, causing the world to forget even their names and identities for a time. Gnomes who wander far from home are said to have "gone looking for the Ladies."

Rock gnome communities are most common in the Western Heartlands and along the coast of the Shining Sea, but gnome wanderers travel between communities across Faerûn in order to trade with or learn from outsiders, including members of other races.

Rock gnomes who leave their communities often find work by using their racial aptitudes to their advantage. Their heritage and their interest in precious stones leads many rock gnomes to become skilled gemcutters and jewelers. Rock gnomes also use their affinity with machines to work as tinkers, alchemists, and engineers. In human communities, gnome tutors and sages are popular, since their comparatively long life spans enable them to acquire and pass on knowledge for generations.

Rock gnomes in Faerûn have the racial traits of rock gnomes in the *Player's Handbook*.

DEEP GNOMES (SVIRFNEBLIN)

Also known as svirfneblin, the deep gnomes of the Underdark are a stark contrast to their surface kin, dour and serious compared to the cheerful and generally optimistic rock gnomes and forest gnomes. They share their cousins' obsession with privacy, and their homes below the surface of Faerûn are well guarded and deeply hidden.

Owing to the hostility of their Underdark neighbors, particularly the drow, the settlements and kingdoms of svirfneblin are in constant danger of being relocated, conquered, or destroyed. Such was the fate of Blingdenstone, one of the grandest deep gnome strongholds, which existed for more than two thousand years until it was overrun a little more than a century ago by the dark elves of Menzoberranzan. The deep gnomes recently reclaimed their old home, and now struggle to rid it of malign influences that have crept into the tunnels and warrens in their absence.

Deep gnomes are lean with dark, earthen skin tones of gray. Males are bald and beardless, while females have hair on their heads. Both sexes have little or no body hair and a stone-like look to their skin.

Deep gnome adventurers are just as curious and daring as those of other races. Some find their purpose living among other subterranean races, and a few make their way to the surface. Those who study the arcane arts of illusion in particular often range far from home, seeking knowledge unavailable in their own lands.

SVIRFNEBLIN SUBRACE TRAITS

The svirfneblin subrace has the gnome traits in the *Player's Handbook*, plus the subrace traits below. Unlike other gnomes, svirfneblin tend to be neutral, they weigh 80 to 120 pounds, and they reach maturity at 25 and live 200 to 250 years.

Ability Score Increase. Your Dexterity score increases by 1.

Superior Darkvision. Your darkvision has a radius of 120 feet.

Stone Camouflage. You have advantage on Dexterity (Stealth) checks to hide in rocky terrain.

Extra Language. You can speak, read, and write Undercommon.

GNOMISH DEITIES

Gnomes honor a small pantheon of seven primary deities, known as the Lords of the Golden Hills, plus two other entities.

WISE PROTECTORS

The Watchful Protector, Garl Glittergold, is the king of gnomish gods, a deity of humor, gemcutting, protection, and trickery. His pranks serve to protect gnomes and to teach his victims humility and wisdom. Garl's second, Gaerdal Ironhand, is the gnomes' war god, who espouses vigilance and defense.

NATURE GODS

Baervan Wildwanderer is the gnomish god of forests and woodlands, accompanied by his companion Chiktikka Fastpaws, a great raccoon said to be the wiser of the two. Segojan Earthcaller is god of the wilds beneath the earth, rather than upon it, as well as god of burrows and the plants and animals found therein.

SHADOW AND STONE

Baravar Cloakshadow is the god of illusion and deception, given the respectful title of Sly One. Callarduran Smoothhands is the god of stone and the Underdark, patron of the svirfneblin.

CRAFT AND INVENTION

Flandal Steelskin, the god of mining and smithcraft, is known as the Steelsmith. He is also the gnomes' god of physical improvement and good health. The fearless Nebelun the Meddler is the god of invention and luck, revered by many gnomes even though he isn't considered one of the Lords of the Golden Hills. "Nebelun's head!" is a common gnomish exclamation of discovery.

THE CRAWLER BELOW

The last member of the gnomish pantheon is Urdlen, which appears not as a gnome, but an elephantine, blind, pale mole. Urdlen is the great-clawed god of bloodlust and evil, of greed and uncontrolled impulses. Young gnomes are warned to "never let Urdlen burrow into your heart," as a caution against giving in to wicked impulses.

Half-Elves

An elf who looks upon a half-elf sees a human, and a human who beholds the same person sees an elf. Though this characterization is simplistic, it gets to the heart of what it means to be a half-elf in Faerûn.

To elves who have an extreme viewpoint on the matter, half-elves are emblematic of the decline of elven civilization, a dilution of the race's heritage and culture that will lead to its eventual dissolution. To the humans at the other end of the spectrum, half-elves have an unfair advantage over their fully human peers, and are seen as privileged or favored regardless of the actual circumstances of their birth.

For most folk in Faerûn, the issue isn't so cut and dried. Half-elves are generally tolerated wherever they go, or wherever they take up residence—with the proviso that a society that doesn't look kindly on elves or humans is likely to feel the same way about someone who has the blood of both races. Conversely, a society that holds humans or elves in high esteem doesn't usually bestow the same status on half-elves (though such individuals are generally not ostracized).

Young Race, Old Roots

In the distant past, half-elves were scarce because humans and elves came into contact only infrequently. The ancient elven kingdoms of Cormanthyr and Myth Drannor had significant populations of half-elves. It is only in the past thousand years or so, as the races have intermingled more and more, that the number of half-elves has increased so that they are now found throughout Faerûn.

Not surprisingly, half-elves enjoy the company of others of their kind, such that where half-elves congregate, they are likely to be joined by others. Most of the half-elves in the North and along the Sword Coast are of moon elf heritage mixed with Illuskan or Tethyrian blood. In other parts of Faerûn, half-elves have significant communities in the Yuirwood and throughout Aglarond. Aquatic half-elves are found along the coasts, including near Aglarond, the Dragon Coast, Impiltur, Sembia, and the Vilhon Reach. Drow half-elves are most numerous in the nation of Dambrath, which was conquered by the dark elves years ago, and in the Underdark, where House Ousstyl of Menzoberranzan is particularly infamous for having mated with humans.

Mixed Heritage

Half-elves are a diverse lot, given the number of combinations of elf subraces and human ethnicities in their ranks. Most of them consider their dual nature a blessing more than a disadvantage, because it gives them a set of capabilities and a perspective on the world that full-blooded humans and elves can't hope to match.

At the same time, the mixed heritage of half-elves dictates that they make an effort to fit in with humans or elves when possible. For instance, half-elves born and raised in human settlements tend to have human names, while half-elves in elven communities generally have elven names. In some places half-elf children are named according to the "other" parent, or with a mix of human and elven names, as a way of setting half-elves apart from the rest of their community.

Half-elves speak both Common and Elvish. In addition, half-elves from the Yuirwood commonly speak Aglarondan.

Half-elves in Faerûn have the racial traits of half-elves in the *Player's Handbook,* although some variations are possible; see the "Half-Elf Variants" sidebar.

The Gods of Two Peoples

There are no half-elven gods, so half-elves follow elven or human deities of their choosing—although just as many religious half-elves believe that their gods choose them. Half-elves often revere the gods of the culture in which they were raised, although some rebel

---

Half-Elf Variants

Some half-elves in Faerûn have a racial trait in place of the Skill Versatility trait. If your DM allows it, your half-elf character can forgo Skill Versatility and instead take the elf trait Keen Senses or a trait based on your elf parentage:

- A half-elf of **wood elf** descent can choose the wood elf's Elf Weapon Training, Fleet of Foot, or Mask of the Wild.
- A half-elf of **moon elf** or **sun elf** descent can choose the high elf's Elf Weapon Training or Cantrip.
- A half-elf of **drow** descent can choose the drow's Drow Magic.
- A half-elf of **aquatic** heritage can choose a swimming speed of 30 feet.

against their upbringing, seeking out the gods of the other aspect of their heritage, or feeling a calling or need to do so.

As with any people, half-elves often choose a favored deity based on their calling or profession: Corellon Larethian, Azuth, or Mystra for wizards, Solonor Thelandira or Mielikki for rangers, Milil or Corellon for poets and bards, and so forth.

Many half-elves worship Sune or Hanali Celanil in appreciation for the love their parents felt for one another, and the two goddesses are seen as boon companions. Some half-elves are drawn to outsiders such as Auril, Eldath, Erevan Ilesere, and Ilmater, or to nature gods like Mielikki, Rillifane Rallathil, and Silvanus. Half-elves from Aglarond often choose Chauntea, Selûne, or one of the Seldarine as their patron.

Half-Orcs

Half-orcs have existed in the world since before the dawn of recorded history, when orcs and humans first came into contact. Yet, in all that time, they have found few places for themselves in Faerûnian civilization—or, perhaps more accurately, civilization has never made room for them.

Most of the common folk have an aversion to half-orcs based largely on their appearance: anyone who looks that much like an orc, they reason, must be like an orc and should be kept at a distance. Because half-orcs are typically stronger and hardier than their human peers, they can find employment in towns and cities, but their appearance marks them as outsiders . In response to being ostracized, half-orcs either embrace their otherness and take pride in their physical superiority, pull back and try not to draw too much attention to themselves, or give up trying to fit in anywhere and adopt a nomadic lifestyle.

Half-orcs in Faerûn have the racial traits of half-orcs in the *Player's Handbook*. They speak both Common and Orc. The rare written examples of the Orc language use the Dethek alphabet.

Blood Will Tell

Half-orcs ultimately owe their plight to the deity Gruumsh, the creator of the orcs. Legend has it that when Gruumsh discovered all the territories of the world had been claimed by other races, he swore the orcs would avenge themselves by taking what they wanted by force. The great orc hordes continue to do just that today, appearing periodically from out of the wilderness to raid and scavenge.

As a result, the word "orc" has no pleasant connotation in the minds of other Faerûnians. At the same time, the word "half" is a mark of derision among orcs. Some half-orcs raised among orcs react to this stigma by being more brutal than others of their tribe, which can put them in roles of leadership, but outsider half-orcs aren't welcomed into orc society because they aren't of pure orc blood. And they aren't accepted into other societies because of their orc heritage.

Half-orcs are seen as off-putting and intimidating by other people, which is both a blessing and a curse, because while they are often left alone by those who fear them, they also become targets of discrimination, or outright attacks, from those who feel threatened by them. This prejudice against the race makes half-orcs slow to trust even those who show them courtesy—because they all have stories of when they were tricked by such behavior. Their orc blood—the Mark of Gruumsh—makes them quick to anger and inclined to lash out at those who treat them unfairly.

Having grown up among orcs or under the shadow of their heritage, half-orcs rarely have experience with pleasant society, and they often come off as coarse, blunt, or rude in dealings with other people. With the directness of an orc, they speak their minds with no apparent concern for how their opinions are received. No matter where they live, half-orcs usually find themselves defined by others in terms of their usefulness as heavy laborers and soldiers. It is the rare and fortunate few who are judged by their character and their deeds rather than their ancestry.

Half-Orc Homelands

In lands far from the Sword Coast, such as Thesk and Chessenta, there are large communities of half-orcs, where generations of them have lived as a people in their own right. Yet there are few such places in the North. A small community was growing near the

Kingdom of Many Arrows, but the recent war with the orcs of that realm caused this burgeoning population to disperse.

Today no civilized place in the North has a significant population of half-orcs, although at least a few of them reside in or on the outskirts of any stable community. Ironically, it is among the largest and most civilized of these places that half-orcs are likely to find acceptance—in the great cities where people are often more cosmopolitan in their outlook.

In Waterdeep, for instance, half-orcs make up a tiny percentage of the population, yet even at that they still number in the hundreds. Half-orcs who call Waterdeep home appreciate the acceptance, or at least tolerance, they receive in the city, whether they were born there, arrived overland from elsewhere on the continent, or entered the city by way of ships bringing trade.

HALF-ORC DEITIES

As befits their dual nature, many half-orcs revere deities from both the human and the orc pantheons. Alone or among themselves, half-orcs offer prayers to orc deities, particularly Ilneval, who is thought of as a patron of half-orcs and other orc crossbreeds.

FAERÛNIAN GODS

Half-orcs trying to fit in with human society often adopt a human deity out of expediency (though rarely just for the sake of appearances). They favor Faerûnian deities of war and trickery, such as Bane, Mask, and Tempus.

FIRST FAMILY

The orc pantheon, known as the Tribe of He Who Watches, is a group of brutal and cruel gods, dominated by their father and chieftain, Gruumsh One-Eye. This god of conquest, strength, and survival is the hated rival of the elven deity Corellon Larethian. It is said that Gruumsh owes the loss of his eye to Corellon's aim with an arrow.

The mother-deity of the orcs is Luthic, mate of Gruumsh, and the goddess of fecundity, caverns, and witchery.

Bahgtru, the son of Gruumsh, is the god of pure, brute strength, renowned for his power but disdained by some for his oafishness.

HORDE LEADER

The patron deity of half-orcs is the war god Ilneval. He has the title of War Master in the pantheon, revered by those who believe in the wisdom of attacking with overwhelming numbers.

BLACK AND WHITE

The two most sinister members of the orc pantheon lie at opposite ends of the visual spectrum. One is Shargaas, the Night Lord, god of darkness, night, and stealth. The other is Yurtrus the White-Handed, Lord of Maggots, the fearsome deity of plagues and death.

TIEFLINGS

Humans with the blood of fiends, most tieflings in Faerûn share a common connection due to the machinations of the archdevil Asmodeus a century ago.

THE MARK OF ASMODEUS

During the Spellplague, Asmodeus consumed the divine spark of Azuth and thereby achieved godhood. Subsequently, Asmodeus and a coven of warlocks, the Toril Thirteen, performed a rite wherein the archdevil claimed all tieflings in the world as his own, cursing them to bear "the blood of Asmodeus." This act marked all tieflings as "descendants" of the Lord of the Nine Hells, regardless of their true heritage, and changed them into creatures that resembled their supposed progenitor. The other folk of Faerûn, unnerved by the appearance of these devil-beings, became suspicious of all tieflings and occasionally hostile to them.

In spite of what some people believe, however, Asmodeus exerts no power over his "children," and tieflings today are as free-willed—and willful—as they ever have been. Some do choose to serve the Lord of the Nine Hells and his schemes, while others align themselves with different fiendish factions, or none at all, doing their best to stay out of infernal politics.

Since the ritual that spread the curse of Asmodeus a century ago, tieflings have been born on Faerûn that belong to other infernal bloodlines, but those that bear the mark of the archdevil (and their descendants) remain the most numerous examples of their kind by far.

Tieflings in Faerûn generally have the racial traits of tieflings in the *Player's Handbook*, except that those not

---

TIEFLING VARIANTS

Since not all tieflings are of the blood of Asmodeus, some have traits that differ from those in the *Player's Handbook*. The Dungeon Master may permit the following variants for your tiefling character, although Devil's Tongue, Hellfire, and Winged are mutually exclusive.

Appearance. Your tiefling might not look like other tieflings. Rather than having the physical characteristics described in the *Player's Handbook*, choose 1d4 + 1 of the following features: small horns; fangs or sharp teeth; a forked tongue; catlike eyes; six fingers on each hand; goat-like legs; cloven hoofs; a forked tail; leathery or scaly skin; red or dark blue skin; cast no shadow or reflection; exude a smell of brimstone.

Feral. Your Intelligence score increases by 1, and your Dexterity score increases by 2. This trait replaces the Ability Score Increase trait.

Devil's Tongue. You know the *vicious mockery* cantrip. When you reach 3rd level, you can cast the *charm person* spell as a 2nd-level spell once with this trait. When you reach 5th level, you can cast the *enthrall* spell once with this trait. You must finish a long rest to cast these spells once again with this trait. Charisma is your spellcasting ability for them. This trait replaces the Infernal Legacy trait.

Hellfire. Once you reach 3rd level, you can cast the *burning hands* spell once per day as a 2nd-level spell. This trait replaces the *hellish rebuke* spell of the Infernal Legacy trait.

Winged. Bat-like wings jut from your shoulder blades. You have a flying speed of 30 feet while you aren't wearing heavy armor. This trait replaces the Infernal Legacy trait.

---

descended from Asmodeus might exhibit different qualities; see the "Tiefling Variants" sidebar.

A Race without a Home

As offspring of the infernal, tieflings call no place in Faerûn their own, although some places and nations are more tolerant of them than most.

In the North, the largest population of tieflings is found in Neverwinter. Since the Ashmadai, a violent cult dedicated to Asmodeus, is also active in the city, mistrust of tieflings isn't unusual even here, since folk never know if a tiefling is a member of the Ashmadai or was drawn to Neverwinter by the opportunity to blend in that a metropolis provides.

Small and scattered groups of tieflings are found elsewhere across Faerûn, particularly in cosmopolitan cities (where they can be anonymous to some degree) and in rough and poor settlements that welcome anyone who can help them survive and prosper.

Tieflings are common in Calimshan, to the south, where many of them fought for the djinn as mercenaries and now serve other masters with the coin to pay them. In the east, many tieflings dwell in Aglarond—escaped slaves from Thay or their descendants—and in Mulhorand, where tieflings are believed to carry the blood of the ancient Mulhorandi gods themselves.

Lone Faithful

Although many Faerûnian folk believe that all tieflings worship Asmodeus and the Lords of the Nine Hells, the truth is that only a fraction of them do so, but enough are devil- or demon-worshipers to lend the weight of truth to all the rumors and suspicion.

Tieflings who revere a god other than Asmodeus often worship deities who watch over and care for outsiders, including Ilmater, Mask, Selûne, Shar, and Tymora. Gods of knowledge, survival, cunning, and warfare are also common attractions for tieflings who value those qualities. Beshaba has tiefling worshipers who consider the accident of their birth as a kind of cruel joke they have chosen to embrace.

Equally intriguing and disturbing to followers of some faiths in Faerûn are stories spread by tieflings who claim to have visions in which the gods of Faerûn appear to them modeled in the tieflings' own image. One such is the entity they call the "pale horned goddess of the moon" (Selûne); another is the "dark, devilish lady of fortune" (Tymora)—an indication, tieflings say, that one's outward appearance and bloodline are less important to the gods than the heart and soul within.

Tiefling Names

A great many tiefling parents follow the naming conventions of the culture in which their offspring are born, such as using human names if they live in a human settlement (the better to seem like "normal" citizens). Others take names derived from the Infernal language that have been passed down since ancient times.

In addition, some Faerûnian tieflings have names drawn from the language of cultures where they are relatively common and generally accepted, such as Calish-

ite and Mulhorandi, which are foreign-sounding to folk in the North and along the Sword Coast.

Al-Khem and Beni-Asmodai are two common Calishite tiefling surnames that proclaim the race's heritage, along with first names such as Haroun, Ishaq, and Nizam (male) or Hania, Rashaa, and Zaar (female).

Mulhorandi surnames that begin with "Sia" or "Zia" followed by a god's name indicate a bearer of that god's bloodline, such as Zianhur and Siasobek. First names commonly seen among Mulhorandi tieflings include Aybtep ("horned"), Bahati ("wise soul"), Het ("smoke"), Kamen ("dark"), Katsu ("star born"), and Kohl ("dark eyed").

CHAPTER 4: CLASSES

THE TWELVE CLASSES PRESENTED IN THE *Player's Handbook* are all found in the Forgotten Realms. The material in this chapter describes the place of those classes in Faerûn, particularly on the Sword Coast and in the North. The chapter also includes new class-feature options for most of the classes, as well as some new spells.

BARBARIANS

CLOSEST TO THE DARK ELVES, PWENT LOWERED HIS *head, with its long helmet spike, and impaled one elf through the chest, blasting through the fine mesh of drow armor easily and brutally. The second drow managed to deflect the next battlerager's charge, turning the helmet spike aside with both his swords. But a mailed fist, the knuckles devilishly spiked with barbed points, caught the drow under the chin and tore a gaping hole in his throat. Fighting for breath, the drow managed to score two nasty hits on his opponent's back, but those two strikes did little in the face of the flurry launched by the wild-eyed dwarf.*

—R.A. Salvatore, *Siege of Darkness*

Many of the lands of the Sword Coast and the North are savage, where day-to-day survival is a struggle. Such lands breed hardy tribes and fierce warriors, such as the Reghed and Uthgardt barbarians of the North and the seafaring Northlanders of the Moonshae Isles and the northernmost reaches of the Sword Coast.

Barbarians of these lands are most often humans or half-orcs, occasionally half-elves born of contact between savage human tribes and the elves of the North or Western Heartlands, or tieflings from tribes known to consort with fiends. Dwarf barbarians are famed and feared warriors among the fiercely proud clans that have reclaimed territories like Mithril Hall and Gautlgrym. Barbarians of most other races hail from warmer southern lands, rather than the Savage North, although southern foundlings are sometimes adopted in the North and raised by tribes there.

PRIMAL PATHS

Barbarians in the Forgotten Realms have the following Primal Path options, in addition to those in the *Player's Handbook*. Reghed and Northlander barbarians tend to follow the Path of the Berserker, while Uthgardt barbarians are nearly always followers of the Path of the Totem Warrior.

PATH OF THE BATTLERAGER

Known as *Kuldjargh* (literally "axe idiot") in Dwarvish, battleragers are dwarf followers of the gods of war and take the Path of the Battlerager. They specialize in wearing bulky, spiked armor and throwing themselves into combat, striking with their body itself and giving themselves over to the fury of battle.

RESTRICTION: DWARVES ONLY

Only dwarves can follow the Path of the Battlerager. The battlerager fills a particular niche in dwarven society and culture.

Your DM can lift this restriction to better suit the campaign. The restriction exists for the Forgotten Realms. It might not apply to your DM's setting or your DM's version of the Realms.

BATTLERAGER ARMOR

When you choose this path at 3rd level, you gain the ability to use spiked armor (see the "Spiked Armor" sidebar) as a weapon.

While you are wearing spiked armor and are raging, you can use a bonus action to make one melee weapon attack with your armor spikes against a target within 5 feet of you. If the attack hits, the spikes deal 1d4 piercing damage. You use your Strength modifier for the attack and damage rolls.

Additionally, when you use the Attack action to grapple a creature, the target takes 3 piercing damage if your grapple check succeeds.

RECKLESS ABANDON

Beginning at 6th level, when you use Reckless Attack while raging, you also gain temporary hit points equal to your Constitution modifier (minimum of 1). They vanish if any of them are left when your rage ends.

BATTLERAGER CHARGE

Beginning at 10th level, you can take the Dash action as a bonus action while you are raging.

SPIKED RETRIBUTION

Starting at 14th level, when a creature within 5 feet of you hits you with a melee attack, the attacker takes 3 piercing damage if you are raging, aren't incapacitated, and are wearing spiked armor.

PATH OF THE TOTEM WARRIOR

If you follow the Path of the Totem Warrior from the *Player's Handbook*, you have access to the options presented here.

TOTEM SPIRIT

These options are available to you when you choose a totem animal at 3rd level.

SPIKED ARMOR

Spiked armor is a rare type of medium armor made by dwarves. It consists of a leather coat and leggings covered with spikes that are usually made of metal.

Cost: 75 gp
AC: 14 + Dexterity modifier (max 2)
Stealth: Disadvantage
Weight: 45 lb.

Uthgardt Totems

The totems of the Uthgardt barbarians of the North (described in chapter 5) correspond to the spirits of the Path of the Totem Warrior as shown in the following table.

Totem	Spirit
Black Lion	Tiger
Black Raven	Eagle
Blue Bear	Bear
Gray Wolf	Wolf
Great Worm	Wolf
Griffon	Eagle
Red Tiger	Tiger
Sky Pony	Eagle, with the Elk Aspect of the Beast
Thunderbeast	Bear, with the Tiger Totemic Attunement
Tree Ghost	Bear, with *speak with plants* in place of the normal rituals for the Spirit Seeker feature

As with the spirits in the *Player's Handbook*, the options here require a physical object incorporating some part of the totem beast, and you might acquire minor physical attributes associated with your totem spirit, such as a prominent nose if you have an elk totem spirit or catlike eyes if you have a tiger totem spirit.

Also, your totem spirit might be an animal similar to one listed here but more suitable to your homeland, such as a horse or stag, rather than an elk, or a lion, panther, or other big cat, rather than a tiger.

Elk. While you're raging and aren't wearing heavy armor, your walking speed increases by 15 feet. The spirit of the elk makes you extraordinarily swift.

Tiger. While raging, you can add 10 feet to your long jump distance and 3 feet to your high jump distance. The spirit of the tiger empowers your leaps.

Aspect of the Beast

These options are available to you when you choose a totem animal at 6th level.

Elk. Whether mounted or on foot, your travel pace is doubled, as is the travel pace of up to ten companions while they're within 60 feet of you and you're not incapacitated (see chapter 8 in the *Player's Handbook* for more information about travel pace). The elk spirit helps you roam far and fast.

Tiger. You gain proficiency in two skills from the following list: Athletics, Acrobatics, Stealth, and Survival. The cat spirit hones your survival instincts.

Totemic Attunement

These options are available to you when you choose a totem animal at 14th level.

Elk. While raging, you can use a bonus action during your move to pass through the space of a Large or smaller creature. That creature must succeed on a Strength saving throw (DC 8 + your Strength bonus + your proficiency bonus) or be knocked prone and take bludgeoning damage equal to 1d12 + your Strength modifier.

Tiger. While you're raging, if you move at least 20 feet in a straight line toward a Large or smaller target right before making a melee weapon attack against it, you can use a bonus action to make an additional melee weapon attack against it.

Bards

Bards hold a special place of responsibility and respect in the Forgotten Realms. They are bearers of news, gossip, and messages in their travels from place to place, in addition to being living storehouses of history and folklore. Bards know a great deal, and they tend to be willing to share what they know, or at least barter for it.

The arrival of a renowned bard is a special occasion, akin to the visit of a dignitary. A bard can reasonably expect at least a hot supper and a clean place to sleep from a local landlord or inn in exchange for a few songs or stories. A noble might host a bard in fine style—while also being careful to guard any secrets the noble's household doesn't want retold or sung across Faerûn.

Not all wandering performers are true bards, nor are all bards inclined to sing for their supper, although most will, given the need. Bards literally have magic to them, and the powers they command through their performance and lore earns them additional respect.

In the Savage North, singers and storytellers called skalds are keepers of the history and great legends of the Northlanders and the Reghed. These warrior-poets are the singers of the songs and sagas that fire the blood of warriors in battle, and composers of the new songs and sagas relating the mighty deeds of heroes and villains. However, spellcasting is taboo among Reghed and Norhtlanders unless it is considered a gift of their gods. Characters with the bard class who rise to prominence among these folk must align themselves with their clan's priests and shamans or risk being outcast. Most skalds are members of the College of Valor, as described in the Bard College class feature in the *Player's Handbook*.

THE HARPERS

Bards in the North and the Dalelands benefit from the existence of the Harpers, that legendary society recruiting bards and other independent agents to struggle against the forces of evil. Even though most bards in the region aren't Harpers (and many who are don't advertise that fact), common folk in the North often behave as if all bards are legendary wandering heroes, and are as likely to ask a bard for the solution to a problem troubling their community as they are a wandering fighter or wizard. This reputation cuts both ways, however, as some enemies of the Harpers suspiciously assume any humble minstrel might secretly be a Harper agent.

BARDIC COLLEGES

In addition to the tradition of apprenticing with a master bard, the Sword Coast has some bardic colleges where masters teach students the bardic arts. They hark back to the great bardic colleges of the distant past, particularly the seven elder colleges: Fochlucan, Mac-Fuirmidh, Doss, Canaith, Cli, Anstruth, and Ollamh. These seven are said to be the origin of the *instrument of the bards*, each of which is named after one of the colleges. See chapter 7 of the *Dungeon Master's Guide* for the game statistics of these magic instruments.

Long ago, bards who sought the rank of master bard attended each of the elder colleges, seeking to learn its musical and magical secrets. Traditionally, the colleges were attended in the order given above, starting with Fochlucan. That tradition fell when the colleges went into decline, but some bards dream of restoring it.

COLLEGE OF FOCHLUCAN

The original College of Fochlucan once stood on the northeastern edge of Silverymoon. Many years after it closed its doors, the site was reopened as Ultrumm's Music Conservatory. The conservatory later moved to Southbank, and the House of the Harp occupied the college's original location under the guidance of Master Bard Forell "Flamebeard" Luekuan, who sought to revive the ancient traditions and teachings of Fochlucan. Years of cultivation and support from Silverymoon, as well as the Harpers, yielded a faculty able to revive the college, and the House of the Harp adopted the Fochlucan name once again. Most of its bards study and practice the methods of the College of Lore, as described in the Bard College class feature in the *Player's Handbook*.

The College of Fochlucan is naturally allied with the Harpers, although its master bards are careful to stress that its mission is separate from that of the Harpers.

COLLEGE OF NEW OLAMN

Housed in two Cliffride villas overlooking the sea near Waterdeep, the College of New Olamn is a prestigious bardic college established in the Year of the Staff (1366 DR) by wealthy Waterdhavian patrons and named for the old College of Ollamh. Students of the college undergo training in their chosen instruments, along with rigorous practice in memorization and the study of ancient songs, sagas, and history. Most bards of New Olamn belong to the College of Lore, as described in the Bard College class feature in the *Player's Handbook*.

The Cliffride, a gravel path up Mount Waterdeep's northern spur, is used to bring goods to the college, but most visitors and students use the Mount Melody Walk—a tunnel through the mountain itself—to reach it. The tunnel regularly resounds with music, thanks to the Neverending String of Pearls, an ongoing concert where bardic students perform in a small alcove in the tunnel, which carries and echoes their music.

COLLEGE OF THE HERALD

Based at the great lore-house of Herald's Holdfast, northwest of Silverymoon, the College of the Herald is dedicated to the preservation of ancient history and legends. The Heralds are charged with collecting and organizing bodies of lore, which they make available to all of good and peaceful intent. Established by the Harper Aliost Oskrunnar in 922 DR, the Heralds are allies of the Harpers but remain neutral in most conflicts, dedicated to preserving knowledge above all else.

The College of the Herald is less concerned with musical performance (although it contains a considerable library of songs) and more with history, heraldry, and folklore, making it a key center of learning for bards of the College of Lore, as described in the Bard College class feature in the *Player's Handbook*.

MUSICAL INSTRUMENTS

In addition to the common musical instruments listed in chapter 5, "Equipment," of the *Player's Handbook*, bards in the Realms play the following instruments:

Birdpipes: Pan pipes or satyr pipes, also known as the shalm, these are sacred to Lliira and popular with wood elf and wild elf bards.

Glaur: Short, curved horns like a cornucopia. Played with valves, glaur sound like trumpets, while those without valves, known as gloon, have a more mournful sound.

Hand Drum: A double-headed skin drum fitted with handles along its side.

Longhorn: A Faerûnian flute of sophisticated make, found only in areas with skilled artisans, as in great cities or elven enclaves.

Shawm: A double-reed instrument similar to an oboe or a bassoon, popular with gnomes, who have developed some bellows-powered versions.

Songhorn: A recorder, a simple type of flute, usually carved from wood.

Tantan: A tambourine, a popular instrument with halflings and humans south of the Dalelands.

Thelarr: Also known as a whistlecane, a simple and easy-to-make wind instrument cut from a reed. They are so simple, in fact, that skilled bards frequently make and give them away to children—to the parents' delight or regret.

Tocken: A hanging set of carved oval bells, usually played with a pair of light wooden hammers (or open handed). They are most common in underground cultures, where the resonant tones can carry.

Wargong: A metal gong, traditionally made from a shield, particularly the shield of an enemy. Both goblins and dwarves make and play wargongs, their sound echoing through tunnels in the Underdark.

Yarting: A southern instrument from Amn and Calimshan that is a Faerûnian analog to the guitar. Numerous variations have spread across the continent.

Zulkoon: A complex pump organ that originated with the zulkirs of Thay, who use it in the casting of their spells. It is considered to have a dramatic, but sinister, sound.

THE MOONSTARS

Over a century ago, the Harpers endured a schism. Khelben "Blackstaff" Arunsun was denounced by other Harper leaders for empowering Fzoul Chembryl, then the evil leader of the Zhentarim, with a powerful artifact. That Khelben did so in order that Fzoul destroy a dangerous lich mattered little. Khelben and Laeral Silverhand, his wife, left the Harpers then, taking with them certain agents and folding them into to a different organization, which Khelben had been secretly working to create for some time due to an old prophecy of the elves of Cormanthor. This group was the Moonstars, called Tel'Teukiira in Elvish. Although the Moonstars worked in concert at times with the Harpers, they also worked at cross purposes, and the Moonstars membership included many whom the Harpers considered too evil, such as a vampire. The Moonstars performed many good deeds, but their methods were often more brutal and pragmatic than the Harpers' lofty ideals allowed. When Khelben died, the Moonstars seemed to collapse, and for many years the organization was assumed defunct. Yet during the Sundering, Moonstar sleeper agents reactivated the organization on a surprisingly massive scale, with members active in Candlekeep, Waterdeep, and Myth Drannor. The organization has since gone underground again. Their relationship to the present-day Harpers, Laeral Silverhand, and the current Blackstaff of Waterdeep, Vajra, remains unclear.

Clerics

The gods are most active through their chosen clerics, who carry out the gods' work on the Material Plane. A typical cleric in Faerûn serves a single divine patron, but some individuals feel called to serve a group, such as the elemental gods Akadi, Grumbar, Kossuth, and Istishia, while others serve deities that are intertwined gods, such as the elves' Angharradh.

Some clerics in Faerûn belong to an established religious hierarchy, but many do not. The gods choose whomever they will, and sometimes a devoted worshiper is blessed with all the abilities of a cleric, despite not being a priest of any kind. That cleric might be a contemplative hermit, a wandering prophet, or simply a devout peasant. Religious orders often try to recruit such clerics and bring them into the fold, but not all of those clerics wish to be bound to a hierarchy.

Conversely, not everyone who pursues a religious vocation is a true cleric. Some acolytes discover a different path for their lives than the path of the cleric. They serve their faiths in other roles, such as priests, scholars, or artisans, while some go on to vocations that have nothing to do with religion. A few souls who are denied the path of the cleric become embittered and seek favor with sinister or forbidden gods or forge pacts with other powerful entities. Religious scholars in the Realms debate whether divine rejection led such a person to embrace a dark path or whether the person was rejected because the gods foresaw the potential for darkness in the person's future. The gods remain silent on the matter.

Some clerics are homebodies who serve a particular community of the faithful, but adventuring clerics tend to have a certain crusading zeal to do their deity's work in the wider world. This work may include ministering to far-flung communities, as well as seeking out and defeating threats to the civilized world.

Divine Domain

Clerics in the Forgotten Realms have the following Divine Domain option, in addition to those in the *Player's Handbook*.

Arcana Domain

Magic is an energy that suffuses the multiverse and that fuels both destruction and creation. Gods of the Arcana domain know the secrets and potential of magic intimately. For some of these gods, magical knowledge is a great responsibility that comes with a special understanding of the nature of reality. Other gods of Arcana see magic as pure power, to be used as its wielder sees fit.

The gods of this domain are often associated with knowledge, as learning and arcane power tend to go hand-in-hand. In the Realms, deities of this domain include Azuth and Mystra, as well as Corellon Larethian of the elven pantheon. In other worlds, this domain includes Hecate, Math Mathonwy, and Isis; the triple moon gods of Solinari, Lunitari, and Nuitari of Krynn; and Boccob, Vecna, and Wee Jas of Greyhawk.

Arcana Domain Spells

Cleric Level	Spells
1st	detect magic, magic missile
3rd	magic weapon, Nystul's magic aura
5th	dispel magic, magic circle
7th	arcane eye, Leomund's secret chest
9th	planar binding, teleportation circle

Arcane Initiate

When you choose this domain at 1st level, you gain proficiency in the Arcana skill, and you gain two cantrips of your choice from the wizard spell list. For you, these cantrips count as cleric cantrips.

Channel Divinity: Arcane Abjuration

Starting at 2nd level, you can use your Channel Divinity to abjure otherworldly creatures.

As an action, you present your holy symbol, and one celestial, elemental, fey, or fiend of your choice that is within 30 feet of you must make a Wisdom saving throw, provided that the creature can see or hear you. If the creature fails its saving throw, it is turned for 1 minute or until it takes any damage.

A turned creature must spend its turns trying to move as far away from you as it can, and it can't willingly end its move in a space within 30 feet of you. It also can't take reactions. For its action, it can only use the Dash action or try to escape from an effect that prevents it from moving. If there's nowhere to move, the creature can use the Dodge action.

After you reach 5th level, when a creature fails its saving throw against your Arcane Abjuration feature, the creature is banished for 1 minute (as in the *banishment* spell, no concentration required) if it isn't on its plane of origin and its challenge rating is at or below a certain threshold, as shown on the Arcane Banishment table.

ARCANE BANISHMENT

Cleric Level	Banishes Creatures of CR ...
5th	1/2 or lower
8th	1 or lower
11th	2 or lower
14th	3 or lower
17th	4 or lower

SPELL BREAKER

Starting at 6th level, when you restore hit points to an ally with a spell of 1st level or higher, you can also end one spell of your choice on that creature. The level of the spell you end must be equal to or lower than the level of the spell slot you use to cast the healing spell.

POTENT SPELLCASTING

Starting at 8th level, you add your Wisdom modifier to the damage you deal with any cleric cantrip.

ARCANE MASTERY

At 17th level, you choose four spells from the wizard spell list, one from each of the following levels: 6th, 7th, 8th, and 9th. You add them to your list of domain spells. Like your other domain spells, they are always prepared and count as cleric spells for you.

DRUIDS

The druids of the Realms venerate nature in all its forms, as well as the gods of the First Circle, those deities closest to the power and majesty of the natural world. That group of gods includes Chauntea, Eldath, Mielikki, Silvanus, as well as Auril, Malar, Talos, and Umberlee, for nature is many-sided and not always kind.

Unlike clerics, who typically serve a single deity, druids revere all the gods of the First Circle in their turn, and see them as embodiments of the natural world, which moves in cycles: creation and destruction, waxing and withering, life and death. Thus, Grumbar isn't just god of the earth to a druid; he is the fertile soil and the rolling hills themselves. Malar isn't just the Beastlord, but the hunger and the hunting instinct of a predatory beast.

Although they are most strongly associated with sylvan forests, druids care for all aspects of the land, including frozen mountains, burning deserts, rolling hills, and rough coasts.

DRUID CIRCLES

Druidic ways are ancient and largely practiced in secret, away from the eyes of the uninitiated. In many lands, the Old Ways of the First Circle have given way to new churches and temples, but druids and their followers still gather to honor the cycles of nature and to ensure the natural balance isn't threatened. People who dwell in or near wild lands do well to learn if a druid circle operates nearby, seeking the circle's blessing before hunting or farming on the lands they protect.

The druid habit of gathering in clearings, wooded groves, or around sacred pools gave rise to the tradition of circles. In a circle, all are equal, and while respect is given to age and accomplishment, the circle reaches decisions as a whole. Those who disagree are free to argue their point, or even to leave the circle, if they wish, but the circle acts as one for the good of all. Druid circles often include non-druid allies, such as rangers, wood elves, and the fey creatures of the land where the circle meets, all given equal voice.

Numerous circles are found across Faerûn, usually made up of no more than a dozen or so druids, plus their allies. They include the High Dance, guarding the

Dancing Place in the high valleys of the Thunder Peaks, alongside their fey allies. The Watchers of Sevreld meet in Old Mushroom Grove in the High Forest, northeast of Secomber, and the Starwater Circle gathers around their namesake pool in the northern forest of Mir.

THE CIRCLE OF SWORDS

Protectors of the Neverwinter Wood, the Circle of Swords drives destructive humanoids like hobgoblins, bugbears, and their kin from the wood, while also safeguarding it against exploitation at the hands of civilized folk and protecting the wood's ancient ruins and sacred sites from looters.

In the Druid Circle class feature in the *Player's Handbook*, the Circle of the Moon is common for Circle of Swords druids, although some belong to the Circle of the Land (Forest).

THE EMERALD ENCLAVE

Less a druid circle and more a loose confederation of circles and their allies, the Emerald Enclave is devoted to protecting the redoubt of civilization in the North from destruction. Elsewhere in the world, the Emerald Enclave must pursue a more balanced path, but the vast wilderness of the North holds far more danger to people than they pose to it.

Founded in the Vilhon Reach over a thousand years ago, the Emerald Enclave has spread across much of Faerûn. Its members include druids, rangers, barbarians, and others who live in the wilderness and know and respect its ways. They wear an article of emerald green clothing as a symbol of their membership, often bearing the emblem of a stag's head.

In the Druid Circle class feature in the *Player's Handbook*, Emerald Enclave druids belong to the Circle of the Land and Circle of the Moon in equal measure.

THE MOONSHEA CIRCLES

The Ffolk of the Moonshea Isles venerate the land as the great goddess they call the Earthmother. Their circles gather around sacred pools known as moonwells, their link between the natural world and the goddess, ringed by standing stone circles, raised by their ancient ancestors.

In the Druid Circle class feature in the *Player's Handbook*, Moonshea druids most often belong to the Circle of the Land (Coast, Forest, and Mountain).

MOONWELLS

The water of a moonwell, drunk directly from cupped hands, restores 1d8 hit points, plus the drinker's Wisdom bonus, if any. If the drinker has threatened the balance of nature since the last full moon, the water instead deals 1d8 poison damage to the drinker. This damage is also dealt by a corrupted moonwell. Either effect occurs once only per day per drinker. On the nights of the full moon, drinking the water of a moonwell can, at the DM's discretion, have additional effects, such as conferring the benefits of a *lesser restoration* spell.

Moonwell water placed in a container or taken more than 30 feet away from the well no longer has any of these properties; it is simply water.

On the three nights of the full moon, three or more druids gathered around a moonwell can cast *commune* and *scrying* once each without expending spell slots and without material components, provided that one of the druids is at least 9th level and the rest are at least 4th level. At the DM's option, the druids can use a moonwell on such nights to cast different spells.

FIGHTERS

"SLOW TO LEARN, AREN'T THEY?" A WHITE-HAIRED OLD *knight who'd lost his helm in the last fray drawled. "This is getting to be like a proper romp in the Dragonjaws, it is! I'll have to get my minstrel to write a ballad about this ..."*

"I hope he sings swiftly," a Purple Dragon armsman growled. "Here they are!"

The howling spilled over the bodies in another rushing tide of flapping leather, slashing swords, and beady goblin eyes. Men planted themselves—no running and leaping now—to hew steadily, like harvesters with scythes and many fields in front of them, in a rhythm of death.

—Troy Denning, *Death of the Dragon*

Whether doughty warriors, idealistic young soldiers, or hard-bitten mercenaries, fighters are found everywhere in the Forgotten Realms. Even the most peaceful lands have militia for protection against their enemies, and many great rulers in the Realms' past were fighters of some sort. There are always opportunities for those who know how to handle themselves in a fight.

Able-bodied folk in many parts of the Sword Coast and the North learn at least the rudiments of combat as part of a local militia, serving in times of need, while a few go on to become professional soldiers, guards, or the like. Officers tend to come from the nobility, although there are opportunities for capable leaders to demonstrate their skills and rise through the ranks.

Fighters who don't make a career of soldiering find other ways to demonstrate their prowess. Mercenaries find employment with those who need skilled warriors but who lack the time or means to train them. Such employers include adventuring companies, which are almost always in need of a reliable fighter.

Merchants and guilds hire guards to protect caravans, ships, and their warehouses and guildhalls. Such work affords the opportunity for frequent travel and danger.

A good deal of danger comes from fighters who abandon legitimate employment to become bandits—raiding caravans, robbing travelers, and pillaging isolated homesteads, manors, and villages. Out-of-luck fighters might also take part in gladiatorial fights or similar blood sports to make a living off their skills, although such matches are virtually unknown on the Sword Coast and in the North, as compared to southern nations like Amn and Calimshan.

MARTIAL ARCHETYPE

Fighters in the Forgotten Realms have the following Martial Archetype option, in addition to those in the *Player's Handbook*.

PURPLE DRAGON KNIGHT

Purple Dragon knights are warriors who hail from the kingdom of Cormyr. Pledged to protect the crown, they take the fight against evil beyond their kingdom's borders. They are tasked with wandering the land as knights errant, relying on their judgment, bravery, and fidelity to the code of chivalry to guide them in defeating evildoers.

A Purple Dragon knight inspires greatness in others by committing brave deeds in battle. The mere presence of a knight in a hamlet is enough to cause some orcs and bandits to seek easier prey. A lone knight is a skilled warrior, but a knight leading a band of allies can transform even the most poorly equipped militia into a ferocious war band.

A knight prefers to lead through deeds, not words. As a knight spearheads an attack, the knight's actions can awaken reserves of courage and conviction in allies that they never suspected they had.

RESTRICTION: KNIGHTHOOD

Purple Dragon knights are tied to a specific order of Cormyrean knighthood.

Banneret serves as the generic name for this archetype if you use it in other campaign settings or to model warlords other than Purple Dragon knights.

RALLYING CRY

When you choose this archetype at 3rd level, you learn how to inspire your allies to fight on past their injuries.

When you use your Second Wind feature, you can choose up to three creatures within 60 feet of you that are allied with you. Each one regains hit points equal to your fighter level, provided that the creature can see or hear you.

ROYAL ENVOY

A Purple Dragon knight serves as an envoy of the Cormyrean crown. Knights of high standing are expected to conduct themselves with grace.

At 7th level, you gain proficiency in the Persuasion skill. If you are already proficient in it, you gain proficiency in one of the following skills of your choice: Animal Handling, Insight, Intimidation, or Performance.

Your proficiency bonus is doubled for any ability check you make that uses Persuasion. You receive this benefit regardless of the skill proficiency you gain from this feature.

INSPIRING SURGE

Starting at 10th level, when you use your Action Surge feature, you can choose one creature within 60 feet of you that is allied with you. That creature can make one melee or ranged weapon attack with its reaction, provided that it can see or hear you.

Starting at 18th level, you can choose two allies within 60 feet of you, rather than one.

BULWARK

Beginning at 15th level, you can extend the benefit of your Indomitable feature to an ally. When you decide to use Indomitable to reroll an Intelligence, a Wisdom, or a Charisma saving throw and you aren't incapacitated, you can choose one ally within 60 feet of you that also failed its saving throw against the same effect. If that creature can see or hear you, it can reroll its saving throw and must use the new roll.

MONKS

THE FAT MAN STRAIGHTENED HIS BLACK-AND-GOLD
vest, lowered his round head, and charged.

Danica waited until he was right in front of her, and to
the onlookers it appeared as if the woman would be buried
beneath mounds of flesh. At the last moment, she dipped
her head under the fat man's lunging arm, caught his hand,
and casually stepped behind him as he lumbered past. A
subtle twist of her wrist stopped him dead in his tracks, and
before he even realized what was happening, Danica kicked
the back of both his knees, dropping him to a kneel.

—R.A. Salvatore, *Canticle*

Some of the earliest monastic orders in Faerûn arose in
the southern lands of Amn and Calimshan, their practices migrating north and east at the same time similar
practices filtered westward from distant Kara-Tur.

The oldest orders have branched or fractured into
smaller offshoots over time, such that there are now dozens of them. Most are no more than a few dozen members living in an isolated community in the wilderness.
Some monastic communities have members numbering
in the hundreds, with a presence closer to civilization,
and often with correspondingly greater influence, for
those orders concern themselves with worldly affairs.

As most monastic orders in Faerûn arose from human
nations, the majority of monks in those communities
tend to be human. Monasteries have long been sanc-
tuaries for foundlings and outcasts of various sorts, so
nonhuman monks are not unheard of.

MONASTIC ORDERS

The following orders can be found in various parts of
the Forgotten Realms.

THE DARK MOON

A monastic order devoted to Shar, the Dark Moon works
openly in lands where her worship is accepted and in
secret wilderness and underground hideaways where
it isn't. Its followers seek "knowledge and conversation
with the shadow," believing true wisdom is found in
darkness and loss, both literally and spiritually. Its
adherents most often follow the Way of Shadow, as described in the Monastic Tradition class feature in the
Player's Handbook.

THE HIN FIST

A halfling monastic order from Luiren, adherents of
the Hin Fist turn their people's natural confidence into
a spiritual path for mastering themselves and their
potential. A few Hin Fist masters have established monasteries in lands outside Luiren, where the teachings
available only to halflings have been opened to students
of other races who are willing to follow the path laid out
by Yondalla. Hin Fist monks generally follow the Way of
the Open Hand, as described in the Monastic Tradition
class feature in the *Player's Handbook.*

ORDER OF THE YELLOW ROSE

Also known as the Disciples of Saint Sollars the
Twice-Martyred, the Order of the Yellow Rose is a solitary monastery of Ilmater worshipers in the Earthspur
Mountains of Damara. It is known for loyalty to its allies and destruction to its enemies. Greatly respected
on matters of truth and diplomacy, the monks work
hard to survive in their remote sanctuary. The monks
of the Monastery of the Yellow Rose use the remorhaz
to test their disciples. Young monks must prove the
power of their mind to overcome fear and pain by riding
the beasts.

The faith of Ilmater fosters far more orders of monks
that other gods. Other Ilmatari monastic orders include
the Followers of the Unhindered Path, the Disciples of
St. Morgan the Taciturn, and the Sisters of St. Jasper of
the Rocks.

Monks of Ilmater often travel as wanderers, begging for alms, seeking enlightenment, and relieving the suffering of others. They tend to follow the Way of the Open Hand, as described in the Monastic Tradition class feature in the *Player's Handbook*.

THE SUN SOULS

The Sun Soul monks follow a monastic tradition that they believe has its roots in the ancient empire of Netheril. In their philosophy, living things harbor a fragment of the sun's mystic essence within them. Just as the body has a shadow, so too does the spirit have a light. That light is called the sun soul. Brothers and sisters of the Order of the Sun Soul train to tap into the "spiritual light within" and manifest it as supernatural feats of prowess and endurance. Members of this order follow the Way of the Sun Soul, which is described in the "Monastic Traditions" section below.

To get in touch with their internal light, Sun Soul monks follow a strict code of ascetic conduct called the Precepts of Incandescence. It emphasizes three pillars:

Seek physical perfection. To open the way for the sun soul to manifest, one should strive to make the body beautiful. Fitness, cleanliness, and well-honed physicality create a clearer window through which the light can shine.

Seek spiritual virtue. Recognize the light in others, not just the darkness. Grant and take each new chance to be virtuous.

Shine light into darkness. Share the soul's light with the world. Light up dark places with your presence and banish shadow.

Due to the precepts' similarity to the teachings of some faiths, the Order of the Sun Soul has long had associations with temples and the faithful of three particular deities: Sune, Selûne, and Lathander. The dictate to seek physical perfection and recognize hidden virtue has similarity to Sune's teachings about physical and spiritual beauty. Followers of Selûne recognize their goddess's exhortation to battle darkness and seek virtue. And of course, Lathander's association with the sun links to the Sun Soul philosophy, but more critically for worshipers of Lathander, they see the idea of granting and taking new chances as similar to Lathander's emphasis on new beginnings.

LONG DEATH MONKS

Followers of the Way of the Long Death worship the principle of death more so than any deity of death. These monks seek the secrets of life by studying death itself. It is the condition of being dead that concerns them most, and not what lies beyond; the afterlife holds little interest for them. Their monasteries are full of decaying, dying, and dead animal and plant specimens, which they study with detached interest. They frequently purchase rare specimens from adventurers and merchants that they can't obtain easily themselves. But such studies are only part of the monks' daily life: They seek to understand death as it pertains especially to intelligent living beings, and to this end they eagerly welcome the diseased and the dying so that they might watch and record their deaths. If such unfortunates seek release from pain through death, the monks provide it. They view death as a gift that they bestow on those who are ready for it. Their means of determining readiness vary from one sect (or even one monk) to another.

The monks suffer no moral qualms about these deeds, for death is the most natural thing in the world, from their perspective, and to expire in service to its principle is one of the most profoundly holy experiences a living being can hope to enjoy. It is for this reason that the monks themselves do not fear death.

Most of the order's members are either scholars who share mutual fascination with death and dying or clergy who worship one of the deities concerned with death. Some of the monks consider themselves to be nothing less than visionaries whose work will pave the way for a better future for all Faerûn. When death is truly understood, it can be harnessed and used as a tool for the betterment of all, or so they rationalize to themselves.

Monks of this tradition follow the Way of the Long Death, which is described in the "Monastic Traditions" section below.

THE YIELDING WAY

The monastic order of Eldath is the Disciples of the Yielding Way, sometimes known as the Brothers and Sisters of the Open Palm. These monks guard sacred sites where many priests dwell, and they travel the countryside gathering information for isolated groves and fastnesses. They don't ever seek to provoke violence, but are quite deadly when defending themselves, their charges, and their holy sites.

MONASTIC TRADITIONS

Monks in the Forgotten Realms have the following Monastic Tradition options, in addition to those in the *Player's Handbook*.

WAY OF THE LONG DEATH

Monks of the Way of the Long Death are obsessed with the meaning and mechanics of dying. They capture creatures and prepare elaborate experiments to capture, record, and understand the moments of their demise. They then use this knowledge to guide their understanding of martial arts, yielding a deadly fighting style.

TOUCH OF DEATH

Starting when you choose this tradition at 3rd level, your study of death allows you to extract vitality from another creature as it nears its demise. When you reduce a creature within 5 feet of you to 0 hit points, you gain temporary hit points equal to your Wisdom modifier + your monk level (minimum of 1 temporary hit point).

HOUR OF REAPING

At 6th level, you gain the ability to unsettle or terrify those around you as an action, for your soul has been touched by the shadow of death. When you take this action, each creature within 30 feet of you that can see you must succeed on a Wisdom saving throw or be frightened of you until the end of your next turn.

MASTERY OF DEATH

Beginning at 11th level, you use your familiarity with death to escape its grasp. When you are reduced to 0 hit points, you can expend 1 ki point (no action required) to have 1 hit point instead.

TOUCH OF THE LONG DEATH

Starting at 17th level, your touch can channel the energy of death into a creature. As an action, you touch one creature within 5 feet of you, and you expend 1 to 10 ki points. The target must make a Constitution saving throw, and it takes 2d10 necrotic damage per ki point spent on a failed save, or half as much damage on a successful one.

WAY OF THE SUN SOUL

Monks of the Way of the Sun Soul learn to channel their own life energy into searing bolts of light. They teach that meditation can unlock the ability to unleash the indomitable light shed by the soul of every living creature.

RADIANT SUN BOLT

Starting when you choose this tradition at 3rd level, you can hurl searing bolts of magical radiance.

You gain a ranged spell attack that you can use with the Attack action. The attack has a range of 30 feet. You are proficient with it, and you add your Dexterity modifier to its attack and damage rolls. Its damage is radiant, and its damage die is a d4. This die changes as you gain monk levels, as shown in the Martial Arts column of the Monk table.

When you use the Attack action on your turn to use this special attack, you can spend 1 ki point to make two additional attacks with it as a bonus action.

SEARING ARC STRIKE

At 6th level, you gain the ability to channel your ki into searing waves of energy. Immediately after you take the Attack action on your turn, you can spend 2 ki points to cast the 1st-level spell *burning hands* as a bonus action.

You can spend additional ki points to cast *burning hands* as a higher level spell. Each additional ki point you spend increases the spell's level by 1. The maximum number of ki points (2 plus any additional points) that you can spend on the spell equals half your monk level (round down).

SEARING SUNBURST

At 11th level, you gain the ability to create an orb of light that erupts into a devastating explosion. As an action, you magically create an orb and hurl it at a point you choose within 150 feet, where it erupts into a sphere of radiant light for a brief but deadly instant.

Each creature in that 20-foot-radius sphere must succeed on a Constitution saving throw or take 2d6 radiant damage. A creature doesn't need to make the save if the creature is behind total cover that is opaque.

You can increase the sphere's damage by spending ki points. Each point you spend, up to a maximum of 3, increases the damage by 2d6.

SUN SHIELD

At 17th level, you become wreathed in a luminous, magical aura. You shed bright light in a 30-foot radius and dim light for an additional 30 feet. You can extinguish or restore the light as a bonus action.

If a creature hits you with a melee attack while this light shines, you can use your reaction to deal radiant damage to the creature. The radiant damage equals 5 + your Wisdom modifier.

PALADINS

Some people are warriors of superior virtue. They exemplify a host of traits that folk consider honorable, just, and good. These warriors aspire to be the best people they can. When such a warrior also has great devotion to a particular deity, that god can reward the faithful with a measure of divine power, making that person a paladin.

Different paladin orders in the Forgotten Realms emphasize different elements of righteous behavior, but all paladins are expected to hold true to a common set of virtues:

Liberality. Be generous and tolerant.
Good faith. Be honest and keep promises.

Courtesy. Treat others with respect despite how they treat you. Give honor to those above your station. Earn the respect of those below your station.

Lawfulness. Laws exist to bring prosperity to those under them. Unjust laws must be overturned or changed in a reasonable fashion.

Bravery. Gain glory through battle. Defend any charge unto death.

Pride in one's actions. Lead by example. Let your deeds speak your intentions.

Humility in one's deeds. Do not boast or accept rewards undue to you.

Unselfishness. Share resources, especially with those who have the most need.

Good-temperedness. Render service cheerfully and without disdain.

Wisdom. Cause the most good through the least harm.

Piety. Be faithful to the precepts of your god.

Kindness. Protect the weak. Grant mercy to those who seek redemption.

Honor. Hold true to the code. Death before dishonor.

Every paladin grades and emphasizes these virtues based on his or her own personal ethos and religious background. A paladin of Sune would emphasize aspects of courtly love and courtesy, whereas a paladin of Tyr would be more concerned with justice and fair treatment of foes.

Most paladins in the Forgotten Realms, like clerics, are devoted to a particular deity. The most common paladin deities are those that embody action, decision, watchfulness, and wisdom. Torm and Tyr are both popular deities for paladins, as is Ilmater, who stresses self-sacrifice and the alleviation of suffering. Although less common, there are paladins of the following deities: Helm, Hoar, Lathander, Sune, Corellon Larethian, the Red Knight, Clangeddin Silverbeard, Arvoreen, and Mystra.

Their devotion to a higher ideal makes paladins popular folk heroes in the Realms. Many tales are woven about noble knights and oath-sworn champions, although pragmatists note that the tales often end with a tremendous sacrifice on the part of said champions.

The most common patrons of paladins of the Oath of Devotion and the Oath of the Crown (which is described below) are Helm, Torm, and Tyr—protection, courage, and justice—although Ilmater has his share of devoted champions. Those green knights sworn to the Oath of the Ancients might honor Arvoreen or Corellon, while avengers of the Oath of Vengeance follow patrons like Hoar, although there are also avengers of Helm and Tyr, meting out harsh justice.

Paladin Orders

The following orders can be found in various parts of the Forgotten Realms.

Order of the Companion

Based in Elturgard in the Western Heartlands, the Order of the Companion is sworn to guard that nation. It formed in the wake of the Spellplague and helped to create Elturgard, centered on the city of Elturel, overlooking the River Chionthar. The Companions safeguard civilization against dangerous and wild forces, particularly unnatural creatures. Of the options in the Sacred Oath class feature, the Oath of the Crown (described below) and the Oath of Devotion (described in the *Player's Handbook*) are equally represented among their ranks.

Order of the Gilded Eye

The monastery and cathedral of Helm's Hold stands on the edge of the Neverwinter Wood in the North as a safe haven for travelers. The Order of the Gilded Eye safeguards the hold and serves the surrounding community, but their mission has a much broader focus: to guard the world from dangers originating on other planes of existence, especially on the Lower Planes. Many paladins and non-paladins have joined the order in response to its call to cast fiendish incursions out of the world. In recent years, many have ventured forth from Helm's Hold to do the order's work in the wider world.

Of the options in the Sacred Oath class feature in the *Player's Handbook*, paladins of the Gilded Eye most often follow the Oath of Devotion, although a few zealots are followers of the Oath of Vengeance.

Order of Samular

The Holy Order of Samular, also known as the Knights of Samular, is made up of warriors in the service of Tyr. The order is based at Summit Hall, while also maintaining a chapter house in Waterdeep. Legendary paladin Samular Caradoon founded the order in 952 DR after the Second Troll War and the deaths of his brothers Renwick "Snowcloak" and Amphail the Just during the war. When Tyr fell silent and the paladins in his service lost their powers, many turned to other gods such as Torm, but the Kights of Samular stayed true to Tyr. Their patience was recently rewarded when, upon Tyr's return to the world, many of their dwindling number were invested with the powers of a paladin. Known for their support of the law, many paladins of the order follow the Oath of the Crown, which is described below.

Sacred Oath

Paladins in the Forgotten Realms have the following Sacred Oath option, in addition to those in the *Player's Handbook*.

Oath of the Crown

The Oath of the Crown is sworn to the ideals of civilization, be it the spirit of a nation, fealty to a sovereign, or service to a deity of law and rulership. The paladins who swear this oath dedicate themselves to serving society and, in particular, the just laws that hold society together. These paladins are the watchful guardians on the walls, standing against the chaotic tides of barbarism that threaten to tear down all that civilization has built, and are commonly known as guardians, exemplars, or sentinels. Often, paladins who swear this oath are members of an order of knighthood in service to a nation or a sovereign, and undergo their oath as part of their admission to the order's ranks.

TENETS OF THE CROWN

The tenets of the Oath of the Crown are often set by the sovereign to which their oath is sworn, but generally emphasize the following tenets.

Law. The law is paramount. It is the mortar that holds the stones of civilization together, and it must be respected.

Loyalty. Your word is your bond. Without loyalty, oaths and laws are meaningless.

Courage. You must be willing to do what needs to be done for the sake of order, even in the face of overwhelming odds. If you don't act, then who will?

Responsibility. You must deal with the consequences of your actions, and you are responsible for fulfilling your duties and obligations.

OATH SPELLS

You gain oath spells at the paladin levels listed.

OATH OF THE CROWN SPELLS

Paladin Level	Spells
3rd	command, compelled duel
5th	warding bond, zone of truth
9th	aura of vitality, spirit guardians
13th	banishment, guardian of faith
17th	circle of power, geas

CHANNEL DIVINITY

When you take this oath at 3rd level, you gain the following Channel Divinity options.

Champion Challenge. As a bonus action, you issue a challenge that compels other creatures to do battle with you. Each creature of your choice that you can see within 30 feet of you must make a Wisdom saving throw. On a failed save, a creature can't willingly move more than 30 feet away from you. This effect ends on the creature if you are incapacitated or die or if the creature is more than 30 feet away from you.

Turn the Tide. As a bonus action, you can bolster injured creatures with your Channel Divinity. Each creature of your choice that can hear you within 30 feet of you regains hit points equal to 1d6 + your Charisma modifier (minimum of 1) if it has no more than half of its hit points.

DIVINE ALLEGIANCE

Starting at 7th level, when a creature within 5 feet of you takes damage, you can use your reaction to magically substitute your own health for that of the target creature, causing that creature not to take the damage. Instead, you take the damage. This damage to you can't be reduced or prevented in any way.

UNYIELDING SPIRIT

Starting at 15th level, you have advantage on saving throws to avoid becoming paralyzed or stunned.

EXALTED CHAMPION

At 20th level, your presence on the field of battle is an inspiration to those dedicated to your cause. You can use your action to gain the following benefits for 1 hour:

- You have resistance to bludgeoning, piercing, and slashing damage from nonmagical weapons.
- Your allies have advantage on death saving throws while within 30 feet of you.
- You have advantage on Wisdom saving throws, as do your allies within 30 feet of you.

This effect ends early if you are incapacitated or die. Once you use this feature, you can't use it again until you finish a long rest.

RANGERS

MONTOLIO HELD OUT HIS ARM, AND THE GREAT OWL *promptly hopped onto it, carefully finding its footing on the man's heavy leather sleeve.*

"You have seen the drow?" Montolio asked.

The owl responded with a whoo, then went off into a complicated series of chattering hoots and whoos. Montolio took it all in, weighing every detail. With the help of his friends, particularly this rather talkative owl, the ranger had monitored the drow for several days, curious as to why a dark elf had wandered into the valley. At first, Montolio had assumed that the drow was somehow connected to Graul, the chief orc of the region, but as time went on, the ranger began to suspect differently.

—R.A. Salvatore, *Sojourn*

Long have rangers walked the wilds of the Sword Coast and the Savage Frontier. Like druids, their practices date back to the earliest days of humanity. And long before humans set foot in the North, elf rangers strode through its forests and climbed its mountains. The traditions and outlook of these people are now shared by members of many races. In particular, lightfoot halflings frequently hear the call of the wild and become rangers, often acting as guides and protectors of roving halfling bands, and shield dwarves forced to wander far from old clanholds sometimes follow the ranger's path.

Not every prospector wandering far hills or trapper hunting through uninhabited lands becomes a ranger. True rangers go out into nature and find it holy, and like paladins, they are touched by something divine. Their gods and creeds might differ, but rangers share similar values about the sanctity of nature. While by no means always aligned with one another, rangers are bound into a loose community of sorts—one that often connects with circles of druids.

In the North and throughout much of the Heartlands, rangers use special marks to indicate campsites, dangerous areas, evil creatures, foul magic, goblinoid activity, hidden caches of supplies, safe passage, shelter, and graves or tombs. Many of these symbols were derived from elven lore or borrowed from groups like the Harpers. While by no means a secret language, these trail marks are often obtuse to non-rangers, and even druids might not understand them.

As a whole, rangers serve to help societies survive and thrive in the wilderness. Much of the Sword Coast and

ELF RANGERS

Elf rangers are usually associated with a particular community such as Evereska or the tribes in the Misty Forest. Rather than being wandering explorers, elf rangers typically act as scouts and guardians of elven realms. Such elves usually devote themselves to Rillifane Rallathil or Solonor Thelandria. Elf rangers driven to roam might instead favor Fenmarel Mestarine, god of lone wanderers, or Shevarash, elven god of vengeance.

HALFLING RANGERS

Most halflings who revere nature and its raw beauty come from lightfoot stock. Their bands spend at least as much time on the road and river as in village and town, and the role of a ranger is a natural fit with the lifestyle of most lightfoots. Lightfoot rangers tend to favor the god Brandobaris in his aspect as patron of exploration. Halflings more inclined toward nature itself typically prefer Sheela Peryroyl. Those who devote themselves more to the protection of settlements or travelers honor Arvoreen. The few strongheart halflings who become rangers tend to favor those latter two deities.

DWARF RANGERS

Most dwarves prefer to hunker down under a mountain, rather than roam the wilderness of the surface or the Underdark. Most often, a dwarf ranger is either a shield dwarf cast out of a clanhold or a clanless dwarf seeking a place in the world. Sometimes dwarf rangers are prospectors who explore the world seeking new veins of ore. In any case, there are two deities who appeal to such dwarves: Marthammor Duin and Dumathoin.

ROGUES

There are those whose abilities lie not with sword or the Art, but with quiet motion, dexterous action, and stealth. Such talents often lead to illegal endeavors, which plague most major cities, but can be placed to good use in dealing with dangerous monsters and lost treasure.

Most large cities in the Realms have a number of thieves' dens that compete with one another. A few places, such as Baldur's Gate, have an organized group of rogues that controls all such activity. Most thieves' dens are secret gathering spots, often beneath the city, and move after they're discovered.

The city of Waterdeep had once been home to the most powerful guild of thieves in the North: the Shadow Thieves. The Lords of Waterdeep smashed that guild, forcing its leaders to flee the city (the group still operates out of Amn). There are still thieves and even assassins in Waterdeep, but they are broken into innumerable small groups or operate alone.

The most common respite for such robbers is what they call the Honest Trade—adventuring, where roguish abilities may be used without censure and are later lionized in song and legend. Many thieves take to this life, adhering to a code that keeps them out of trouble in civilized areas but still keeps them rich; they vow to burglarize ancient tombs and monstrous lairs instead of the homes and businesses of the wealthy in civilized lands.

the North are unsettled. Rangers are driven to explore these lands, searching for fertile soil in which the seeds of civilization might grow, seeking resources (such as metals) that will benefit settled lands, or rooting out evil before it can spread. Other rangers spy on enemy troops or hunt down dangerous beasts or criminals. Given that so much of the North is frontier, rangers play a critical role in keeping communities safe and are often admired within them.

HUMAN RANGERS

Human rangers of the Moonshaes are devoted to the Earthmother, and those that work closely with druid circles on the mainland often honor the gods of the First Circle, but most rangers among humans favor the goddess Mielikki. However, they consider the goddess too wild and primal for them to pray to directly. Instead, they pray to Gwaeron Windstrom to bring their words to the goddess. Gwaeron is said to sleep in a grove of trees west of the town of Triboar, and most of his followers travel to that place at least once in their lives as a holy pilgrimage. Evil human rangers usually honor Malar for his ferocity and hunting skill.

Some rogues have learned it is easier to pick someone's pocket when you have a royal writ, which is to say many rogues are diplomats, courtiers, influence-peddlers, and information-brokers, in addition to the better-known thieves and assassins. Such rogues blend more easily into civilized society, more often acting as grease in the wheels than a wrench in the works.

ROGUISH ARCHETYPES

Rogues in the Forgotten Realms have the following Roguish Archetype options, in addition to those in the *Player's Handbook*.

MASTERMIND

Your focus is on people and on the influence and secrets they have. Many spies, courtiers, and schemers follow this archetype, leading lives of intrigue. Words are your weapons as often as knives or poison, and secrets and favors are some of your favorite treasures.

MASTER OF INTRIGUE

When you choose this archetype at 3rd level, you gain proficiency with the disguise kit, the forgery kit, and one gaming set of your choice. You also learn two languages of your choice.

Additionally, you can unerringly mimic the speech patterns and accent of a creature that you hear speak for at least 1 minute, allowing you to pass yourself off as a native speaker of a particular land, provided that you know the language.

MASTER OF TACTICS

Starting at 3rd level, you can use the Help action as a bonus action. Additionally, when you use the Help action to aid an ally in attacking a creature, the target of that attack can be within 30 feet of you, rather than 5 feet of you, if the target can see or hear you.

INSIGHTFUL MANIPULATOR

Starting at 9th level, if you spend at least 1 minute observing or interacting with another creature outside combat, you can learn certain information about its capabilities compared to your own. The DM tells you if the creature is your equal, superior, or inferior in regard to two of the following characteristics of your choice:

- Intelligence score
- Wisdom score
- Charisma score
- Class levels (if any)

At the DM's option, you might also realize you know a piece of the creature's history or one of its personality traits, if it has any.

MISDIRECTION

Beginning at 13th level, you can sometimes cause another creature to suffer an attack meant for you. When you are targeted by an attack while a creature within 5 feet of you is granting you cover against that attack, you can use your reaction to have the attack target that creature instead of you.

SOUL OF DECEIT

Starting at 17th level, your thoughts can't be read by telepathy or other means, unless you allow it. You can present false thoughts by making a Charisma (Deception) check contested by the mind reader's Wisdom (Insight) check.

Additionally, no matter what you say, magic that would determine if you are telling the truth indicates you are being truthful, if you so choose, and you can't be compelled to tell the truth by magic.

SWASHBUCKLER

You focus your training on the art of the blade, relying on speed, elegance, and charm in equal parts. While some warriors are brutes clad in heavy armor, your method of fighting looks almost like a performance. Duelists and pirates typically belong to this archetype.

A Swashbuckler excels in single combat, and can fight with two weapons while safely darting away from an opponent.

FANCY FOOTWORK

When you choose this archetype at 3rd level, you learn how to land a strike and then slip away without reprisal. During your turn, if you make a melee attack against a creature, that creature can't make opportunity attacks against you for the rest of your turn.

SWASHBUCKLERS AND TWO-WEAPON FIGHTING

The Swashbuckler relies on a good understanding of the D&D rules to realize its potential, specifically when it comes to fighting with two weapons. Other characters must use an action to Disengage if they want to escape a melee, but the Fancy Footwork feature of the Swashbuckler bundles a more limited version of Disengage within your attack. This allows you to use your bonus action to fight with two weapons, and then safely evade each foe you attacked.

RAKISH AUDACITY

Starting at 3rd level, your unmistakable confidence propels you into battle. You can add your Charisma modifier to your initiative rolls.

In addition, you don't need advantage on your attack roll to use your Sneak Attack if no creature other than your target is within 5 feet of you. All the other rules for the Sneak Attack class feature still apply to you.

PANACHE

At 9th level, your charm becomes extraordinarily beguiling. As an action, you can make a Charisma (Persuasion) check contested by a creature's Wisdom (Insight) check. The creature must be able to hear you, and the two of you must share a language.

If you succeed on the check and the creature is hostile to you, it has disadvantage on attack rolls against targets other than you and can't make opportunity attacks against targets other than you. This effect lasts for 1 minute, until one of your companions attacks the target or affects it with a spell, or until you and the target are more than 60 feet apart.

If you succeed on the check and the creature isn't hostile to you, it is charmed by you for 1 minute. While charmed, it regards you as a friendly acquaintance. This effect ends immediately if you or your companions do anything harmful to it.

ELEGANT MANEUVER

Starting at 13th level, you can use a bonus action on your turn to gain advantage on the next Dexterity (Acrobatics) or Strength (Athletics) check you make during the same turn.

MASTER DUELIST

Beginning at 17th level, your mastery of the blade lets you turn failure into success in combat. If you miss with an attack roll, you can roll it again with advantage. Once you do so, you can't use this feature again until you finish a short or long rest.

SORCERERS

The Weave of magic infuses every part of the Realms, and some people have the natural ability to perceive, touch, and shape the Weave. Some inherit this ability from a magical ancestor such as a dragon or an angel, others gain it by accident from exposure to wild magical power, and others manifest this power by chance or the hand of fate, perhaps portended by events at their conception or birth.

Due to their varied origins and delayed manifestation of powers, sorcerers can be found almost anywhere and among almost any people. Larger cities on the Sword Coast—including Baldur's Gate, Neverwinter, and Waterdeep—all have a few sorcerers, since people with magic gravitate to places where their abilities are valued. Sorcerers are slightly more common among cultures steeped in magic, such as among the elves of Evermeet and the humans of Halruaa. The witches of Rashemen are sorcerers who lead that country's society, but their Thayan neighbors often persecute the sorcerers who appear in Thay, seeing sorcery as a threat to the nation's power structure, which is based on the study of wizardry. Magic-hating cultures, such as the Northlanders and Uthgardt, exile or kill the sorcerers who manifest among them.

WILD MAGIC

The Forgotten Realms has a long history of magical disasters and uncontrolled surges of power that alter creatures or the land itself. Whether caused by a Netherese wizard trying to become god of magic, deities being forced to walk the earth during the Time of Troubles, or the chaos of the Spellplague, the magical chaos unleashed by such events has created a legacy of wild magic sorcerers. This legacy often lies dormant for generations, then suddenly manifests under the right (or wrong) circumstances. These wild mages are more common recently in lands directly affected by the Spellplague, including Halruaa, Mulhorand, and pockets of Cormyr and the Sword Coast.

DRACONIC MAGIC

Dragons are known to take humanoid form and live among lesser creatures for decades. Some of these dragons have liaisons with humanoids, or invest their allies or minions with dragon magic. These invested creatures might become draconic bloodline sorcerers, or pass their abilities on to their descendants. Draconic bloodline sorcerers have appeared in most parts of the world due to the actions of individual dragons or experimentation by dragon cults, but they are significantly more common around Chessenta, which was once ruled by a dragon, and the land of Murghôm near Thay, where dragon princes have ruled for the last eighty years.

MAGIC OF THE STORM

During the Sundering, a constant storm called the Great Rain covered the Sea of Fallen Stars, darkening the skies and causing massive floods. Thousands of people died from drowning, lightning strikes, or bursts of wind that hit like fists and capsized ships. A few survivors of these events found themselves blessed or cursed with innate magic—storm sorcerers able to bend lightning, thunder, and wind to their will. Most of these new mages appeared near the Inner Sea, but clouds from the Great Rain sometimes traveled much farther away. Although not all storm sorcerers gained their powers from the Great Rain, most common folk associate them with its destructive weather and treat them with caution.

SORCEROUS ORIGIN

Sorcerers in the Forgotten Realms have the following Sorcerous Origin option, in addition to those in the *Player's Handbook*.

STORM SORCERY

Your innate magic comes from the power of elemental air. Many with this power can trace their magic back to a near-death experience caused by the Great Rain, but perhaps you were born during a howling gale so powerful that folk still tell stories of it, or your lineage might include the influence of potent air creatures such as vaati or djinn. Whatever the case, the magic of the storm permeates your being.

Storm sorcerers are invaluable members of a ship's crew. Their magic allows them to exert control over wind and weather in their immediate area. Their abilities also prove useful in repelling attacks by sahuagin, pirates, and other waterborne threats.

WIND SPEAKER

The arcane magic you command is infused with elemental air. You can speak, read, and write Primordial. (Knowing this language allows you to understand and be understood by those who speak its dialects: Aquan, Auran, Ignan, and Terran.)

TEMPESTUOUS MAGIC

Starting at 1st level, you can use a bonus action on your turn to cause whirling gusts of elemental air to briefly surround you, immediately before or after you cast a spell of 1st level or higher. Doing so allows you to fly up to 10 feet without provoking opportunity attacks.

HEART OF THE STORM

At 6th level, you gain resistance to lightning and thunder damage. In addition, whenever you start casting a spell of 1st level or higher that deals lightning or thunder damage, stormy magic erupts from you. This eruption causes creatures of your choice that you can see within 10 feet of you to take lightning or thunder damage (choose each time this ability activates) equal to half your sorcerer level.

STORM GUIDE

At 6th level, you gain the ability to subtly control the weather around you.

If it is raining, you can use an action to cause the rain to stop falling in a 20-foot-radius sphere centered on you. You can end this effect as a bonus action.

If it is windy, you can use a bonus action each round to choose the direction that the wind blows in a 100-foot-radius sphere centered on you. The wind blows in that direction until the end of your next turn. This feature doesn't alter the speed of the wind.

STORM'S FURY

Starting at 14th level, when you are hit by a melee attack, you can use your reaction to deal lightning damage to the attacker. The damage equals your sorcerer level. The attacker must also make a Strength saving throw

ARCANE SPELLCASTERS

The common folk of Faerûn often make little distinction between sorcerers, warlocks, and wizards. Most mages see little point in kindling rivalries with other types of arcane spellcasters—magic is magic, regardless of the means—and for the most part, sorcerers, wizards, and warlocks respect each other as fellow practitioners of the Art, understanding the power it represents.

against your sorcerer spell save DC. On a failed save, the attacker is pushed in a straight line up to 20 feet away from you.

WIND SOUL

At 18th level, you gain immunity to lightning and thunder damage.

You also gain a magical flying speed of 60 feet. As an action, you can reduce your flying speed to 30 feet for 1 hour and choose a number of creatures within 30 feet of you equal to 3 + your Charisma modifier. The chosen creatures gain a magical flying speed of 30 feet for 1 hour. Once you reduce your flying speed in this way, you can't do so again until you finish a short or long rest.

WARLOCKS

Given their dealings with often sinister otherworldly patrons in exchange for power, warlocks don't have a sterling reputation in the Realms. Even well-meaning warlocks are viewed with suspicion and justifiable caution. Some wizards feel the very existence of warlocks taints the view of their noble Art and causes the common folk to view all practitioners of magic with doubt.

Some warlocks, particularly those of fey or fiendish bloodlines, are born with a propensity for their power, drawing the attention of potential patrons even from childhood. Others seek out a pact, sometimes because they can't find the power they desire elsewhere. Some warlocks forge multiple pacts, although they must eventually come to favor one over the others, as their patrons are jealous and possessive beings.

PATRONS IN THE REALMS

The gods are far from the only forces at work in the Realms, and ambitious warlocks have many potential patrons able to offer them arcane power.

THE ARCHFEY

In the vast wilderness of the Realms one can still find connections to the Feywild. These are fey crossings, places of mysterious natural beauty in the world that have a near-perfect mirror in the Feywild. You can pass through a fey crossing by entering a clearing, passing through the surface of a pool, stepping into a circle of mushrooms, or crawling under the trunk of a tree. A few warlocks seek out such places to bargain with the Archfey of that realm for power. Noteworthy Archfey patrons include the following:

Titania, the Summer Queen, is perhaps the mightiest of the archfey. With a smile, she can ripen a crop, and with a frown, summon wildfires. She rules the seelie of the Summer Court.

Oberon, the Green Lord, an unrivaled hunter and woodland warrior, is Titania's lover and frequently her foe. Oberon is attuned to every bough of each tree and each branch of every stream in the forests of the Feywild. If Oberon has a weakness, it is the wild nature of his heart. His mood swings like a weather vane in a wind storm.

Hyrsam, the Prince of Fools, is thought to be the first satyr. He can sing the shine off gold, and his jokes and antics can cause stones to cry with laughter. Yet Hyrsam is also the soul of savagery and the wild. Hyrsam the Fool is a prankster and prone to mischief, but when such jokes turn vicious and deadly, Hyrsam the Savage is at play.

The Queen of Air and Darkness rules the unseelie of the Gloaming Court from an onyx throne that sits empty except for the hovering Night Diamond, a black gem the size of a human head that dully glimmers with captured stars. The Queen of Air and Darkness is an invisible presence around it, her voice thundering from the Night Diamond or whispering secrets directly in the ears of her courtiers, and sometimes both at once.

The Prince of Frost was once known as the Sun Prince, but his heart grew cold when his betrothed betrayed him and escaped, her soul becoming one of the stars. Ever since, the wrathful prince has sought to reunite with his betrothed whenever she is reincarnated in mortal form.

THE FIEND

Numerous fiends forge pacts with mortal warlocks in the Realms—so many that warlocks are almost synonymous with infernal power in Faerûn. These fiends include the Archdevils of the Nine Hells and their most powerful dukes, the Demon Lords of the Abyss, and the ultroloths who rule over yugoloth armies. Such deals need not be struck directly with the power in question, however. Often a weaker fiend serves as an intermediary, and the warlock might not know whom he or she serves. Notable fiendish patrons peculiar to the Forgotten Realms include the following:

Baazka is the pit fiend behind the most recent incursion of infernal forces from Dragonspear Castle. Its plans for the Sword Coast were thwarted along with those of allied Red Wizards, but its ambitions in the region remain.

Belaphoss is a demon that serves Demogorgon. It considers itself the greatest servitor of the Prince of Demons and thus a rival for Demogorgon's power.

Eltab was once bound beneath the city of Eltabbar in Thay, caged even by the layout of the city's streets and canals, which formed a glyph of imprisonment. The demon is now loose in the world, seeking revenge.

Errtu the balor has plagued Drizzt Do'Urden for more than a century, largely over possession of an artifact called the Crenshinibon. Having lost the last battle and been banished from the world, the balor now seeks indirect means of revenge.

Gargauth is a mysterious infernal power who seeks godhood while trapped in the world within a magical shield.

Lorcan is a cambion who collects warlocks like one might collect butterflies. His favorite collection, the Troil Thirteen, includes warlocks of blood descent from the thirteen who first made a pact with Asmodeus.

Malkizid is a solar who fell from grace when he betrayed the Seldarine. Ever since then, Malkizid has delighted in every wrong he can do to elves, but he gains the greatest pleasure when he manipulates the elves into harming each other.

Wendonai is the balor lord who first tempted the dark elves to summon demons in the ancient wars between the elf peoples. It also turned them to the worship of Lolth and continued to advise and tutor them for long after the Descent.

THE GREAT OLD ONE

Beyond the planes known to great wizards and sages lies the Far Realm of the Great Old Ones, beings outside time, space, and sanity. That realm is reachable by profane rituals and in the dreams of some of those drawn to those entities' power. Some of the blasphemous names associated with that place and its madness include the following:

Dendar the Night Serpent, Eater of the World, is said to be the spawn of the first nightmare, devourer of foul visions, and harbinger of the end of the world. Her warlocks frequently dream of Dendar's hiss and the dry rasp of her scales when they first realize their potential.

Ghaunadaur, That Which Lurks, Underdark god of aberrations, also known as the Elder Eye. It is worshiped (if such a word can be used) by slimes, oozes, and similar creatures.

Kezef the Chaos Hound is a black, skeletal mastiff covered in swarming maggots, its blood a black acid. The gods imprisoned Kezef in an unbreakable leash forged by Gond and a glowing ward conjured by Mystra, for which the Chaos Hound bit off Tyr's hand.

Moander is a dark power of corruption and decay. Those touched by its influence first receive a dream, the "seed of Moander," wherein the following words are heard: "Question not the words of Moander, lest you be stricken by the Eating From Within. Go forth and possess beings of power and influence for me. Slay, and let the rot cover all. Fear me, and obey."

Tyranthraxus, also called the Possessing Spirit and the Flamed One, seeks to rule the world through the bodies of others. Similar to the Earthmother, it uses magical pools as windows into the world to spread its influence.

Zargon, the Returner, also called the Invincible Tyrant, is said to be an undying and unkillable evil. Some stories claim Zargon was the original master of the Nine Hells. Others claim him to be a powerful Demon Prince exiled from the Abyss. Perhaps neither of these stories are true, but it can surely be said that Zargon is a power that inspires madness and terror.

OTHERWORLDLY PATRON

Warlocks in the Forgotten Realms have the following Otherworldly Patron option, in addition to those in the *Player's Handbook*.

THE UNDYING

Death holds no sway over your patron, who has unlocked the secrets of everlasting life, although such a prize—like all power—comes at a price. Once mortal, the Undying has seen mortal lifetimes pass like the seasons, like the flicker of endless days and nights. It has the secrets of the ages to share, secrets of life and death. Beings of this sort include Vecna, Lord of the Hand and the Eye; the dread Iuz; the lich-queen Vol; the Undying Court of Aerenal; Vlaakith, lich-queen of the githyanki; and the deathless wizard Fistandantalus.

In the Realms, Undying patrons include Larloch the Shadow King, legendary master of Warlock's Crypt, and Gilgeam, the God-King of Unther.

EXPANDED SPELL LIST

The Undying lets you choose from an expanded list of spells when you learn a warlock spell. The following spells are added to the warlock spell list for you.

UNDYING EXPANDED SPELLS

Spell Level	Spells
1st	*false life, ray of sickness*
2nd	*blindness/deafness, silence*
3rd	*feign death, speak with dead*
4th	*aura of life, death ward*
5th	*contagion, legend lore*

AMONG THE DEAD

Starting at 1st level, you learn the *spare the dying* cantrip, which counts as a warlock cantrip for you. You also have advantage on saving throws against any disease.

Additionally, undead have difficulty harming you. If an undead targets you directly with an attack or a harmful spell, that creature must make a Wisdom saving throw against your spell save DC (an undead needn't make the save when it includes you in an area effect, such as the explosion of *fireball*). On a failed save, the creature must choose a new target or forfeit targeting someone instead of you, potentially wasting the attack or spell. On a successful save, the creature is immune to this effect for 24 hours. An undead is also immune to this effect for 24 hours if you target it with an attack or a harmful spell.

Defy Death

Starting at 6th level, you can give yourself vitality when you cheat death or when you help someone else cheat it. You can regain hit points equal to 1d8 + your Constitution modifier (minimum of 1 hit point) when you succeed on a death saving throw or when you stabilize a creature with *spare the dying*.

Once you use this feature, you can't use it again until you finish a long rest.

Undying Nature

Beginning at 10th level, you can hold your breath indefinitely, and you don't require food, water, or sleep, although you still require rest to reduce exhaustion and still benefit from finishing short and long rests.

In addition, you age at a slower rate. For every 10 years that pass, your body ages only 1 year, and you are immune to being magically aged.

Indestructible Life

When you reach 14th level, you partake of some of the true secrets of the Undying. On your turn, you can use a bonus action to regain hit points equal to 1d8 + your warlock level. Additionally, if you put a severed body part of yours back in place when you use this feature, the part reattaches.

Once you use this feature, you can't use it again until you finish a short or long rest.

Wizards

The First Hilt parried a clumsy axe swing and caught the rhythm of the wizard's spell. It was one with which he was well familiar. Using his free hand, the bladesinger mirrored his opponent's casting then sent his considerable power out to surround the overmatched wizard, binding it to himself. Argent energy flew from the human's outstretched hand only to fizzle into nothingness as the bladesinger quenched the spell.

—Keith Francis Strohm, *Bladesinger*

Scholars and practitioners of what they call "the Art" (see chapter 1 for details), wizards are the most disciplined spellcasters in the Forgotten Realms. They need to be, as their powers come from years of careful study and practice. Some wizards apprentice and study with an experienced master, while others attend formal academies or universities of wizardry, such as those in Evermeet or Halruaa, or in the great cities of the North like Waterdeep or Silverymoon.

With the intensity of their study and practice, wizards tend to become increasingly solitary as they advance in their Art, having fewer peers with whom they can share their insights, if they choose to share them with anyone at all. Thus great wizards often take up residence in isolated towers or strongholds, exhibiting ever more eccentric behavior as time goes on. Some say this is a mark of madness brought on by delving too deeply into arcane lore, but they never say it too loudly anywhere a wizard might overhear.

The greatest wizards of the Realms find means of extending their lives far beyond the span of any race except the elves. Archwizards may be centuries old, having seen civilizations rise and fall across Faerûn. Other wizards seeking this longevity turn to lichdom, dwelling in isolated tombs and strongholds as they withdraw from the world in body as well as mind.

Wizardly Groups

Many wizardly groups exist in the Forgotten Realms, but two, in particular, stand out.

The Red Wizards

The most infamous group of wizards in the Realms are the Red Wizards of Thay. Garbed in their distinctive red robes, the Red Wizards have sought to expand their power and to extend Thay's influence across the Realms, particularly in lands in the East. They shave their heads and wear complex tattoos reflecting their ambitions and achievements and their favored school of magic.

In Thay, the Red Wizards have ultimate power, although they give governance of day-to-day affairs to those without skill in the Art. Every Red Wizard devotes study to one of the eight schools of magic and serves that school's zulkir, the leader and ultimate master of that style of magic. The zulkirs and their underlings constantly vie with one another for power and influence, and this competition frequently sends Red Wizards far from Thay to seek new spells, recover lost artifacts, and create wealth that can flow back to Thay. The power the Red Wizards hold in Thay gives them a measure of diplomatic legitimacy in the lands of the Sword Coast and the North, but their presence is rarely welcome and is universally viewed with suspicion.

War Wizards

The potential for wizards to influence the outcome of battle is something no ruler in Faerûn can afford to ignore, and most great armies seek to recruit and include wizards among their ranks. Evokers are the most common, simply for the potential their spells have of inflicting the most damage to the greatest number of enemies. Still, all schools of magic find their applications in warfare.

The War Wizards of Cormyr are perhaps the best known application of the Art to the field of battle. As much soldiers as they are scholars, many of them were members of the Purple Dragons before they began their training in the Art. In addition to field duty in times of war, the War Wizards also protect the royalty of Cormyr, and each one swears a magic oath of service to the Crown. In this role, War Wizards serve as bodyguards, advisors, and even spies. Members of the royal family, Purple Dragon Knights, and officers of the Purple Dragons frequently wear magic rings that allow a War Wizards to know where they've gone and to scry upon them. Removing such a ring, even for innocent reasons, can call a cadre of battle-ready War Wizards to teleport nearby with attack spells already in the midst of being cast.

Arcane Tradition

Wizards in the Forgotten Realms have the following Arcane Tradition option, in addition to those in the *Player's Handbook*.

Bladesinging

Bladesingers are elves who bravely defend their people and lands. They are elf wizards who master a school of sword fighting grounded in a tradition of arcane magic. In combat, a bladesinger uses a series of intricate,

elegant maneuvers that fend off harm and allow the bladesinger to channel magic into devastating attacks and a cunning defense.

Restriction: Elves Only

Only elves and half-elves can choose the bladesinger arcane tradition. In the world of Faerûn, elves closely guard the secrets of bladesinging.

Your DM can lift this restriction to better suit the campaign. The restriction reflects the story of bladesingers in the Forgotten Realms, but it might not apply to your DM's setting or your DM's version of the Realms.

BLADESINGER STYLES

From its inception as a martial and magical art, Bladesinging has been tied to the sword, more specifically the longsword. Yet many generations of study gave rise to various styles of Bladesinging based on the melee weapon employed. The techniques of these styles are passed from master to students in small schools, some of which have a building dedicated to instruction. Even the newest styles are hundreds of years old, but are still taught by their original creators due to the long lives of elves. Most schools of Bladesinging are in Evermeet or Evereska. One was started in Myth Drannor, but the city's destruction has scattered those students who survived.

Styles of Bladesinging are broadly categorized based on the type of weapon employed, and each is associated with a category of animal. Within that style are specializations named after specific animal types, based on the types of spells employed, the techniques of the master, and the particular weapon used. Bladesingers who apprentice to a master typically get a tattoo of their chosen style's animal. Some bladesingers learn multiple styles and bear many tattoos, wearing a warning on their skin of their deadly skills.

Cat. Styles that employ a sword belong to this family. The lion style, the eldest, trains practitioners in the use of the longsword and doesn't favor any particular type of spells. Leopard style focuses on the shortsword and spells of illusion and stealth. Red tiger, a style just three centuries old, has its bladesingers using the scimitar in a whirling dance of defense from which they launch into sudden leaps and attacks.

Bird. Styles that focus on the use of a hafted weapon, such as an axe or hammer, have been grouped together as bird styles, yet they vary wildly. All relatively new styles, they use weapons not typically favored by elves. Eagle-style bladesingers use small handaxes, and many maneuvers in the style involve fluid ways to throw the weapon and draw a new one. Raven style uses a war pick, and spells associated with it grant the bladesinger more agility in combat.

Snake. Practitioners of these styles use a flail, chain, or whip. Viper style uses a whip, despite its inelegance as a weapon, and has almost as long a history as the lion style. Its masters punctuate their bladesong with a stunningly rapid rhythm of whip cracks, which can keep many foes at bay and allow the bladesinger space to cast the cruel spells of poison and disease favored by the style.

TRAINING IN WAR AND SONG

When you adopt this tradition at 2nd level, you gain proficiency with light armor, and you gain proficiency with one type of one-handed melee weapon of your choice.

You also gain proficiency in the Performance skill if you don't already have it.

BLADESONG

Starting at 2nd level, you can invoke a secret elven magic called the Bladesong, provided that you aren't wearing medium or heavy armor or using a shield. It graces you with supernatural speed, agility, and focus.

You can use a bonus action to start the Bladesong, which lasts for 1 minute. It ends early if you are incapacitated, if you don medium or heavy armor or a shield, or if you use two hands to make an attack with a weapon. You can also dismiss the Bladesong at any time you choose (no action required).

While your Bladesong is active, you gain the following benefits:

- You gain a bonus to your AC equal to your Intelligence modifier (minimum of +1).
- Your walking speed increases by 10 feet.
- You have advantage on Dexterity (Acrobatics) checks.
- You gain a bonus to any Constitution saving throw you make to maintain your concentration on a spell. The bonus equals your Intelligence modifier (minimum of +1).

You can use this feature twice. You regain all expended uses of it when you finish a short or long rest.

EXTRA ATTACK

Starting at 6th level, you can attack twice, instead of once, whenever you take the Attack action on your turn.

SONG OF DEFENSE

Beginning at 10th level, you can direct your magic to absorb damage while your Bladesong is active. When you take damage, you can use your reaction to expend one spell slot and reduce that damage to you by an amount equal to five times the spell slot's level.

SONG OF VICTORY

Starting at 14th level, you add your Intelligence modifier (minimum of +1) to the damage of your melee weapon attacks while your Bladesong is active.

CANTRIPS FOR SORCERERS, WARLOCKS, AND WIZARDS

Practitioners of the Art have developed the following cantrips for those who favor casting spells in melee. War Wizards of Cormyr, bladesingers, and warlocks of the Pact of the Blade are especially fond of these spells.

These cantrips are on the sorcerer, warlock, and wizard spell lists.

BOOMING BLADE
Evocation cantrip

Casting Time: 1 action
Range: 5 feet
Components: V, M (a weapon)
Duration: 1 round

As part of the action used to cast this spell, you must make a melee attack with a weapon against one creature within the spell's range, otherwise the spell fails. On a hit, the target suffers the attack's normal effects, and it becomes sheathed in booming energy until the start of your next turn. If the target willingly moves before then, it immediately takes 1d8 thunder damage, and the spell ends.

This spell's damage increases when you reach higher levels. At 5th level, the melee attack deals an extra 1d8 thunder damage to the target, and the damage the target takes for moving increases to 2d8. Both damage rolls increase by 1d8 at 11th level and 17th level.

Green-Flame Blade

Evocation cantrip

Casting Time: 1 action
Range: 5 feet
Components: V, M (a weapon)
Duration: Instantaneous

As part of the action used to cast this spell, you must make a melee attack with a weapon against one creature within the spell's range, otherwise the spell fails. On a hit, the target suffers the attack's normal effects, and green fire leaps from the target to a different creature of your choice that you can see within 5 feet of it. The second creature takes fire damage equal to your spellcasting ability modifier.

This spell's damage increases when you reach higher levels. At 5th level, the melee attack deals an extra 1d8 fire damage to the target, and the fire damage to the second creature increases to 1d8 + your spellcasting ability modifier. Both damage rolls increase by 1d8 at 11th level and 17th level.

Lightning Lure

Evocation cantrip

Casting Time: 1 action
Range: 15 feet
Components: V
Duration: Instantaneous

You create a lash of lightning energy that strikes at one creature of your choice that you can see within range. The target must succeed on a Strength saving throw or be pulled up to 10 feet in a straight line toward you and then take 1d8 lightning damage if it is within 5 feet of you.

This spell's damage increases by 1d8 when you reach 5th level (2d8), 11th level (3d8), and 17th level (4d8).

Sword Burst

Conjuration cantrip

Casting Time: 1 action
Range: 5 feet
Components: V
Duration: Instantaneous

You create a momentary circle of spectral blades that sweep around you. Each creature within range, other than you, must succeed on a Dexterity saving throw or take 1d6 force damage.

This spell's damage increases by 1d6 when you reach 5th level (2d6), 11th level (3d6), and 17th level (4d6).

CHAPTER 5: BACKGROUNDS

HE BACKGROUNDS DESCRIBED IN THE *Player's Handbook* are all found in Faerûn's various societies, in some form or another. This chapter offers additional backgrounds for characters in a Forgotten Realms campaign, many of them specific to Faerûn or to the Sword Coast and the North in particular.

As in the *Player's Handbook*, each of the backgrounds presented here provides proficiencies, languages, and equipment, as well as a background feature and sometimes a variant form. For personality traits, ideals, bonds, and flaws, most of the backgrounds in this chapter use a thematically similar background in the *Player's Handbook* as their foundation.

CITY WATCH

You have served the community where you grew up, standing as its first line of defense against crime. You aren't a soldier, directing your gaze outward at possible enemies. Instead, your service to your hometown was to help police its populace, protecting the citizenry from lawbreakers and malefactors of every stripe.

You might have been part of the City Watch of Waterdeep, the baton-wielding police force of the City of Splendors, protecting the common folk from thieves and rowdy nobility alike. Or you might have been one of the valiant defenders of Silverymoon, a member of the Silverwatch or even one of the magic-wielding Spellguard.

Perhaps you hail from Neverwinter and have served as one of its Wintershield watchmen, the newly founded branch of guards who vow to keep safe the City of Skilled Hands.

Even if you're not city-born or city-bred, this background can describe your early years as a member of law enforcement. Most settlements of any size have their own constables and police forces, and even smaller communities have sheriffs and bailiffs who stand ready to protect their community.

Skill Proficiencies: Athletics, Insight
Languages: Two of your choice
Equipment: A uniform in the style of your unit and indicative of your rank, a horn with which to summon help, a set of manacles, and a pouch containing 10 gp

FEATURE: WATCHER'S EYE

Your experience in enforcing the law, and dealing with lawbreakers, gives you a feel for local laws and criminals. You can easily find the local outpost of the watch or a similar organization, and just as easily pick out the dens of criminal activity in a community, although you're more likely to be welcome in the former locations rather than the latter.

VARIANT: INVESTIGATOR

Rarer than watch or patrol members are a community's investigators, who are responsible for solving crimes after the fact. Though such folk are seldom found in rural areas, nearly every settlement of decent size has at least one or two watch members who have the skill to investigate crime scenes and track down criminals. If your prior experience is as an investigator, you have proficiency in Investigation rather than Athletics.

SUGGESTED CHARACTERISTICS

Use the tables for the soldier background in the *Player's Handbook* as the basis for your traits and motivations, modifying the entries when appropriate to suit your identity as a member of the city watch.

Your bond is likely associated with your fellow watch members or the watch organization itself and almost certainly concerns your community. Your ideal probably involves the fostering of peace and safety. An investigator is likely to have an ideal connected to achieving justice by successfully solving crimes.

CLAN CRAFTER

The Stout Folk are well known for their artisanship and the worth of their handiworks, and you have been trained in that ancient tradition. For years you labored under a dwarf master of the craft, enduring long hours and dismissive, sour-tempered treatment in order to gain the fine skills you possess today.

You are most likely a dwarf, but not necessarily—particularly in the North, the shield dwarf clans learned long ago that only proud fools who are more concerned for their egos than their craft turn away promising apprentices, even those of other races. If you aren't a dwarf, however, you have taken a solemn oath never to take on an apprentice in the craft: it is not for non-dwarves to pass on the skills of Moradin's favored children. You would have no difficulty, however, finding a dwarf master who was willing to receive potential apprentices who came with your recommendation.

Skill Proficiencies: History, Insight
Tool Proficiencies: One type of artisan's tools
Languages: Dwarvish or one other of your choice if you already speak Dwarvish
Equipment: A set of artisan's tools with which you are proficient, a maker's mark chisel used to mark your handiwork with the symbol of the clan of crafters you learned your skill from, a set of traveler's clothes, and a pouch containing 5 gp and a gem worth 10 gp

FEATURE: RESPECT OF THE STOUT FOLK

As well respected as clan crafters are among outsiders, no one esteems them quite so highly as dwarves do. You always have free room and board in any place where shield dwarves or gold dwarves dwell, and the individuals in such a settlement might vie among themselves to determine who can offer you (and possibly your compatriots) the finest accommodations and assistance.

SUGGESTED CHARACTERISTICS

Use the tables for the guild artisan background in the *Player's Handbook* as the basis for your traits and motivations, modifying the entries when appropriate to suit

knowledge and to make yourself available to help those in other places who seek your expertise. You might be one of the few who aid Herald's Holdfast, helping to catalogue and maintain records of the information that arrives daily from across Faerûn.

Skill Proficiencies: History, plus your choice of one from among Arcana, Nature, and Religion

Languages: Two of your choice

Equipment: The scholar's robes of your cloister, a writing kit (small pouch with a quill, ink, folded parchment, and a small penknife), a borrowed book on the subject of your current study, and a pouch containing 10 gp

FEATURE: LIBRARY ACCESS

Though others must often endure extensive interviews and significant fees to gain access to even the most common archives in your library, you have free and easy access to the majority of the library, though it might also have repositories of lore that are too valuable, magical, or secret to permit anyone immediate access.

You have a working knowledge of your cloister's personnel and bureaucracy, and you know how to navigate those connections with some ease.

Additionally, you are likely to gain preferential treatment at other libraries across the Realms, as professional courtesy shown to a fellow scholar.

SUGGESTED CHARACTERISTICS

Use the tables for the sage background in the *Player's Handbook* as the basis for your traits and motivations, modifying the entries when appropriate to suit your identity as a cloistered scholar.

Your bond is almost certainly associated either with the place where you grew up or with the knowledge you hope to acquire through adventuring. Your ideal is no doubt related to how you view the quest for knowledge and truth—perhaps as a worthy goal in itself, or maybe as a means to a desirable end.

COURTIER

In your earlier days, you were a personage of some significance in a noble court or a bureaucratic organization. You might or might not come from an upper-class family; your talents, rather than the circumstances of your birth, could have secured you this position.

You might have been one of the many functionaries, attendants, and other hangers-on in the Court of Silverymoon, or perhaps you traveled in Waterdeep's baroque and sometimes cutthroat conglomeration of guilds, nobles, adventurers, and secret societies. You might have been one of the behind-the-scenes law-keepers or functionaries in Baldur's Gate or Neverwinter, or you might have grown up in and around the castle of Daggerford.

Even if you are no longer a full-fledged member of the group that gave you your start in life, your relationships with your former fellows can be an advantage for you and your adventuring comrades. You might undertake missions with your new companions that further the interest of the organization that gave you your start in life. In any event, the abilities that you honed while

your identity as a clan crafter. (For instance, consider the words "guild" and "clan" to be interchangeable.)

Your bond is almost certainly related to the master or the clan that taught you, or else to the work that you produce. Your ideal might have to do with maintaining the high quality of your work or preserving the dwarven traditions of craftsmanship.

CLOISTERED SCHOLAR

As a child, you were inquisitive when your playmates were possessive or raucous. In your formative years, you found your way to one of Faerûn's great institutes of learning , where you were apprenticed and taught that knowledge is a more valuable treasure than gold or gems. Now you are ready to leave your home—not to abandon it, but to quest for new lore to add to its storehouse of knowledge.

The most well known of Faerûn's fonts of knowledge is Candlekeep. The great library is always in need of workers and attendants, some of whom rise through the ranks to assume roles of greater responsibility and prominence. You might be one of Candlekeep's own, dedicated to the curatorship of what is likely the most complete body of lore and history in all the world.

Perhaps instead you were taken in by the scholars of the Vault of the Sages or the Map House in Silverymoon, and now you have struck out to increase your serving as a courtier will stand you in good stead as an adventurer.

Skill Proficiencies: Insight, Persuasion
Languages: Two of your choice
Equipment: A set of fine clothes and a pouch containing 5 gp

FEATURE: COURT FUNCTIONARY

Your knowledge of how bureaucracies function lets you gain access to the records and inner workings of any noble court or government you encounter. You know who the movers and shakers are, whom to go to for the favors you seek, and what the current intrigues of interest in the group are.

SUGGESTED CHARACTERISTICS

Use the tables for the guild artisan background in the *Player's Handbook* as the basis for your traits and motivations, modifying the entries when appropriate to suit your identity as a courtier.

The noble court or bureaucratic organization where you got your start is directly or indirectly associated with your bond (which could pertain to certain individuals in the group, such as your sponsor or mentor). Your ideal might be concerned with the prevailing philosophy of your court or organization.

FACTION AGENT

Many organizations active in the North and across the face of Faerûn aren't bound by strictures of geography. These factions pursue their agendas without regard for political boundaries, and their members operate anywhere the organization deems necessary. These groups employ listeners, rumormongers, smugglers, sellswords, cache-holders (people who guard caches of wealth or magic for use by the faction's operatives), haven keepers, and message drop minders, to name a few. At the core of every faction are those who don't merely fulfill a small function for that organization, but who serve as its hands, head, and heart.

As a prelude to your adventuring career (and in preparation for it), you served as an agent of a particular faction in Faerûn. You might have operated openly or secretly, depending on the faction and its goals, as well as how those goals mesh with your own. Becoming an adventurer doesn't necessarily require you to relinquish membership in your faction (though you can choose to do so), and it might enhance your status in the faction.

Skill Proficiencies: Insight and one Intelligence, Wisdom, or Charisma skill of your choice, as appropriate to your faction
Languages: Two of your choice
Equipment: Badge or emblem of your faction, a copy of a seminal faction text (or a code-book for a covert faction), a set of common clothes, and a pouch containing 15 gp

FACTIONS OF THE SWORD COAST

The lack of large, centralized governments in the North and along the Sword Coast is likely directly responsible for the proliferation of secret societies and conspiracies in those lands. If your background is as an agent for one of the main factions of the North and Sword Coast, here are some possibilities.

The Harpers. Founded more than a millennium ago, disbanded and reorganized several times, the Harpers remain a powerful, behind-the-scenes agency, which acts to thwart evil and promote fairness through knowledge, rather than brute force. Harper agents are often proficient in Investigation, enabling them to be adept at snooping and spying. They often seek aid from other Harpers, sympathetic bards and innkeepers, rangers, and the clergy of gods that are aligned with the Harpers' ideals.

The Order of the Gauntlet. One of the newest power groups in Faerûn, the Order of the Gauntlet has an agenda similar to that of the Harpers. Its methods are vastly different, however: bearers of the gauntlet are holy warriors on a righteous quest to crush evil and promote justice, and they never hide in the shadows. Order agents tend to be proficient in Religion, and frequently seek aid from law enforcement friendly to the order's ideals, and the clergy of the order's patron gods.

The Emerald Enclave. Maintaining balance in the natural order and combating the forces that threaten that balance is the twofold goal of the Emerald Enclave. Those who serve the faction are masters of survival and living off the land. They are often proficient in Nature, and can seek assistance from woodsmen, hunters, rangers, barbarian tribes, druid circles, and priests who revere the gods of nature.

The Lords' Alliance. On one level, the agents of the Lords' Alliance are representatives of the cities and other governments that constitute the alliance. But, as a faction with interests and concerns that transcend local politics and geography, the Alliance has its own cadre of individuals who work on behalf of the organizations, wider agenda. Alliance agents are required to be knowledgeable in History, and can always rely on the aid of the governments that are part of the Alliance, plus other leaders and groups who uphold the Alliance's ideals.

The Zhentarim. In recent years, the Zhentarim have become more visible in the world at large, as the group works to improve its reputation among the common people. The faction draws employees and associates from many walks of life, setting them to tasks that serve the goals of the Black Network but aren't necessarily criminal in nature. Agents of the Black Network must often work in secret, and are frequently proficient in Deception. They seek aid from the wizards, mercenaries, merchants and priesthoods allied with the Zhentarim.

FEATURE: SAFE HAVEN

As a faction agent, you have access to a secret network of supporters and operatives who can provide assistance on your adventures. You know a set of secret signs and passwords you can use to identify such operatives, who can provide you with access to a hidden safe house, free room and board, or assistance in finding information. These agents never risk their lives for you or risk revealing their true identities.

Suggested Characteristics

Use the tables for the acolyte background in the *Player's Handbook* as the basis for your traits and motivations, modifying the entries when appropriate to suit your identity as a faction agent. (For instance, consider the words "faith" and "faction" to be interchangeable.)

Your bond might be associated with other members of your faction, or a location or an object that is important to your faction. The ideal you strive for is probably in keeping with the tenets and principles of your faction, but might be more personal in nature.

Far Traveler

Almost all of the common people and other folk that one might encounter along the Sword Coast or in the North have one thing in common: they live out their lives without ever traveling more than a few miles from where they were born.

You aren't one of those folk.

You are from a distant place, one so remote that few of the common folk in the North realize that it exists, and chances are good that even if some people you meet have heard of your homeland, they know merely the

name and perhaps a few outrageous stories. You have come to this part of Faerûn for your own reasons, which you might or might not choose to share.

Although you will undoubtedly find some of this land's ways to be strange and discomfiting, you can also be sure that some things its people take for granted will be to you new wonders that you've never laid eyes on before. By the same token, you're a person of interest, for good or ill, to those around you almost anywhere you go.

Skill Proficiencies: Insight, Perception
Tool Proficiencies: Any one musical instrument or gaming set of your choice, likely something native to your homeland
Languages: Any one of your choice
Equipment: One set of traveler's clothes, any one musical instrument or gaming set you are proficient with, poorly wrought maps from your homeland that depict where you are in Faerûn, a small piece of jewelry worth 10 gp in the style of your homeland's craftsmanship, and a pouch containing 5 gp

Why Are You Here?

A far traveler might have set out on a journey for one of a number of reasons, and the departure from his or her homeland could have been voluntary or involuntary. To determine why you are so far from home, roll on the table below or choose from the options provided. The following section, discussing possible homelands, includes some suggested reasons that are appropriate for each location.

Why Are You Here?

d6	Reason	d6	Reason
1	Emissary	4	Pilgrim
2	Exile	5	Sightseer
3	Fugitive	6	Wanderer

Where Are You From?

The most important decision in creating a far traveler background is determining your homeland. The places discussed here are all sufficiently distant from the North and the Sword Coast to justify the use of this background.

Evermeet. The fabled elven islands far to the west are home to elves who have never been to Faerûn. They often find it a harsher place than they expected when they do make the trip. If you are an elf, Evermeet is a logical (though not mandatory) choice for your homeland.

Most of those who emigrate from Evermeet are either exiles, forced out for committing some infraction of elven law, or emissaries who come to Faerûn for a purpose that benefits elven culture or society.

Halruaa. Located on the southern edges of the Shining South, and hemmed in by mountains all around, the magocracy of Halruaa is a bizarre land to most in Faerûn who know about it. Many folk have heard of the strange skyships the Halruaans sail, and a few know of the tales that even the least of their people can work magic.

Halruaans usually make their journeys into Faerûn for personal reasons, since their government has a strict stance against unauthorized involvement with other nations and organizations. You might have been exiled for breaking one of Halruaa's many byzantine laws, or you could be a pilgrim who seeks the shrines of the gods of magic.

Kara-Tur. The continent of Kara-Tur, far to the east of Faerûn, is home to people whose customs are unfamiliar to the folk of the Sword Coast. If you come from Kara-Tur, the people of Faerûn likely refer to you as Shou, even if that isn't your true ethnicity, because that's the blanket term they use for everyone who shares your origin.

The folk of Kara-Tur occasionally travel to Faerûn as diplomats or to forge trade relations with prosperous merchant cartels. You might have come here as part of some such delegation, then decided to stay when the mission was over.

Mulhorand. From the terrain to the architecture to the god-kings who rule over these lands, nearly everything about Mulhorand is alien to someone from the Sword Coast. You likely experienced the same sort of culture shock when you left your desert home and traveled to the unfamiliar climes of northern Faerûn. Recent events in your homeland have led to the abolition of slavery, and a corresponding increase in the traffic between Mulhorand and the distant parts of Faerûn.

Those who leave behind Mulhorand's sweltering deserts and ancient pyramids for a glimpse at a different life do so for many reasons. You might be in the North simply to see the strangeness this wet land has to offer, or because you have made too many enemies among the desert communities of your home.

Sossal. Few have heard of your homeland, but many have questions about it upon seeing you. Humans from Sossal seem crafted from snow, with alabaster skin and white hair, and typically dressed in white.

Sossal exists far to the northeast, hard up against the endless ice to the north and bounded on its other sides by hundreds of miles of the Great Glacier and the Great Ice Sea. No one from your nation makes the effort to cross such colossal barriers without a convincing reason. You must fear something truly terrible or seek something incredibly important.

Zakhara. As the saying goes among those in Faerûn who know of the place, "To get to Zakhara, go south. Then go south some more." Of course, you followed an equally long route when you came north from your place of birth. Though it isn't unusual for Zakharans to visit the southern extremes of Faerûn for trading purposes, few of them stray as far from home as you have.

You might be traveling to discover what wonders are to be found outside the deserts and sword-like mountains of your homeland, or perhaps you are on a pilgrimage to understand the gods that others worship, so that you might better appreciate your own deities.

The Underdark. Though your home is physically closer to the Sword Coast than the other locations discussed here, it is far more unnatural. You hail from one of the settlements in the Underdark, each of which has its own strange customs and laws. If you are a native of one of the great subterranean cities or settlements, you are probably a member of the race that occupies the place—but you might also have grown up there after being captured and brought below when you were a child.

If you are a true Underdark native, you might have come to the surface as an emissary of your people, or perhaps to escape accusations of criminal behavior (whether warranted or not). If you aren't a native, your reason for leaving "home" probably has something to do with getting away from a bad situation.

FEATURE: ALL EYES ON YOU

Your accent, mannerisms, figures of speech, and perhaps even your appearance all mark you as foreign. Curious glances are directed your way wherever you go, which can be a nuisance, but you also gain the friendly interest of scholars and others intrigued by far-off lands, to say nothing of everyday folk who are eager to hear stories of your homeland.

You can parley this attention into access to people and places you might not otherwise have, for you and your traveling companions. Noble lords, scholars, and merchant princes, to name a few, might be interested in hearing about your distant homeland and people.

SUGGESTED CHARACTERISTICS

PERSONALITY TRAIT

d6	Personality Trait
1	I have different assumptions from those around me concerning personal space, blithely invading others' space in innocence, or reacting to ignorant invasion of my own.
2	I have my own ideas about what is and is not food, and I find the eating habits of those around me fascinating, confusing, or revolting.
3	I have a strong code of honor or sense of propriety that others don't comprehend.
4	I express affection or contempt in ways that are unfamiliar to others.
5	I honor my deities through practices that are foreign to this land.
6	I begin or end my day with small traditional rituals that are unfamiliar to those around me.

IDEALS

d6	Ideal
1	**Open.** I have much to learn from the kindly folk I meet along my way. (Good)
2	**Reserved.** As someone new to these strange lands, I am cautious and respectful in my dealings. (Lawful)
3	**Adventure.** I'm far from home, and everything is strange and wonderful! (Chaotic)
4	**Cunning.** Though I may not know their ways, neither do they know mine, which can be to my advantage. (Evil)
5	**Inquisitive.** Everything is new, but I have a thirst to learn. (Neutral)
6	**Suspicious.** I must be careful, for I have no way of telling friend from foe here. (Any)

BONDS

d6	Bond
1	So long as I have this token from my homeland, I can face any adversity in this strange land.
2	The gods of my people are a comfort to me so far from home.
3	I hold no greater cause than my service to my people.
4	My freedom is my most precious possession. I'll never let anyone take it from me again.
5	I'm fascinated by the beauty and wonder of this new land.
6	Though I had no choice, I lament having to leave my loved one(s) behind. I hope to see them again one day.

FLAWS

d6	Flaw
1	I am secretly (or not so secretly) convinced of the superiority of my own culture over that of this foreign land.
2	I pretend not to understand the local language in order to avoid interactions I would rather not have.
3	I have a weakness for the new intoxicants and other pleasures of this land.
4	I don't take kindly to some of the actions and motivations of the people of this land, because these folk are different from me.
5	I consider the adherents of other gods to be deluded innocents at best, or ignorant fools at worst.
6	I have a weakness for the exotic beauty of the people of these lands.

INHERITOR

You are the heir to something of great value—not mere coin or wealth, but an object that has been entrusted to you and you alone. Your inheritance might have come directly to you from a member of your family, by right of birth, or it could have been left to you by a friend, a mentor, a teacher, or someone else important in your life. The revelation of your inheritance changed your life, and might have set you on the path to adventure, but it could also come with many dangers, including those who covet your gift and want to take it from you—by force, if need be.

Skill Proficiencies: Survival, plus one from among Arcana, History, and Religion
Tool Proficiencies: Your choice of a gaming set or a musical instrument
Languages: Any one of your choice
Equipment: Your inheritance, a set of traveler's clothes, the tool you choose for this background's tool proficiency, and a pouch containing 15 gp

FEATURE: INHERITANCE

Choose or randomly determine your inheritance from among the possibilities in the table below. Work with your Dungeon Master to come up with details: Why is your inheritance so important, and what is its full story? You might prefer for the DM to invent these details as part of the game, allowing you to learn more about your inheritance as your character does.

The Dungeon Master is free to use your inheritance as a story hook, sending you on quests to learn more about its history or true nature, or confronting you with foes who want to claim it for themselves or prevent you from learning what you seek. The DM also determines the properties of your inheritance and how they figure into the item's history and importance. For instance, the object might be a minor magic item, or one that begins with a modest ability and increases in potency with the passage of time. Or, the true nature of your inheritance might not be apparent at first and is revealed only when certain conditions are met.

When you begin your adventuring career, you can decide whether to tell your companions about your inheritance right away. Rather than attracting attention to yourself, you might want to keep your inheritance a secret until you learn more about what it means to you and what it can do for you.

INHERITANCE

d8	Object or Item
1	A document such as a map, a letter, or a journal
2–3	A trinket (see "Trinkets" in chapter 5 of the *Player's Handbook*)
4	An article of clothing
5	A piece of jewelry
6	An arcane book or formulary
7	A written story, song, poem, or secret
8	A tattoo or other body marking

SUGGESTED CHARACTERISTICS

Use the tables for the folk hero background in the *Player's Handbook* as the basis for your traits and motivations, modifying the entries when appropriate to suit your identity as an inheritor.

Your bond might be directly related to your inheritance, or to the person from whom you received it. Your ideal might be influenced by what you know about your inheritance, or by what you intend to do with your gift once you realize what it is capable of.

KNIGHT OF THE ORDER

You belong to an order of knights who have sworn oaths to achieve a certain goal. The nature of this goal depends on the order you serve, but in your eyes it is without question a vital and honorable endeavor. Faerûn has a wide variety of knightly orders, all of which have a similar outlook concerning their actions and responsibilities.

Though the term "knight" conjures ideas of mounted, heavily armored warriors of noble blood, most knightly orders in Faerûn don't restrict their membership to such individuals. The goals and philosophies of the order are more important than the gear and fighting style of its members, and so most of these orders aren't limited to fighting types, but are open to all sorts of folk who are willing to battle and die for the order's cause.

The "Knightly Orders of Faerûn" sidebar details several of the orders that are active at present and is designed to help inform your decision about which group you owe allegiance to.

Skill Proficiencies: Persuasion, plus one from among Arcana, History, Nature, and Religion, as appropriate for your order

Tool Proficiencies: One type of gaming set or musical instrument

Languages: One of your choice

Equipment: One set of traveler's clothes, a signet, banner or seal representing your place or rank in the order, and a pouch containing 10 gp

FEATURE: KNIGHTLY REGARD

You receive shelter and succor from members of your knightly order and those who are sympathetic to its aims. If your order is a religious one, you can gain aid from temples and other religious communities of your deity. Knights of civic orders can get help from the community—whether a lone settlement or a great nation—that they serve, and knights of philosophical orders can find help from those they have aided in pursuit of their ideals, and those who share those ideals.

This help comes in the form of shelter and meals, and healing when appropriate, as well as occasionally risky assistance, such as a band of local citizens rallying to

---

KNIGHTLY ORDERS OF FAERÛN

Many who rightfully call themselves "knight" earn that title as part of an order in service to a deity, such as Kelemvor's Eternal Order or Mystra's Knights of the Mystic Fire. Other knightly orders serve a government, royal family, or are the elite military of a feudal state, such as the brutal Warlock Knights of Vaasa. Other knighthoods are secular and nongovernmental organizations of warriors who follow a particular philosophy, or consider themselves a kind of extended family, similar to an order of monks. Although there are organizations, such as the Knights of the Shield, that use the trappings of knighthood without necessarily being warriors, most folk of Faerûn who hear the word "knight" think of a mounted warrior in armor beholden to a code. Below are a few knightly organizations.

Knights of the Unicorn. The Knights of the Unicorn began as a fad of romantically minded sons and daughters of patriar families in Baldur's Gate. On a lark, they took the unicorn goddess Lurue as their mascot and went on various adventures for fun. The reality of the dangers they faced eventually sank in, as did Lurue's tenets. Over time the small group grew and spread, gaining a following in places as far as Cormyr. The Knights of the Unicorn are chivalric adventurers who follow romantic ideals: life is to be relished and lived with laughter, quests should be taken on a dare, impossible dreams should be pursued for the sheer wonder of their completion, and everyone should be praised for their strengths and comforted in their weaknesses.

Knights of Myth Drannor. Long ago, the Knights of Myth Drannor were a famous adventuring band, and Dove Falconhand, one of the famous Seven Sisters, was one of them. The band took its name to honor the great but fallen city, just as the new Knights of Myth Drannor do today. With the city once again in ruins, Dove Falconhand decided to reform the group with the primary goal of building alliances and friendship between the civilized races of the world and goodly people in order to combat evil. The Knights of Myth Drannor once again ride the roads of the Dalelands, and they've begun to spread to the lands beyond. Their members, each accepted by Dove herself, are above all valiant and honest.

Knights of the Silver Chalice. The Knights of the Silver Chalice was formed by edict of the demigod Siamorphe in Waterdeep a century ago. Siamorphe's ethos is the nobility's right and responsibility to rule, and the demigod is incarnated as a different noble mortal in each generation. By the decree of the Siamorphe at that time, the Knights of the Silver Chalice took it upon themselves to put a proper heir on the throne of Tethyr and reestablish order in that kingdom. Since then they have grown to be the most popular knighthood in Tethyr, a nation that has hosted many knighthoods in fealty to the crown.

aid a sorely pressed knight in a fight, or those who support the order helping to smuggle a knight out of town when he or she is being hunted unjustly.

SUGGESTED CHARACTERISTICS

Use the tables for the soldier background in the *Player's Handbook* as the basis for your traits and motivations, modifying the entries when appropriate to suit your identity as a knight of your order.

Your bond almost always involves the order to which you belong (or at least key members of it), and it is highly unusual for a knight's ideal not to reflect the agenda, sentiment, or philosophy of one's order.

MERCENARY VETERAN

As a sell-sword who fought battles for coin, you're well acquainted with risking life and limb for a chance at a share of treasure. Now, you look forward to fighting foes and reaping even greater rewards as an adventurer. Your experience makes you familiar with the ins and outs of mercenary life, and you likely have harrowing stories of events on the battlefield. You might have served with a large outfit such as the Zhentarim or the soldiers of Mintarn, or a smaller band of sell-swords, maybe even more than one. (See the "Mercenaries of the North" sidebar for a collection of possibilities.)

Now you're looking for something else, perhaps greater reward for the risks you take, or the freedom to choose your own activities. For whatever reason, you're leaving behind the life of a soldier for hire, but your skills are undeniably suited for battle, so now you fight on in a different way.

Skill Proficiencies: Athletics, Persuasion
Tool Proficiencies: One type of gaming set, vehicles (land)
Equipment: A uniform of your company (traveler's clothes in quality), an insignia of your rank, a gaming set of your choice, and a pouch containing the remainder of your last wages (10 gp)

FEATURE: MERCENARY LIFE

You know the mercenary life as only someone who has experienced it can. You are able to identify mercenary companies by their emblems, and you know a little about any such company, including the names and reputations of its commanders and leaders, and who has hired them recently. You can find the taverns and festhalls where mercenaries abide in any area, as long as you speak the language. You can find mercenary work between adventures sufficient to maintain a comfortable lifestyle (see "Practicing a Profession" under "Downtime Activities" in chapter 8 of the *Player's Handbook*).

SUGGESTED CHARACTERISTICS

Use the tables for the soldier background in the *Player's Handbook* as the basis for your traits and motivations, modifying the entries when appropriate to suit your identity as a mercenary.

> ### MERCENARIES OF THE NORTH
>
> Countless mercenary companies operate up and down the Sword Coast and throughout the North. Most are small-scale operations that employ a dozen to a hundred folk who offer security services, hunt monsters and brigands, or go to war in exchange for gold. Some organizations, such as the Zhentarim, Flaming Fist, and the nation of Mintarn have hundreds or thousands of members and can provide private armies to those with enough funds. A few organizations operating in the North are described below.
>
> **The Chill.** The cold and mysterious Lurkwood serves as the home of numerous groups of goblinoids that have banded together into one tribe called the Chill. Unlike most of their kind, the Chill refrains from raiding the people of the North and maintains relatively good relations so that they can hire themselves out as warriors. Few city-states in the North are willing to field an army alongside the Chill, but several are happy to quietly pay the Chill to battle the Uthgardt, orcs, trolls of the Evermoors, and other threats to civilization.
>
> **Silent Rain.** Consisting solely of elves, Silent Rain is a legendary mercenary company operating out of Evereska. Caring little for gold or fame, Silent Rain agrees only to jobs that either promote elven causes or involve destroying orcs, gnolls, and the like. Prospective employers must leave written word (in Elvish) near Evereska, and the Silent Rain sends a representative if interested.
>
> **The Bloodaxes.** Founded in Sundabar nearly two centuries ago, the Bloodaxes were originally a group of dwarves outcast from their clans for crimes against the teachings of Moradin Soulforger. They began hiring out as mercenaries to whoever in the North would pay them. Since then the mercenary company has broadened its membership to other races, but every member is an exile, criminal, or misfit of some sort looking for a fresh start and a new family among the bold Bloodaxes.

Your bond could be associated with the company you traveled with previously, or with some of the comrades you served with. The ideal you embrace largely depends on your worldview and your motivation for fighting.

URBAN BOUNTY HUNTER

Before you became an adventurer, your life was already full of conflict and excitement, because you made a living tracking down people for pay. Unlike some people who collect bounties, though, you aren't a savage who follows quarry into or through the wilderness. You're involved in a lucrative trade, in the place where you live, that routinely tests your skills and survival instincts. What's more, you aren't alone, as a bounty hunter in the wild would be: you routinely interact with both the criminal subculture and other bounty hunters, maintaining contacts in both areas to help you succeed.

You might be a cunning thief-catcher, prowling the rooftops to catch one of the myriad burglars of the city. Perhaps you are someone who has your ear to the street, aware of the doings of thieves' guilds and street gangs. You might be a "velvet mask" bounty hunter, one who blends in with high society and noble circles in order to catch the criminals that prey on the rich, whether pickpockets or con artists. The community where you plied your trade might have been one of Faerûn's great metropolises, such as Waterdeep or Baldur's Gate, or a less populous location, perhaps Luskan or Yartar—any place that's large enough to have a steady supply of potential quarries.

As a member of an adventuring party, you might find it more difficult to pursue a personal agenda that doesn't fit with the group's objectives—but on the other hand, you can take down much more formidable targets with the help of your companions.

Skill Proficiencies: Choose two from among Deception, Insight, Persuasion, and Stealth
Tool Proficiencies: Choose two from among one type of gaming set, one musical instrument, and thieves' tools
Equipment: A set of clothes appropriate to your duties and a pouch containing 20 gp

FEATURE: EAR TO THE GROUND

You are in frequent contact with people in the segment of society that your chosen quarries move through. These people might be associated with the criminal underworld, the rough-and-tumble folk of the streets, or members of high society. This connection comes in the form of a contact in any city you visit, a person who provides information about the people and places of the local area.

SUGGESTED CHARACTERISTICS

Use the tables for the criminal background in the *Player's Handbook* as the basis for your bounty hunter's traits and motivations, modifying the entries when appropriate to suit your identity as a bounty hunter.

For instance, your bond might involve other bounty hunters or the organizations or individuals that employ you. Your ideal could be associated with your determination always to catch your quarry or your desire to maintain your reputation for being dependable.

UTHGARDT TRIBE MEMBER

Though you might have only recently arrived in civilized lands, you are no stranger to the values of cooperation and group effort when striving for supremacy. You learned these principles, and much more, as a member of an Uthgardt tribe.

Your people have always tried to hold to the old ways. Tradition and taboo have kept the Uthgardt strong while the kingdoms of others have collapsed into chaos and ruin. But for the last few generations, some bands among the tribes were tempted to settle, make peace, trade, and even to build towns. Perhaps this is why Uthgar chose to raise up the totems among the people as living embodiments of his power. Perhaps they needed a reminder of who they were and from whence they came. The Chosen of Uthgar led bands back to the old ways, and most of your people abandoned the soft ways of civilization.

Barbarian Tribes of Faerûn

Though this section details the Uthgardt specifically, either it or the outlander background from the *Player's Handbook* can be used for a character whose origin lies with one of the other barbarian tribes in Faerûn.

You might be a fair-haired barbarian of the Reghed, dwelling in the shadow of the Reghed Glacier in the far North near Icewind Dale. You might also be of the nomadic Rashemi, noted for their savage berserkers and their masked witches. Perhaps you hail from one of the wood elf tribes in the Chondalwood, or the magic-hating human tribes of the sweltering jungles of Chult.

You might have grown up in one of the tribes that had decided to settle down, and now that they have abandoned that path, you find yourself adrift. Or you might come from a segment of the Uthgardt that adheres to tradition, but you seek to bring glory to your tribe by achieving great things as a formidable adventurer.

See the "Uthgardt Lands" section of chapter 2 for details on each tribe's territory and its activities that will help you choose your affiliation.

Skill Proficiencies: Athletics, Survival
Tool Proficiencies: One type of musical instrument or artisan's tools
Languages: One of your choice
Equipment: A hunting trap, a totemic token or set of tattoos marking your loyalty to Uthgar and your tribal totem, a set of traveler's clothes, and a pouch containing 10 gp

Feature: Uthgardt Heritage

You have an excellent knowledge of not only your tribe's territory, but also the terrain and natural resources of the rest of the North. You are familiar enough with any wilderness area that you find twice as much food and water as you normally would when you forage there.

Additionally, you can call upon the hospitality of your people, and those folk allied with your tribe, often including members of druid circles, tribes of nomadic elves, the Harpers, and the priesthoods devoted to the gods of the First Circle.

Suggested Characteristics

Use the tables for the outlander background in the *Player's Handbook* as the basis for your traits and motivations, modifying the entries when appropriate to suit your identity as a member of an Uthgardt tribe.

Even if you have left your tribe behind (at least for now), you hold to the traditions of your people. You will never cut down a still-living tree, and you may not countenance such an act being done in your presence. The Uthgardt ancestral mounds—great hills where the totem spirits were defeated by Uthgar and where the heroes of the tribes are interred—are sacred to you.

Your bond is undoubtedly associated with your tribe or some aspect of Uthgardt philosophy or culture (perhaps even Uthgar himself). Your ideal is a personal choice that probably hews closely to the ethos of your people and certainly doesn't contradict or compromise what being an Uthgardt stands for.

Waterdhavian Noble

You are a scion of one of the great noble families of Waterdeep. Human families who jealously guard their privilege and place in the City of Splendors, Waterdhavian nobles have a reputation across Faerûn for being eccentric, spoiled, venal, and, above all else, rich.

Whether you are a shining example of the reason for this reputation or one who proves the rule by being an exception, people expect things of you when they know your surname and what it means. Your reasons for taking up adventuring likely involve your family in some way: Are you the family rebel, who prefers delving in filthy dungeons to sipping *zzar* at a ball? Or have you taken up sword or spell on your family's behalf, ensuring that they have someone of renown to see to their legacy?

Work with your DM to come up with the family you are part of—there are around seventy-five lineages in Waterdeep, each with its own financial interests, specialties, and schemes. You might be part of the main line of your family, possibly in line to become its leader one day. Or you might be one of any number of cousins, with less prestige but also less responsibility.

Skill Proficiencies: History, Persuasion
Tool Proficiencies: One type of gaming set or one musical instrument
Languages: One of your choice
Equipment: A set of fine clothes, a signet ring or brooch, a scroll of pedigree, a skin of fine *zzar* or wine, and a purse containing 20 gp

Feature: Kept in Style

While you are in Waterdeep or elsewhere in the North, your house sees to your everyday needs. Your name and signet are sufficient to cover most of your expenses; the inns, taverns, and festhalls you frequent are glad to record your debt and send an accounting to your family's estate in Waterdeep to settle what you owe.

This advantage enables you to live a comfortable lifestyle without having to pay 2 gp a day for it, or reduces the cost of a wealthy or aristocratic lifestyle by that amount. You may not maintain a less affluent lifestyle and use the difference as income—the benefit is a line of credit, not an actual monetary reward.

Suggested Characteristics

Use the tables for the noble background in the *Player's Handbook* as the basis for your traits and motivations, modifying the entries when appropriate to suit your identity as a member of a Waterdhavian family.

Like other nobles, you were born and raised in a different world from the one that most folk know—one that grants you privilege but also calls you to fulfill a duty befitting your station. Your bond might be associated with your family alone, or it could be concerned with another noble house that sides with or opposes your own. Your ideal depends to some extent on how you view your role in the family, and how you intend to conduct yourself in the world at large as a representative of your house.

APPENDIX: CLASS OPTIONS IN OTHER WORLDS

HE CLASS OPTIONS IN THIS BOOK ARE designed for the Forgotten Realms, but they can be easily transported to other official D&D worlds or to a world of your own creation. This appendix offers suggestions for modifying names and other elements of the character options in chapter 4.

None of the statements here should be treated as canonical for the D&D settings discussed. Instead, take them in the spirit of advice given from one DM to another on how to integrate these new character options into your campaign.

DRAGONLANCE

Use the following guidelines to adapt this book's class options to a campaign set on Krynn.

BARBARIAN

Barbarians are most common among Kagonesti elves and human nomad tribes. Both groups have a healthy respect for the land and its creatures, and the tiger and elk totems both have devotees among them. While the folk of Ansalon know of elk, the griffon replaces the tiger as an object of respect.

The battlerager has no equivalent in the Dragonlance saga. A character opting for the Path of the Battlerager might be part of a gnomish attempt at inventing a new sort of armor, an effort that yielded a dangerous but effective fighting style. It's up to the player whether the barbarian's rage stems from a set of tactics developed for use with the gnome-created spiked armor or from sheer frustration at having to turn to the mad tinker gnomes for help.

CLERIC

The Arcana Domain has no established place in Dragonlance. The gods of magic are patrons of the Wizards of High Sorcery. Spellcasters revere the deity appropriate to their order through the study and mastery of arcane magic, rather than through divine power. However, clerics devoted to the neutral gods Gilean (god of knowledge) and Zivilyn (god of wisdom) might have the Arcana Domain.

FIGHTER

The Purple Dragon Knight is an ideal match for the Knights of Solamnia, specifically a Knight of the Rose. As leaders of their order, Knights of the Rose are expected to provide wisdom, inspiration, and guidance to the knights in all situations.

MONK

Few monks are found on Krynn, but those active in the world fall into two camps.

The Way of the Long Death provides a good match for those evil monks who worship Sargonnas. The minotaurs who follow Sargas sometimes follow this path, but most prefer the martial aspect of the Way of the Open Hand.

The Way of the Sun Soul could be used to represent followers of Sirrion, god of creativity, passion, fighters, and fire. Sirrion is said to sculpt the fire of the soul, and these monks seek to sculpt their minds and bodies so that all three act in unison, making instinct and action one and the same.

PALADIN

The Oath of the Crown is a perfect match for any paladin who is a member of the Knights of the Sword or Knights of the Skull. Both orders swear fealty to an organization and combine spellcasting and martial skill.

ROGUE

The Mastermind matches well with any character of cunning, intelligence, and insight who might be involved in court intrigue. But it also serves as a good way to portray a cunning pirate captain from the Blood Sea Isles.

The Swashbuckler provides another option for characters who hail from that region. Serving as pirates or mariners plying the Blood Sea, a Swashbuckler's emphasis on speed and light armor is ideal for an environment where heavy armor is little more than a deadly anchor.

WARLOCK

The warlock character class has yet to be depicted in the Dragonlance setting. That said, warlocks of various types might be individuals who make promises to the gods in return for power, and the Undying patron is a good match for a character who seeks to follow in the footsteps of a long dead but mighty wizard.

WIZARD

Bladesinging is a good option for elf warriors of the Qualinesti or Silvanesti. Like the heroic Gilthanas, a bladesinger combines a study of arcane magic with a mastery of the blade.

EBERRON

Use the following guidelines to adapt this book's class options to a campaign set on Eberron.

BARBARIAN

The Path of the Battlerager is a great fit for a warforged barbarian trained for close quarters battle and with a chassis modified to incorporate spikes, blades, and other weapons. These warforged made ideal shock troops during the Last War. The few that survive have little choice but to continue martial pursuits, as their frames are suited for little else.

The new totem warrior options are an obvious choice for barbarians with an affinity for a tiger or an elk. The option can also reflect an Argonnessen barbarian's ties to a specific dragon type. Use the tiger totem for a red dragon totem and the elk for a silver dragon totem.

Cleric

The Arcana Domain maps to the portfolios overseen by Aureon of the Sovereign Host and the Shadow from the Dark Six. Blood of Vol cultists who are clerics can also take this domain.

Fighter

With the Last War in the recent past, the Purple Dragon Knight's role as a combat leader can apply to any fighter who served in one of Khorvaire's militaries as an officer. Soldiers from Karrnath, with its strong martial tradition, are especially likely to choose this option.

Monk

The Way of the Long Death captures the cruel and sinister nature of monks devoted to the Mockery. In contrast, the Way of the Sun Soul is the perfect option for monks dedicated to the Silver Flame, especially those who also take levels in the paladin class.

Paladin

The Oath of the Crown represents paladins who place loyalty to their sovereign ruler above all other concerns. The military tradition of Karrnath produces paladins who take this oath, especially those whose fanaticism leads them to join the Order of the Emerald Claw.

Rogue

Both the Mastermind and the Swashbuckler are perfectly at home in the city of Sharn. In addition, the ranks of the dragonmarked houses are filled with scheming, adventurous entrepreneurs best captured by the Mastermind's abilities.

While the Mastermind lacks a specific ability in investigation, pairing it with the right skill selections and ability scores (a high Wisdom is a must) yields a good model for an inquisitive.

Sorcerer

Storm Sorcery is a natural match for House Lyrandar. Drawing on the power conferred by that house's dragonmark, a Lyrandar storm sorcerer can help guide ships through the air and across the sea. Such sorcerers are likely elite members of the house, since they can guarantee safe passage through dangerous weather.

Warlock

The elves of Aerenal are an ideal match for the Undying. Some of these elves enter pacts with their deathless ancestors, pledging service and obedience in return for ancient secrets of the elves that unlock magical powers, as well as mastery over the undead.

Wizard

Bladesingers can be found in Aundair, serving as specially trained agents of the Arcane Congress. Bladesingers are specifically tasked with protecting the congress's secrets and ensuring that they never fall into the wrong hands. At times, they are dispatched to distant lands in search of magic items long thought lost or to deal with nascent, magical threats before they grow too dangerous.

Greyhawk

Use the following guidelines to adapt this book's class options to a campaign set on Oerth.

Barbarian

Barbarians are common throughout the northern reaches of Oerik. From the lands of the Wolf Nomads to the enclaves of the Ice Barbarians, these characters venture south in search of loot, glory, and power. Others are exiles, forced to leave their homeland under penalty of death.

The Path of the Battlerager lacks a direct analog on Oerth. Most likely, a battlerager could be of any race and formerly trained as a pit fighter by the vicious Slave Lords. The Slave Lords are a much-feared cabal who direct raids on seaside communities, carrying off prisoners to a wretched life of servitude. A battlerager might be one such unfortunate victim. A prisoner who shows signs of martial aptitude might be trained in an exotic fighting style sure to fetch a high price from a bloodthirsty buyer.

The tiger totem is an easy match for barbarians who hail from the realm of the Tiger Nomads. The elk totem is most common among the Rovers of the Barrens, preserving an ancient Flan tradition.

Cleric

The Arcana Domain is a perfect match for clerics of Boccob. They are charged with using their abilities to seek out lost magic items and to help counter the slow but relentless disappearance of magic from Oerth.

Fighter

The Purple Dragon Knight's focus on combat leadership makes it the ideal model for the Knights of the Watch. Charged with protecting the lands of Bissel, Gran March, Geoff, and Keoland from Baklunish incursions, these knights combine strict discipline, a near-monastic way of life, and ample study of battle tactics and strategy to remain vigilant against attack.

Monk

Monks are relatively rare on Oerth, with the notable exception of the sinister Scarlet Brotherhood.

Among the Scarlet Brotherhood, the Way of the Long Death is a secretive technique taught to those who combine the brotherhood's expertise in unarmed fighting with its preference for assassination to remove troublesome enemies.

The Way of the Sun Soul is a perfect fit for monks who worship Pholtus or Pelor. The monastic orders among the Baklunish lands could easily yield an order of monks dedicated to Al'Akbar.

PALADIN

The Oath of the Crown can represent a wide variety of paladins associated with various knightly orders across the Flanaess. The Knights of the Hart are the perfect faction for this type of paladin. In addition, paladins associated with the Great Kingdom likely take this oath.

ROGUE

The City of Greyhawk is known as the City of Thieves for good reason. Its thieves' guild exerts power across the world. Nestled at the center of the Flanaess's economic network, the guild and the city it rules has a hand in almost every business deal across the region.

The Mastermind archetype is the perfect way to represent an ambitious member of Greyhawk's thieves' guild. Willing to take a personal risk on a job but more comfortable directing muscle, this flavor of rogue is a great match for a character who wants to follow in the footsteps of Nerof Gasgol and rise to political and economic power.

Rakes and bravos are common throughout the cities of the Flanaess. A Swashbuckler can thus originate from almost any city, but among the Rhennee in particular, Swashbucklers are common. As travelers along waterways, they have learned that a quick, mobile approach to combat works best.

WARLOCK

Warlocks are relatively rare in Greyhawk, but as Iuz has ascended to power, he has begun to offer power directly to those who choose to serve him. Some of the other mysterious powers of Oerth, most notably Vecna and Tharizdun, also offer pacts to warlocks who dare contact them.

Both Iuz and Vecna fit the Undying patron's role. Iuz, in particular, uses offers of power to corrupt and subvert folk among his enemies. He offers easy bargains and great power to those in the realms of Furyondy and Veluna who are willing to subvert those states from within. Some warlocks relish their role as turncoats, a few others turn against Iuz, and still others take his power and use it to their own ends.

WIZARD

Bladesingers form an elite cadre of warrior-mages in the kingdom of Celene. Some of these agents work beyond Celene's borders, wielding blade and magic against the queen's enemies. The art of the blade song is unknown beyond that kingdom; no non-elf has learned its secrets.

HOMEMADE WORLDS

Running your campaign in a world of your own creation? Here are tips for introducing some of this book's character options to your world, skipping options that have obvious applications in a world.

BARBARIAN

The Path of the Battlerager is somewhat difficult to incorporate into a setting because of its idiosyncratic nature. It provides a good match for pit fighters, berserkers, and gladiators. Its reliance on armor provides a good cultural touchstone for dwarf characters, as befits its role in the Realms. Alternatively, you could use the battlerager as the basis for a militant religious order in your world, especially one focused on cruelty or fury.

For the tiger and elk totems, conversion is simply a matter of replacing them with more suitable animals (if necessary).

CLERIC

The concept of a goddess of magic is important to the Realms. If your campaign lacks a deity concerned with magic, the Arcana Domain works well for religious orders charged with hunting down or policing arcane spellcasters. If your world strikes a conflict between arcane and divine magic, this domain provides the divine faction's mage hunters.

FIGHTER

The Purple Dragon Knight captures the essence of a bold battlefield strategist. It provides a framework for a mercenary captain, a member of an elite order of warriors, or a noble charged with leading vassals into battle.

MONK

You've probably noticed that the Way of the Long Death and the Way of the Sun Soul are both handy tools for modeling monastic orders at opposite ends of the alignment spectrum. A particularly sinister order is a good match for the Long Death, while a heroic order follows the Way of the Sun Soul.

PALADIN

The Oath of the Crown's utility for your campaign comes from its ability to capture neutral paladins, those whose code of conduct is focused on the law rather than on moral principles. Its divine spellcasting makes it tricky to use as a tool for every knightly order, but it's a great option for a theocracy. You could also decide that the spells a paladin casts aren't divine in origin, but arcane.

SORCERER

Storm Sorcery is a good match for an arcane order supported by a powerful seagoing culture. These sorcerers might form an elite cadre of sea captains, helping a kingdom dominate the sea through trade or raiding.

WARLOCK

The Undying patron is a great option for the agents of a powerful lich king, necromancer, or other undead ruler. These warlocks are also useful for portraying any cult or organization focused on a powerful, undead figure from your campaign's past.

WIZARD

The bladesinger's flavor makes it more than just a warrior/mage in the Forgotten Realms. In your campaign, consider using it to model an order of elf knights or an elite group of warriors trained to protect the rulers of a magocracy.

INDEX